FERGUSON

CAREER RESOURCE GUIDE TO

Internships

and

Summer Jobs

VOLUME 2

Carol Turkington

Ferguson

An imprint of Infobase Publishing

Ferguson Career Resource Guide to Internships and Summer Jobs

Copyright © 2006 by Carol Turkington

Ferguson
An imprint of Infobase Publishing
132 West 31st Street
New York NY 10001

Library of Congress Cataloging-in-Publication Data
Turkington, Carol.
Ferguson career resource guide to internships and summer jobs / Carol Turkington.
    p.   cm.
  Includes index.
  ISBN 0-8160-6019-3 (set) (hc : alk. paper)
  ISBN 0-8160-6020-7 (vol. 1)— ISBN 0-8160-6021-5 (vol. 2)
  1. Internship programs—United States. 2. College students—Employment—United States. 3. High school students—Employment—United States. 4. Summer employment—United States. I. Title.
  LC1072.I58T87 2006
  311.25'922—dc22

Text design by David Strelecky
Cover design by Salvatore Luongo

Printed in the United States of America

VB FOF 10 9 8 7 6 5 4 3 2 1

This book is printed on acid-free paper.

CONTENTS

ANIMALS

ART

ENTERTAINMENT

HISTORICAL AREAS

SPORTS

TECHNICAL

PART IV: FURTHER RESOURCES
APPENDIXES

INDEXES

PART III
DIRECTORY

HEALTH

ABBOTT LABORATORIES ENVIRONMENTAL, HEALTH, AND SAFETY INTERNSHIP

Abbott Laboratories
100 Abbott Park Road
Abbott Park, IL 60064-3500
(847) 937-6100
http://www.abbott.com

What You Can Earn: Interns receive competitive pay based on experience; eligible interns who plan to drive will be reimbursed per mile for the most direct route to Abbott. Those who fly will receive an airline ticket via the most direct route to and from your Abbott location. Upon arrival, the company will reimburse you for your taxi fare. Subsidized housing may be provided for interns with a permanent address of more than 40 miles from Abbott Laboratories.

Application Deadlines: March 1.

Educational Experience: At least a rising sophomore with an occupational safety and health, industrial hygiene, or environmental engineering major; must be enrolled in school for the fall term after the internship; excellent academic record with at least a 3.0 GPA.

Requirements: Leadership abilities, extracurricular activities, relevant course work, and proficiency in Abbott's core competencies (integrity, innovation, initiative, teamwork, and adaptability) are also considered.

OVERVIEW

More than a century ago, 30-year-old Wallace C. Abbott, M.D., began making a new form of medicine. Using the active part of a medicinal plant, he formed tiny pills that provided a measured amount of the drug. Soon he was producing pills under the banner of his new company, Abbott Labs. Since then, the company has contributed a host of major medical breakthroughs across the healthcare spectrum. These achievements are the direct result of a commitment to innovative thinking and measurable results. For more than a century, innovation and success in the areas of pharmaceuticals, nutritionals, and diagnostics has enabled Abbott to provide total, integrated solutions for some of the world's most prevalent medical conditions, including: AIDS, cancer, and diabetes.

As an intern in the environmental, health, and safety department, you'll get hands-on experience as you provide support to the safety program, development/implementation, industrial hygiene laboratory activities, emergency preparedness building plans, hazard communication and/or incident investigation support.

During the summer, interns gather for career development activities, a summer social, and an intern program closing event with Abbott's senior executives. Many of these events provide more information about long-term career opportunities and will help you network with experts in your field. In addition, the Abbott Intern Sports League offers Abbott interns the chance to get together outside of work and participate in various league and weekends sports. During the course of the summer, intern and intern/manager tournaments are organized to promote fun and networking. Tournaments include flag football, basketball, volleyball, softball, and bowling.

Abbott Laboratories actively recruits at many universities. To learn when the company will be recruiting on your campus, visit http://www.abbott.com/career/abt_on_campus.cfm.

HOW TO APPLY

You can use this Web site to submit your resume to apply for a summer internship: https://jobs.brassring.com/EN/ASP/TG/cim_home.asp?sec=1&partnerid=281&siteid=50.

ADMINISTRATION ON AGING INTERNSHIP

Administration on Aging
U.S. Department of Health and Human Services
Room 4708
Washington, DC 20201
donna.blake@aoa.hhs.gov
http://www.aoa.gov/about/jobs/jobs_internship_
   pf.asp

What You Can Earn: Unpaid.
Application Deadlines: Rolling.
Educational Experience: Full-time undergraduate and graduate students
Requirements: Serious interest in working with the elderly.

OVERVIEW

For more than 35 years, the Administration on Aging (AoA) has provided home and community-based services to millions of older persons through the programs funded under the Older Americans Act. These include the Meals on Wheels program, nutrition services, and transportation, adult day care, legal assistance, and health promotion programs. AoA ombudsmen work at nursing homes to monitor care and conditions and provide a voice for those who are unable to speak for themselves. The National Family Caregiver Support Program provides a variety of services to help people caring for family members who are chronically ill or who have disabilities.

Internships with the AoA give students the chance to gain valuable professional federal experience with one of the most comprehensive aging services and research programs in the federal government. These internships are primarily located at the headquarters in Washington, D.C., but there are also potential placements available in nine regional offices at Seattle, San Francisco, Denver, Dallas, Chicago, Kansas City (Missouri), Atlanta, New York City, and Boston. The internship positions are available throughout the year.

HOW TO APPLY

To apply, e-mail or mail a resume with cover letter summarizing your interests in the field of aging and public policy to the address above.

AMERICAN CANCER SOCIETY INTERNSHIP

American Cancer Society
Manager of Student Programs
1599 Clifton Road NE
Atlanta, GA 30329
Internships@cancer.org
Fax: 404-982-3677

What You Can Earn: Up to $2500; no housing allowance.
Application Deadlines: Rolling.
Educational Experience: Full-time undergraduate and graduate students who can demonstrate a relationship between their major and the work of the American Cancer Society.
Requirements: Must have completed freshman year of college and will return to college after the internship; minimum cumulative 3.0 GPA; serious interest in pursuing a career in the nonprofit sector.

OVERVIEW

The American Cancer Society is a nationwide community-based voluntary health organization dedicated to eliminating cancer as a major health problem by preventing cancer, saving lives, and diminishing suffering from cancer through research, education, advocacy, and service. With more than two million volunteers nationwide, the American Cancer Society is one of the oldest and largest voluntary health agencies in the United States, with over 3,400 local offices.

The purpose of this internship program is to develop public awareness of the American Cancer Society and the inner workings of nonprofit agencies. During your eight-week session, you'll get hands-on experience in the activities of nonprofit agencies and in-depth knowledge of the Society's efforts in cancer control, volunteer involvement, and community outreach. Internships are offered in three separate sessions during the year: fall (September through December); spring (January through May); summer (June through Aug).

To find a list of the internship positions available by state, visit the Web page of the ACS (http://www.cancer.org/docroot/AA/AA_5.asp?sitearea=AA&level=1) and click on the state in which you're interested in working. If no positions are available, you should check the Web site for the next internship season (spring, summer or fall).

HOW TO APPLY

If you're interested, you should submit an internship application, indicating the complete title and location of the position in which you're interested, your resume (including honors, awards, and so on), and a typed, double-spaced, one-page essay about why you're applying and your area of interest. After being preselected, you'll need to submit two letters of recommendation from faculty and an official school transcript.

You should e-mail (preferred), fax, or mail your application form, resume, and essay by the appropriate deadline to the preceding address. Apply as soon as possible, because positions fill quickly. The ACS will accept applications until positions are filled or until the application deadline.

AMERICAN FOUNDATION FOR THE BLIND INTERNSHIP

American Foundation for the Blind
Internship Coordinator
11 Penn Plaza, Suite 300
New York, NY 10001

Fax: (212) 502-7772
communications@afb.net
http://www.afb.org

What You Can Earn: Stipend; college credit is possible.
Application Deadlines: Rolling.
Educational Experience: Undergraduate students with concentrations in communications or a desire to pursue a career in a communications field.
Requirements: Motivated, diligent, and organized. An openness to working in an environment where the staff make-up is varied and includes people with disabilities is imperative. Flexibility and the ability to multitask are important.

OVERVIEW

The American Foundation for the Blind (AFB)—the organization to which Helen Keller devoted her life—is a national nonprofit whose mission is to ensure that the 10 million Americans who are blind or visually impaired enjoy the same rights and opportunities as other citizens.

The AFB offers a summer internship in the communications department, where you'll help coordinate AFB's images and messages through marketing, media outreach, and events. As an intern, you'll help the communications department with a variety of long-term projects such as implementation of a photo database using the program Extensis Portfolio, monitoring and evaluating media coverage, assisting with the development of a print production archive, evaluating readership and expanding the audience of AFB's monthly e-newsletter, and organizing project information for a department timeline. Short-term duties include drafting press releases, building media lists, and related administrative duties. Hours are flexible, but typically include Monday through Thursday from 9:00 A.M. to 5:00 P.M. from early June through mid-August.

HOW TO APPLY

To apply, send your resume with a cover letter to the preceding e-mail address.

AMERICAN LUNG ASSOCIATION INTERNSHIP

American Lung Association
Internship Coordinator
61 Broadway, 6th Floor
New York, NY 10006
(212) 315-8844
Fax: (212) 315-8872
cbruff-graves@lungusa.org
http://www.lungusa.org

What You Can Earn: A stipend is available.
Application Deadlines: Rolling.
Educational Experience: None specified.
Requirements: Excellent computer and communication skills and ability to work independently.

OVERVIEW

The American Lung Association is the oldest voluntary health organization in the United States. Founded in 1904 to fight tuberculosis, the American Lung Association today fights lung disease in all its forms, with special emphasis on asthma, tobacco control, and environmental health. It's funded by contributions from the public, along with gifts and grants from corporations, foundations, and government agencies. The association teaches children how to understand and control asthma, funds scientists seeking better treatments and cures for all lung diseases, works to prevent kids from smoking and gives help to smokers who want to quit, and champions the cause of cleaner air for all.

A number of internships are available in different departments, including in online marketing, cultural diversity, and design and production.

Cultural Diversity Internship

Interns will work 15 hours a week to help the cultural diversity office. Duties will include helping to identify, catalog, and develop hard copy files for articles and documents housed in the cultural diversity office. You'll also help establish a computer catalog that lists article titles, and you'll help research diversity-indicator data from the field in order to develop comparative data charts for each field association. Finally, you'll help organize the operational and archival files.

Candidates should have basic computer skills, including the creation and saving of Word documents, and must be well organized and able to work independently with minimal supervision.

Design and Production

In this 15-hour a week internship, you'll have the chance to work with desktop publishing software, including Quark, Illustrator, and Photoshop, and scanning and archiving the existing photo library, with the addition of all digital images used on past publications. Your responsibilities will include scanning and performing file conversions, storage, and retrieval using the PC operating system. You'll also help adjust images and graphics using curves, cloning, and channel adjustments in Photoshop and set up, and maintain and update photo archives in Acrobat Reader.

Candidates should have basic PC platform skills, including scanning, photo manipulation and archiving, organizational skills, and some knowledge of Quark and PDF technology.

Online Marketing Internship

This intern will address the online marketing of press and advocacy materials on http://www.lungusa.org and www.lungnet.org for the American Lung Association. The intern will also help with online marketing tasks for major reports and e-fundraising initiatives. Interns should expect to work Tuesdays and Thursdays through the summer.

Candidates should be reliable, have strong communication skills, html experience, and a keen interest in the mission of the American Lung Association.

HOW TO APPLY

To apply, send and e-mail and letter of interest to the preceding address.

AMERICAN PUBLIC HEALTH ASSOCIATION INTERNSHIP

American Public Health Association
800 I Street, NW
Washington, DC 20001
(202) 777-2742
Fax (202) 777-2534
comments@apha.org
http://www.apha.org/wfpha/intrnshp.htm

What You Can Earn: Unpaid.
Application Deadlines: July 15 for fall session (September 1 to December 15); December 1 for spring session (January 15 to May 1); April 15 for summer session (June 1 to August 15).
Educational Experience: Sophomore in college or above (including grad students) studying international health and development.
Requirements: None specified.

OVERVIEW

The American Public Health Association (APHA) is the oldest and largest organization of public health professionals in the world, representing more than 50,000 members from more than 50 occupations of public health. APHA has been influencing policies and setting priorities in public health for more than 125 years. Throughout its history, it has been in the forefront of numerous efforts to prevent disease and promote health.

If public health is your interest, you may be interested in an internship with the APHA, which offers unpaid internships in its International Health section for students and graduates interested in international public health issues.

As an international health intern, you'll work primarily with the World Federation of Public Health Associations (WFPHA), an international, nongovernmental organization of public health societies from 60 countries, located in APHA headquarters in downtown Washington, D.C.

Interns are given substantial responsibility for performing activities such as developing policy resolutions for consideration by the WFPHA General Assembly, researching and writing articles for the newsletter, establishing contact with health and development NGOs around the world, planning international conferences, and fund-raising.

Each internship is structured to suit your needs and interests, as well as to fulfill the requirements of WFPHA. In addition to working for WFPHA, you'll have an opportunity to interact with staff and interns of APHA's government relations and scientific staff as well as individuals involved in the International Health section of APHA. During the course of the internship, you'll further develop your writing and research skills and become more familiar with the key issues and actors in international health and development. Although you won't get to travel, you'll experience lots of networking opportunities using the most up-to-date electronic communication facilities.

HOW TO APPLY

Fill out and submit an online application available at http://www.apha.org/career/intern_app/index.cfm.

AMERICAN RED CROSS INTERNSHIP

American Red Cross
Internship Coordinator
8111 Gatehouse Road, Second Floor
Falls Church, VA 22042
carnoj@usa.redcross.org
http://www.redcross.org/services/
    youth/0,1082,0_416_,00.html

What You Can Earn: Paid and unpaid.
Application Deadlines: Rolling.

Educational Experience: High school, college and graduate school students eligible.
Requirements: U.S. citizenship.

OVERVIEW

The American Red Cross employees, interns, and volunteers help keep the public prepared to respond to disasters and personal emergencies. The Red Cross provides training in lifesaving skills such as CPR and first aid, collects and distributes half the nation's blood supply, and helps victims of more than 67,000 disasters annually. Internships are available at the national office of the American Red Cross in Washington, D.C., (see below) and in many of the 1,100 chapters across the country (call your local ARC chapter to check on area internships).

While most internships are available only to college students, The American Red Cross offers paid and nonpaid internship positions for high school students as well as undergraduate and graduate students. These internships offer students the opportunity to gain career-related work experience related to their academic programs.

If you participate in the American Red Cross internship programs, you'll be working on professional projects, assignments, and activities during your tenure with a staffer. Work assignments can include working in the Holland Lab as a research assist, working in International Services as a project manager, or working as a historical resource assistant. All work assignments are designed to provide student interns with stimulating and challenging work that will help both you and the ARC.

Internship Positions

The following positions are examples of typical summer internship positions and include a wide range of scientific, administrative, and organization-related opportunities. (See sections on "government" or "media" for other ARC-related internships.)

*Biomedical Services: Plasma Services
(Marketing and Sales)*
At this Washington, D.C.-based internship, you'll help develop marketing and sales materials, man-

age sales contests and sales performance, process sales data and monitor sales trends, and review all plasma services hospital products Web sites. You also may review all current and audit collateral materials, and provide administrative support for sales and marketing function. Undergraduate students are preferred; you must know Microsoft Office (Word, Excel, PowerPoint).

Biomedical Services: Plasma Services (Sales Training and Development)
In this Washington, D.C.-based internship, you'll create and redesign training manuals for the plasma hospital group and the bio-surgical sales team. You'll develop individual training plans for the sales territory managers, develop learning challenges for the field, and roll out the new computer sales tracking system). Also, you also may run and analyze reports. Interns must be familiar with Microsoft Word; Excel and PowerPoint familiarity are plusses.

Biomedical Services: Process Improvement
In this Washington, D.C., position, you'll support business process improvement projects to improve quality and decrease the cost of operations. You'll be trained on Six Sigma tools and will support the use of those tools with project teams. Undergraduate students are preferred. You should know Microsoft Office (especially PowerPoint).

Biomedical Services: Quality & Regulatory Affairs (Policy Development)
In this Washington, D.C., internship, you will undertake the primary responsibility for researching one or more issues and for developing issue papers, drafts, and final policies for the policy review board (PRB) to review. You'll conduct field surveys, literature searches, executive interviews, and reviews of existing documentation to complete the preparation of materials and then present the results to the PRB. You should be familiar with Microsoft Word.

Biomedical Services: Quality & Regulatory Affairs (Regulatory Compliance and Quality Systems)
In this Washington, D.C., internship, you'll research and develop one or more tools (such as affinity dia-

grams, control charts, or Pareto charts), developing a presentation about them and implementing their use. You'll use the new tools to create process maps, analyze performance data, and monitor various processes/systems for trends and new developments. You should have experience with Microsoft Word, Excel, Visio, and PowerPoint.

Biomedical Services: Regulatory Affairs (Technical Policy and Promotion)

In this Washington, D.C., internship, depending on the assignment selected, you may prepare a response to the Food and Drug Administration on a proposed new guidance or rule, help implement good manufacturing practices for tissues, and review advertising and promotional materials. Graduate students are preferred. You should have experience with Microsoft Word, Access, and Excel.

Biomedical Services: Safety and Environment

In this Washington, D.C., internship, you'll research and evaluate state Environmental Protection Agency (EPA) regulations and identify potential operational impact. You'll also integrate facility EPA data collected by the National Safety Officers into the database and analyze data and identify regulatory compliance issues at each facility. Also, you may work on the current safety and environment Web site. Graduate students are preferred. You should have experience with Microsoft Office (Word, Access, Excel, and Publisher).

Communication and Marketing: Hispanic Initiative

In this Washington, D.C., internship, you'll develop Web banners for Spanish Web sites and other Web-appropriate materials that would help promote Red Cross services through the Internet, providing help in developing written pieces for redcross.org in Spanish. You'll also translate and develop culturally sensitive pieces in Spanish and prepare PowerPoint presentations to use in reaching Hispanic communities. You must know Spanish and be familiar with Microsoft Office, Word, PowerPoint, and Internet graphics design.

Communication and Marketing: New Markets and Market Research #1

In this Washington, D.C., internship, you'll work on the Presidential Strategic Initiative—New Generation Outreach. You'll help work on chapters with questions and support materials, coordinate materials for distribution, research market concepts, and perform online searches for backup research. You also may help with presentations.

Alternatively, you may participate in the analysis of various customer surveys and conduct secondary research to improve understanding of various customer segments. You'll set up questionnaires to be administered as surveys on the Internet and download and analyze results, preparing PowerPoint presentations to brief service leadership. You should know Microsoft Office and the Internet. Statistical Package knowledge is a plus.

Corporate Diversity Department

In this Washington, D.C., internship, you'll help the corporate diversity associate in coordinating the presidential intern program, acting as liaison between corporate diversity and all presidential interns. you'll update and maintain the Presidential Intern database and various other departmental databases, help with program evaluation and planning, and support other corporate diversity department projects that may arise within the 10 weeks. You should know Microsoft Office and Internet search engines.

Development: Donor Relations

In this Washington, D.C., internship, you'll research the best ways to communicate with and obtain information from chapters, and design, test and facilitate a method to gather and measure chapter understanding and knowledge. You'll also help in donor research and prospecting, and write or edit proposals, stewardship reports, or donor acknowledgement letters.

Development: Major Gifts

In this Washington, D.C. internship, you'll develop and research prospect lists, working with the research department to expand and filter prospects. You'll prepare communication materials for presentation to the field and work directly with foundations and companies on proposals, working with front-line fund-raisers on multimillion dollar proposals, cultivation, and education materials for prospects and donors. Undergraduate students are preferred.

General Services Division: Finance

In this Lorton, Va., internship, you'll help with a variety of department projects. Undergraduate students are preferred. You should know Microsoft Word 2000 Professional.

International Services: Tracing—Dissemination and Support

In this Washington, D.C., internship, you'll work with caseworker staff to learn database entry and general support to family tracing services. You'll help compile statistical data to help determine allocation of resources, need for capacity building in chapters, current products and services, and service delivery expectations. You'll also provide casework for Africa or other regions. You must know Microsoft Word; Microsoft Office, Internet, database knowledge is preferred. A second language is a plus.

International Services: Tracing—Measles Initiative

In this Washington, D.C., internship, you'll support Youth Campaign efforts with respect to distribution of materials, outreach and support of programs, and data entry. You'll also help with logistical arrangements for measles promotional material and assist with development of PowerPoint and other promotional materials. You must know Microsoft Word, Access, and database programs. Microsoft Office and Internet experience is preferred, and knowledge of French is a plus.

Information Technology: Architecture and Planning

In this Washington, D.C., internship, you'll help establish a process assets library, an online repository of documented information for QMS documents, process-related information, lessons learned, FAQs, project profiles, software-process improvements, tools used in projects, technical papers, training material, process- improvement proposals, and so on. Graduate students are preferred. You must know Microsoft Word, Excel, Outlook, and PowerPoint. IBM Rational tools (such as ClearCase, ClearQuest, Requisite Pro, Rose, and SoDA) are preferred; knowledge of HTML, DHTML, Dreamweaver, and MS FrontPage is a plus.

Office of the President and CEO (Executive Unit)

In this Washington, D.C., internship, you'll help the Director of Administration with various projects concerning budget, contracts, and overall operation of administrative procedures. You'll also help the assistant deputy chief of staff prepare materials for the ARC president's meetings. You must know Microsoft Word, PowerPoint, and Excel and be comfortable with Internet research. Spanish is a plus.

Preparedness: Research and Product Development

In this Washington, D.C., or Falls Church, Va., internship, you'll research the effectiveness of CPR education, conduct literature searches of library and Internet resources, and report conclusions and recommendations for research applications. Graduate students are preferred. You must know Microsoft Office and computer search engines.

Preparedness: Youth and Young Adult Programs and Services

In this Falls Church, Va., or Washington, D.C., internship, you'll review National Youth Council projects, programs, and initiatives, and assess program implementation, outcomes, and process improvement. Budget analysis and projections of current and future programs are important, and you'll help develop report findings and presentations. You should know Microsoft Word, Excel, PowerPoint, and Outlook.

Real Estate Development/Management: Administration

In this Washington, D.C., internship, you'll participate in administrative projects associated with finalizing construction and help with the 17th Street renovation project. You will help with contracts and lease administration and help with administrative projects for the Data Center relocation. Undergraduate students are preferred. You must know Microsoft Word, Excel, and PowerPoint.

Presidential Intern Program for Undergraduate and Graduate College Students

The American Red Cross corporate diversity department offers internships for undergraduate and graduate college students to learn about key professional positions with the American Red Cross. The presidential intern program is open to students currently enrolled in undergraduate or graduate studies (or who have just graduated the spring immediately prior to their appointment). Students are recruited from Washington, D.C.-area colleges and universities, but applications are accepted from any undergraduate or graduate student. You must be eligible to work in the United States.

HOW TO APPLY

You should e-mail a request for applications and a list of current available internships to the preceding address.

BOYS HOPE, GIRLS HOPE INTERNSHIP

Recruitment & Volunteer Coordinator

12120 Bridgeton Square Drive
Bridgeton, MO 63044
(877) 878-HOPE

What You Can Earn: $200 a month for a year, plus room and board, health insurance, and transportation assistance for a year, plus $2500 Commitment to Service Award at the completion of one year of service.

Application Deadlines: Rolling.
Educational Experience: College graduate (any major) at least 21 years old.
Requirements: Willing to devote a minimum of one year in service; good physical and mental health; openness to travel, change, growth, and challenges; ability to be a positive mentor and role model for kids; reliable, flexible, mature, and dedicated; motivated by a desire to be of service.

OVERVIEW

Founded in 1977 by Father Paul Sheridan, Boys Hope Girls Hope is a privately funded, nonprofit, multidenominational organization that gives at-risk children a stable home, good parenting, high-quality education, and support. Many of the children come from home environments marked by drug abuse, poverty, or neglect; others come from caring families who can't meet the child's needs. Boys Hope Girls Hope serves children in 38 homes in 17 U.S. cities and in Brazil, Guatemala, Ireland.

Boys Hope Girls Hope offers a unique program that places children in noninstitutional, family-like homes staffed with live-in residential counselors and supports children financially and emotionally through college and beyond. The program also offers children long-term adult relationships and positive mentoring and provides referral and follow-up services to children not qualified for our program. After-care services are provided for youth who can return to their families.

If you choose to intern as a residential counselors at Boys Hope Girls Hope, you'll help academically capable and motivated children in need meet their full potential by living with the students and staff, assuming the role of a big brother/sister. Responsibilities may include tutoring students, helping them explore college and career opportunities, and providing positive role modeling, guidance, support, care, and nurturing. You'll also work together with the other staff in the daily operation of the home, including chauffeuring students, shopping, cooking, and cleaning. Also, you may be asked to help local programs with special needs or the national headquarters with office support.

HOW TO APPLY

To request an application, contact the organization at their Web site: http://www.boyshopegirlshope.org/m-contactus2.html.

CENTER FOR ADOLESCENT HEALTH AND THE LAW INTERNSHIP

Director, Center for Adolescent Health & the Law
310 Kildaire Road, Suite 100
Chapel Hill, NC 27516
english@cahl.org

What You Can Earn: Unpaid.
Application Deadlines: May 6.
Educational Experience: Law students and graduate students in public health and public policy.
Requirements: Excellent research skills, including Internet research and research in computerized databases such as Medline, LEXIS, and Westlaw; excellent writing skills, including the ability to adapt legal and policy information for broader audiences; strong interpersonal skills and attention to detail; ability to work independently but willingness to ask questions when direction is needed.

OVERVIEW

The Center for Adolescent Health & the Law is a national legal and policy organization that promotes the health of teenagers and their access to comprehensive health care. Based in Chapel Hill, N.C., the center is a nonprofit organization that conducts research, analyzes legal and policy issues, prepares publications, and provides training and technical assistance. The center's work focuses on consent and confidentiality and financial issues, specifically, state minor consent laws and the confi-

dentiality provisions they contain, federal medical privacy regulations (HIPAA Privacy Rule), other state and federal confidentiality protections, and the policies governing adolescents' participation in health research studies. The center devotes particular attention to attempts to repeal, limit, or undermine these laws, which it believes are critically important in maintaining adolescents' access to reproductive health services and other essential healthcare.

To diminish the financial barriers that limit adolescents' access to healthcare, the center focuses on laws and policies to ensure that adolescents are eligible for and enroll in Medicaid and the State Children's Health Insurance Program (SCHIP), that the programs cover the full range of services adolescents need, and that adolescents actually receive the services. The center also has a particular interest in strategies to promote the sustainability and financial viability of safety-net providers and sites that serve adolescents.

Much of the center's work involves consent and confidentiality policies and financing care. The center's work emphasizes the needs of vulnerable populations of teenagers such as those from low-income families, young people who have been in state custody, and homeless and disconnected youth. The center works closely with a broad national community of healthcare professionals, lawyers, and others interested in protecting and expanding adolescents' access to comprehensive health services, including the Society for Adolescent Medicine, the American Academy of Pediatrics, and the American Medical Association; and with advocacy groups such as the National Health Law Program, the Planned Parenthood Federation of America, and the ACLU.

Summer interns will help the center analyze legal and policy issues that influence the ability of homeless or "unaccompanied" youth to access healthcare and will conduct in-depth analyses of state minor consent laws. Interns also will develop materials on teen healthcare confidentiality to advocates and healthcare professionals, analyze the laws and policies that affect teenagers, and analyze federal health reform proposals related to Medicaid, SCHIP, and the uninsured. Interns also will help develop short user-friendly fact sheets, policy briefs, and charts related to these issues.

HOW TO APPLY
Submit a resume with cover letter and contact information for three references, along with a brief writing sample, via e-mail or regular mail, to the preceding address.

CENTER FOR FOOD SAFETY INTERNSHIP

Center for Food Safety
660 Pennsylvania Ave. SE, Suite 302
Washington, DC 20003
(202) 547-9359
Fax: (202) 547-9429
office@centerforfoodsafety.org
http://www.centerforfoodsafety.org

What You Can Earn: College Credit or $8.50 an hour (40+ hours a week)
Application Deadlines: May 10.
Educational Experience: None specified.
Requirements: Highly-motivated person able to work in fast-paced environment; minimum commitment of three months.

OVERVIEW
The Center for Food Safety (CFS) is a nonprofit public interest and environmental advocacy organization working to address the impacts of the industrial food production system on human health, animal welfare, and the environment. CFS works to achieve its goals through litigation, grassroots campaigns, public education, and media outreach. The CFS uses multifaceted strategies (including legal actions, submission of policy comments, and public education) to accomplish its goals of curtailing industrial agricultural production methods that harm human health and the environment and promoting sustainable alternatives. Legal and policy staff work to monitor and change policies established by the three primary federal agencies involved in regulating the nation's food supply (the Food and Drug Administration, the U.S. Department of Agriculture, and the Environmental Protection Agency).

CFS also provides technical help to many legislative initiatives supported by other nonprofit organizations around the country. Public outreach and advocacy staff work to educate CFS members and consumers about key food and agriculture actions and issues and to mobilize their support for all CFS legal, policy, and grassroots actions.

Interns with this organization work in a fast-paced environment on cutting-edge genetic engineering and other food-safety issues. Interns attend hearings, agency meetings, and press conferences and also perform research, data entry, and help with membership correspondence and public-outreach efforts. The start date is flexible but typically begins in late May or early June.

HOW TO APPLY
Submit your resume and a cover letter explaining your experience or interest in food safety, animal welfare, and environmental issues to the preceding address. Writing samples are optional.

CIIT CENTERS FOR HEALTH RESEARCH

Coordinator Education Program
CIIT Centers for Health Research
PO Box 12137
Research Triangle Park, NC 27709
(919) 558-1200
bramlage@ciit.org
http://www.ciit.org/training_edu/undergrade.asp

What You Can Earn: $480/week plus travel allowance.
Application Deadlines: March 1.
Educational Experience: College juniors, college seniors, graduate students, and college graduates.
Requirements: None specified.

OVERVIEW

CIIT is a private, nonprofit research institute established in 1974 by 11 chemical companies to address concerns about the effects of chemicals on the environment and human health. CIIT has evolved over the years to become a leader in environmental health sciences research and education.

The CIIT Centers for Health Research (CIIT) has a strong commitment to the training of future scientists. In addition to its highly competitive and long-standing postdoctoral, predoctoral, and undergraduate programs, CIIT offers a 12-week summer internship program to encourage promising college students to consider careers in the sciences. The CIIT cooperative education program gives undergraduate students the opportunity to integrate their academic studies with related job experience at CIIT.

The summer internship program was introduced in 1989 to encourage promising college students to consider careers in the sciences. Under the guidance of scientific staff, interns are exposed to various facets of on-going research projects at CIIT, including literature review, experiments, data analysis, and interpretation of results. Many of CIIT's summer interns have gone on to earn graduate degrees in toxicology and related fields.

HOW TO APPLY

To apply for a summer internship, download an Application for Education Program form at: http://www.ciit.org/careers/applications/education_app.doc. Submit the application along with letters from two faculty members familiar with your abilities and interests, together with school transcripts.

DOCTORS WITHOUT BORDERS INTERNSHIP

Doctors Without Borders
Attn: (Dept. name) Internship Search
333 7th Avenue, Second Floor
New York, NY 10001-5126
Fax: (212) 679-7016
employment-usa@newyork.msf.org

What You Can Earn: Unpaid but work-study funds and/or course credit will be available for those who qualify, as well as some transportation reimbursement.
Application Deadlines: December 15 for spring internship (February 27 to May 15); April 15 for summer (June 1 to August 15); July 15 for fall (September 15 to December 15).
Educational Experience: None specified.
Requirements: Commitment of 20 hours a week; specific requirements depend on individual departments (check Web site for details).

OVERVIEW

The purpose of this program is to offer practical administrative and clerical experience, along with a basic introduction to the field of international medical humanitarian aid and advocacy. All internships will take place in the New York office.

Each internship position will support the work of a specific department. Interns may choose to work in any of the following departments, including Campaign for Access to Essential Medicines, communications, development, foundations & corporate relations, major gifts, human resources, press, and executive.

Campaign for Access to Essential Medicines

This intern will provide administrative and research support to the program associate for the campaign for an applicant interested in policy advocacy and international affairs. The campaign works to lower the prices of existing medicines, to bring abandoned drugs back into production, to stimulate research and development for diseases that primarily affect the poor, and to overcome other barriers to access. The campaign operates within the program department, which promotes awareness of humanitarian crises and international policy related to healthcare.

As a campaign intern, you'll research events and target audiences, help manage data and files, help prepare information for advocacy meetings and mailings, organize and maintain hard copy and electronic files, and reply to requests for information and help from the public. This internship is ideal for anyone with a particular focus on policy advocacy and the crisis of access to essential medicines in the developing world. Applicants should have a working knowledge of MS Word and Excel, excellent attention to detail and proofreading ability, an interest in medical humanitarian aid and the struggle for access to essential medicines, and the initiative and confidence to ask questions in a fast-paced work environment.

Executive

This internship is ideal for anyone considering a career in international relations or administration of nongovernmental organizations. The intern will help the association coordinator and the executive director, board of directors, and executive staff. As an intern, you'll compile background materials for monthly meetings of the board, provide logistical support to the executive associate when these meetings are held in New York (in September, November, February, May, and June), maintain the archive of official MSF documents, and conduct ongoing research under the direction of the executive associate on trademark and intellectual property issues. You'll collect research materials (books and articles via New York area libraries, Lexis-Nexis, and the Internet) for occasional articles for books and journals and maintain an archive of these articles and supporting research files. You'll also update and maintain materials on the association Web site, help edit and distribute the *Insider*, the quarterly newsletter of MSF, update the association database, establish and maintain

contact with returned field workers, and help the association coordinator prepare for the annual general assembly, held in June.

You should be able to work independently on multiple tasks; have excellent writing, computer, administrative, and communication skills; understand issues pertaining to international relations and humanitarian movements; and be familiar with social science research methods. Knowledge of French is a plus for this internship.

Human Resources

The HR intern will respond to requests for information on volunteering requirements and general MSF information. As an intern, you'll learn about the organization's changing human resource needs and help cultivate the pool of prospective applicants. You'll also help gather information on U.S.-based training possibilities for volunteers. You'll be expected to respond to information requests from the general public, help the HR assistant write letters to prospective volunteers or rejection letters to applicants, and research U.S. training programs pertinent to the field. You'll also do some filing and other administrative support tasks and help with the Welcome Days and other in-house training as needed.

You should have strong writing, organizational, and computer skills; experience or interest in human resources for a nongovernmental organization; and the ability to conduct research on training options and analyze the information collected. Knowledge of American medical practices and qualifications is a plus, and fluency in English and French is an asset.

Foundations and Corporate Relations

This internship is designed to help develop and maintain relationships with foundation and corporate donors, while providing a practical learning experience to students interested in foundation fund-raising for a large nonprofit organization. The Foundations & Corporations intern will support the research and administrative activities of a small department team, learning how an organization cultivates foundations for funding and how different foundations organize their grant-making. This internship is ideal for anyone interested in administration, grant-writing, and fund-raising for a nonprofit, nongovernmental organization.

As intern in this department, you'll help research current and prospective corporate and foundation donors, process foundation reports and proposals, and file and do other administrative support tasks. You'll also review and correct donor database records, process new donations, help to record donations, help respond to foundation requests for information, and help write occasional letters.

Applicants should have strong writing and computer skills and a genuine commitment to the principles and work of MSF.

Major Gifts

Interns in this department will support staff, learning how an organization approaches and cultivates individuals in order to generate large donations. This internship is ideal for anyone considering a career in development (fund-raising) and in the administration of nongovernmental organizations. Interns in this department will help manage major donor events, help with large and small mailings, and review and correct donor database records.

Applicants should have strong organizational and computer skills (such as Excel) and a genuine commitment to the principles and work of MSF.

Press

The Communications Department works to help the public understand the humanitarian crises and endemic health problems in developing countries addressed by the organization's medical teams in the field. The organization communicates this information through in-house publications, including a quarterly newsletter and Web site, and via public-education activities such as interactive exhibits, speaking events, screenings, and distributing teaching tools.

An intern in this department will work closely with the press officer and communications assistant, offering whatever support is needed. This position is ideal for a student interested in both humanitarian aid and public relations or journalism. The press intern will help conduct media research and daily monitoring of coverage, maintain media contacts, support media projects in response to developing humanitarian news stories, help organize press conferences, track and file news clippings, and help put together a triannual media highlights kit.

Applicants should be able to work independently on a number of separate, simultaneous tasks, be familiar with U.S. TV and print media, have a working knowledge of Word and Excel, and be proficient in writing and Internet research. Knowledge of French or Spanish is a plus.

HOW TO APPLY

Submit resume with cover letter to the preceding address.

ELIZABETH GLASER PEDIATRIC AIDS FOUNDATION INTERNSHIP

Elizabeth Glaser Pediatric AIDS Foundation
2950 31st Street, Suite 125
Santa Monica, CA 90405
(310) 314-1459
research@pedaids.org
http://www.pedaids.org (go to Grant Applications icon)

What You Can Earn: $2,000.
Application Deadlines: March 31.

Educational Experience: Must be enrolled as a full-time student (high school seniors, college, graduate, and medical school students with at least a 3.0 GPA. Postdoctoral fellows (M.D., Ph.D. or equivalent) are not eligible for this award. Students in masters or doctorate programs will not be allowed to perform this internship as part of their dissertations or theses.

Requirements: Must apply through a sponsor who has expertise in pediatric HIV/AIDS; must work a minimum of four hours a week.

OVERVIEW

The Foundation creates a future of hope for children and families worldwide by eradicating pediatric AIDS, providing care and treatment to people with HIV/AIDS, and accelerating the discovery of new treatments for other serious and life-threatening pediatric illnesses.

The Foundation provides an opportunity for interns to engage in clinical and research programs related to pediatric HIV/AIDS, providing motivation for you to consider future careers in pediatric HIV/AIDS. Awards are designed to help you work with a sponsor, conducting basic research or research into clinical care by using a proposal that you develop.

To apply, you must find a sponsor who has expertise in pediatric HIV/AIDS. You can find a sponsor by checking a local hospital or clinic in the departments of pediatrics, infectious disease, or social work where pediatric HIV/AIDS research is being conducted. Sponsors must be an M.D., a Ph.D., or a licensed clinical social worker. The internship may be performed any time during the year.

HOW TO APPLY

The sponsor and the student must complete an application downloaded from http://www.ped-aids.org/fs_search.html. No faxed applications will be accepted. Applicants must send the original and five copies (a total of six stapled and collated versions) of the application. Applications will be reviewed by a subcommittee of the Elizabeth Glaser Pediatric AIDS Foundation Grant Review Committee. The student and sponsor will be notified by mail.

FRONTIER NURSING SERVICE INTERNSHIP

Frontier Nursing Service
132 FNS Drive
Wendover, KY 41775
http://www.frontiernursing.org/Courier/
    TodaysCourier.shtm

What You Can Earn: Unpaid; housing costs are $250 for two months service.
Application Deadlines: Rolling.
Educational Experience: Not specified.
Requirements: Negative TB test within the past year.

OVERVIEW

The Frontier Nursing Service was founded in 1925 by Mary Breckinridge, an aristocrat so devastated after the death of her two children that she divorced her husband and set out to reduce the mortality rate for mothers and children in Leslie County, Kentucky, in the heart of the Appalachian Mountains. Born in 1881, in Memphis, she was the great-granddaughter of Thomas Jefferson's attorney, the granddaughter of the Vice President of the United States under President Buchanan, and the daughter of a U.S. Ambassador to Russia. Married at age 23, her first husband died of appendicitis within two years. In 1910 she was awarded a nursing degree and two years later married a second time. After her second child died at birth and her first died at age four of appendicitis, Mrs. Breckinridge divorced her second husband. In 1925 Mrs.

Breckinridge founded the Kentucky Committee for mothers and Babies, and in 1928 the name was changed to the Frontier Nursing Service. Between 1927 and 1930, six outpost clinics were built and staffed with nurse midwives. These clinics covered nearly 700 hundred square miles, caring for nearly 10,000 people.

Today, the FNA works to safeguard the lives and health of mothers and children by providing and preparing trained nurse-midwives and nurse-practitioners for rural areas where there is inadequate medical service, giving skilled care to women in childbirth and nursing care to the sick. The FNS also owns and operates hospitals, clinics, nursing centers, and educational programs for nurse-midwives and nurse-practitioners and carries out preventive public health measures to educate the rural population in the laws of health and to educate parents in baby hygiene and child care. Its experts also provide social service and help the needy obtain medical, dental, and surgical services at a price they can afford.

Although the internship program (the FNS calls them "couriers") has changed over the years, the FNS is still preparing the young for their future by offering opportunities for interns to accompany family nurse-practitioners, nurse-midwives and/or physicians as they provide care or home health nurses as they travel to patients' homes.

Couriers may also choose to spend time at the Frontier School of Midwifery & Family Nursing, the largest nurse-midwifery school in the United States. If the medical field doesn't interest you but you'd still like to help in this area, you can become involved with community projects such as the adult learning center, the safe house for abused mothers and children, or the local animal shelter.

HOUSING

Housing is provided on the historical grounds for a $250 fee. You'll live at the historical headquarters of FNS called Wendover, which sits on the side of a hill about 10 minutes from Hyden, KY, along the narrow, winding Wendover Road. The Wendover complex consists of the Big House, the Garden House, and the Barn. The Big House is the original home of Mary Breckinridge and has been designated a National Historic Landmark; today, it's a licensed Bed & Breakfast Inn. The Garden House is used for the administrative offices on the first floor and housing for the female interns on the second floor. The Barn is renovated with rooms for male interns and guests.

HOW TO APPLY

Download the short application at http://www.frontiernursing.org/Courier/CourierApp.pdf. Submit the application, along with a short written article summarizing your future goals and explaining why you want to work in a rural area, three references, and a doctor's health form (also downloadable at the Web site) to the preceding address.

GAY MEN'S HEALTH CRISIS INTERNSHIP

Gay Men's Health Crisis Inc.
Attn: Derry Duncan
The Tisch Building
119 West 24 Street
New York, NY 10011
(212) 367-1510
http://www.gmhc.org/careers.html#internships

What You Can Earn: Unpaid but GMHC will support academic institution requirements for students by completing all paperwork required by the intern's school or program.
Application Deadlines: Rolling.
Educational Experience: Students from undergraduate, graduate, certificate, and job-training programs affiliated with an accredited academic institution or job-training program. High school students interested in an internship are assigned to

supervised onsite internships without direct client contact.

Requirements: High school students must have a signed parental consent form.

OVERVIEW

The Gay Men's Health Crisis (GMHC) is the nation's oldest and largest AIDS service organization and provides internship opportunities designed to nurture talent while providing support in the fight against AIDS. As an AIDS service organization dedicated to providing education, advocacy, and direct services to men, women, and children infected or affected by HIV/AIDS, GMHC has supervised internships in a variety of departments, including AIDS hotline, public policy, human resources, communications, marketing, accounting, child life, HIV prevention, recreation, women and family services, treatment education, and support services.

All interns will have direct supervision from a GMHC staff member committed to ensuring that interns have appropriate and clearly directed assignments related to students' academic programs as well as being relevant to agency operations.

HOW TO APPLY

Submit your resume with a cover letter stating your area of interest and academic requirements to the preceding address.

GOULD FARM INTERNSHIP

Gould Farm
Human Resources Director
PO Box 157
Monterey, MA 01245
(413) 528-1804, ext. 17
Fax: (413) 528-5051
http://www.gouldfarm.org/opportunity.htm

What You Can Earn: $57 a week stipend, free room and board, medical benefits with a one-year commitment; recent grads can usually defer student loans through volunteer work here.
Application Deadlines: Rolling.
Educational Experience: Mature individuals with experience in any of a variety of disciplines.
Requirements: Interest in working with individuals experiencing mental illness.

OVERVIEW

Gould Farm is a psychiatric rehabilitation program on 650 acres of farmland and woodland in Monterey in the Berkshire Hills of Western Massachusetts. For many years, the farm has been providing respectful treatment for individuals over age 18 with mental illness, especially those with schizophrenia, schizo-affective disorder, bipolar disorder, and depression. The farm is a diverse community of patients (called "clients" or "guests"), staff and their families, and interns and offers guests a strong clinical team as well as residential advisors with training and experience in the field of mental health.

As a community, staff and interns live, work, and provide job skills, training, and education for guests on 100 acres. All join in the work, which follows the cycle of the seasons, tapping trees for maple syrup in late winter, preparing the ground and planting seeds in the spring, gardening in the summer, and pressing apples for cider in autumn. The farm's intensive work program is balanced with educational opportunities, community events, traditional celebrations, and a variety of therapeutic supports.

Guests are provided with counseling, goal-setting, planning and evaluation meetings, and medications, all integrated into the normal structure of work and community life. Once guests have improved, they begin to prepare to leave the farm by moving to outlying satellite clinics in the Boston area, eventually moving on to independent living. The farm's new Harvest Barn provides job training to help guests who are leaving the program. Working at the farm's Roadside Store is also helpful.

Gould Farm offers a rehabilitation program steeped in the tradition of social service and fellowship within a compassionate, respectful family environment where people with mental illness learn to build more meaningful lives for themselves. Services are rooted in the belief that every person has something valuable to contribute to the community regardless of his or her mental or emotional limitations. The farm was founded in 1900 by William J. Gould, a visionary and pioneer in social reform who came up with a plan for emotional rehabilitation based on the principles of respectful discipline, wholesome work, and kindness. Will and his wife Agnes bought a farm in Western Massachusetts and set up America's oldest therapeutic community for people with mental illness.

Gould Farm provides opportunities for volunteer interns, especially those looking for quality work experiences before applying for graduate school or starting a career. Volunteer commitments usually last for one to two years, and all positions are live-in and full-time (40 hours per week.) Volunteers are supervised by a senior staff member. The greatest need for volunteers occurs in May and September.

Internships are available in a variety of areas, including residential support, maintenance/forestry & grounds, gardening/farming, kitchen/food services, administrative support, and the Boston-area program support.

Administrative Support
Here, you'll help make the farm run, helping out with childcare, activities, transportation, reception, special events, and outreach work.

Boston Area Program Support
Interns who live in the farm's smaller communities in the Boston suburbs provide support, guidance, and advocacy for clients who are on their way to leading more independent lives. Volunteers work with clients in both residential and nonresidential programs.

Gardening/Farming
Guests and interns work together on daily or seasonal tasks, including sowing seeds in the greenhouse, planting in the garden, and helping with the chores of a working farm, including tending to cows, chickens, and pigs.

Kitchen/Food Services
Volunteers in the kitchen work alongside guests to prepare three healthy meals a day for the community. At the Roadside Store & Café, interns gain experience in both restaurant management and human services as they work with guests. Both positions involve working with the clinical staff on treatment plans for guests.

Maintenance/Forestry and Grounds
Here, you'll work beside guests on a variety of work projects including trail maintenance, painting, repairs, forest management, housekeeping and cooking. Seasonal projects include making maple syrup, splitting firewood, and pressing cider.

Residential Support
This volunteer position includes teaching daily-living skills, assisting in crisis management, informal counseling, input into treatment planning, some asleep overnight coverage, and participation in activities.

HOW TO APPLY
Applications for volunteer positions are accepted year-round; to apply for an internship position, call or send a cover letter and resume to the preceding address.

HARVARD SCHOOL OF PUBLIC HEALTH MINORITY INTERNSHIP

Undergraduate Internship Program for Minority Students
Division of Biological Sciences
Harvard School of Public Health

665 Huntington Ave., Building 1-1312
Boston, MA 02115-6021
(617) 432-4470
Fax: (617) 432-0433
dbs@hsph.harvard.edu
http://www.hsph.harvard.edu/sip

What You Can Earn: Stipend of at least $3,200 over the nine-week internship, travel allowance of up to $475, and free dormitory housing.
Application Deadlines: February 14.
Educational Experience: Minority college students who will be juniors or seniors in the fall immediately after their summer internship ends.
Requirements: U.S. citizenship or permanent residency; a member of an ethnic group currently underrepresented in science: African American, Mexican American, Chicano, Native American (American Indian, Aleut, Eskimo), Pacific Islander (Polynesian or Micronesian), or Puerto Rican.

OVERVIEW

Sponsored by the National Institutes of Health, this Harvard internship is designed to expose minority college science students to the rewards of laboratory research directed toward solving important public health problems such as cancer, cardiovascular disease, or infections. The overall mission of the program is to recruit qualified students for graduate-level training leading to research careers in the biological sciences.

During this internship, you'll apply state-of-the art technology in your own research projects under the direction of a Harvard faculty member. Research projects focus on biological science questions that are important to the prevention of disease, such as cancer, cardiovascular disease, infections (malaria, parasites, and AIDS), lung diseases, aging, diabetes, obesity, and so on. As part of your internship, you'll write a paper and complete an oral presentation.

The internship faculty includes specialists in the fields of immunology and infectious diseases, genetics and complex diseases, molecular and cellular toxicology, environmental health sciences, nutrition, and cardiovascular research.

HOW TO APPLY

An application may be downloaded from the Web site at http://www.hsph.harvard.edu/sip/summer2005.pdf or requested at the previous address. You should submit all in one packet: a completed application form along with a one-page statement describing your long-term career goals in biological research, an official college transcript, and two letters of reference. Confidential letters of reference should be sent in a sealed envelope, which has been signed over the seal. Applicants should be notified by mid-March.

HEAD START NATIONAL INTERNSHIP

National Head Start Association
1651 Prince Street
Alexandria, VA 22314
(703) 739-0875
Fax: (703) 739-0878
ballen@nhsa.org
http://www.nhsa.org

What You Can Earn: Unpaid but partial subway (Metro) reimbursement provided.
Application Deadlines: Rolling.
Educational Experience: Undergrad or grad student majoring in political science, psychology, family studies, sociology, child development, or public administration. Minorities and women are strongly urged to apply.
Requirements: Excellent written and oral communication skills; ability to work well with others.

OVERVIEW

The National Head Start Association (NHSA) is a private nonprofit membership organization dedicated exclusively to meeting the needs of Head Start children and their families, representing more than 900,000 children, 190,000 staff, and nearly 2,700 Head Start programs in the United States. Created in 1965, Head Start is the most successful, longest-running, national school readiness program in the United States. It provides comprehensive education, health, nutrition, and parent-involvement services to low-income children and their families. More than 21 million preschool aged children have benefited from Head Start.

As an intern, you may help draft articles for newsletters, such as *NHSA News* and the *Legislative Update;* perform research and literature reviews; attend and report on research-related events, such as congressional hearings on Capitol Hill and research-related press conferences or events; help staff with survey research projects; and maintain a library of reports and journal articles on related topics

HOW TO APPLY
E-mail a resume, a cover letter, and a writing sample (no more than three pages) to the preceding address.

HEALTHY MOTHERS, HEALTHY BABIES COALITION OF WASHINGTON INTERNSHIP

Healthy Mothers, Healthy Babies Coalition of Washington
(800) 322-2588
kayk@hmhbwa.org
http://www.hmhbwa.org

What You Can Earn: Unpaid.
Application Deadlines: Rolling.
Educational Experience: Master's degree and/or enrolled in a master's program in public health, public administration, nutrition or social work; candidates should also have some experience or knowledge of survey design, methodology, and implementation.
Requirements: Must be able to work 15 to 25 hours a week.

OVERVIEW
Healthy Mothers, Healthy Babies Coalition of Washington (HMHB) is committed to ensuring optimal health for all families through information hotlines. This private nonprofit organization serves as a catalyst for improvements in maternal, child, and family heath. Healthy Mothers, Healthy Babies provides information and referral for social and health services across Washington State. Information and Referral Specialists help callers with answers to questions about health insurance, prenatal resources, nutrition and food resources, breast-feeding, immunization, family planning, child care, children with special needs, child development, and parent/sibling support.

Healthy Mothers, Healthy Babies works with interns on a project-by-project basis.

HOW TO APPLY
For additional information, contact Kay Knox at the preceding e-mail address.

INJURY CENTER INTERNSHIP

Association of Schools of Public Health
1101 15th Street, NW, Suite 910
Washington, DC 20005
(202) 296-1099
Fax: (202) 296-1252
http://www.asph.org/document.
    cfm?page=751&JobProg_ID=12

What You Can Earn: Stipend of $2,500 is provided for the 12-week period.
Application Deadlines: Rolling.
Educational Experience: Grad students at ASPH-accredited schools of public health; doctoral candidates are not eligible to apply.
Requirements: U.S. citizenship or permanent resident.

OVERVIEW

The Internship Program is part of a cooperative agreement between the Association of Schools of Public Health (ASPH) and the Centers for Disease Control and Prevention (CDC) to support injury-related internship experiences. If you're chosen as an intern, you'll have the chance to gain practical experience by participating in projects under the direction of the school's experts in injury control and prevention. While participating in this program, you'll be exposed to state-of-the-art prevention research and given the chance to apply knowledge to real world public health situations.

Examples of unintentional injuries include car accidents, man-made or natural disasters, drowning, falls, suffocation, poisoning, fire and burns, cuts, and so on. Examples of intentional injuries include partner/spousal abuse, sexual violence, homicide, assault, school violence, suicide, child abuse or neglect, elder abuse, and so on. Injuries will not include job-related accidents.

Internship positions are for 12 weeks, usually beginning in the summer or fall; the actual start date of the internship and weekly schedule (not to exceed 20 hours/week) are mutually agreed upon by the student and internship mentor. Internship opportunities will be located at ASPH Accredited Schools of Public Health.

HOW TO APPLY

Full details regarding applications, program information, and internship descriptions are available at your school's public health office. A downloadable application is available at the preceding Web address.

As part of the application process, you will propose a project that must be related to injury control and prevention activities and endorsed either by your school's injury center director, faculty mentor and department chair, or the sponsoring individual at the organization where the project will be completed.

All applications to the internship program undergo a two-phase review process. In the first stage, applications are reviewed by injury prevention professionals on the following criteria: project proposal (60 percent), public health interest/background/experience (20 percent), academic achievement/transcript (10 percent), and letters of recommendation (10 percent).

Applications approved by the professional review are forwarded to the U.S. Centers for Disease Control, where applications are assessed to decide which of the candidates applying for individual projects are most suited for the internships. You'll be notified about four weeks after the deadline for applications.

NATIONAL HEALTHY MOTHERS, HEALTHY BABIES COALITION INTERNSHIP

National Healthy Mothers, Healthy Babies Coalition
Attn: Intern Coordinator
121 North Washington Street, Suite 300
Alexandria, VA 22314
(703) 836-6110
Fax: (703) 836-3470
info@hmhb.org

What You Can Earn: Unpaid but college credit is available.
Application Deadlines: Rolling.

Educational Experience: Undergraduate or graduate students or recent graduates available at least 20 hours per week for at least three months.

Requirements: Strong oral/written communication, organizational/interpersonal skills; commitment to maternal and child health; and experience in or desire to work with underserved populations.

OVERVIEW

The National Healthy Mothers, Healthy Babies Coalition (HMHB) is a leader in maternal and child health, reaching about 10 million healthcare professionals, parents, and policymakers through more than 100 local, state, and national organizations. Enhanced by a network of 90 local coalitions, HMHB acts as a catalyst for change and creates partnerships among community groups, nonprofit organizations, professional associations, and businesses and government agencies. By promoting optimal health for mom and baby, HMHB works to strengthen families and build healthy communities.

From the beginning, HMHB has focused on raising public awareness of the basic components of prenatal care, emphasizing early care; good nutrition; drug, tobacco, and alcohol avoidance; and the importance of breast-feeding. The coalition has targeted low income and underserved communities, where early prenatal care is absent and infant mortality rates are high.

HMHB interns work to make a difference for mothers, babies, and their families as they take part in the opportunity to learn more about maternal and child health issues. Winter, spring, summer, and fall internships are available, and students with special academic project requirements are welcome. A limited number of opportunities for interns are available year round. During their internship, students work on various projects such as drafting articles for HMHB publications and helping with the Web site and listservs; researching the Internet, publications, and also utilizing personal contacts; attending and assisting with meetings, conferences, and seminars; working on an in-depth project in a core program area or on a specific issue; and handling reports, copying, mailings, and other duties.

HOW TO APPLY

Call or send an e-mail to request an application from the intern coordinator at the preceding address.

NATIONAL MENTAL HEALTH ASSOCIATION INTERNSHIP

National Mental Health Association
2001 North Beauregard Street, 12th Floor
Alexandria, VA 22311
(703) 684-7722
http://www.nmha.org/contact/index.cfm

What You Can Earn: Unpaid but college credit is available.

Application Deadlines: Rolling.

Educational Experience: Undergraduate and graduate students.

Requirements: Unspecified.

OVERVIEW

The National Mental Health Association is the country's oldest and largest nonprofit organization addressing all aspects of mental health and mental illness. With more than 340 affiliates nationwide, NMHA works to improve the mental health of all Americans, especially the 54 million people with mental disorders, through advocacy, education, research, and service. The association's internship program provides an ideal opportunity for students interested in mental health issues to gain real-world work experience relevant to their academic and career goals. Each intern collaborates with a supervisor to develop a focused curriculum/work plan. Once on the job, the type of work given to the intern integrates the curriculum/work plan and includes challenging projects and tasks that are both meaningful and stimulating.

To enhance the internship experience and help prepare students for future career success, interns are also trained how to identify their unique skills and abilities and develop career goals. Interns are also invited to attend any of the association's professional development workshops for staff that include many different mental health, skill-building, and information technology topics.

As the country's oldest and largest nonprofit organization addressing all aspects of mental health and mental illnesses, the association helps prepare students for an exciting future in the field by providing opportunities to explore career options in mental health advocacy, public policy, education, research and service.

Adult Mental Health Services

This internship position provides the opportunity to learn about community-based programs managed by people with mental illnesses. Interns will research and develop materials related to organizational development and fund-raising. In addition, this internship will provide the opportunity to learn about community-based services such as housing, employment, supported education, integrated services, and peer-support services. This position is intended for individuals interested in learning more about the mental health field, particularly those interested in learning about the perspectives of national advocacy organizations and consumer-run programs.

Communications/Media

Here interns will work in the association's communications department. Applications should be studying communications, public policy, social work, psychology, and marketing. Interns will work on the association's Mental Health Media Awards program and "May is Mental Health Month" outreach, among other public relations projects. Ideal candidates will have excellent oral and written communication skills, strong organizational skills, research skills, and the ability to work in fast-paced environment. Knowledge of mental health issues is a plus. Proficiency in Word, Excel, and the Internet is required.

Development Department

In this department, interns will work on a variety of fund-raising projects, including corporate, foundation, and individual fund-raising. The internship offers the opportunity to work in a variety of areas within the organization and will include projects such as developing marketing materials for the department, coordinating end-of-year fundraising programs, and assisting with the launch of a new national fund-raising program.

Federal Affairs

The intern will work on federal policy issues and legislation and provide research and other support to the federal policy team and grass-roots advocates. Issue areas will include expanding access to treatment, children's mental health, mental health parity, Medicaid, and the Medicare prescription drug program. This internship is located in Washington, D.C., four blocks from Capitol Hill.

Healthcare Reform

In this department, enthusiastic, mature interns with knowledge of health policy will be responsible for tracking state legislation, conducting policy research for conferences and products, providing technical assistance to advocates, and helping coordinate special events. Good writing skills, attention to detail, and the ability to work independently are important. Graduate students are preferred for this internship.

Marketing/Publications

The primary duties of this internship will be to provide customer service to those ordering NMHA publications, help with the implementation of sales and marketing plans, create sales reports, and help plan the organization's annual meeting. This internship offers a great opportunity to learn about the sale of products in a nonprofit environment, as well as coordinating the content and attendance of a large organizational meeting.

National Association of Mental Health Planning and Advisory Councils

The intern will help coordinate projects, helping to research material for presentations and technical assistance activities and managing logistics associated with meetings and travel. Research supporting brochure development on topics related to mental health also may be part of the internship. Depending on intern experiences and interests, the intern may help with Web site development and database management.

Public Education

In this internship, interns will work on the association's public awareness and education programs that address the needs of children and families, college students, mental health consumers, communities of color, older adults, and the general public. Interns will help research and develop materials such as fact sheets, brochures, Web site copy, reports and kits, and participate in other activities as necessary.

Research and Services

The intern is assigned to work on the development of a children's mental health agenda, helping assess all NMHA child-related activities in all departments. This also may involve a survey of selected MHA affiliates and states on their capacity and readiness to engage in systems-reform activities related to children's mental health. Finally, activities might include some basic research on funding sources for children's mental health advocacy.

HOW TO APPLY

You should apply online at http://www.nmha. org/intern/internship_apply.cfm, including your resume.

NEW ENGLAND HEALTHCARE INSTITUTE INTERNSHIP

New England Healthcare Institute
One Cambridge Center, Ninth Floor
Cambridge, MA 02142
(617) 225-0857
careers@nehi.net

What You Can Earn: Competitive salary.
Application Deadlines: April 15.
Educational Experience: Bachelor's degree required; graduate-level interns strongly preferred who have one to three years of work experience in consulting, healthcare, or academic research settings.
Requirements: Demonstrated interest/experience in healthcare; ability to synthesize information from multiple sources (academic journals, newspapers, online publications, interviews); attentiveness to detail; ability to interact with senior-level leaders in the healthcare industry and community, and ability to carry out projects. Strong computer and Internet proficiency and excellent verbal and written communication skills; ability to work in a highly collaborative team environment.

OVERVIEW

Headquartered in Cambridge, Mass., the New England Healthcare Institute (NEHI) is a regional applied health policy research institute dedicated to identifying, analyzing, and resolving critical healthcare issues facing the people of New England. NEHI represents all sectors of the healthcare industry, including members of the biotechnology, pharmaceutical, medical device, hospital, physician, physician, researcher, employer, and insurer communities.

Interns will provide research assistance in one or more of NEHI´s focus areas: speeding the adoption of healthcare innovations, reducing health care inefficiency, and improving the healthcare economy in New England. Interns will conduct literature reviews and background research, participate in interviews of experts and senior industry leaders, analyze data and synthesize findings, and help develop policy initiatives. Interns will help identify potential partners, keep up to date on healthcare and health policy issues that affect NEHI´s research and policy development, and support the NEHI team.

HOW TO APPLY

E-mail a cover letter and resume to the preceding address, referencing "Summer Internship" in the subject line of the e-mail.

PENNSYLVANIA DEPARTMENT OF HEALTH PUBLIC HEALTH INTERNSHIP

Pennsylvania Department of Health
Bureau of Human Resources
PO Box 90
Health and Welfare Building
Harrisburg, PA 17108
(717) 787-6002
dhhr@state.pa.us

What You Can Earn: $10.31 an hour
Application Deadlines: Rolling.
Educational Experience: Must be enrolled as a full-time student in an accredited college or university that offers or leads to a B.A., B.S., or graduate degree and be in good academic standing. Applicant must be a Pennsylvania resi-

dent or be attending an academic institution in Pennsylvania.
Requirements: Must demonstrate leadership qualities, international experiences and perspectives, a good academic record, and strong writing and oral skills. Knowledge of a foreign language is a must. Candidates should also have a mature sense of purpose and commitment and must be interested in a career in public or nonprofit service.

OVERVIEW

Created in 1905, the Pennsylvania Department of Health (DOH) is responsible for protecting the health of the people by preventing and suppressing disease and injury. The department also works closely with local health agencies in cities, counties and municipalities. The department plans and coordinates health resources throughout the state, regulating a variety of facilities such as hospitals, nursing homes, surgical facilities, and other in-patient and out-patient facilities. In addition, the department supports outreach, education, prevention and treatment, and helps provide essential services to support programs for women and children, nutrition, immunization, diagnosis and treatment of certain blood and communicable diseases, cancer control and prevention, and the prevention and treatment of substance abuse.

The DOH offers a number of internships to college students depending on the needs of DOH, the availability of funds, and the qualifications of applicants. DOH Public Health Internships provide valuable work experience in public health, social sciences, information technology and health related sciences. Internships are primarily in the Harrisburg area.

HOW TO APPLY

To apply for a DOH internship, e-mail, or mail your resume to the Bureau of Human Resources at the address above.

POPULATION INSTITUTE INTERNSHIP

Education Coordinator, The Population Institute
107 Second Street, NE
Washington, DC 20002
(202) 544-3300, ext. 121
(202) 544-0068
web@populationinstitute.org
http://www.populationinstitute.org

What You Can Earn: $24,000 a year plus health, dental, and life insurance, 10 days of annual leave, and one sick day per month.
Application Deadlines: April 15.
Educational Experience: Must have completed at least two years of college and be between 21 and 25 years old; graduate students are also accepted.
Requirements: Must demonstrate leadership qualities, international experiences and perspectives, a good academic record, and strong writing and oral skills. Knowledge of a foreign language is a must. Candidates should also have a mature sense of purpose and commitment and must be interested in a career in public or nonprofit service.

OVERVIEW

The Population Institute is an international, educational, nonprofit organization trying to slow population growth to achieve a world population in balance with a healthy global environment. Established in 1969, the Institute has members in 172 countries and headquarters on Capitol Hill in Washington, D.C. The Institute tries to help others understand the social, economic, and environmental consequences of rapid population growth and promotes international and U.S. support for voluntary family-planning programs.

Its internship program was established in 1980 for qualified upper-level undergraduate and graduate students interested in the fields of nonprofit international relations and development.

The program is a yearlong, full-time professional development program. You'll participate fully in all activities, working with experienced professionals in seeking practical solutions to population-related problems.

Two to three staff assistants work as public policy coordinators, helping with legislative education projects, providing information to legislators and key staff, and following up on community leaders recruited during field trips across the nation. One fellow is hired as a media coordinator responsible for maintaining a press list and working with the media in writing, reporting, proofreading, and editing. One to two interns are hired as field coordinators to plan and implement educational tours around the nation for Institute speakers. One fellow may be recruited to manage special programs, such as World Population Awareness Week, depending on funding.

HOW TO APPLY

Send your cover letter, resume, three recommendations (two from academic sources), and official transcripts to the preceding address. Application material may be sent separately, but do not e-mail any application materials.

PROJECT HOPE (HEALTH OPPORTUNITIES FOR PEOPLE EVERYWHERE) INTERNSHIP

Project HOPE Recruitment
255 Carter Hall Lane
Millwood , VA 22646
Fax: (540) 837-9052
recruitment@projecthope.org
http://www.projecthope.org/employment/
  volunteeropps.htm

What You Can Earn: Unpaid.
Application Deadlines: Rolling.
Educational Experience: Graduate students or medical students.
Requirements: Dedication, responsibility, attention to detail, and interest in serving others.

OVERVIEW

Identifiable to many by the S.S. *HOPE*, the world's first peacetime hospital ship, Project HOPE now conducts land-based medical training and healthcare education programs on five continents, including North America. Project HOPE's mission is to improve healthcare around the world by implementing health education programs, conducting health-policy research, and providing humanitarian assistance in areas of need, contributing to human dignity, promoting international understanding, and enhancing social and economic development. The essence of Project HOPE is teaching; the basis is partnership.

Volunteers have been at the heart of Project HOPE's work since the days when the S.S. HOPE first sailed. The project is able to bring medical education and healthcare training to the developing world through the efforts of volunteer physicians, nurses, surgeons, biomedical engineers, allied healthcare workers, and others who give their time and talents to travel overseas for short-term and long-term training assignments. More than 5,000 healthcare professionals have donated their services in this manner to Project HOPE's programs during its 47-year history.

The breadth of Project HOPE programs throughout the world offers a unique educational laboratory for students of the health sciences. Internship opportunities vary throughout the year. With programs in 32 countries around the world, Project HOPE offers an opportunity to interns to gain a global perspective through clinical and/or academic teaching experience, exposure to health issues and needs in developing countries, development of healthcare systems and research, and experience in program planning and evaluation. Fundamental to its success

and the achievement of Project HOPE's mission are its core values of integrity, excellence, respect, and compassion.

HOW TO APPLY
Visit the preceding Web site to apply.

PULMONARY HYPERTENSION ASSOCIATION INTERNSHIP

Medical Services Manager
Pulmonary Hypertension Association
850 Sligo Avenue, Suite 800
Silver Spring, MD 20910
(301) 565-3004 x.107
Fax: (301) 565-3994
justine@phassociation.org
http://www.phassociation.org

What You Can Earn: Unpaid but includes $50-a-week stipend for administrative work.
Application Deadlines: May 15.
Educational Experience: None specified.
Requirements: Good communication, writing, and editing skills; interest in healthcare issues and in working with a nonprofit organization; experience with the Internet and/or library research; ability to organize information and document research for future reporting; ability to think creatively and strategically and multitask; ability to work well with a team.

OVERVIEW
The Pulmonary Hypertension Association (PHA) is a nonprofit association of patients, caregivers, and medical professionals looking for a cure for pulmonary hypertension and providing support, education, advocacy, and awareness. The associa-

tion supports research to develop better treatments; offers support groups, hotlines, and electronic communications; provides information to the general public and the medical community; and works on targeted projects.

The association internship offers students a structured experience working with PHA staff, helping the medical services manager provide medical services to physicians, researchers, and patients. As an intern with this association, you'll gain valuable experience in the field of managing a nonprofit health organization, help develop the medical resources section of the Web site and other educational tools such as brochures and DVDs, research medical topics, and interview researchers, physicians, and other medical professionals who work with PHA. You'll also help develop communication materials for medical professionals and patients and help coordinate events and meetings for medical professionals and patients.

This is a three- to six-month unpaid internship (20 to 40 hours a week), but you can earn a $50 weekly stipend for administrative work (mailings, faxing, filing, photocopying, and so on). Administrative work rarely exceeds 25 percent per week.

HOW TO APPLY
To apply, e-mail, fax, or mail a cover letter explaining your interest in working for PHA, a resume, and a three- to six-page writing sample to the preceding address.

SILENT SPRING INSTITUTE INTERNSHIP

Silent Spring Institute
Administrative Manager
29 Crafts Street
Newton, MA 02458
careers@silentspring.org

What You Can Earn: Unpaid.
Application Deadlines: Rolling.
Educational Experience: Undergraduate or graduate students with excellent academic records; chemistry, biology, or statistics coursework is an asset.
Requirements: Energetic, flexible, constructive outlook; excellent attention to accuracy; ability to work independently within a multidisciplinary team. Commitment to careful and impartial research.

OVERVIEW
Silent Spring Institute is a partnership of scientists, physicians, public health advocates, and community activists working together to identify and change the links between the environment and women's health (especially breast cancer). This collaboration began when activists from the Massachusetts Breast Cancer Coalition recognized the need for a new type of research organization to find preventable causes of breast cancer. Silent Spring Institute is named in recognition of *Silent Spring*, Rachel Carson's pioneering book that tied the use of pesticides to adverse effects on wildlife.

The organization's research projects investigate a number of issues key to determining how women are exposed to pollutants with potentially long-term health risks. This research is funded by organizations and individuals committed to furthering research on issues that affect women's health and, in particular, on potential environmental links to breast cancer.

Responsibilities will be tailored to the skills and interests of the applicant.

Each intern will work directly as an assistant to a supervising staff member, and interns are encouraged to develop an independent project to be completed during the internship. Responsibilities may include literature searches, interviewing, environmental sampling, data management, and writing. Undergraduate and masters interns are expected to spend approximately 20 percent of their time on office-support tasks (telephones and so on). Interns are expected to maintain regular work hours, with some flexibility to accommodate major assignments and exams.

HOW TO APPLY

To apply, e-mail or mail a cover letter describing your interests and experience related to this internship and which time period you're interested in, along with your resume and a copy of academic transcript (photocopy is fine) to the preceding address.

SURGEONS OF HOPE FOUNDATION INTERNSHIP

Surgeons of Hope
825 Eighth Avenue, 35th Floor
New York, NY 10019
(212) 474-5994
Fax: (212) 474-5996
aheifetz@ surgeonsofhope.org
http://surgeonsofhope.org

What You Can Earn: Unpaid.
Application Deadlines: Rolling.
Educational Experience: Must either be enrolled in a college degree program or have a bachelor's degree.
Requirements: Ability to speak, read, and write in French is helpful; good knowledge of computers and the Internet; must be organized and a creative thinker.

OVERVIEW

The Surgeons of Hope Foundation (SoH) is a nonprofit whose purpose is to bring surgical and medical care to needy children in developing countries. SoH works to transfer necessary medical, technical, and managerial skills to specially devised hospitals, which will use these resources to treat patients locally. The hospitals are designed to become financially independent within the first few years of operation. SoH works with its French partner, La Chaîne de l'Espoir (CdE), which, along with its network of affiliate organizations in Europe, has more than 15 years of experience in the field of pediatric surgery and has operated on more than 6,000 children in developing countries.

The organization's goal is to extend hospital projects and their resource base. Through the creation of a lasting cooperation between the United States and Europe, SoH-CdE seeks to mobilize human, material, and financial resources to train more local surgical teams and operate on more children.

If you're interested in international issues, like to write and create documents using a variety of applications, and want to gain experience working for a nonprofit, this internship could be for you. Part-time (15-20 hours per week) summer interns will help write and edit the Web site, press packages, and other public relations tools.

HOW TO APPLY

To apply, send a copy of your resume and cover letter to development and marketing coordinator of SoH.

WAKEMED HEALTH AND HOSPITALS INTERNSHIP

Ylenia Taylor, Human Resources Specialist
WakeMed
3000 New Bern Avenue
Raleigh, NC 27601
(919) 350-4470
http://www.wakemed.org

What You Can Earn: $9.39 to $12.21 an hour
Application Deadlines: April 15.

Educational Experience: At least a junior or senior attending an accredited college or university in a baccalaureate degree program or graduate degree program in public health, health policy administration, or business with an emphasis in healthcare and an overall 3.0 GPA.

Requirements: Available to work 12 consecutive weeks during the summer and able to provide your own transportation and housing. Preference will be given to African-American and Hispanic students.

OVERVIEW

WakeMed is a 752-bed private, nonprofit healthcare system based in Raleigh, N.C. The Raleigh campus is a multiservice facility with 515 beds and a 24-hour adult emergency department treating more than 90,000 patients a year. Wake County's state-designated trauma center is home to North Carolina's only 24-hour freestanding children's emergency department. The Raleigh campus also houses a world-famous Heart Center, which brings all cardiac-related services under one roof. WakeMed is one of the state's leading providers of care for cardiac disease and is one of *Modern Maturity*'s Top Ten Cardiovascular Surgery Programs. A leader in the care of neurological injury and illness, WakeMed also provides a comprehensive program that includes the county's only neurological intensive care unit and the only inpatient unit dedicated to neuroscience.

WakeMed Rehab offers treatment for patients recovering from stroke, spinal cord injuries, brain injuries, arthritis, and neuromuscular disorders in a 68-bed rehabilitation hospital that is the largest and most comprehensive in the area.

WakeMed Health & Hospital's Summer Internship Program is a 12-week program from May through August that provides an opportunity to learn in a fast-paced hospital setting, working alongside an experienced staff of professionals. Interns are mentored by hospital managers who provide each intern with a hospital project and familiarize each intern with procedures and organizational structure and culture.

HOW TO APPLY

Apply online at the preceding address. During the interview process, two professional references and an official copy of your most recent transcript will be required.

WASHINGTON, D.C., DEPARTMENT OF HEALTH INTERNSHIP

Andria Barbee, Special Projects Coordinator
Department of Health
825 North Capitol Street, NE, Suite 4400
Washington, DC 20002
(202) 442-5942
http://dchealth.dc.gov/services/internship_
    program/contact.shtm

What You Can Earn: Paid; exact salary civil service grade depends on year of college (one grade higher for each year of college, through graduate school); academic credit is also available.

Application Deadlines: Rolling.

Educational Experience: Currently enrolled and attending a university, trade/vocational school, or business school that offers a degree, diploma, or certificate with a C average and must be enrolled at least one semester or quarter prior to the submission of an application.

Requirements: Must be in good standing financially at the institution of enrollment.

OVERVIEW

The Washington, D.C., Department of Health works to eliminate disparities in healthcare access and works toward measurable improvement in the health status of all district neighborhoods. The department's goal is to ensure that the District of Columbia leads the nation in healthy lifestyles.

Interns may work full time or part time in the department, depending on the scope of work, availability of funds, and the student's schedule. An initial internship may not exceed one year. Appointments may be renewed based on departmental needs and the availability of funds.

HOW TO APPLY

Download an application in PDF format at http://dchealth.dc.gov/services/internship_program/eligibility.shtm. Complete and submit the application, along with two letters of recommendation from someone who can attest to your knowledge, skills, and experience (such as a professor, advisor, or former employer), to the preceding address.

YAI NATIONAL INSTITUTE FOR PEOPLE WITH DISABILITIES INTERNSHIP

YAI/NIPD Network
460 West 34th Street
New York, NY 10001-2382
http://careers.hodes.com/yai

What You Can Earn: Unpaid but college credit is offered.
Application Deadlines: Rolling.
Educational Experience: Undergraduate or graduate student in any majors, including psychology, social work, human services, education, or sociology; nonstudents also considered.
Requirements: Must have the desire to work with the developmentally disabled population.

OVERVIEW

For almost 45 years, YAI/National Institute for People with Disabilities (YAI/NIPD) has been committed to improving the lives of people with mental retardation and developmental and learning disabilities and helping them reach their potential. YAI is an award-winning, nonprofit, nonsectarian agency with nearly 20,000 people involved in more than 300 community-based programs. With locations in New York City, Long Island, Westchester and Orange County, Northern New Jersey (Bergen County) and Puerto Rico, teams provide a full range of early intervention, preschool, family support, employment training and placement, clinical and residential services, and recreational and camping services.

YAI offers a variety of internship programs to help students learn more about developmental disabilities, providing hands-on experience, supportive supervision, and state-of-the-art training. Interns also can train in an administrative department (research, professional information, human resources, special events, fund-raising/development, and office management).

Participants will receive professional training and supervision, mentorship, professional networking opportunities, and a complimentary pass to YAI's International Conference. Internships are available in a variety of programs such as residential group homes, structured classroom settings, job readiness programs, community-based programs, clinics, and so on. You may find yourself teaching independent-living skills, providing informal counseling, promoting community integration, teaching job-training skills, or helping with recreational activities.

HOW TO APPLY

To check for current intern openings, visit http://careers.hodes.com/yai/and complete the online application form.

HISTORICAL AREAS

ANACOSTIA MUSEUM AND CENTER FOR AFRICAN AMERICAN HISTORY AND CULTURE INTERNSHIP

Anacostia Museum Internship Coordinator
Smithsonian Institution
1901 Fort Place, SE
Washington, DC 20020-0520
(202) 287-3306
http://anacostia.si.edu

What You Can Earn: Unpaid, but funding is available on a competitive basis from the Smithsonian Institution Office of Fellowships.
Application Deadlines: Rolling.
Educational Experience: Undergraduate and graduate students with an interest in African-American history and culture and black individuals in the Americas.
Requirements: Unspecified.

OVERVIEW

The Anacostia Museum and Center for African American History and Culture, part of the Smithsonian, is a national institution devoted to the identification, documentation, protection, and interpretation of the African American experience and the people of African decent and heritage living in the Americas. The museum encourages the collection, protection, and preservation of materials that reflect the history and traditions of families, organizations, individuals, and communities.

Internships are available in the registrar's office and the following departments: research, exhibits design and production, education, public programs, and public affairs.

HOW TO APPLY

Applications will be considered and accepted based on staff availability and museum schedules.

To apply, contact the internship office at the preceding address.

BUCHANAN /BURNHAM INTERNSHIP

Newport Historical Society Internship
82 Touro Street
Newport, RI 02840
jfiles@newporthistorical.org
http://newporthistorical.org/summer.htm

What You Can Earn: $3,000 stipend for the summer, with possible extra money for weekend or evening work at the Museum of Newport History or for working as tour guides through the end of the tour season. Housing is not provided; please note that summer housing is expensive in Newport. Furnished rooms may be available at a rate of $100 to $150/week.
Application Deadlines: March 1.
Educational Experience: Graduate and undergraduate students of African American history; colonial history; Early American decorative arts/architecture; nonprofit management/marketing; museum studies; political history; religious history; women's history; and related majors. Recent graduate and undergraduate grads are also welcome.
Requirements: Enthusiasm for history, research, tour guiding, historic artifacts, and architecture. Experience studying early America, giving tours, speaking in public, teaching, providing visitor service, and conducting historical or marketing research is preferred.

OVERVIEW

Once a leading colonial seaport engaged in worldwide trade, Newport is a remarkably well-preserved and vibrant seaside city.

Buchanan/Burnham interns lead tours and educational programs at three key historic sites owned by the Newport Historical Society, which interprets three historic sites and manages a fourth: the Wanton-Lyman-Hazard House (circa 1697), the Great Friends ("Quaker") Meeting House (1699), the Newport Colony House (1739), and the Seventh Day Baptist Meeting House (1730).

As an intern in Newport, you'll work with mentors from the Newport Historical Society to develop and execute projects to improve the understanding, interpretation, and promotion of these sites. You may be asked to choose projects relevant to the Wanton-Lyman-Hazard House, which the society is refurnishing, reinterpreting, and marketing as an innovative center for exploring Newport's history and material culture. You may choose to conduct marketing research related to the house or study the experiences and material possessions of the Anglicans, apprentices, Baptists, children, husbands, lawyers, merchants, politicians, Quakers, servants, shopkeepers, single women, slaves, soldiers, and wives who lived and worked at the house from the 1690s through the 1910s.

As an intern, you'll have access to the Newport Historical Society's important manuscript and artifact collections, and you'll present your research findings in writing and conduct a lecture or public program related to your research. Intensive training is provided.

As an intern, you'll work from 9:30 A.M. to 4:30 P.M. five days a week (some interns work Tuesdays through Saturdays; others work Sundays through Thursdays), from early June through late August. The first two weeks of your internship will be spent training and attending lectures and field trips, bolstered by occasional ongoing training throughout the summer. The remainder of your time will be divided evenly between working on your independent projects and working as tour guides at the three historic sites. You'll also attend occasional evening lectures and programs.

HOW TO APPLY

To apply, send a resume, a recent transcript, two letters of recommendation, and a letter explaining your reasons for applying, your career goals, and what you hope to accomplish as a Buchanan/Burnham intern to the preceding address.

Admission to the internship program is very competitive. The Newport Historical Society will invite leading candidates for telephone or face-to-face interviews in mid-March; the NHS will notify successful candidates in mid-April.

BUFFALO BILL HISTORICAL CENTER INTERNSHIP

Collections and Registration
720 Sheridan Avenue
Cody, WY 82414
(307) 578-4020
Fax: (307) 578-4090

What You Can Earn: $6.75 per hour, based on a full-time schedule of 40 hours per week.
Application Deadlines: September 1 for fall session; February 1 for spring and summer sessions; however, applications are accepted all year, as new internship opportunities can occur unexpectedly.
Educational Experience: Qualified upper-level undergraduate students and graduate students enrolled in colleges and universities majoring in museum studies, art, anthropology, history, or a related field, with a cumulative GPA of 3.00 or better.
Requirements: Open to students who want practical museum experience in fields such as art and art history; natural history; ecology; environmental history; wildlife biology; geography; geology; history; American studies; historical development of firearms; Plains Indian ethnology; anthropology; Plains Indian culture; technology; education; collections; exhibitions; photography; publications; graphic design; library/archives; and communications.

OVERVIEW

If you're interested in gaining practical museum experience, the Buffalo Bill Heritage Center offers students hands-on involvement with the museum profession by providing a range of internships. Internships are full-time positions that are usually 12 weeks, including orientation and continuing-education sessions about the work of a museum. As an intern here, you'll be expected to complete a special project, and you'll learn how your department operates.

Buffalo Bill Museum Intern

The Buffalo Bill Museum examines both the personal and public lives of W.F. "Buffalo Bill" Cody (1846–1917) and tells his story in the context of the history and myth of the American West. Highly regarded as a research center focusing on the life and times of Buffalo Bill, the collections of the museum also interpret the history of the American cowboy, dude ranching, Western conservation, frontier entrepreneurship, and the source of popular concepts about the West.

As an intern here, you'll help with acquisitions, collections care, and documentation and research. You'll also help interpret western history and Buffalo Bill Cody, including participation in exhibitions and education.

Candidates should have demonstrated verbal/written communication skills and superior research and computer skills. Graduate students are preferred, but exceptional undergraduate candidates will be considered.

Cody Firearms Museum Firearms Research

Interns in the research department will help organize and index the diagrams and schematics of firearms and firearms-related objects currently archived in the McCracken Research Library so that they can be located and retrieved readily by description and/or function.

As an intern in the firearms department, you'll learn firearms nomenclature and appropriate handling techniques, to identify firearms based on action types, frame and barrel inscriptions, and proof marks. You'll help curatorial staff answer questions and maintain a daily journal, including notes on firearms terminology, action types, inscriptions, proof marks, and reference resources. You'll prepare proposed responses to firearms and firearms-related information inquiries, along with gallery-card requests and comments for review by the curatorial staff. In addition, you'll locate reference resources in the McCracken Research Library for additional information about firearms of interest for BBHC visitors and to those making telephone, electronic message, correspondence, and walk-in inquiries.

Candidates should have good computer and organizational skills; superior verbal and written communication skills; good physical strength, endurance and coordination; a high-level interest in the history and technology of firearms, with a strong basic knowledge of each; and self-motivation and the ability to work independently.

Collections Management Intern

As an intern in this department, you'll learn appropriate methods and techniques for museum object care and handling, and you'll fulfill work orders, examine collections for condition, prepare condition reports, and document activities related to collections movement. You'll also pack and crate objects and clean and prepare objects for storage, exhibition, or travel; maintain permanent and temporary exhibitions; and inspect pest traps and complete written reports on the integrated pest-management program. You also may help install or dismantle collections and attend collections workshops or seminars.

Candidates should be able to lift 30 pounds and maintain a static position and have basic knowledge of computer skills.

Education

As an intern in this department, you'll participate in education staff meetings and help department staffers develop programs such as winter workshops, cowboy songs and range ballads, summer gallery presenters, and so on. You'll also help develop guided tours for each of the five museums.

Candidates should have superior verbal/written communication skills and a basic knowledge of learning theory and interpretive techniques and demonstrate computer literacy, especially with Microsoft Word, Excel, Access, and Publisher. Candidates also should be self-directed.

Education Outreach

As an intern here, you'll evaluate current outreach materials and outline suggestions for improvement and evaluate the content, age level, format, and graphic/visual presentation for outreach materials.

Candidates for this internship must have superior verbal/written communication skills, basic knowledge of learning theory, good computer skills, and be organized, self-directed, and able to multitask. Graduate students are preferred, but exceptional undergraduate students will be considered.

Graphics Intern

As an intern in this department, you'll be working in a professional design environment, gaining practical experience in producing printed materials and exhibition graphics. You'll help produce printed materials and exhibition graphics, scan photographic prints and transparencies for use in printed publications, retouch photographic scans digitally, typeset and mount exhibition labels and vinyl lettering for exhibition graphics, produce graphic print projects, and archive print projects and exhibition labels.

Candidates should be fluent with the Macintosh and able to work with QuarkXPress, Adobe Illustrator, and Photoshop in a Mac environment. Candidates should be able to learn computer applications quickly and to troubleshoot common hardware and software problems. Excellent written/oral communication skills are also important.

Photography Intern

In this department, you'll help the photography staff with the various functions of the studio and photo lab as you learn skills in the area of studio photography. You'll also help with the demands of lab work and digital needs. You'll participate in photography documentation and learn more about the value of objects and collections documented with photography in a museum setting. You'll also learn the present guidelines of the photography department.

Candidates should already have taken one year of photography courses before the internship begins. Candidates also should have a working knowledge of photographic equipment, skills in studio photography, and an active interest in the field of documentation.

Plains Indian Museum Intern

The Plains Indian Museum tells the story of the lives of Plains Indians, their cultures, traditions, values, and histories, as well as the story of their lives today. Since 1979, the museum has been a leader in promoting public recognition of the importance of Plains Indian art. Most of the art from the Plains Indian Museum is from the early reservation period (circa 1880–1930) and relates primarily to Northern Plains tribes, such as the Lakota, Crow, Arapaho, Shoshone, and Cheyenne.

Interns in this museum help with collections care and storage and provide documentation and research on publications, exhibition content, and text. They also help interpret the Plains Indian Museum permanent and special exhibitions and its related educational programming.

Candidates should have verbal/written communication skills and demonstrated research and computer skills.

Public Relations

As an intern here, you'll work in a professional communications environment, gaining practical experience in public relations, marketing, and advertising in a museum setting. Your jobs may include conducting research, writing news releases, converting mailing lists to e-mail lists, getting permission from media to mail news releases to them via e-mail, and performing some office duties. You also may act as Historical Center ambassador to welcome bus groups who visit.

Candidates should have experience with the Internet, Excel spreadsheets, and Word.

Registration Intern

As an intern in this department, you'll work with the registrar and associate registrar to learn appropriate museum policies and procedures for collections documentation and management of collections records and information. You'll help catalog a variety of collections, maintain the appropriate documentation, enter catalog information in the ARGUS collection management program, examine collections for condition, and prepare condition reports.

Candidates should be able to lift 30 pounds, have average physical strength and endurance, and have basic computer skills.

Research Library Intern

As an intern in this area, you'll learn how to organize and describe archival manuscript and photograph collections and how to retrieve modern information both from in-house resources and from Internet/Web-based bibliographic databases.

Candidates should have superior verbal and written communication skills and be self-directed. Graduate students are preferred, but exceptional undergraduate students will be considered.

Whitney Gallery of Western Art Database Research and Development

As an intern in this department, you'll research, update, and develop a database for the Whitney Gallery of Western Art at the Historical Center, which focuses on works by Western American artist Frederic Remington. You'll update the current catalogue, develop a cross-reference database for accompanying digital images, and develop a finding guide for the database.

Candidates should have taken accredited courses in art history, have good verbal and written communication skills, and have excellent computer skills (especially Access, Microsoft Word, and scanning). Graduate students are preferred, but exceptional undergraduate candidates will be considered.

Whitney Gallery of Western Art Intern

The Whitney Gallery of Western Art includes masterworks by revered artists such as George Catlin, Alfred Jacob Miller, Thomas Moran, Albert Bierstadt, Frederic Remington, Charles M. Russell, W.R. Leigh, Joseph Henry Sharp, N.C. Wyeth and many others. The H. Peter and Jeannette Kriendler Gallery of Contemporary Western Art displays a stunning collection of modern artworks, a testament to how the West continues to inspire powerful creative works. Some of the artists featured in the gallery include Harry Jackson, James Bama, Deborah Butterfield, and Fritz Scholder. As an intern here, you'll help with acquisitions, collections care, documentation, and research and help with the interpretation of Western American art, including exhibitions and education.

Candidates should have good verbal and written communication skills and superior research and computer skills. Graduate students are preferred, but exceptional undergraduate candidates will be considered.

HOW TO APPLY

Download an application at http://www.bbhc.org/edu/internshipApp2005.doc. In addition, include three letters of recommendation (Northwest College Students need only include one letter of recommendation), plus a cover letter, resume, and school transcripts. Applicants may be requested to submit a proposal and/or to participate in an interview.

Students applying for the Native American internship should include the name of the tribe in which they are enrolled; and one of the letters of recommendation must be from an official of the tribe in which they are enrolled.

COLONIAL WILLIAMSBURG INTERNSHIP

Department of Archaeological Research

Colonial Williamsburg Foundation
PO Box 1776
Williamsburg, VA 23187

(757) 220-7330
mlopez@cwf.org
http://www.history.org/history/argy/programs/
  argyintern.cfm

What You Can Earn: Unpaid. Generally, internships are not paid, although grants and specific donations occasionally provide limited funding. You'll be given information on low-cost housing in the area.

Application Deadlines: Rolling.

Educational Experience: No specific recommendations, although a major in history or anthropology or archaeology would be helpful.

Requirements: Prospective interns must be enrolled in a university program as an undergraduate or graduate student.

OVERVIEW

If you long to experience life as our ancestors did in colonial times, an internship at Colonial Williamsburg could be a great choice. Colonial Williamsburg is located in Williamsburg, Virginia, the world's largest living history museum. This restored 18th-century city was the largest, wealthiest, and most populated outpost in the New World. Today, the 301-acre historic area includes hundreds of restored, reconstructed, and historically furnished buildings peopled by costumed interpreters telling the stories of men and women of the 18th-century city—African American, Anglo American, and Native American, slave, indentured, and free—and the challenges they faced.

Internships are available at Williamsburg's Department of Archaeological Research for the academic calendar year and the summer. Here, in one of the largest and oldest living history museums, archaeologists and other scholars are engaged in projects related to colonial historical archaeology, including landscape reconstruction, African-American archaeology, environmental archaeology, comparative colonialism, foodways, animal husbandry, and material life.

Colonial Williamsburg provides ample opportunities for interns to study material life in the late 17th, 18th, and 19th centuries. Archaeological excavations, CAD-based analyses integrating archaeological data, maps, and historical information, and environmental studies of pollen, parasites, phytoliths, and macrobotanical remains have helped chronicle the growth of the colonial capital of Williamsburg. This town served as a service center for local areas as well as a meeting place for wealthy planters who arrived twice yearly for the sessions of the Burgesses and the General Court.

You may volunteer your time to work beside professionals to learn excavation techniques, conduct documentary research, develop collections-management skills, or identify and analyze artifacts, faunal remains, or archaeobotanical remains. Alternatively, you may complete a more focused research project and earn college credit at their university.

Undergraduate interns will work with a professional archaeologist to excavate an archaeological site. This option may or may not be available, depending upon the status of current field programs. Generally, the intern will be required to have some excavation experience.

Graduate interns will develop a course of study, depending on experience, to investigate state-of-the-art techniques and programs for recording and presenting the archaeological record in three dimensions. This might include using Computer Aided Design (CAD) and GIS software.

Interns may choose from a variety of projects, described as follows.

African-American Archaeology

Colonial Williamsburg has been a leader in the field of African-American archaeology for many years, which complements the museum's commitment to the interpretation of the African-American past. This work began with early excavations at the Carter's Grove slave quarter and continues with recent research at sites within the Historic Area, at plantations that existed at the outskirts of Williamsburg, and at sites elsewhere in the British colonial empire (including Bermuda and Barbados). Internship opportunities include studies of existing archaeological collections, ongoing research on slaves and slave owners, or the development of strategies for interpreting findings to the public.

Conservation

Conservation is important to ensure both the survival of excavated materials and the recovery of significant information about the manufacture, use, and processing of individual items. There are several ongoing projects in the lab that you could choose to work on:

Analysis and Remediation of Past Treatments

Conservation methods have changed over time, and some have had a detrimental effect on the collection. If you choose this project, you'll help survey the collection to determine its condition and then conduct experiments to determine the best method to retreat affected portions of the collection. You also may help retreat materials.

The Burial Environment

The Archaeological Conservation Lab and the Department of Archaeological Research are developing a program to study the effects of the burial environment on several classes of archaeological objects and to determine the factors affecting the preservation and deterioration of artifacts. Interns will monitor sites, conduct data analysis, do documentary research, or work with materials excavated from recent sites.

Recently Excavated Material Treatments

This internship could involve X-raying artifacts, filing treatment reports, photographing artifacts, and researching specific classes of artifacts and their manufacture.

Curation/Collections Management

Collections management and curatorial responsibilities include the processing, documentation, preservation, and analysis of the archaeological collection of the Colonial Williamsburg Foundation. The collection is maintained as a research tool to provide support of the foundation's education and preservation mission, to afford accessibility for

scholars, and to contribute to the overall understanding of Williamsburg's history.

Environmental Archaeology

Environmental research is a significant component of archaeology at Williamsburg, since faunal analysis and archaeobotany (including the analysis of seeds, wood, and phytoliths) play an important role in the reconstruction of Colonial life. Since this work requires specialized training, interns interested in laboratory technical work are expected to focus on areas to which they have a strong commitment. However, there are other opportunities for interns, including documentation on gardens, horticulture, animal husbandry, landscapes, database design, or public presentation. Ongoing projects that you may wish to pursue include:

- **Documentary database:** If you chose this project, you will learn about animal husbandry, agriculture, plant types, gardening, hunting, and fishing in Colonial Chesapeake by researching early documents and helping to enter these records into a computer database.
- **Archaeobotanical research:** Depending on your skill, you could learn the basics of archaeobotanical research, including flotation, processing samples, or the identification of plant remains such as seeds, wood, and nutshell. Other projects include processing soil samples for phytoliths, exploring the use of root and tuber crops, signatures of animal dung, and so on.
- Nonlaboratory projects include developing interpretive programs or exhibits, data analysis, and documentary research.

General Laboratory

This internship is designed as an introduction to archaeological laboratory procedures and curatorial practices. This is the one for you if you want to gain basic experience in a variety of activities.

Project-Based Internship

Project-focused internships include options for work in documentation/archives, artifact processing, curatorial practices, material culture analysis/research, and cataloging. This internship is a good choice if you have specific material culture research plans.

HOW TO APPLY

After your application has been reviewed, you will be notified in writing. You should send a completed application to the Department of Archaeological Research at the Colonial Williamsburg Foundation, along with a current resume and two letters of recommendation. If you want to earn academic credit, at least one reference must be from a current professor at your university.

D. C. BOOTH HISTORIC FISH HATCHERY INTERNSHIP

Curator, D. C. Booth HNFH
423 Hatchery Circle
Spearfish, SD 57783-2643
http://dcbooth.fws.gov/internship.htm

What You Can Earn: Salary depends on funding, education, and experience.
Application Deadlines: Rolling.
Educational Experience: Upper level or graduate students in museum studies or historic preservation preferred.
Requirements: Interns must promise to stay three to five months.

OVERVIEW

The D. C. Booth Historic National Fish Hatchery, located on a 10-acre site in Spearfish, S.D., is one of the oldest fish hatcheries in the west. Operated by the U.S. Fish and Wildlife Service, it was established in 1896 and is listed on the National Register of Historic Places.

The museum collection at D. C. Booth gets bigger every day. The collection includes tools and equipment used in fish culture and distribution, uniforms, photographs, personal papers, and archaeological material—as well as two hatchery trucks and a 33-foot long boat used on Lake Yellowstone by hatchery personnel.

In 1989, Congress appropriated funding for construction of a state-of-the-art museum property storage building, public restrooms, concession, and underwater viewing area at D. C. Booth with the Fish and Wildlife Service resuming operations of the facility to interpret the history and technology of fish culture.

The museum, historic house, and gift shop are open mid-May through mid-September, but the grounds are open throughout the year for the 140,000 visitors. Volunteers provide most of the summer staffing for visitor contact and tours of the buildings.

As an intern here, you'll interact with the public, with Fish and Wildlife Service staff, and with volunteer staff, as well as working with the historic buildings and structures.

Part- or full-time interns will work with the museum collection under the supervision of the curator, maintaining inventory, cataloging, preserving, storing, researching, archiving, processing, photographing, and exhibiting. Work will include involvement in several aspects of collection management.

HOW TO APPLY

Send a detailed resume of your work, career goals, and academic requirements (if any) to the preceding address. Include at least three references with their name, address and telephone number.

EISENHOWER NATIONAL HISTORIC SITE INTERNSHIP

Supervisor Historian
250 Eisenhower Farm Lane
Gettysburg, PA 17325

(717) 338-9114
carol_hegeman@nps.gov.
http://www.nps.gov/eise/home.htm

What You Can Earn: $1,520 for 12 weeks.
Application Deadlines: Rolling but internship positions are often committed by late winter.
Educational Experience: None specified.
Requirements: None specified.

OVERVIEW

The Eisenhower National Historic Site is the presidential and retirement home of Dwight D. Eisenhower. The 189-acre farm, which Eisenhower bought in 1950, supported a herd of prize Angus cattle. Eisenhower used the farm as a combination presidential retreat, temporary White House, and meeting place for world leaders. Bordering the Gettysburg Battlefield, the working farm today includes 690 acres.

Three-month interpretive and curatorial internships are both available at the site. As an interpretive intern, you'll research, prepare, and present 15- to 20-minute orientation tours to visitors at the site and 20- to 30-minute detailed lectures about Eisenhower's life and work. You'll work in the Eisenhower home as you give short talks in the living room and answer visitor questions. You'll also help children participating in the Jr. Secret Service Agent program.

If you choose to work as a curatorial intern, you'll assist the curator to catalog, clean, and reorganize artifacts.

Both internships involve a 40-hour week, with two consecutive days off each week. However, interpretive interns also must work on Saturday and Sunday, since the site is open seven days a week. Formal and informal on-the-job training is provided.

HOW TO APPLY

To schedule an interview and a tour of the site, contact the supervisor historian at the preceding phone number or e-mail address. Or mail your resume to the preceding address.

EL PUEBLO DE LOS ANGELES HISTORICAL MONUMENT MULTICULTURAL SUMMER INTERNSHIP

Curator, El Pueblo de Los Angeles Historical Monument
125 Paseo de la Plaza, Suite 400
Los Angeles, CA 90012
(213) 485-6855
Fax: (213) 485-8238
westrada@mailbox.lacity.org or scheng@mailbox.lacity.org

What You Can Earn: $3,500 for a 10-week period.
Application Deadlines: Mid-May.
Educational Experience: Currently enrolled undergraduates who are members of underrepresented groups in professions related to museums and the visual arts and who have completed at least one semester of college by the start of the internship but are not graduating before the end of the year in which the internship takes place. Candidates are welcome from all areas of undergraduate study and are not required to have demonstrated a previous commitment to museum studies or the visual arts.
Requirements: Must be a resident of or attend college in Los Angeles County; must be able to communicate effectively, both orally and in writing. Computer literacy is strongly desired.

OVERVIEW

The El Pueblo de Los Angeles Historical Monument is the oldest section of Los Angeles, the birthplace of Los Angeles, and home to world-famous Olvera Street, with 27 historic buildings clustered around an old plaza.

The El Pueblo Park Association and El Pueblo de Los Angeles Historical Monument sponsor two interns funded by the Getty Grant Program for 40 hours a week from late June to late August.

Interns will receive training in the storage and care of archival materials and collections management. Interns also will participate in El Pueblo's ongoing community-oriented projects and activities, such as the Oral History Project, and institutional research. The Getty Grant Program will host the interns at four events, which will be held at various cultural sites during the grant period.

HOW TO APPLY

To apply, mail a letter of interest, a resume, and two letters of recommendation to the preceding address. Electronic and faxed submissions are not recommended.

GEORGIA STATE PARK AND HISTORIC SITES INTERNSHIP

**Training Coordinator, Georgia Department of
   Natural Resources, PR&HS**
Georgia Public safety Training Center
1000 Indian Springs Drive
Forsyth, GA 31029
(478) 993-4546
Ralph_Delgiorno@dnr.state.ga.us

What You Can Earn: $5.15 an hour; housing will be provided when available.
Application Deadlines: Rolling.
Educational Experience: College students in a field related to one of the internships; must be in good academic standing.
Requirements: Desire to learn more about the management of state parks and historic sites.

OVERVIEW

The Georgia Department of Natural Resources operates 15 historic sites and 46 state parks, some with lodges and/or golf courses. Together, they offer a variety of natural, cultural, and historical resources, ranging from alpine vistas at Black Rock Mountain State Park to the colonial-era ruins at Wormsloe Historic Site, all of which require interns.

Unless previously arranged, you'll be expected to be on active duty 40 hours a week, with some weekends, nights, and holidays. Since the busiest times are weekends and holidays, it's in your best interest to observe and participate during high-use times.

Most sites, but not all, are in a position to offer comfortable housing at no cost. During application, interns will be asked if they require housing. A signed housing contract will be required prior to occupancy.

Culinary Arts

Working at parks with lodges, you'll learn about food and beverage operations, guest services, banquet services, kitchen operations, menu planning, and budgeting. In most cases, park lodging is available.

Golf Operations

Under the supervision of a PGA Class A professional, you'll learn about clubhouse operations, golf car fleet and turf-grass management, customer relations, tournaments, business planning, course/facility design, marketing, merchandising, inventory, and volunteer management. At some parks, intern lodging is available. Candidates must be pursuing a career in golf-course management.

The turf-grass management intern program will expose you to all aspects of golf-course maintenance, including turf-grass basics, equipment maintenance, and pest management. At some parks, intern lodging is available.

Historic Site Management

Here, you'll be involved with the daily operation of some of the most interesting historic sites in the Southeast, where you'll help with interpretive programming, artifact preservation, operating procedures, budgeting, maintenance, resource management, and volunteer coordination. At some historic sites, lodging may be available.

Hospitality

Working at parks with lodges, you'll learn skills specific to the hospitality industry, such as guest services, front-desk operations, food and beverage operations, banquet services, human resources, group sales, housekeeping and maintenance, and retail sales and programming. In most cases, park lodging is available to hospitality interns.

Interpretation

In this internship, you'll work with programming staff, planning activities such as guided hikes, holiday celebrations, campfire programs, and nature crafts. At some parks and sites, intern lodging is available. You'll also learn aspects of state-park management. You can request assigned at either a park or historic site.

Resource Management

Here you'll be actively involved with ongoing resource-management programs such as invasive plant control, landscaping with native plants, botanical and aquatic surveys, forestry improvement, prescribed burning, and wildlife management. You may be assigned to a park, and housing may be available, or you may be given work at the Atlanta office, which would require commuting. Resource-management interns will be assigned a management project for direct application and experience on their assigned park.

State Park Management

Here you'll get hands-on experience in a variety of departments, including front-desk operations, operating procedures, budgeting, reports and administration, maintenance, housekeeping, law enforcement, interpretive programming, and resource management. If placed at a park with a lodge, you'll also gain experience in hospitality. At some parks, intern lodging is available.

Candidates should have an interest in natural sciences, resource management, recreation, criminal justice, or business administration.

HOW TO APPLY

Applications can be initiated either by you or your academic coordinator. First, download an application at http://www.gastateparks.org/net/forms/apply.aspx?alias=georgiaparks.internapp&s=0.0.1.5 and submit it directly to the training coordinator at the preceding address. The coordinator will carefully review the information. The training coordinator will contact you of your application status, usually within two weeks.

Once approved by the training coordinator, you'll be asked to supply the following:

- Internship application and information form
- Letter from your academic advisor approving the placement
- Current resume
- Official university transcript

Upon receiving the application information, the training coordinator will contact the successful applicant with an offer for an internship placement. In some cases, a screening interview is requested prior to an offer. In all cases, a site interview with the manager is required. This gives both the intern and the park staff an opportunity to meet and discuss the requirements of the internship and tour the park to make certain the placement is a good match for all concerned.

GREY TOWERS NATIONAL HISTORIC SITE INTERNSHIP

Grey Towers National Historic Site
151 Grey Towers Drive
PO Box 188

Milford, PA 18337
(570) 296-9661
Fax: (570) 296-9675
http://www.fs.fed.us/na/gt/volunteering/
    mortimerintern.shtml

What You Can Earn: $2,500 stipend for the 10- to 12-week program.
Application Deadlines: Early May.
Educational Experience: Motivated undergraduate students who are at least sophomores majoring in ornamental horticulture, forestry, landscape architecture, or environmental disciplines.
Requirements: Ability to operate equipment, including lawn mowers and string trimmers; a valid drivers license; ability to identify both native and ornamental woody and herbaceous plant species; ability to read landscape plans and drawings; practical knowledge of the appropriate methods and techniques of horticultural science, plant nutrition, and plant growth; sensitivity to historic values as they apply to maintaining and restoring historic gardens and landscapes. A car is not required but is recommended for those interested in personal sightseeing and convenience.

OVERVIEW

Grey Towers is a French-style mansion designed by Richard Morris Hunt and built in 1886 on a 101-acre landscaped and wooded site now administered by the U.S. Forest Service. Grey Towers was the home of Gifford Pinchot, first Chief of the U.S. Forest Service and Pennsylvania Governor for two terms. Grey Towers was completed in 1886 by Gifford's father, James, a wealthy wallpaper merchant and supporter of the arts, including Richard Morris Hunt, a leading architect of the era. Hunt designed their summer home to utilize both local materials and reflect the French heritage of the Pinchot family, who had first settled in Milford in 1818.

For 20 years the Pinchots enjoyed summers at Grey Towers, entertaining guests for afternoon teas and dinner parties. It was here that James Pinchot, upset by destructive logging practices then com-mon, encouraged his eldest son Gifford to consider a career in forestry.

In 1963, Gifford Bryce Pinchot—grandson of James—donated Grey Towers and 102 acres to the Forest Service, the federal agency founded by his father and now administers the site. The Forest Service works closely with the Pinchot Institute for Conservation, a national nonprofit group committed to leadership in forest policy. Today, conferences and seminars at the estate bring together a diversity of leading conservation and environmental thinkers to help guide the future of natural-resource conservation.

The Elisabeth S. Mortimer internship was created in 1994 when Elisabeth and Charles Mortimer made a donation to the Pinchot Institute for Conservation to establish an internship at Grey Towers with a focus on gardening, one of Mrs. Mortimer's greatest passions. The internship gives students hands-on experience to challenge and broaden their knowledge of practical applications of horticultural theory learned in the classroom.

As an intern here, you'll help the horticulturist manage, maintain, and restore the historic landscape and gardens. Your duties may include planting, preparing, and maintaining annual and perennial flower beds, maintaining woody ornamentals and tress, and maintaining groomed lawns. You'll also help develop and present horticulture exhibits and interpretive programs on landscape history, plant identification, and garden design for public events and help implement and broaden the horticultural garden volunteer team. You also may be asked to help research and review historic documents and photographs, as related to garden restoration and maintenance.

Grey Towers, at the foot of the Pocono Mountains, overlooks the town of Milford, Pennsylvania, and is close to New York City. Government on-site housing is provided, which will be shared with other seasonal volunteers.

HOW TO APPLY

A resume and cover letter that also indicates your field of study and expected graduation date should be faxed, e-mailed, or mailed to the preceding address.

HERMITAGE FOUNDATION MUSEUM INTERNSHIP

Hermitage Foundation
7637 North Shore Road
Norfolk, Virginia 23505
(757) 423-2052
Fax: (757) 423-2410
info@hermitagefoundation.org

What You Can Earn: Unpaid
Application Deadlines: Rolling; internships are offered throughout the year.
Educational Experience: Students interested in a career in the museum, historic house, history, library, art education, museum gallery, gardens and grounds, landscape design, or horticulture fields.
Requirements: Sense of responsibility and enthusiasm.

OVERVIEW

The Hermitage Museum is an early-20th century residence surrounded by 12 acres of formal gardens and natural woodlands in a residential neighborhood of Norfolk, Virginia. The house, a combination brick, stucco, and timber building, was built by wealthy New Yorkers William and Florence Sloane in 1907, when the family came to Hampton Roads, where Mr. Sloane operated textile mills. Named "The Hermitage," the house served as a five-room vacation home at first but soon became the Sloane's principal residence.

Today, the museum and its contents remain as they were when the Sloanes lived there with their two sons, Russian wolfhounds, horses, and sheep, giving visitors a sense of the life and artistic interests of a wealthy family during the early 1900s. Today, the Hermitage Foundation maintains and operates the house and grounds as a museum open to the public.

Under Mrs. Sloane's direction, the house was remodeled and expanded over the years to its final 42 rooms. The Sloanes were educated art collectors and were among the leading founders of the Norfolk Society of Arts and the Norfolk Museum of Arts and Sciences, corresponding with prominent artists.

The Sloanes established the Hermitage Foundation in 1937 as a museum to encourage development of arts and crafts and to promote the arts within the community. Ultimately, they contributed the house and its contents, the Hermitage grounds, and all outbuildings on the property to the foundation. The Hermitage house museum opened to the public in 1947, although Mrs. Sloane still lived in the house until her death in 1953; one of her sons lived in the house and led the Hermitage Foundation until the early 1970s.

The Hermitage Foundation offers a number of internships in several departments at the foundation, including collections and archives; gardens and grounds; site restoration and renovation; landscape design/horticulture; and public programs/art education/museum gallery.

HOW TO APPLY

Interested students should submit a resume, at least one academic recommendation, and a list of relevant coursework to the appropriate contact (the curator of collections, the curator of gardens and grounds, or the public programs manager).

THE HERMITAGE (HOME OF ANDREW JACKSON) INTERNSHIP

The Hermitage, Internships
4580 Rachel's Lane
Nashville, TN 37076
(615) 889-2941
Fax: (615) 889-9289
internships@thehermitage.com

What You Can Earn: Room, board, and a stipend of $250 per week.
Application Deadlines: Early April.
Educational Experience: Advanced undergraduates and early-phase graduate students who have had field training in archaeology.
Requirements: Should be in good physical condition and should be aware that this internship primarily involves long hours of digging in hot, humid, and dirty settings.

OVERVIEW

The Hermitage is a historic site museum, visited by 250,000 people each year, one of the oldest and largest historic site museums in the country. Its mission is to interpret the life and times of Andrew Jackson, the seventh U.S. president, by allowing visitors to view his home and the surrounding farm where he lived between 1804 and 1845.

Jackson bought the farm on July 5, 1804, for $3,400, hiring a Nashville craftsman to decorate the farmhouse with French wallpaper and painted trim. After moving to the farm in August, the Jacksons renamed the property "Hermitage" and began growing cotton with the help of nine African American slaves. By 1820 he added 35 more slaves and had converted the farm into a prosperous 1,000-acre plantation, adding a distillery, dairy, carriage shelter, cotton gin and press, and slave cabins. Eventually, brick and log cabins for housing 95 African American slaves dotted the Hermitage landscape. Andrew Jackson took office as seventh president of the United States in 1829. While Jackson was president, his son Andrew Jackson Jr. and Jackson's Nashville friends saw to Hermitage affairs. In 1837, Jackson retired from the U.S. presidency and returned to the Hermitage, where he died June 8, 1845. At the time of his death, 161 African American slaves operated the cotton plantation and lived in dozens of slave cabins on the 1,050-acre plantation.

The Hermitage hosts interns in historical archaeology, doing archaeological fieldwork and investigating the First Hermitage, the location of dwelling sites occupied originally by Andrew Jackson's family and later by enslaved African American families. Interested students may apply for terms of two, five, or 10 weeks.

The five- and 10-week terms offer an opportunity for more experience in a research-oriented setting, with strong emphasis on direct interaction with museum visitors. The two-week term offers exposure to the archaeological study and public interpretation of the recent past and does not require previous archaeological experience.

HOW TO APPLY

You can apply for this internship by letter to the preceding address. Include a summary of your education and research experience and a statement explaining your specific interest in the program. You should include the term for which you are applying and your session preference and dates of availability. You should also send two letters of recommendation under separate cover.

If you'd like to be notified once your application is received, please enclose a self-addressed, stamped postcard. All applicants will be notified of selection decisions no later than May 1.

HISTORIC DEERFIELD SUMMER FELLOWSHIP

Historic Deerfield Summer Fellowship
Office of Academic Programs
Historic Deerfield, Inc.
PO Box 321
Deerfield, MA 01342
(413) 774-5581
(413) 775-7207 for questions about fellowship
Fax: (413) 775-7224
sfp@historic-deerfield.org
http://www.deerfield-fellowship.org/apply.html

What You Can Earn: All interns will receive a $7,500 fellowship to cover tuition, books, field trip expenses, and room and board for nine weeks. In addition, a limited number of awards from $800 to $1500 will be given to offset lost summer income to students of exceptional promise with demonstrated financial need.

Application Deadlines: February for a summer internship (check with the program for precise application deadlines); decisions will be announced in March.

Educational Experience: A background in history or anthropology is helpful. The internship offers six credits.

Requirements: Students must have must have completed two or more years of college and must have undergraduate status as of January 1 of the year of the program.

OVERVIEW

Every summer since 1956, six to 10 college students have experienced the world of Historic Deerfield, a museum of New England history and art in Deerfield, Massachusetts. The nine-week living/earning program offers students a chance to take part in the behind-the-scenes workings of a museum, to study early New England life using the Historic Deerfield collections and historic houses, and to join staff in an investigation of early American history and material life. The internship also provides six hours of academic credit through the History Department of the University of Massachusetts at Amherst.

If you sign on as a Deerfield Fellow, you will study and work in Historic Deerfield's museum houses, the state-of-the-art Flynt Center of Early New England Life, Deerfield's old main street, and historic sites in New England. The program provides hands-on research of daily life and cultural history of New England using the museum's collections of historic artifacts and American decorative arts and the manuscripts and printed collections of the Memorial Libraries.

Professional and academic staff at Historic Deerfield, the Pocumtuck Valley Memorial Association, and nearby five colleges also make presentations about their areas of academic expertise and their work in the world of museums.

As a summer fellow, you'd participate in seminar sessions in a classroom setting, on walking tours, and in the museum houses, studying topics such as dating New England architecture; history of daily life in New England as seen through the study of furniture; ceramics in early New England life; gravestone carving; Native Americans in the Connecticut River Valley; probate inventories; the archaeological heritage of Deerfield; the Colonial Revival in New England; and the advantages and challenges of teaching early American history through objects.

You'll also be expected to give guided tours five afternoons in each of three historic houses, using information gathered in seminars and working with Historic Deerfield's guiding staff. You'll also work with other fellows to develop, research, and enact one public program for Historic Deerfield. In addition, you'll go on weekly field trips to other historic cities and museums in New England, including Old Sturbridge Village, Plimoth Plantation, Boston, and the Pequot Museum in Connecticut. At the end of the summer, you'll take a week-long trip to visit historic areas in the South, including the Winterthur Museum in Delaware; Annapolis; and Colonial Williamsburg in Virginia. At each stop, you'll meet with museum staff members for in-depth discussions about their interpretive philosophies and the issues facing museums today.

To build practical research and writing skills, you'll also write a short paper analyzing an object in the collections, and you'll work on a research project using primary sources from the manuscript, printed, and artifact collections at Historic Deerfield and the Pocumtuck Valley Memorial Association. The research topics should deal with some aspect of the history or material culture of the Connecticut River Valley or with objects in the Deerfield collections. Many summer fellowship papers have become the basis for senior theses or published articles.

HOW TO APPLY

You should submit a Summer Fellowship Application form along with an official transcript, a resume, and at least two letters of recommendation from college faculty members (additional letters may come from field-related professionals). You should also include a personal statement discussing why you want to come to Deerfield and how your academic experiences and other interests have prepared you for this program. A nonrefundable fee of $15 should be included with the application.

For application forms and further information, contact Historic Deerfield Summer Fellowship (see the preceding contact information).

HISTORIC PRESERVATION INTERNSHIP TRAINING PROGRAM

Internship Training Program
Heritage Preservation Services
National Park Service
1201 Eye Street NW, 2255,
Washington, DC 20005
(202) 354-2025
Fax: (202) 371-1616
nps_hps-info@nps.gov

What You Can Earn: $12 an hour for 10 weeks at 40 hours a week.
Application Deadlines: Mid-March.
Educational Experience: Undergraduates and graduate students in historic-preservation programs and related disciplines.
Requirements: Excellent computer and word-processing skills, familiarity with historic construction methodology, building-fabric investigation and analysis, and skills in assessing building-fabric pathologies. Experience with field documentation and architectural drawing and design skills are a bonus. Must be willing to travel throughout the metro Washington, D.C., area (MD, VA, WV, D.C., and PA) and possibly further.

OVERVIEW

The historic preservation internship training program gives undergraduate and graduate students opportunities to undertake short-term research and administrative projects with the National Park Service either during the summer or the school year. The internship training program trains future historians, archeologists, architects, curators, planners, and archivists by fostering an awareness of the National Park Service cultural resource management activities and providing the opportunity to work under the direction of experienced professionals in the field of historic preservation.

Operated jointly with the National Council for Preservation Education, the internship training program places students in National Park Service cultural programs headquarters and field offices and in units of the park system with historic preservation and cultural resource-management responsibilities.

You'll learn about and contribute to the national historic preservation programs operated in partnership with state historic preservation offices and National Park Service efforts to preserve and manage historic properties. The National Park Service leads the nation in implementation of the national historic preservation program, offering students the opportunity to become familiar with the range of programs related to historic-preservation practice. Under the guidance of National Park Service professionals, you'll help with projects and activities that provide experience while contributing to the mission of the service.

Interns also will help senior historical architects and other preservation craftspersons in ongoing historic-preservation projects throughout the National Park System. Duties may include field inspection, documentation, fabric investigation, and condition assessments on a variety of historic structures. You'll also be responsible for preparing condition-assessment reports. As time permits, you may work with field crews to monitor ongoing preservation treatments and construction administration. A registered architect will supervise interns.

Since its inception in 1992, the Historic Preservation internship training program has sponsored more than 400 internship opportunities to work on historic preservation projects.

HOW TO APPLY

All application materials should be submitted in duplicate and mailed to the National Council for Preservation Education, Attention: Michael A. Tomlan, 210 West Sibley Hall, Cornell University, Ithaca, New York, 14853-6701 (mat4@cornell.edu).

LIVING HISTORY FARMS INTERNSHIP

Living History Farms
2600 111th Street
Urbandale, IA 50322
(515) 278-5286
info@lhf.org
http://www.lhf.org/intern.html

What You Can Earn: $2,000 plus six hours of history credits (tuition free).
Application Deadlines: March 1.
Educational Experience: Must be at least a sophomore in college, majoring in history, agriculture, museum studies, leisure studies, folk art, child development, education, or related courses; PR/marketing interns should be majoring in journalism, English, marketing, public relations, or a related field.
Requirements: None specified.

OVERVIEW

Living History Farms in Urbandale, Iowa, tells the story of how Iowans transformed the fertile prairies of the Midwest into the most productive farmland in the world. At the 550-acre open-air museum, visitors travel at their own pace through 300 years and five historical time periods as interpreters provide seasonal activities and demonstrations. A complete visit lasts three to four hours.

The 1700 Ioway Indian Farm shows how Iowa's first farmers worked the rich black soil. On the 1850 Pioneer Farm, oxen do much of the heavy work and the family lives in a log cabin. The 1875 town of Walnut Hill recreates a bustling frontier community with craftsmen and merchants in 16 shops along the town's main street. At the 1900 Farm, draft horses supply the power for field work while the family lives in a white-frame farm house. The Henry A. Wallace Exhibit Center depicts the history of the 20th century. Sites are connected by walking trails and tractor-drawn carts. Each site is authentically farmed or worked by interpreters in historical clothing. Many educational programs are available for school and adult groups. Day camps and historical dinners also are available.

If you've got a yen to don period clothing and interpret history or work with kids, consider interning at Living History Farms, which provides summer internships for 20 to 25 students as historical interpreters, day-camp counselors, or public information and marketing interns.

All interns begin the program with an intensive orientation session (day-camp counselors also receive three weeks of training prior to the start of camp). Throughout the summer, you'll also attend four evening seminars that explore some aspect of history, museum operations, or related topics. You'll be required to write three short papers and complete a special project.

Living History Farms pays all tuition costs associated with the summer internship program; credit is offered through the history department of Graceland University. At the conclusion of the internship, you may transfer the credit hours to your own academic program.

Day-Camp Counselors

As a day-camp counselor, you'll supervise groups of eight to 12 children in first through seventh grades each week during the summer. Day-camp sessions at Living History Farms run from Monday through Friday, with each day spent at a different historical site enjoying games, crafts, and projects that reflect the various time periods. Interns receive three weeks of intensive training prior to the first camp session.

Historical Interpretation

If you intern as an historical interpreter, you'll dress in period clothing supplied by Living History Farms as you explain and demonstrate what life in Iowa was like in an earlier time. Living History Farms operates four sites where the daily routines of the past are recreated: a 1700 Ioway Indian Farm, an 1850 Pioneer Farm, an 1875 town and a 1900 Farm with horse-powered equipment. As an historical interpreter, you'll work at a minimum of two sites, and you'll be supervised by the museum staff. All historical interpreters work five days a week, including weekends.

Public Information and Marketing

Marketing interns help the public relations department promote the museum's educational programs, membership, special events, fund raising, volunteer opportunities, historic dinners, group travel, rental facilities, and retail.

HOW TO APPLY

Download an application at http://www.lhf.org/internapplication.pdf. Send the completed application, along with a letter stating the reasons for your interest in the program, to the preceding address. Day-camp counselors also must provide the name, address, and phone number of one person who has observed them working with children (such as babysitting/childcare, youth groups, Sunday/Bible school, and so on).

In-person interviews, scheduled in March, are required for all applicants. Living History Farms will notify all applicants of hiring decisions in early April.

If you have questions about the internship program, you should contact:

- Historical interpreters: Leo Landis, 515-278-5286 ext. 130

- Day camp counselors: Carol Wise, 515-278-5286 ext. 138
- Public information/marketing: Tracy Bainter, 515-278-5286 ext. 114
- All other applications: Nancy Wente, 515-278-5286 ext. 119

MINNESOTA HISTORICAL SOCIETY INTERNSHIP

Minnesota Historical Society
345 West Kellogg Blvd.
St. Paul, MN 55102-1906
(651) 296-6126
http://www.mnhs.org/about/interns

What You Can Earn: Unpaid.
Application Deadlines: Rolling.
Educational Experience: Advanced undergraduate and graduate students interested in arranging work experience for academic credit; see departments for specific requirements.
Requirements: Must register for internship credits at your college to be considered for admission.

OVERVIEW

At its founding in 1849—nine years before Minnesota's statehood—the Minnesota Historical Society was composed of a small group of people, including the territorial governor, with a deep appreciation for the past and a vibrant vision for the future. Today, the society is one of the premier historical organizations in the nation, offering a broad array of programs and services to more than 1.6 million people. The society tells the stories of hundreds of generations. Collections include nearly 550,000 books; 37,000 maps; 250,000 photographs; 165,000 historical artifacts; 800,000 archaeological items; 38,000 cubic feet of manuscripts; 45,000 cubic feet of government records; and 5,500 paintings, prints, and drawings. The completion of the new $76.4 million history center in 1992, after 10 years of planning and almost three years of construction, brought together the archives, collections, and libraries.

Internships at the Minnesota Historical Society are based on learning objectives defined by the intern, the intern's faculty adviser, and the society's internship supervisor. The student and supervisor carefully plan a project that will be mutually beneficial and that will help the student develop practical skills. The learning objectives will serve as a basis for evaluation and should describe in detail the internship project and define the signers' mutual responsibilities, the duration of the internship, an arrangement for academic credit, and the evaluation procedure.

Internships typically involve from four to 40 hours a week, which can be modified to suit your needs. With the exception of internships at some of the historic sites, weekend and evening schedules may be needed only if the intern supervisor finds it appropriate for an intern to work during such hours.

The intern and intern supervisor will each write a final evaluation of the internship and submit copies to the sponsoring academic institution and the appropriate division head at the society.

There are a variety of areas in which you can arrange internships: archaeology; conservation; exhibits; finance/accounting; historic preservation; historic sites; human resources; marketing/communications; museum education; oral history; processing; publications; reference services; and volunteer services.

Archaeology
In this department, you'll be able to work with an archaeologist on long- and short-term projects in a broad range of cultural and heritage resources throughout the state. This may include conducting field or laboratory research, computer analysis, collections research, site preservation, public interpretation, and/or historic research.

Candidates should have a background in anthropology, archaeology, American studies, history, or related fields. Contact Pat Emerson, 612-725-2410; e-mail: patricia.emerson@mnhs.org.

Conservation
This department preserves information and objects that make up the physical evidence of the history of the state. It maintains five labs (photographic, microfilm, book and paper, textile and objects). The department provides preservation and conservation services to all Minnesota Historical Society divisions and departments and also provides advice and technical information to help other state agencies, museums, historical societies, libraries and archives, and the general public preserve material culture.

An internship in this department can be arranged that relates to your major or your experience, such as in conserving objects, textiles, books, and paper. Contact Sherelyn Ogden, 651-205-4661; e-mail: sherelyn.odgen@mnhs.org.

Exhibits
The exhibits department orchestrates the planning, artifact acquisition, research, content, development, design, and construction of exhibitions. Staff includes exhibition developers, designers, project managers, curators, and production staff. This department offers research internships to students in American history, American studies, and related fields, who work under the direction of an exhibit developer to learn how to turn historical materials into exhibits for general audiences. The department also offers internships to students in design who are interested in acquiring museum exhibit experience. Contact Dan Spock at 651-296-3830; e-mail: daniel.spock@mnhs.org.

Finance and Accounting
The finance department supports the work of the Minnesota Historical Society by providing accounting, financial reporting, contracting and purchasing, and other financial services. You can arrange an internship in this area related to your academic major and interest in practical experience. You may work in general ledger fund accounting, budget analysis and reporting, cash

forecasting, or systems and procedures analysis, as well as on special projects. Academic preparation in accounting or a related business field is required. Contact Deborah Mayne, 651-297-7365; e-mail: deborah.mayne@mnhs.org.

Historic Preservation, Field Services, and Grants

This department administers the National Register of Historic Places program for Minnesota and conducts an ongoing statewide survey for properties of historical, architectural, archaeological, cultural, and engineering significance. Students majoring in fields such as law, landscape, archaeology, interior design, architecture, city planning, and other related areas may be interested in internships in this department, learning more about research, library work, grants programs, and data management for historic properties in the state's inventory as well as in other areas of historic-preservation work. Special joint projects with other departments are also possible.

Contact Britta Bloomberg, 651-296-5471; e-mail: britta.bloomberg@mnhs.org.

Historic Sites

The historic sites department administers 32 state historic sites throughout Minnesota, which represent some of the most compelling aspects of Minnesota history, and provides a place for visitors to hear the stories and visit the real places where Minnesota history happened. This department offers a wide variety of internship opportunities in the development, operation, and interpretation of these historic sites, giving you experience in research, interpretation, or collections management. You may perform historical research in areas important to the interpretation of historic sites; develop interpretive training materials; plan, develop, and implement public programs; or gain experience in site interpretation. You also may help clean, sort, and catalog artifacts or assist with some restoration projects. Other projects may be arranged in cooperation with historic sites department staff or with the manager of a particular site. Contact Jim Mattson, 651-296-4450; e-mail jim.mattson@mnhs.org.

Human Resources

This department is responsible for policy development and implementation; compensation-plan design and administration; recruitment, selection, orientation, and training; compliance with federal, state, and local regulations; managerial, supervisory, and general staff development; in-house consulting; position classification; and performance management. The department also administers multiple benefit programs, including workers' comp; health, dental, and life insurance; pretax 125 plans; unemployment; leave programs; retirement plans; and deferred compensation.

A variety of internships are available in this department for graduate students interested in gaining experience in a nonprofit setting. Internships are available in benefits administration, employee safety and health, staff training and development, recruitment and selection, EEO/Affirmative Action initiatives, compensation and classification practices, and other personnel issues. Contact Pat Gaarder, 651-297-1905; e-mail: pat.gaarder@mnhs.org.

Marketing and Communications

This department promotes the programs and services of the society through public relations, publications, marketing communications, and information services. A variety of internship opportunities exist here, so you can design an internship around your own interests, in such areas as customer service at the information desk, marketing, news release/newsletter writing, editing, media and public relations, promotion, design, and print production. Alternatively, you can design general internships in the fields of marketing and communications. You would assist office staff in their efforts to promote the Minnesota Historical Society (both the History Center and the Historic Sites), and you'd learn all aspects of the communication effort. Contact Lory Sutton, 651-297-1827; e-mail: lory.sutton@mnhs.org.

Museum Education

The Minnesota History Center Museum and Mill City Museum create and promote learning experiences in history and related fields. This department offers internships in public-program development and execution, museum teaching, museum interpretation, applied research, and public-history administration. You also can arrange an internship producing educational materials about Minnesota history for use in elementary and secondary schools and design materials for programs in the museum setting.

Candidates should be upper-level undergraduate and graduate students with backgrounds in American history, humanities, education, public administration, or related fields. Contact Danielle Dart, 651-296-3252; e-mail: danielle.dart@mnhs. org.

Oral History

Internships in oral history provide opportunities to participate in research for oral history projects; in identification and contact of potential narrators; in the transcription, editing, and preparation of oral history interviews; and in related aspects of oral history program management. Recent projects include those on environmental issues, agriculture and rural life, and the resort industry. Contact James Fogerty, 651-296-9989; e-mail: james. fogerty@mnhs.org.

Processing

The processing department organizes the society's collection of books, periodicals, state archives, manuscripts, maps, photographs, newspapers, films and videos, sound recordings, works of art, and newspapers and creates tools such as catalogs and inventories that help patrons locate and use these collections. If you're interested in exploring how to organize and catalog historical-research materials, you may find an internship in this department to be rewarding. Here you can specialize in one or more of the following collection areas: manuscripts, government archives, sound and visual collections, and books and periodicals. Joint projects doing related work with other departments also may be arranged. Contact Lydia Lucas, 651-297-5542; e-mail: lydia.lucas@mnhs.org.

Publications

The publications and research department houses the Minnesota Historical Society Press, which publishes scholarly and popular books about Minnesota and the Upper Midwest; the Society's quarterly journal, *Minnesota History*; and the research department. Specialized internships may be arranged with the Minnesota Historical Society Press for students with experience in research, editing, or marketing. If you meet these qualifications, you can arrange a special project with staff at the Minnesota Historical Society.

Contact Pamela J. McClanahan, 651-297-4461; e-mail: pamela.mcclanahan@mnhs.org.

Reference Services

The reference department provides the public with access to the Minnesota Historical Society's collections. Reference staff assists researchers in the society's library and also answers questions through telephone, mail, fax, and e-mail services. Specialized internships may be arranged in this department, especially if you're interested in archives or libraries.

Contact Kathryn Otto, 651-297-3874; e-mail: kathryn.otto@mnhs.org.

Volunteer Services

In this department, interns can learn more about volunteer administration, including planning, screening, placement, recruitment, and supervisor training of volunteers. Interns also may work with the program manager to create special projects.

Candidates should have previous or current classes in volunteer management, marketing, and/ or human resources. Contact Jean Nierenhausen, 651-296-2155; e-mail: jean.nierenhausen@mnhs. org.

HOW TO APPLY

After you decide which of the society's programs interests you, you should connect with the contact person listed in the given department, who will give you an application to complete. Once your application has been received, the contact person will notify you regarding an interview. Usually, the intern supervisor will interview the candidate in person or by telephone prior to acceptance into the internship program.

The learning objective of your internship will be included in a written internship agreement, which is signed by you, your faculty sponsor, the society's department head, and your internship supervisor at the Minnesota Historical Society. You should allow two to three months to provide time for project development and to consult with academic advisers.

MOUNT VERNON SUMMER INTERNSHIP

Historic Mount Vernon
3200 Mount Vernon Memorial Highway
Mount Vernon, VA 22121
http://www.mountvernon.org
(703) 799-8611

What You Can Earn: $200 a week, free lodging on the estate, plus round-trip travel.
Application Deadlines: February 28 and 29.
Educational Experience: Students between the ages of 18 and 22 who have academic backgrounds in agricultural history or American history.
Requirements: At least minimal public speaking or teaching experience.

OVERVIEW

When George Washington lived there, Mount Vernon was an 8,000-acre plantation divided into five farms, each with its own overseers, slaves, livestock, equipment, and buildings. The farm where Washington and his family lived was called the "Mansion House Farm," the part of the plantation that visitors see today. From the Potomac River on the east to the estate's west-gate entrance ran the pleasure grounds and wide vistas. Along the north-south line were the out-buildings, or dependencies, where much of the work was done.

Today, about 500 acres of this historic estate have been preserved 16 miles south of Washington, D.C., on the banks of the Potomac River. Visitors can see 20 structures and 50 acres of gardens as they existed in 1799, along with a museum, the tombs of George and Martha Washington, Washington's greenhouse, an outdoor exhibit devoted to Washington's agriculture, the nation's most important memorial to the accomplishments of 18th-century slaves, and a collection featuring many decorative and domestic artifacts.

Mount Vernon is owned and maintained in trust for the people of the United States by the Mount Vernon Ladies' Association, a private, nonprofit organization founded in 1853, the oldest national historic preservation organization in the country.

There are a variety of ways that interns can work at the site. Most interns will be stationed primarily at the Pioneer Farmer Site, which interprets George Washington's farming practices. As an intern here, you'll interpret the site to the public while demonstrating a variety of farm-related tasks. You'll also wear 18th-century costumes that would have been typical for a male or female farmer of the yeoman's class. You'll be interpreting typical practices at the farm, which included seven-year crop rotation, a variety of fertilization experiments and methods, and the use of devices that Washington invented to improve planting, cultivating, harvesting, and processing crops, which were highly innovative in their day. One of the site's big attractions is an exact replica of a 16-sided treading barn that Washington designed and had built for use at Mount Vernon. The barn lessened the time and manpower needed to thresh wheat, which was Washington's major cash crop.

Other interns will be stationed primarily at George Washington's gristmill, which demonstrates to the public how the grain that Washington grew on his farms was milled into flour. The mill is an exact working replica of Washington's original water-powered gristmill, which occupied the same site on Dogue Run, about three miles from the main Mount Vernon estate. These interns also will be dressed in 18th-century costumes.

HOW TO APPLY

For more information and to receive an application, call the preceding number.

NATIONAL COUNCIL FOR PRESERVATION EDUCATION INTERNSHIPS

National Council for Preservation Education
210 West Sibley Hall
Cornell University
Ithaca, NY 14853-6701
mat4@cornell.edu
http://www.cr.nps.gov/hps/tps/Intern/
summer2005.html

What You Can Earn: $12 an hour for 10 weeks at 40 hours a week.
Application Deadlines: Early March.
Educational Experience: Highly qualified undergraduate seniors and graduate students pursuing a degree in historic preservation or a closely allied field such as anthropology, archaeology, architectural history, architecture, ethnography, history, landscape architecture, museology, or planning. Individual internships below may require more specific educational experience.
Requirements: Excellent computer and word-processing skills; see individual internships below for specific requirements.

OVERVIEW

Under a cooperative agreement between the National Council for Preservation Education and the National Park Service, a number of internships are offered in the summer. The National Council is a nationwide, nonprofit organization that represents more than 50 institutions regularly involved in historic-preservation education at the undergraduate and graduate levels.

Archeology and Ethnography Program

Interns here will work with the departmental consulting archeologist as a research assistant on small research projects, organizing and cataloging office records and archives, databases, resource protection, and related projects. You also may help develop materials for archeology training and research and develop educational materials for archeology outreach, in addition to working on aspects of Web development, including links verification and technical editing.

Cultural Landscape Program, National Capital Region

As an intern in this program, you'll help historical landscape architects and other preservation professionals complete various cultural-landscape reports associated with different national parks in the Washington, D.C., metropolitan area. You'll research the landscape history of a historic property and make site visits and do field work to document the existing conditions with photographs and maps, analyze the landscape features, and prepare treatment plans.

Candidates should have a working knowledge of MS Word and experience with ArcView and/ or CAD. This is a good opportunity for students majoring in all preservation fields with an interest in the study of historic landscapes (vernacular, designed, and ethnographic) and historic landscape design solutions.

Everglades National Park (Homestead, Florida)

As an intern here, you'll help catalog archives and museum objects from Big Cypress National Preserve and Biscayne, Dry Tortugas, and Everglades National Parks. You'll also rehouse museum collections to meet professional museum-storage standards.

Candidates should have a background in archives management or museum studies, attention to detail, and a willingness to learn.

General Services Administration Internships

Art-in-Architecture Program

As an intern here, you'll help with the Art-in-Architecture program that commissions works of art by living artists to enhance the architectural design of historic and contemporary federal buildings and U.S. courthouses throughout the nation. You'll help maintain the National Artists Registry, which includes statements of qualifications, slides, and other visual material, and research and catalog federally owned works of art in GSA's historic and contemporary buildings.

Candidates should be familiar with art history and artistic media and materials.

Design Excellence Program

The Design Excellence program hires many of the finest architects, designers, and artists working in America today to design future landmarks for the United States. Through collaborative partnerships with private-sector designers, GSA is producing facilities that reflect the dignity, enterprise, vigor, and stability of the federal government. As an intern in this program, you'll help maintain the buildings library database, digitizing/scanning images of buildings and helping research, inventory, and catalog building models.

Fine Arts Program

As a fine arts intern, you'll help research and develop interpretive information on historic buildings, artists, and works of art installed in federal buildings nationwide (information may be in the form of plaques, brochures, or other publications). You'll also create computer images of artwork using digitizing/scanning and computer graphics equipment and maintain automated databases and archives of fine arts installed in GSA's historic and contemporary buildings. In addition, you'll help research, inventory, and catalog federally owned artwork in nonfederal repositories nationwide and prepare a compre-

hensive checklist/catalog of artwork from the WPA period (1933–1943).

Historic Buildings Program

As an intern in this program, you'll help the historic buildings program manager and staff coordinate activities to maintain the function, integrity, and economic viability of 430 public buildings controlled by GSA and to increase GSA leasing of historic buildings and reuse of historic buildings on sites the government acquires for new construction. You'll conduct research, help take care of GSA's historic buildings, and provide guidance to GSA headquarters and regional staff. You'll also coordinate with preservation specialists in educational, nonprofit, and public institutions outside of GSA to exchange preservation solutions and learn about new initiatives.

Candidates should be familiar with historic preservation theory and practice and have experience with software programs for digital-image manipulation and desktop publishing.

Sunbelt Regional Office

As an intern in Atlanta with the regional historic preservation program, you'll help with work of the Southeast Sunbelt regional office, with responsibilities based on your knowledge and experience. You'll help conduct and coordinate the inventory, evaluation, nomination, preservation planning, and maintenance of GSA's historic buildings. You also may review and comment on construction and rehabilitation project plans that affect historic properties; perform computer database research and analysis; gather background information and prepare documentation for a variety of specific projects or buildings; plan, coordinate, and attend meetings; and maintain and update project files. A special project will focus on inventory and planning for preservation and display of original construction drawings for GSA's oldest buildings, working with other preservation or art organizations.

Candidates should have experience in historic preservation theory and practice and knowledge of software programs for digital-image manipulation and desktop publishing. Research, writing, survey, and building evaluation experience would be beneficial.

General Services Administration/Fort Worth

As a regional historic preservation intern, you'll help the greater Southwest regional office coordinate activities to maintain the function, integrity, and economic viability of more than 50 public historic buildings controlled by the region and to increase GSA leasing of historic buildings and reuse of historic buildings on sites the government buys for new construction. You'll help historic preservation staff with research, and you'll work on maintaining historic buildings and complying with cultural resource management laws and executive orders. Special projects require knowledge and experience with photographic image scanning for the purpose of developing both electronic and physical photo archives. Images will be used for project review and compliance, interpretation, and educational purposes.

Candidates should have experience with software programs for digital-image scanning and manipulation. Knowledge of historic preservation and archival theory and practice is helpful, as is experience in creating presentations and desktop publishing.

General Services Administration/Auburn, Washington

As a regional historic preservation specialist intern, you'll help the Pacific Northwest and Arctic regional office coordinate activities to maintain the function, integrity, and economic viability of 30 public historic buildings controlled by GSA. You'll help conduct research, take care of historic buildings, and provide guidance to regional staff. You'll also exchange preservation solutions and learn about new initiatives with preservation specialists in educational, nonprofit, and public institutions outside GSA. In addition, you'll provide preservation help to project managers and realty asset managers on a variety of restoration projects in different construction phases. The region currently has four very high-profile restoration projects underway, including restoration of the

National Historic Landmark Pioneer Courthouse in Portland, OR.

Candidates should be familiar with historic preservation theory and practice and have experience with software programs for digital-image manipulation and desktop publishing.

Harry S Truman National Historic Site

As an intern at the Harry S. Truman park headquarters in Independence, MO, you'll help with a variety of tasks related to photography of museum artifacts. You'll work with the National Park Service Automated National Catalog System museum collection database and with site-specific artifacts, reports, and procedures, as well as with collections-management policies, photographic standards, and park documents. In addition, you'll develop experience working with photographic collections as you organize, label, and create finding aids and with standard 35mm SLR camera equipment in a studio setting. You'll also help with routine tasks such as museum housekeeping and environmental monitoring. You'll be responsible for evaluating museum objects before moving and photographing them.

You'll work independently on some tasks after an initial orientation and training period, and you'll have the chance to have extra supervised learning experiences related to museum collections care and management.

Candidates must have experience in handling artifacts.

Historic Architecture Program, National Capital Region

As an intern here, you'll work as a member of the historic structures survey and condition assessment team. You'll be responsible for field investigations and research of historic structures, developing determinations of National Register eligibility in consultation with state historic preservation offices in Virginia, Maryland, West Virginia, and the District of Columbia. You'll also be responsible for entering the collected information into the Web-based national computerized database.

You'll document historic resources in written form, through digital photographs and by locating resources with GPS equipment. You'll focus on resources at the Chesapeake and Ohio Canal National Historic Park, the Antietam National Battlefield Park, and the Manassas National Battlefield Park.

Candidates should be advanced students or recent graduates in architectural history, architecture or historic preservation.

Interior Museum Program, Bureau of Reclamation/Boise—Snake River Area

As an intern with this program, you'll help the Snake River area office assemble information on and create a database of archeological properties previously recorded on reclamation lands in the Snake River area. In addition, you'll help complete file searches to identify previously recorded historic properties and associated consultation records, photocopy site records, organize records, create a bibliography of reports, and enter information into an Access database. Although the program is located in Boise, ID, there might be occasional travel to other locations in Idaho or Oregon.

Candidates should have experience in records research and data organization and experience using Access database software. Candidates also must have a valid driver's license.

Interior Museum Program, Bureau of Reclamation/Boise— Pacific Northwest Archeology Survey

As an intern here, you'll help the Pacific Northwest regional office collect archeological site and survey data and enter it into an Access database. You'll help complete file searches to identify previously recorded historic properties and associated consultation records, photocopy and organize site records, create a bibliography of reports, and enter information into an Access database. This program is located in Boise, but there may be occasional travel to other locations in Idaho, Oregon, or Washington.

Candidates must have a valid driver's license, experience in records research and data organization, and experience using Access database soft-

ware. Preference will be given to students with archeological training and experience.

Interior Museum Program, Bureau of Reclamation/Denver— Archaeology Collections Management

As a curatorial assistant intern, you'll help the curatorial staff at the Denver University Museum of Anthropology manage archeology collections recovered in Colorado and complete the catalog records.

Candidates should have experience with contemporary museum registration practices and archeological collections.

Interior Museum Program, Bureau of Reclamation/Denver— Teton Dam Project

As an intern here, you'll review, arrange, and create an electronic index of the historical records relating to the Teton Dam failure in Idaho during 1976. This failure resulted in the Dam Safety Act of 1978, which established a safety of dams' inspection program for all federal and most state agencies with dam-management responsibilities. These records have significant historical value at the national, regional, and local levels. They'll be transferred to the Rocky Mountain Region of the National Archives in Denver.

Candidates should be familiar with Access database software or related computer skills.

Interior Museum Program, Bureau of Reclamation/Flagstaff, Arizona

As an intern here, you'll help staff of the Museum of Northern Arizona with curation tasks associated with reclamation collections from the Glen Canyon Region.

Candidates should be familiar with the archeology of the Southwestern United States and basic museum methods and should have basic computer skills and a valid driver's license.

Interior Museum Program, Bureau of Reclamation/Flatiron

As an intern here, you'll help the Eastern Colorado area office complete file searches to identify previously recorded historic properties and associated consultation records. The program is located at the Flatiron office, west of Loveland, Colorado. You'll photocopy site records, organize records, create a bibliography of reports, and enter data into a GIS-based database with the archeological data gathered by or on reclamation land. An existing GIS mapping system will be extended to include data on archeological sites, including site condition, in an Access database. You may need to do some fieldwork assessment of site conditions as well.

Candidates must have experience with ArcGIS and Access database management software.

Interior Museum Program, Bureau of Reclamation/Lincoln, Nebraska

As a curatorial assistant intern here, you'll help the curatorial staff of the Nebraska State Historical Society (NSHS) identify, repackage, and label materials from primarily prehistoric collections from Bureau of Reclamation projects in Nebraska. You'll recopy and reconcile records associated with the materials. Your tasks are part of a comprehensive plan to manage these collections to standards set forth in an existing agreement between the NSHS and the reclamation bureau.

Interior Museum Program, Bureau of Reclamation/Mills, Wyoming

As an intern here, you'll help the Wyoming area office organize heritage-assets information from projects in the area. The goal is to develop an electronic database of archeological and historical sites and museum property collections to make it easier to retrieve data. You'll help compile data by reviewing existing records, reports, correspondence, and other documents. You also may conduct files searches in state and other federal agency files; enter data into the electronic data base; organize early project photographs; and update the cultural resource management bibliography, entering that information into an Access database.

Candidates must have a valid driver's license, as some travel may be necessary.

Interior Museum Program, Bureau of Reclamation/Oklahoma City, Oklahoma

As an intern here, you'll help the Oklahoma-Texas area office gather and organize data on heritage assets and archeological collections from projects in the area. You'll also help organize files and photographs, copy files to archival paper, and enter data into a database.

Candidates must have a valid driver's license.

Interior Museum Program, Bureau of Reclamation/Phoenix, Arizona

As an intern here, you'll help reclamation archeologists relocate and assess known archeological sites and update the Phoenix Area Office Cultural Resources Access/ArcGIS database. You'll plot sites with a handheld GPS unit, and that data will be used to update the database. You'll also take digital photographs of sites and archeological features as appropriate. Field observations will be recorded according to predefined reclamation criteria, and archeological site assessments will then be used to refine the database.

Candidates should have experience with spatial and tabular database operation; prior use of Global Positioning Systems is a plus.

Interior Museum Program, Bureau of Reclamation/Salt Lake City, Utah

As an intern in this program, you'll help the curatorial staff manage archeological collections at the University of Utah Museum of Natural History. Staff has been working to relocate the collection to an area of the museum with better storage and improved humidity and temperature controls. You'll help inventory, assess, analyze, stabilize, and rehouse perishable artifacts and check the database to make sure records exist. You'll also be trained by museum professionals in proper museum practices for handling objects and taught how to best conserve, stabilize, and store different types of objects.

Candidates should have basic computer skills and a valid driver's license.

Interior Museum Program, Bureau of Reclamation/Santa Fe, New Mexico

As an intern here, you'll help the staff of the Museum of New Mexico, Museum of Indian Arts and Culture conduct a basic inventory of reclamation collections at the museum and check items found in the collections during the past five years to verify that no new sensitive objects (such as previously missing funerary objects) have surfaced. You'll also work on processing archeological records associated with reclamation collections and prepare more detailed and descriptive cataloging on whole (or nearly complete) vessels stored in boxes in the bulk collections, as well as taking digital photos of them.

Candidates should be familiar with the archeology of the Southwestern United States and basic museum methods. Good writing skills and experience in archival processing and database development is preferred.

Interior Museum Program, Bureau of Reclamation/Wichita, Kansas— Bonny Reservoir Collections

As an intern with this program, you'll work with an archeological collection that was excavated and collected at Bonny Reservoir in eastern Colorado. This program is located at Wichita State University, in Wichita, Kansas. Your tasks will include writing site descriptions from field notes; organizing and preparing a report on the archeological survey; and organizing, duplicating, and cataloging field notes, maps, photographs, and artifacts from the various sites. No driver's is license required.

Interior Museum Program, Bureau of Reclamation/Wichita, Kansas— Kansas Collections

As a curatorial assistant intern, you'll help the curatorial staff at the anthropology department at Wichita State University manage archeological collections recovered in Kansas. You'll help identify, catalog, document, and repackage materials.

Candidates should have experience with contemporary museum registration practices and archeological collections.

Interior Museum Program, Bureau of Reclamation/Yakima, Washington— Columbia Basin Project

As an historic properties researcher intern, you'll help the Columbia Basin Project office compile and enter information on a collection of historic structures into an Access database. You may help complete field work to update photographs and record condition of structures.

Candidates must have a driver's license and should have experience in relational databases and be familiar with the vocabulary of historic preservation.

Interior Museum Program, Bureau of Reclamation/Yakima, Washington —Yakima Irrigation Project

As an intern here, you'll index, catalog, and conserve a collection of photographs, maps and construction drawings, and documents of the Bureau of Reclamation's Yakima Irrigation Project. The goal is to scan a large collection of historic photographs to be included in the bureau's online photo archives. You'll use flat-top, negative, and large-format sheet scanners and Adobe Photoshop imaging software for this project.

Candidates should be proficient with scanners, digital photography and imaging software. Related interests in western water development, federal reclamation programs, and public history are useful but not mandatory.

Interior Museum Program, U.S. Fish and Wildlife Service

As an intern here in Shepherdstown, W.Va., you'll help with activities at the National Conservation Training Center Museum, which houses a collection of objects and documents related to service history. You'll help access and catalog museum objects under the supervision of the museum curator and enter catalog records into the agency Rediscovery Museum property database. You'll also have other preservation and conservation duties and environmental-monitoring procedures in museum storage and display areas.

Midwest Archeological Center (Archeological Study of Hopeton Earthworks)

As an intern with this center, you'll spend 40 hours a week helping with geoarcheological and geophysical studies being conducted in association with excavations at the prehistoric Hopeton Earthworks at the Hopewell Culture National Historical Park in Ross County, Ohio. The archeological center itself is located in Lincoln, NE. You also may help teach and supervise undergraduate students enrolled in an archeological field school at the same site. In addition, you'll participate in an ongoing geophysical survey of the site, including basic training in geophysical survey techniques.

Candidates must have experience in archeological work.

Midwest Regional Office Cultural Landscapes Inventory (CLI) and List of Classified Structures (LCS) Program

As an intern in Omaha, you'll work with historical landscape architects and architectural historians to research, evaluate, and enter data (including scanning images) into a word-processing program and then into the CLI and LCS databases. Other duties may include helping with research and preparation of National Register documentation for sites located within the National Park Service Midwest Region. Some evaluation of historic structures may be included. You also may help redraft hand-drawn site maps to produce quality scans.

You may travel to a Midwest national park to help document a cultural landscape or historic structure; cost for this travel will be paid by the NPS.

Candidates should have strong computer, research, and writing skills, plus knowledge of the National Register process and vernacular/cultural landscapes/historic structures. Familiarity with the National Register form is helpful.

Midwest Regional Office Historic Inventory Program (Omaha)

You'll help organize, preserve, and produce a finding aid for access to a list of classified structures and cultural landscapes inventory program records and resource documentation, including correspon-dence, reports, field notes, black-and-white photographic prints and negatives, and maps. You'll also update a file plan or finding aid for current files and label folders as necessary and may digitize inventory images for inclusion in the collection database and do limited research.

Candidates should have strong organizational skills and be familiar with fundamental archival theories and methodologies.

NPS Museum Management Program

As an intern in this program, you'll help manipulate and analyze data of 12 million electronic records in the museum collection's database, adding preautomation catalog records dating from the beginning of the National Park Service to the automated database. You also may help with inventory and management of the Washington office art collection.

Candidates should be familiar with (or willing to learn) museum collection management software.

Ozark National Scenic Riverways

As an intern here, you'll work with the museum curator and regional office archivist in Van Buren, MO, to organize, preserve, and provide access to the Riverways collection of records and resource documentation. This includes the administrative history collection, correspondence, reports, manuscripts, field notes, black-and-white photographic prints and negatives, maps, and blueprints.

You'll evaluate and improve the environmental condition and conservation of the collection and identify and research rare books and documents to be moved to secure archival storage. You'll also identify items needing repair or other special treatment and research repair options. In addition, you may help catalog elements of park collections into the Automated National Cataloging System database.

Candidates must have a museum studies or archives management background and strong organizational skills and familiarity with fundamental archival theories and methodologies.

Yosemite National Park, Heritage Structures Preservation Team and Cultural Resources Division

As an intern here, you'll help the park preservation team with fieldwork on National Register structures. You'll be located in El Portal, CA, at the west park entrance, but you may have field assignments anywhere in the park.

This position is geared toward hands-on treatment of historic structures and preservation practices as they apply to the carpentry and masonry trades. You'll be working with park preservation specialists on preservation projects to develop hands-on techniques in historic fabric repair and conservation, on structures ranging from vernacular log cabins to rustic and Victorian architecture. Work may include both office and fieldwork, depending on your skills and the planning requirements of the preservation program. You also may be expected to handle technical writing, develop treatment plans, research the historic structures database information collection, draft architectural plans, and do onsite investigation work.

Construction skills, AutoCAD skills, computer skills, and backcountry outdoor skills are a plus.

Yosemite National Park Archeology Program

At this internship in Yosemite National Park, CA, you'll help with archeological field, limited laboratory, and database work in support of archeological inventory projects. You'll learn archeological survey work, conducting systematic transects, identifying archeological material, and using topographic maps and compasses. You'll also learn to document surface archeological remains through detailed mapping and photography, geographic positioning using Global Positioning System equipment, and describing archeological materials. Lab work will include entering site information into database systems and electronic site forms.

You'll be working in middle and high elevations of the Sierra Nevada, and you should expect to hike long distances over rough terrain at high elevation and with heavy packs.

Candidates should be in excellent physical condition, possess a background in archeological method and theory, and understand basic field techniques of archeological resource documentation.

HOW TO APPLY

To download an application in Word format, visit http://www.cr.nps.gov/hps/tps/Intern/summer2005.doc. Submit to the preceding address two copies of the following: an application; a transcript; a reference from a faculty member or advisor; and a short essay indicating why you are applying for this internship, the position in which you're most interested, and how this position will further your preservation studies and career goals.

NATIONAL TRUST FOR HISTORIC PRESERVATION INTERNSHIP

Office of Human Resources
1785 Massachusetts Avenue, NW
Washington, DC 20036
Fax: 202-588-6059
jobs@nthp.org
http://www.nationaltrust.org/about_the_trust/
    jobs/internships.html

What You Can Earn: Unpaid but academic credit is possible.
Application Deadlines: Rolling.
Educational Experience: College sophomores or above.
Requirements: None specified.

OVERVIEW

In the late 1940s, leaders of the growing American preservation movement recognized a need for a national organization to support and encourage grassroots efforts. A group of interested citizens began working to establish a National Trust for Historic Preservation, which was signed into law by President Truman in 1949. The National Trust supports preservation through a wide range of programs and activities. The trust operates a nationwide collection of historic sites and demonstrates how preservation can revitalize historic downtowns through programs such as the National Main Street Center and the Community Partners, which use preservation to provide affordable housing in older residential neighborhoods. The National Trust also provides technical and financial assistance to state and local organizations.

The National Trust's two-dozen historic sites are located all over the country; some are operated directly by the National Trust, while others are managed by local partners. Its 25 historic sites range from quiet oak-shaded bayous in Louisiana to crowded city streets in New York, from a simple California adobe to a massive castle overlooking the Hudson River, from Frank Lloyd Wright's Pope-Leighey House of 1940 to James Madison's Montpelier, built almost two centuries earlier. These buildings, the collections they house, and the landscapes that surround them are a legacy from the past and a gift to the future.

During the Trust's 10-week summer program in Washington, D.C., between 15 and 20 interns work on individual projects and have the opportunity to attend weekly educational sessions on topics relating to preservation, National Trust programs, and nonprofit management. Projects are available in various departments in the National Trust's main office and at some of the D.C.-area historic sites, including the Decatur House, the Woodrow Wilson House, and the Woodlawn/Pope-Leighey House.

As an intern with the National Trust, you may help research and compile case studies on preservation-related topics; develop architectural and collections databases; market the National Trust's annual conference and other workshops; promote cultural-diversity programs; research community-revitalization projects; help develop resources for statewide and local partners; improve the Web site; and work on fund-raising, membership development, communications, and marketing.

Some internships require graduate study or experience in preservation, urban planning, or historic-site management, while others offer entry-level opportunities. Schedules are generally flexible for interns who aren't able to volunteer on a full-time basis.

HOW TO APPLY

To apply for an internship, send a cover letter and resume to the preceding address. If applying by e-mail, specify "Internships" in the subject line.

OLD STURBRIDGE VILLAGE INTERNSHIP

Old Sturbridge Village
1 Old Sturbridge Village Road
Sturbridge, Massachusetts 01566
(508) 347-3362, ext. 265
http://www.osv.org/pages/volunteer.html

What You Can Earn: Unpaid.
Application Deadlines: Rolling.
Educational Experience: Graduates and undergraduates enrolled in degree programs and others with the academic qualifications and professional objectives appropriate for the desired internship project.
Requirements: College enrollment.

OVERVIEW

Old Sturbridge Village is an indoor-outdoor museum that brings to life a working community of the 1830s and offers internship opportunities to students interested in gaining practical experience for academic credit or professional experience. It's the largest outdoor living-history museum in the Northeast, with an historical landscape of more than 200 acres. This includes more than 40 structures, including restored buildings brought from across New England as well as some authentic reconstructions.

Volunteer internships are available in nearly every department throughout the museum. If you're accepted, you could spend your summer helping welcome visitors; interacting with young visitors in games, expressive play, reading, and hands on activities at the Samson's Children's Museum; working in the Village's gardens; helping to perform hands-on activities and Village exploration; assisting with basic archival processing, catalog card filing, and data entry; or participating as a marketing or development team member helping to organize and prepare materials for mailing.

Although the internship is unpaid, after 50 hours of service interns can earn guest passes and museum discounts.

HOW TO APPLY
Applicants should submit a letter of interest and a resume to the Coordinator of Staffing by visiting the Web site http://www.osv.org/pages/SendContact.html?ID=7 to send an e-mail, by downloading an application form at the same Internet address, or by calling the coordinator to request an application at the number listed previously.

PRESERVATION ACTION INTERNSHIP

Preservation Action
1054 31st Street NW
Suite 526
Washington, DC 20007
(202) 298-6180

rsincavage@preservationaction.org
http://preservationaction.org/intern2.htm

What You Can Earn: $100 to $200 a week, depending on experience, plus participation in the National Trust intern brown-bag seminar program and possible financial assistance to attend the annual National Preservation Conference in October.
Application Deadlines: March 15 for summer session (early June through late August).
Educational Experience: Historic preservation students (graduate and undergraduate) seeking experience in their future fields.
Requirements: None specified.

OVERVIEW
Founded in 1974, Preservation Action is the only national organization focused on grassroots lobbying for historic preservation in Washington, D.C. The organization monitors federal legislation and keeps members informed of its work in the preservation area through weekly legislative updates, committee conference calls, quarterly national meetings, phone polls, and in-depth policy reports.

Preservation Action and its educational partner, the Center for Preservation Initiatives, offer a number of internship opportunities for students interested in historic preservation. Both organizations offer unique learning opportunities in the areas of preservation advocacy, congressional affairs, fund-raising for political causes, policy analysis, and political writing and research.

Interns help Preservation Action and the Center for Preservation Initiatives (CPI) manage phone calls about policy issues, poll members to help create a legislative agenda, and write and research CPI's online journal (now in development). Interns also help with the two organization's annual fund-raiser—an auction and party at the annual national conference.

Just like Preservation Action's professional staff, interns have to multitask—answering phones, licking envelopes, and meeting elected officials in Congress.

HOW TO APPLY

To apply, submit your cover letter, resume, and references to the preceding address.

SMITHSONIAN ARCHITECTURAL HISTORY AND HISTORIC PRESERVATION DIVISION INTERNSHIP

Architectural History and Historic Preservation Division
Intern Coordinator
Arts & Industries Building, Room 2263
PO Box 37012
Smithsonian Institution
Washington, DC 20560-7012

What You Can Earn: $2,000, pending availability of funding; college credit is available.
Application Deadlines: April 1 for summer program; July 1 for fall internships; January 1 for spring internships.
Educational Experience: Both undergraduate and graduate students with some previous coursework or experience in art history, architectural history or historic preservation.
Requirements: Weekly tutorial sessions with the director or other staff members, a workplan, and a written paper of 20 pages.

OVERVIEW

If you are interested in history and preservation of the Smithsonian Institution buildings, you might be interested in an internship with the Office of Architectural History and Historic Preservation (AHHP). The Smithsonian buildings vary in date and style, from the Patent Office Building (housing the Museum of American Art and the National Portrait Gallery) of 1839 to the National Museum of the American Indian, now under construction. Although they vary a great deal in style and date, the Smithsonian buildings share a common program of creating a unique complex of American public buildings.

Interns in this program will attend weekly staff meetings and an independent research project under the supervision of the staff. Internships are available in the AHHP office, in architectural history, or in preservation.

An internship in the AHHP office is a structured learning experience under the guidance of the director.

Internships in architectural history focus on the use of primary research materials, integrating original documentation, such as correspondence and memoranda, architectural drawings, photographs, and other such archival materials, into the architectural history of the Smithsonian.

Preservation internships use similar research materials and methodology to address a specific preservation issue at the Smithsonian.

HOW TO APPLY

Applicants should send a cover letter, resume, official transcript, writing sample and two recommendations from either professors or employers to the preceding address.

U.S. CAPITOL HISTORICAL SOCIETY INTERNSHIP

U.S. Capitol Historical Society
200 Maryland Avenue, NE
Washington, DC 20002
(202) 543-8919; (800) 887-9318

uschs@uschs.org
http://www.uschs.org/01_society/subs/01d_
  01.html

What You Can Earn: Small transportation stipend is provided.
Application Deadlines: Rolling.
Educational Experience: Undergraduate or graduate college students.
Requirements: None specified.

OVERVIEW

If you can't tear yourself away from Congressional debates and you love to stroll through the Capitol building, an internship with the U.S. Capitol Historical Society might be a good choice for you.

The society is a private, nonprofit, nonpartisan educational organization created in 1962 to interpret, preserve, and communicate the history of the U.S. Capitol and the U.S. Congress, making these institutions and their history more accessible to more people. The society sponsors annual scholarly conferences and fellowship programs to add new research findings about the country's democratic and cultural traditions. Its staff works closely with the Capitol architect and Congressional committees to enhance the Capitol collections. It also provides special tours, lectures, and symposia for its members and for visiting history enthusiasts, scholars, students, and the general public.

As an intern here, you'll work on a variety of research-related projects and help administer symposia, youth forums, and other programs. Your primary job will be to conduct research for the annual *We the People* historical calendar, which involves collecting several historic facts that occurred each day 200 years ago. As part of this research, you'll need to travel to a variety of off-site locations, including the Library of Congress's Main Reading Room and the Newspapers and Periodicals Reading Room. Sources include the journals of the House and Senate, newspapers, diaries, collected papers, encyclopedias, and almanacs. You'll also prepare and edit calendar text.

HOW TO APPLY

If you're interested in an internship at the Society, e-mail the internship coordinator at the preceding address.

VERMONT FOLKLIFE CENTER INTERNSHIP

Vermont Folklife
3 Court Street
PO Box 442
Middlebury, VT 05753
(802) 388-4964
gsharrow@vermontfolklifecenter.org or
  akolovos@vermontfolklifecenter.org
http://www.vermontfolklifecenter.org

What You Can Earn: $4,000 plus mileage reimbursement for the 12-week term of work; academic credit is possible.
Application Deadlines: May 1
Educational Experience: Graduate-level work in folklore, ethnomusicology, anthropology, or a related field; course work in and experience with ethnographic fieldwork methodologies.
Requirements: Ethnographic fieldwork skills; experience working with analog and digital field audio equipment and photographic equipment; strong writing skills; experience with Windows-based PCs; knowledge of HTML a plus. Must have a valid driver's license and your own car; must own a 35mm SLR camera; must be willing to travel extensively throughout state; some weekend and evening work required.

OVERVIEW

The Vermont Folklife Center in Middlebury, VT, founded in 1984, is dedicated to preserving and presenting the folk arts and cultural traditions of Vermont and the surrounding region. The center researches and preserves the historic and contemporary folklife of the state's communities with audio and video interviews, photography, traditional arts apprenticeships, exhibits, publications, workshops, and educational outreach.

Through ongoing field research, a multimedia archive, and an apprenticeship program, center employees document and conserve cultural heritage that could easily be lost. By producing exhibits, publications, and educational projects, the center brings recognition to the skills, talents, and traditions of Vermonters. The center has focused primarily on preserving the spoken word, assembling an archive of more than 3,800 taped interviews that have been transcribed and electronically indexed.

The center uses graduate student interns interested in conducting fieldwork to identify ethnic and traditional artists in the state of Vermont. The intern will be expected to work 30 hours per week on a variety of fieldwork and programming tasks.

As an intern at the center, you'll conduct fieldwork for state-wide traditional arts surveys, perform fieldwork with refugee communities, conduct site visits for the VFC traditional arts apprenticeship program, help with the administration of survey projects and apprenticeship programs, and help with clerical tasks.

HOW TO APPLY

To schedule an interview and for additional information, contact Dr. Gregory Sharrow or Andy Kolovos at the preceding address.

WYCKOFF FARMHOUSE MUSEUM INTERNSHIP

Development Project Manager
Wyckoff Farmhouse Museum
5816 Clarendon Road
Brooklyn, NY 11203

(718) 629-5400
Fax: (718) 629-3125
development@wyckoffassociation.org
http://www.wyckoffassociation.org

What You Can Earn: Stipend available.
Application Deadlines: Rolling.
Educational Experience: Undergraduate college student familiar with data entry and word processing.
Requirements: Must have experience in MS Excel and MS Word; be comfortable navigating the Internet; pay attention to detail; be organized and a quick learner with the ability to take initiative; and have strong communication and interpersonal skills.

OVERVIEW

Begun in 1652, the Wyckoff Farmhouse is the only structure in Brooklyn that has survived from the period of Dutch rule prior to 1664. The Wyckoff Farmhouse Museum presents the full range of Brooklyn's agrarian history and culture to the public, from its colonial origins through 19th-century immigration to the urban development of the 20th century. The Wyckoff Farmhouse Museum centers on the Pieter Claesen Wyckoff House, a national historical landmark and the oldest structure in New York City, as well as the city's first designated landmark.

The museum's mission is to educate visitors about the diverse peoples of Brooklyn's colonial farms, which it does by integrating performing and visual arts with the presentation of humanities content. Each year, the museum plays host to more than 5,000 school children and sponsors a year-round calendar of free public events, featuring performers and folk-art interpreters as well as an organic community demonstration garden staffed by local high school students. This program is designed to educate visitors and the local community about sustainable living and food-supply issues.

An administrative internship is available at the Wyckoff Farmhouse Museum to work closely with the development project manager and perform a variety of development and membership tasks, as well as perform general office duties. As an administrative intern here, you'll help process members who join or renew their memberships, maintain and update mailing lists and help with mailings, send out thank you letters to those who make contributions, fold and stuff acknowledgement letters, and perform other duties as assigned.

This position lasts between four to six months with work for different lengths of time throughout the year, including the summer. An intern would work an average of 10 hours in any given work week.

HOW TO APPLY

To apply for this internship, fax, e-mail, or mail your resume with a cover letter and two references (with contact information) to the preceding address.

INTERNATIONAL

AIESEC

AIESEC United States
127 W. 26th Street, 10th Floor
New York, NY 10001
(212) 757 3774
Fax: (212) 757 4062
aiesec@aiesecus.org
http://www.us.aiesec.org

What You Can Earn: Stipend varies depending on job and country. AIESEC charges $45 dollars for application processing fees; if you're selected, you'll owe another $455.
Application Deadlines: Rolling.
Educational Experience: University junior or senior.
Requirements: None specified.

OVERVIEW

This international association of students is working to build a better world through a variety of international internships in more than 87 countries, designed to improve cultural understanding, share information and technology, develop entrepreneurs, and help make companies more socially responsible. AIESEC is the world's largest student organization, running an exchange program that enables more than 3,500 students and recent graduates to live and work in another country. You can work with any of AIESEC's global partners throughout the world, including Alcatel, Cadbury Schweppes, DHL, Electrolux, InBev, and P&G.

AIESEC's exchange program will give you the chance to learn about the people and culture of a host country, whether you want to teach English in India, work for a small company in South America, or try to bridge the cultural gaps in Middle Eastern countries. You select an internship in accounting, business administration, development studies, economics, education, finance, human resources, information technology, or marketing .

AIESEC offers a preparation program before you leave the United States to make sure you're ready for the challenge of living and working abroad. In addition, AIESEC will help you obtain travel documentation, insurance, and visas. When you arrive in your host country, AIESEC will make sure you have a smooth transition in your new environment, helping you find a place to live and financial services.

HOW TO APPLY

AIESEC maintains offices at a number of universities around the country. To find the closest university near you to apply, visit http://us.aieseconline.net/apply/sn/default.aspx.

Applicants are screened by a review board including academic representatives, members of the local business community, and AIESEC members. Once you pass the review board, your application will then be entered into the global matching system, where internships and student applications are matched. Your local AIESEC representative will discuss this process with you.

AMERICAN FRIENDS SERVICE COMMITTEE INTERNATIONAL INTERNSHIPS

American Friends Service Committee
1501 Cherry Street
Philadelphia, PA 19102
(215) 241-7151
GSicola@afsc.org
http://www.afsc.org/volunteering/intern_ip_082003.htm

What You Can Earn: Unpaid.
Application Deadlines: Rolling.
Educational Experience: At least a sophomore in college; must have substantial knowledge of inter-

national regions and issues (this could include campus or community organizing in the USA on peace, economic justice, or other international issues; coming from or having visited the countries where the AFSC works; or substantial research and writing on current issues relevant to current AFSC programs).

Requirements: Desire to learn about people and communities around the world and a commitment to working for social and economic justice; commitment to Quaker values of nonviolence and social justice, and commitment to tolerance and understanding class, nationality, religion, age, gender, sexual orientation, and disabilities; ability to work and communicate with a diverse staff.

OVERVIEW

The American Friends Service Committee sponsors peacebuilding and social justice programs in more than 20 countries in Africa, Asia, Europe, Latin America/Caribbean, and the Middle East, providing relief, reconstruction, training, and support to local groups and movements, opportunities for dialogue, and peacebuilding/reconciliation.

Intern projects are based on your personal interests and the organization's current needs, learning skills that will help you in future nonprofit work. In addition, an internship here can open the door to the field of international development and connect you with other individuals working for peace and social justice around the world.

As an intern in the Philadelphia office, you'll research and write on current AFSC themes, help with the emergency and materials assistance program, and monitor national and international media. You'll also provide publications and statements, help with general office work, and undertake other special projects.

HOW TO APPLY

Obtain and submit and application at http://www.afsc.org/volunteering/intern_ip_082003.htm.

AMERICAN INSTITUTE FOR FOREIGN STUDY— CANNES INTERNSHIP

American Institute for Foreign Study—Cannes
9 West Broad Street
Stamford, CT 06902
college.info@aifs.com
http://www.aifsabroad.com/InternAbroad/index.htm#apply

What You Can Earn: Unpaid; your fees may range from $9,000 to $12,700 including room and board, tuition, some travel, and social activities. Exact cost depends on whether or not airfare is included, where you fly from, the time of year, and the type of program you choose. Scholarships are available.

Application Deadlines: Fall semester: May 15; spring semester, October 15.

Educational Experience: Internships are open to college freshmen, sophomores, juniors, and seniors.

Requirements: French proficiency at the 300 level (upper intermediate) is required to participate.

OVERVIEW

Perched on the Mediterranean shoreline, Cannes is a sunny, former fishing village turned international Riviera resort with 75,000 inhabitants. A popular destination, Cannes boasts some of the most beautiful scenery in France.

If you choose this internship, you'll study at the Collège International de Cannes, founded in 1931 by poet and philosopher Paul Valéry. The university draws students from around the world, and was designed to introduce foreign students to the French language and culture. The Collège has trained hundreds of students to enter the French university system and is a supportive place for anyone interested in learning another language or about another culture.

The campus has well-equipped modern facilities with 22 classrooms, audio-visual equipment, a language lab, Internet access, a library, and a theater/cinema/conference hall. It is situated on spacious grounds with views of the sea and is within walking distance of the Old Port and city center. The campus has its own laundry and parking facilities and boasts a café bar with an open-air terrace, gym, large residence hall, and courtyard. The Collège offers diplomas issued by the Ministry of Education, Chambre de Commerce et d'Industrie and certificates in elementary and advanced language qualifications, including the Diplôme d'Etudes en Langue Française and Diplôme Approfondi de Langue Française (DELF/DALF diplomas).

Students are housed in double or triple rooms in Collège residence halls, with breakfast and lunch included. Dinner is optional for a supplemental fee.

The Collège can arrange placements in a wide range of public organizations and private companies depending on your academic major, interests, and suitability. Typical internships include a minimum two hours of work a week at local government and housing projects. Interns also may be placed with local TV, youth clubs, hospitals, or the Cannes Festival Hall. However, no college credit can be obtained.

Cannes Film Festival Internship

Spring semester AIFS students are in Cannes during its world-famous film festival, and AIFS students typically receive a festival badge that allows them to attend screenings. For the past several years, AIFS students have been offered the following opportunities during the festival:

- Internships with a production company from California that supplies crews for CNN, BET, TNT, QVC, and HBO. Although you're not paid, you are given meals and treated as crew members. You'll work every day of the festival after morning classes, helping field crews in shootings, logging, duplicating, editing, and arranging interviews with stars and invitations to functions. This is an excellent opportunity for those interested in careers in communications, public relations, or the arts.
- American Foundation for AIDS Research (AmFAR) Internship with this group may include a gala dinner hosted by Elizabeth Taylor.
- Internship with Cannes TV. Here, you may help translate during live interviews with American film stars and producers for Cannes TV.

HOW TO APPLY

Applications are available by calling (800) 727-2437; alternatively, you may apply online at the preceding address.

AMERICAN INSTITUTE FOR FOREIGN STUDY— FLORENCE INTERNSHIP

**American Institute for Foreign Study—
Florence**
9 West Broad Street
Stamford, CT 06902
college.info@aifs.com
http://www.aifsabroad.com/InternAbroad/index.
htm#apply

What You Can Earn: Unpaid; fees may range from $9,000 to $12,700 including room and board, tuition, some travel and social activities; college credit and scholarships are available. Exact cost depends on whether or not airfare is included, where you fly from, the time of year, and the type of program you choose.
Application Deadlines: Fall semester: May 15; spring semester, October 15.

Educational Experience: Internships are open to college freshmen, sophomores, juniors and seniors.
Requirements: Good knowledge of Italian.

OVERVIEW

More and more international corporations are looking for international experience in their new employees; indeed, international commerce remains the most dynamic sector of the world economy. As a way of meeting that demand, many students are looking for internships abroad to hone their global skills in international management positions.

For more than 39 years, the American Institute For Foreign Study (AIFS) has been a leader in study-abroad programs for American students, sending more than one million students and teachers throughout the world. In addition to more traditional study-abroad programs, the AIFS offers fall and spring internships in Florence, in either business administration or social science.

Classes are offered under the auspices of the American International University in London, an independent, international university of liberal arts and professional studies. Renowned for its emphasis on international and multicultural themes, AIU in Florence has an international student body of more than 1,000 full-time students from 100 countries.

During your stay, you'll live in an Italian household or in a student apartment, complete with restaurant vouchers for five breakfasts and five lunches or dinners a week.

After your interviews and application have been accepted, placement is determined by the director of the program.

Internship in Business Administration (3 credits)

In this internship, you'll work as a part-time volunteer in local companies or small businesses in or near Florence for a minimum of 130 hours. To receive credit, you'll report to the supervising instructor regularly and submit an analytical paper. You may take only Italian plus one other course, such as history, fine arts, social sciences, and so on.

Internship in Social Science (3 credits)

If you have a strong commitment to social work or social sciences, you may obtain part-time placement (minimum 130 hours) in elementary education, assistance to the elderly, work with the handicapped, or health care assistance. The student is placed as a volunteer and is graded. You may take only Italian and one other course.

HOW TO APPLY

Applications are available by calling (800) 727-2437; alternatively, you may apply online at the preceding address.

AMERICAN INSTITUTE FOR FOREIGN STUDY— LONDON INTERNSHIP

American Institute for Foreign Study— London
9 West Broad Street
Stamford, CT 06902
college.info@aifs.com
http://www.aifsabroad.com/InternAbroad/index.htm#apply

What You Can Earn: Unpaid; your fees may range from $9,000 to $12,700 including room and board, tuition, some travel, and social activities; college credit and scholarships are available. Exact cost depends on whether or not airfare is included, where you fly from, the time of year, and the type of program you choose.
Application Deadlines: Fall semester: May 15; spring semester, October 15.
Educational Experience: Internships are open to college freshmen, sophomores, juniors, and seniors.
Requirements: None specified.

OVERVIEW

If you're looking for international corporate experience without having to worry about learning another language, an internship in London could be the way to go. With this program under the auspices of the American Institute For Foreign Study (AIFS), you'll study at Richmond, the American International University in London, an international university of liberal arts and professional studies incorporated in Delaware and accredited by the Commission on Higher Education of the Middle States Association of Colleges and Schools, a regional accrediting body recognized by the U.S. Department of Education.

Summer Internship (up to Nine Credits)

This internship enables you to complement classroom learning with practical experience in the workplace, participate in international, intercultural learning, develop personal skills to help you build a competitive resume and make contacts in career areas. The program's objective is academic training of the highest standard, focusing on the realities of working in a multicultural world.

Richmond has organized the International Internship Program to combine an academic program with the opportunity to work in major British and international institutions. If you're interested in a career in politics, you can work in the House of Commons or in local political organizations. If you're interested in media or journalism, you could to spend a semester at a media or publishing company. For those who want experience in business and finance, internships include banks, investment houses, business analysis, and development in large or small companies. Performing-arts placements are with theaters, music companies, and in entertainment.

During the first three weeks, you'll take a required social science course (Contemporary British Culture) that meets Monday through Friday and is taught by Richmond faculty, many of whom are practicing experts in their fields. During the last nine weeks, you'll intern four days a week for six credits or five days a week for nine credits and meet occasionally in seminars to examine workplace issues. The program runs mid-May to mid-August. Students may take one or two courses, but since some internships are full time, this could limit course selection to evening classes. You can check http://www.richmond.ac.uk to see which courses are offered in the evening.

You'll live with other Richmond students in university housing, use university libraries, computer labs, studios, and other facilities and take part in travel, performances, sports, and social programs. You'll use public transportation to go to work.

HOW TO APPLY

Applications are available by calling (800) 727-2437; alternatively, you may apply online at the preceding address.

AMERICAN INSTITUTE FOR FOREIGN STUDY— SYDNEY INTERNSHIP

American Institute for Foreign Study—Sydney
9 West Broad Street
Stamford, CT 06902
college.info@aifs.com
http://www.aifsabroad.com/InternAbroad/index.htm#apply

What You Can Earn: Unpaid; your fees may range from $9,000 to $12,700 including room and board, tuition, some travel, and social activities; college credit and scholarships are available. Exact cost depends on whether or not airfare is included, where you fly from, the time of year, and the type of program you choose.

Application Deadlines: Fall semester: May 15; spring semester, October 15.

Educational Experience: Internships are open to college freshmen, sophomores, juniors and seniors.

Requirements: You must have a GPA of 3.0 and/or a strong supporting recommendation from the study-abroad adviser of your university.

OVERVIEW

What could provide a greater international internship than spending the summer in the beautiful town of Sydney, Australia, an energetic city built along a gorgeous harbor?

And remember, seasons are reversed down under—Sydney offers students warm sun and beach days from October through April.

This program is a combination of studying and internship, so you'll go to classes at Macquarie University, set on 55 acres of rolling hills in North Ryde, 10 miles northwest of Sydney's center. It combines the best of Australia's open spaces with a modern campus that includes teaching and research facilities and extensive areas for sports and leisure. You can spend time outdoors, reading under the shade of eucalyptus trees, hiking the hills, strolling to the university's complex of shops and restaurants, catching a bus to Sydney's center, or swimming at the beach. Established in 1966, Macquarie is one of the leading research institutions in Sydney, with an annual enrollment of 16,000. It offers a wide range of academic programs and majors that span the humanities, sciences, and social sciences.

During your internship, you'll live in single rooms in Dunmore Lang residential college and have meals in Dunmore Lang dining hall.

You can earn six credits for this internship, which provides you an opportunity to gain valuable work experience within a relevant organization while completing your studies. The internships are normally unpaid positions with companies near the university or a short train or bus ride away. You'll be placed in positions related to your major and/or interests. You'll work 18 hours a week, generally over a three-day period under the direction of a workplace supervisor, and in addition complete an academic project. You may then choose to enroll in either one or two further courses offered by Macquarie University to build a full-time credit load. (A study-abroad student enrolled in one further course will satisfy visa requirements.)

HOW TO APPLY

Applications are available by calling (800) 727-2437; alternatively, you may apply online at the preceding address.

AMERICAN-SCANDINAVIAN FOUNDATION INTERNSHIP

The American-Scandinavian Foundation
Exchange Division
58 Park Avenue
New York NY 10016
(212) 879-9779, ext. 731
Fax: (212) 686-2115
trainscan@amscan.org
http://www.amscan.org

What You Can Earn: Income for a four- to five-hour teaching week is estimated at EU 830 a month, which is taxed at the rate of 35 percent. This is not enough income to live on, so the applicant must bring along at least $1000 a month in personal funds to supplement income and must show proof that a total of $9000 ($1000/month for nine months) is available at the time of application.

Application Deadlines: Rolling.

Educational Experience: College junior or senior with a minimum 2.5 GPA; major must be relevant to the placement offer.

Requirements: Minimum age 20; U.S. citizenship or permanent residency.

OVERVIEW

The American-Scandinavian Foundation (ASF) works to boost international understanding by offering an educational and cultural internship exchange between the United States and Denmark, Finland, Iceland, Norway, and Sweden.

Founded in 1910 by Danish-American industrialist Niels Poulsen, the ASF is a publicly supported nonprofit organization that manages an extensive program of fellowships, grants, trainee placement, publishing, and cultural activities. The foundation is governed by a board of trustees of individuals from the United States and Scandinavia with personal or professional ties to Scandinavia. The five Nordic heads of state serve as the organization's patrons.

Over the years, more than 26,000 young Americans and Scandinavians have participated in ASF's exchange programs of study, research, or practical training. The ASF training program gives American college students insight into the culture and people of Scandinavia. Recently, internships have been offered in the areas of biomedical engineering, chemical engineering, civil engineering, computer science, environmental science and forestry, or paper science. Offers are usually for two to three months in the summer, although they may last for up to 18 months.

HOW TO APPLY

You can apply online at http://www.amscan.org/jobs/index.html.

AUSTRALIAN EMBASSY INTERNSHIP

Internship Coordinator, Public Affairs Office
Embassy of Australia
1601 Massachusetts Ave NW
Washington DC 20036
Fax: (202) 797-3414
E-mail: media@austemb.org
http://www.austemb.org/PAinternships.html

What You Can Earn: Unpaid.
Application Deadlines: Rolling.

Educational Experience: Third-year or fourth-year college students with a personal interest in the fields of public relations, journalism, and/or international relations.
Requirements: Strong initiative and writing and research skills; strong interpersonal skills; an ability to work independently and with a team.

OVERVIEW

If you've always had a yen to live Down Under, you may want to start with an internship at the Australian Embassy in Washington, D.C. The public affairs office in the embassy recruits one intern each in the fall, summer, and spring. Fall and spring interns usually work two days a week, and summer interns are usually full time, although this schedule is flexible.

In this internship, you'll help write embassy news briefs and features for posting on the embassy's Web site; help write the embassy's monthly electronic newsletter (the Australia Report); help compose press releases and embassy fact sheets; undertake research in the library and on the Internet; scan U.S. papers for Australia-related clippings; and handle parcel/package pick-up.

HOW TO APPLY

If you're interested in this internship, you can download the application (it's compatible with Microsoft Word versions 2000 and above), fill it out, and either mail it or e-mail it along with your resume and a cover letter to the preceding address.

BOSTON UNIVERSITY INTERNSHIP ABROAD— AUCKLAND INTERNSHIP

Boston University
Division of International Programs
232 Bay State Road

Boston, MA 02215
(617) 353-9888
abroad@bu.edu
http://www.bu.edu/abroad

What You Can Earn: Unpaid but you can earn 16 credits from Boston University; fee required.
Application Deadlines: October 15 for spring semester (early January to late June); March 15 for fall semester (mid-July to late November).
Educational Experience: Minimum 3.0 GPA in major.
Requirements: None specified.

OVERVIEW

The Auckland programs offer students the opportunity to study and work at the same time in Auckland, the gateway to the South Pacific. The Auckland internship program is hosted by the University of Auckland. In this program, you'll enroll directly in a four-credit course: Aotearoa New Zealand: History, Society, and Politics. You'll also take two four-credit electives at the University of Auckland. Then you'll take a four-credit internship in an area in which you're interested, such as advertising and public relations; arts and arts administration; hospitality administration; journalism; politics and international relations; psychology and social policy; business; or information technology.

While working and studying in New Zealand, you'll live on campus in a three-bedroom apartment at the Railway Campus of the University of Auckland, situated in a vibrant urban environment in the heart of Auckland on the North Island of New Zealand. You'll also have the chance to take excursions to important New Zealand sites as well as spend several days on the island of Rarotonga, a major Maori cultural site and geological area, and capital of the Cook Islands, plus the scenic Bay of Islands, home of New Zealand's original capital city, Russell.

The University of Auckland is about the same size as Boston University and is located near the waterfront of Auckland, New Zealand's largest city. It boasts a comprehensive range of internationally recognized programs of study, outstanding scholars

and teachers, global reach in the dissemination of research publications, extensive involvement in overseas programs, and a richly diverse faculty and student body. (For more information about the University of Auckland, visit http://www.auckland.ac.nz.)

HOW TO APPLY

You can download an application here at http://www.bu.edu/abroad/apply and submit it to the preceding address. Or visit this Web site to apply online: https://app.applyyourself.com/?id=BU-I.

BOSTON UNIVERSITY INTERNSHIP ABROAD— BEIJING INTERNSHIP

Boston University
Division of International Programs
232 Bay State Road
Boston, MA 02215
(617) 353-9888
abroad@bu.edu
http://www.bu.edu/abroad

What You Can Earn: Unpaid; significant tuition fee is involved.
Application Deadlines: October 15 for spring semester (late December through late May).
Educational Experience: Minimum 3.0 GPA (in major and overall), plus four semesters of college-level Chinese (or the equivalent) with grades of B or better.
Requirements: None specified.

OVERVIEW

The Beijing internship program offers an extended semester in China's capital city. The program combines an internship with intensive study of the

Chinese language as it is spoken in both everyday and professional contexts. Study trips to surrounding areas and to local businesses supplement the coursework. All language and culture classes are taught by Chinese faculty in conjunction with CET Academic Programs, an American organization based in Washington, D.C., that has been administering educational programs in Asia for 20 years. Upon successful completion of a semester (20 weeks), students receive 20 Boston University credits.

During the first four to five weeks, you'll be placed into one of two levels of a course titled Chinese in Daily Life. Saturday field trips and a special weekend trip complement the curriculum.

During the next seven to eight weeks, you'll enroll in three courses: Modern China, Professional Chinese, and Advanced Chinese I, II, or III. You'll be placed in classes with students participating in the CET Chinese program in Beijing. Because of differences in language levels among students, CET usually offers up to eight separate levels of Mandarin to suit the abilities of every student. This portion of your internship will end with a study trip to Shanghai, which includes speakers and company visits and offers you the opportunity to observe professional life in China's commercial center. Trips have included visits to the Shanghai Stock Exchange, the U.S. Consulate, the American Chamber of Commerce, and law firms as well as wholly owned Chinese firms. Students also participate in a seminar on China's business strategies and network with expatriate executives.

During the final seven to eight weeks, you'll work a minimum of 25 hours a week at your internship and participate in a one-on-one language tutorial to integrate your language study with the specific requirements of your work experience. You'll also continue the Modern China and Professional Chinese courses. An internship discussion seminar requires you to keep an analytical notebook and present a series of oral and written reports about your internship experiences.

During your internship, you'll live in double-occupancy dorm rooms with Chinese roommates. Single rooms are available but limited.

HOW TO APPLY

You can download an application at http://www.bu.edu/abroad/apply and submit it to the preceding address. Or visit this Web site to apply online: https://app.applyyourself.com/?id=BU-I.

BOSTON UNIVERSITY INTERNSHIP ABROAD— DRESDEN INTERNSHIP

Boston University
Division of International Programs
232 Bay State Road
Boston, MA 02215
(617) 353-9888
abroad@bu.edu
http:// www.bu.edu/abroad

What You Can Earn: Unpaid; fee required.
Application Deadlines: October 15 for spring semester (early January to late April); March 15 for fall semester (late August to mid-December); March 1 for summer semester (mid-May to mid-August)
Educational Experience: Minimum 3.0 GPA in major and overall.
Requirements: None specified.

OVERVIEW

If you're interested in studying and interning in Germany, the Boston University Dresden programs offer a wide variety of options to students, built around a semester or academic year of direct enrollment at Technische Universität Dresden (TUD) in the culturally rich city of Dresden, Germany. German faculty teaches all courses. Upon successful completion of a semester, students earn 16 to 20 Boston University credits.

After the first eight weeks of an intensive four-credit German-language and cultural-immersion course, students are placed in their internships.

Complementary coursework runs in tandem with internships. Students begin their internships during week nine and continue to work for an average of 30 hours a week.

While you're in Germany, you'll also enroll in two or more courses at TUD and attend three to four faculty-directed sessions on the academic component of your internship. During the final week of the program, you'll attend a seminar in which you'll deliver the final presentations on your academic internship projects.

Internship placements vary according to students' interests, backgrounds, work experience, and language abilities, but most are offered in the areas of business, television, human services, international relations, and theater. The program also provides opportunities in a variety of disciplines, so students from all majors are encouraged to apply.

HOW TO APPLY

You can download an application at http://www.bu.edu/abroad/apply and submit it to the preceding address. Or visit this Web site to apply online: https://app.applyyourself.com/?id=BU-I.

BOSTON UNIVERSITY INTERNSHIP ABROAD— DUBLIN INTERNSHIP

Boston University
Division of International Programs
232 Bay State Road
Boston, MA 02215
(617) 353-9888
abroad@bu.edu
http://www.bu.edu/abroad

What You Can Earn: Unpaid but 16 credits are offered; fee required.

Application Deadlines: October 15 for spring semester (early January to late April); March 15 for fall semester (late August to mid-December); March 1 for summer semester (mid-May to mid- August)
Educational Experience: Minimum 3.0 GPA in major and overall.
Requirements: None specified.

OVERVIEW

The Irish internship program offers a semester of study and work in Dublin, based at Dublin City University. The program combines a professional internship with coursework on various aspects of Ireland's dynamic history and contemporary culture, including its art, economy, literature, media, and politics. Courses designed specifically for students in the Boston University program are taught by faculty drawn from Dublin-area universities and professional institutes.

During the first six weeks, you'll be taking two required core courses: Contemporary Irish Society and the History of Ireland (evolution of modern Ireland). Students also meet with the program's internship adviser to be placed according to ability, professional goals, experience, work habits, and availability of local opportunities.

During the final eight weeks, you'll participate in full-time internships with organizations in the greater Dublin area for four days per week, while also enrolling in one of three elective courses: The Arts in Ireland, Modern Irish Literature, or Mass Media in Ireland. Internship areas include: advertising/public relations; arts/arts administration; business/economics; film and radio/television; health/human services; hospitality administration; information technology/telecommunications; journalism; politics/international relations; and prelaw.

Students may choose to live with Irish families or in college apartments on the campus of the National College of Ireland in Dublin city center (http://www.ncirl.ie). The homestays are situated in the suburbs of Dublin, close to DCU.

HOW TO APPLY

You can download an application at http://www.bu.edu/abroad/apply and submit it to the preceding address. Or visit this Web site to apply online: https://app.applyyourself.com/?id=BU-I.

BOSTON UNIVERSITY INTERNSHIP ABROAD— GENEVA INTERNSHIP

Boston University
Division of International Programs
232 Bay State Road
Boston, MA 02215
(617) 353-9888
abroad@bu.edu
http://www.bu.edu/abroad

What You Can Earn: Unpaid but you can earn 16 Boston University credits; tuition fee required.
Application Deadlines: October 15 for spring semester (mid-January to mid-May); March 15 for fall semester (early September to mid-December).
Educational Experience: Minimum 3.0 GPA in major and overall; students who wish to participate in a French-based internship must demonstrate French-language proficiency.
Requirements: None specified.

OVERVIEW

Geneva, Switzerland, is an important center of international diplomacy, business, banking, and humanitarian activities, located on the shores of Lake Geneva and surrounded by the highest peaks of the Alps. Home to more than 100 international organizations, Geneva hosts the World Health Organization, the World Trade Organization, the UN High Commission on Refugees, the International Red Cross, and many more.

The University of Geneva has partnered with Boston University to offer an internship program in Switzerland for students specializing in international relations and other related fields, which will provide a unique opportunity to connect with and play a role in these global organizations through a professional internship and carefully focused coursework. All courses are taught in English at the University of Geneva and include introduction to international law (four credits), the activities of international organizations (four credits), Switzerland and small states (four credits), and the internship (four credits).

For the internship (available in both English and French), you'll probably be placed in one of the many international political, economic, and humanitarian organizations headquartered in Geneva. Additional internships will be available in arts and arts administration, communications, international business and finance, or hospitality.

Most students will live at the Cité Universitaire de Genève, which houses a mix of international students in a modern, high-rise residence and features a cafeteria and athletic facilities. Additionally, female students have the option of living in Home Saint Pierre-Petershöfli, a residence for women ages 18 to 30 featuring a cozy, friendly atmosphere, a large communal kitchen and dining room, and a rooftop terrace with a view of Lake Geneva.

In addition to program field trips to the Swiss capital, Bern, and to Hague in the Netherlands, students have numerous opportunities to explore Europe, including a variety of organized activities and ski trips.

HOW TO APPLY

You can download an application here at http://www.bu.edu/abroad/apply and submit it to the preceding address. Or visit this Web siteto apply online: https://app.applyyourself.com/?id=BU-I.

BOSTON UNIVERSITY INTERNSHIP ABROAD— HAIFA INTERNSHIP

Boston University
Division of International Programs
232 Bay State Road
Boston, MA 02215
(617) 353-9888
abroad@bu.edu
http://www.bu.edu/abroad

What You Can Earn: Unpaid but you can earn between 16 and 20 Boston University credits; fee required.
Application Deadlines: October 15 for spring semester (early January to early June); March 15 for fall semester (late August to early January).
Educational Experience: Minimum 3.0 GPA in major and overall; it's recommended that students have one semester or more of college-level Hebrew language, or the equivalent, before starting the program. However, prior language study is not required.
Requirements: None specified.

OVERVIEW

The Haifa Language and Liberal Arts internship program offers a semester in the Mediterranean seaport of Haifa in Israel, combining language study with other coursework at the University of Haifa and excursions in and outside of Israel.

As part of the internship, you'll enroll in the University of Haifa's department of overseas studies and take four courses (usually three-credit hours each) a semester, including a course in Hebrew or Arabic language (six- and four-credits, respectively), a course related to the culture or history of Israel and the Middle East, and courses in your area of interest in liberal arts. It's also possible to enroll either in the department of English or the department of fine arts. Students proficient in Hebrew may enroll directly in courses offered through other departments in the university.

In addition, you'll participate in internships under the supervision of the department of overseas studies and an on-site supervisor. Placements vary according to your interests, background, and language abilities, but you can consider such fields as medical services; archaeology; business; computer technologies; education; international trade; public relations; social work; conflict resolution; and women's studies. Up to four Boston University credits are awarded for an internship.

To get the most out of your time in Israel, you can take advantage of a chance to live in Israel and earn credit before the regular semester begins, at no additional cost. These opportunities vary from semester to semester but may include a study tour, an Ulpan (intensive Hebrew language program), or a presemester internship.

While at the University of Haifa, you'll live with Israeli students in fully equipped dormitory suites in the new residence hall village.

HOW TO APPLY

You can download an application here at http://www.bu.edu/abroad/apply and submit it to the preceding address. Or visit this Web site to apply online: https://app.applyyourself.com/?id=BU-I.

BOSTON UNIVERSITY INTERNSHIP ABROAD— LONDON INTERNSHIP

Boston University
Division of International Programs
232 Bay State Road
Boston, MA 02215
(617) 353-9888

abroad@bu.edu
http:// www.bu.edu/abroad

What You Can Earn: Unpaid; fee required.
Application Deadlines: October 15 for spring semester (early January to late April); March 15 for fall semester (late August to mid-December); March 1 for summer semester (mid-May to mid-August).
Educational Experience: Undergraduate student.
Requirements: Unspecified.

OVERVIEW

For 22 years, Boston University's London internship program has offered a semester of study and work in England's capital city, combining a professional internship with coursework that examines a particular academic area in the context of Britain's history, culture, and society and its role in modern Europe. Courses in each academic area are taught by British faculty to students enrolled in the Boston University program. Upon successful completion of a semester, students earn 16 Boston University credits.

During the first five weeks of the internship, you'll take one core course in your academic area to prepare for your internship and one elective course. You'll also meet the program's internship advisers to refine your area of work placement according to your ability, professional goals, experience, and work habits.

The final eight weeks is your actual internship phase, when you'll participate in London's professional world through assigned internships designed to complement your particular academic concentration and personal goals. You'll work full time, four days a week, while enrolled in a related, weekly seminar course.

You can choose to focus on one of the following academic areas.

Advertising, Marketing, and Public Relations

In this area, you'll study media and consumer behavior and work in the marketing or public relations departments of British companies, multinational firms, advertising agencies, or public relations agencies. Previous internship placements have included Universal Pictures, L'Oreal, QBO Bell Pottinger, and Fleishman Hillard.

Arts and Arts Administration

Here, you'll study the history and sociology of the arts in Britain and work in one of London's art galleries, theaters, museums, preservation projects, or local arts centers. Internship placements have included Sotheby's, the Royal Academy of Arts, Latchmere Theatre, Flowers Central, and Dali Universe.

Business and Economics

If business is your cup of tea, you can study the current economic, political, and social issues affecting Britain and work in a London organization with an economic dimension. Internship placements have included Thompson Venture Economics, Center for Economic Policy Research, Business Services Association, and Taylor Rafferty.

Film, Radio, and Television

In this area, you'll study communications and society in Britain and work for one of London's radio and television stations or film production companies. Internship placements have included The Travel Channel, TwentyTwenty Television, Raindance Film Showcase, Ruby Films, Prospect Pictures, and Zenith Entertainment.

Hospitality and Tourism

Here, you'll intern in travel, hotel, or restaurant marketing and public relations firms. Internship placements have included the London Hilton, Radison Edwardian, Planet Hollywood, and United Airlines. Placements are limited.

Journalism

If this is your area of interest, you'll study Britain's news media in the context of the political, cultural, and social life of the United Kingdom by participating in the daily operations of a newspaper, magazine, publishing house, or broadcast news organization. Internship placements have included CNN, NBC, *Food and Travel* magazine, *The Financial Times*, *Readers Digest*, the *Sunday Times*, and Simon & Schuster.

Management and Finance

Interns here study international management and work in the accounting, banking, corporate finance, economic research and operations, or personnel management departments of prestigious international organizations. Internship placements have included Deutsche Bank, Citigroup, JP Morgan, and Viacom.

Politics and International Relations

At this internship, you'll study the issues and institutions of British political culture and work in one of London's many political institutions, including Parliament, party organizations, lobbying groups, or political public relations agencies. Internship placements have included Labour and Conservative members of Parliament, Labour Party Headquarters, War on Want, Janes Information Group, Overseas Development Institute, and Free Tibet Campaign.

Prelaw

With this internship, you'll study the history and practice of the law in both the United States and Britain and participate in the daily life of a British law firm or commercial legal department. Internship placements have included such prestigious law firms as Dawson Cornwell, Beachcroft Wansbroughs, and Peter Kandler & Co.

Psychology and Social Policy

In this area, you'll study healthcare and human-services issues and participate in the daily work life of hospital rehabilitation, therapy, or education programs, health center administration, social service departments, community care centers, or social activist organizations. Internship placements have included the Cassell Hospital, Russell Unit Eating Disorders Service, Psychiatric Rehabilitation Services, and Westminster Women's Aid.

HOW TO APPLY

You can download an application at http://www.bu.edu/abroad/apply and submit it to the preceding address. Or visit this Web site to apply online: https://app.applyyourself.com/?id=BU-I.

BOSTON UNIVERSITY INTERNSHIP ABROAD— MADRID INTERNSHIP

Boston University
Division of International Programs
232 Bay State Road
Boston, MA 02215
(617) 353-9888
abroad@bu.edu
http://www.bu.edu/abroad

What You Can Earn: Unpaid but you can earn 16 Boston University credits (eight credits for the summer internship); fee required.
Application Deadlines: October 15 for spring semester (mid-January to mid-May); March 15 for fall semester (early September to mid-December); March 1 for summer semester (late May early July); March 15 for academic year (early September to mid-May).
Educational Experience: Minimum 3.0 GPA in major plus proficiency in Spanish (qualifying for Level II or III).
Requirements: None specified.

OVERVIEW

The Madrid internship program offers a semester or academic year of intensive language and cultural study in Madrid, Spain, and housing in Spanish households, where students have their own room and eat with their hosts. If you select this internship program, you'll enroll in three courses at the Insitutio Internacional; the courses are taught in Spanish by Spanish faculty or the resident director. These courses will depend on your major and on the nature of the internship work. Placements take into consideration your experiences, language abilities, and available opportunities in any given semester, so flexibility is essential.

The Instituto Internacional en España was founded in 1892 by Bostonian Alice Gordon Gulick and was recently named a national monument of historic interest. The Instituto is located in the heart of Madrid and offers a library, cafeteria, auditorium, computer lab with Internet connection, and areas for students to connect to the Internet using their own laptop computers.

You'll also participate in a four-credit, faculty-supervised internship drawn from more than 350 active internship sources in a wide variety of fields, including the arts/architecture; business/economics; politics; comparative law; international organization; health and human services; advertising or public relations; film and television; journalism; or field placement in hospitality administration. During your internship, you'll also undertake a midterm oral briefing (evaluated by the internship director) and a final reflective and analytical written report, evaluating your personal, professional, and academic development during the internship (evaluated by the internship director).

In addition to courses and/or an internship, the programs include day and weekend field trips to such places as Granada, Córdoba, Toledo, Sevilla, and/or Segovia.

Summer Madrid Internship

The summer program offers an intensive seven-week study abroad opportunity that combines an internship, a liberal arts course, and an integrated homestay placement in Madrid. Courses are taught at the Instituto Internacional en España in Madrid, and you'll fulfill your internship in major corporations, institutes, and nonprofit organizations. Areas of internship include advertising and public relations; arts and arts administration; business and economics; film and television; health and human

services; hospitality administration; journalism; politics; law; and teaching.

In addition to working in an internship full time, five days a week, for six weeks, you'll take one liberal arts course. Your internship is assessed on the basis of written work, an evaluation by the on-site supervisor, and a review by the Boston University internship director.

HOW TO APPLY

You can download an application here at http://www.bu.edu/abroad/apply and submit it to the preceding address. Or visit this Web site to apply online: https://app.applyyourself.com/?id=BU-I.

BOSTON UNIVERSITY INTERNSHIP ABROAD— PARIS INTERNSHIP

Boston University
Division of International Programs
232 Bay State Road
Boston, MA 02215
(617) 353-9888
abroad@bu.edu
http://www.bu.edu/abroad

What You Can Earn: Unpaid but 16 credits are possible; fee required.

Application Deadlines: October 15 for spring semester (early January to late April); March 15 for fall semester (late August to mid-December); March 1 for summer semester (mid-May to mid-August).

Educational Experience: Minimum 3.0 GPA (in major and overall), plus completion of fourth-semester French with grades of B or better.

Requirements: None specified.

OVERVIEW

The Paris internship program offers a semester combination of internships in Paris (the center of

French and European business and culture) with intensive French-language study and liberal arts courses. French faculty members from local universities teach courses on contemporary France that are specifically designed for students in the internship program.

After an orientation period, you'll enroll in three courses and begin the internship-placement process. Depending on how good your French is, you'll be placed into one of two sequences: one language course and two electives or two language courses and one elective.

During the second half of the semester, you'll participate in local professional life through faculty-supervised full-time internships that occur Monday through Friday. At the same time, you'll attend small group and individual writing tutorials that monitor your progress in the internship and the drafting of an extensive analytical internship report. At the end of the internship, you'll give an oral defense of your report.

Paris Management Internship Program

During the spring term only, Boston University and the University of Paris IX-Dauphine offer a one-semester management internship program. The program includes two management courses, a special "economic development of Europe" seminar, a French language workshop, and an internship for credit. Students enroll in two management courses at the University of Paris IX-Dauphine and have access to Dauphine facilities and services. This internship provides 18 credits.

The Boston University Paris center, including administrative offices and classrooms, is located in the fifteenth arrondissement, within walking distance of the Eiffel Tower. Students have the option of living in a French household or in student housing at the Fondation des États-Unis, a residence hall in the Cité Universitaire international student complex.

Paris Summer Program

This eight-week, eight-credit program offers an internship track in which you take one liberal arts course and do a full-time internship.

HOW TO APPLY

You can download an application here at http://www.bu.edu/abroad/apply and submit it to the preceding address. Or visit this Web site to apply online: https://app.applyyourself.com/?id=BU-I.

BOSTON UNIVERSITY INTERNSHIP ABROAD— SYDNEY INTERNSHIP

Boston University
Division of International Programs
232 Bay State Road
Boston, MA 02215
(617) 353-9888
abroad@bu.edu
http://www.bu.edu/abroad

What You Can Earn: Unpaid; fee is charged.
Application Deadlines: October 15 for spring semester (early January to late April); March 15 for fall semester (late August to mid-December); March 1 for summer semester (late May to mid-August). Given visa restrictions, serious candidates for the Sydney internship are strongly advised to apply by September 1 for the spring semester.
Educational Experience: Minimum 3.0 GPA.
Requirements: None specified.

OVERVIEW

Boston University's internship abroad program offers a semester of study and work in Sydney, Australia, one of the hubs of the Pacific Rim. This program combines a professional internship with coursework on Australia's dynamic history, contemporary culture, and place in the modern world, including its literature, film, mass media, politics, economy, and art. Courses are taught at the Boston University Sydney Center by faculty drawn from leading Australian universities and industries.

Upon successful completion of a semester, you can earn 16 Boston University credits, which may be transferred to your university with permission from your adviser.

During the first six weeks of your internship in Australia, you'll take two core courses: Australian Culture and Society and a course on Australian art and architecture, film and video production, Australian cinema, or Australian social policy. You'll also meet an appointed Sydney program internship adviser to come up with an internship placement according to your ability, academic history, professional goals, experience, and work style. In addition, the Australian Culture and Society course requires all students to conduct ethnographic research on a selected aspect of Australian society.

During the final eight weeks, you'll begin your actual internship, when you'll participate in Sydney's local work life through internships with Australian and multinational businesses and organizations. You'll work four days a week while taking an elective course in one of the following Australian-focused subjects: politics, literature, mass media, or economics. Throughout this eight-week period, you'll have two required formal meetings with your internship advisers and complete portfolios based on your internship experiences. Internship areas include advertising and public relations; arts and arts administration; business and economics; film, radio and television; health and human services; hospitality administration; journalism; and politics.

You'll live at a student residence near the University of Sydney and the University of Technology, Sydney, a five-minute walk from Boston University's classroom and administrative center. You'll have easy access to public transportation, Darling Harbour, Chinatown, and the City Business District. You'll share double rooms in fully furnished loft apartments with private bathrooms and kitchenettes.

HOW TO APPLY

You can download an application at http://www.bu.edu/abroad/apply and submit it to the preceding address. Or visit this Web site to apply online: https://app.applyyourself.com/?id=BU-I.

CAMP COUNSELORS USA—EUROPEAN DAY CAMPS

Camp Counselors USA
2330 Marinship Way, Suite 250
Sausalito CA 94965
(415) 339-2728; (415) 339-2740; (800) 999-2267
Fax: (415) 339-2744
info@ccusa.com
http://www.ccusa.com/PROGRAMS/RU/intro.aspx#

What You Can Earn: Counselors receive €180 (about $216.50) for each week of camp work; senior counselors may receive a higher rate of pay. It is also possible to earn bonuses for exceptional work. Room and breakfast included; if breakfast is not provided, counselors will receive a €35 ($42) weekly breakfast allowance. Counselors are responsible for their other meals.

Application Deadlines: Rolling.

Educational Experience: Proof of your enrollment in a university/college as a full-time student is required.

Requirements: Some kind of experience working with children; adaptability; flexibility; must be at least age 18 and able to obtain a U.S. visa; creativity and initiative are essential; must work well independently; be professional, dress appropriately, and not smoke or drink alcohol while on duty; able to travel alone; self-sufficient; ability to communicate with children who don't speak English (no need to speak their language, but you must be able to work with children whose English ability is low). Drama and arts/crafts skills are beneficial, as are teaching skills, counseling skills, and even experience in sporting and community groups for children.

OVERVIEW

If you're super-flexible and like the idea of working with children in several different countries, you may be interested in this summer internship as a day-camp counselor in Austria, Germany, and Hungary, designed for children between the ages of six through 15. In the summer, these children attend one-week sessions to improve their English skills while playing games and sports and enjoying arts, crafts, and drama.

As an intern counselor, you'll need to be creative and clever in order to make the program exciting and be instructional and entertaining while fitting into the camp's teaching and learning philosophy. Each weekly group has a maximum of 12 campers with a variety of English-language abilities who attend from Monday through Friday from 9:00 A.M. to 5:00 P.M. During this time, you'll be exclusively responsible for your group.

Most counselors are between 20 and 24 years, though some junior counselors might be as young as 16 and some senior counselors as old as 35. All counselors (even those who can't speak German) are expected to be able to work completely alone if necessary.

Camps are located throughout Austria, Germany, and Budapest, including everything from classrooms, an entire building, or a Boy Scout hall. Some day camps are located in the countryside, while others are much more urban. The ratio of the campers per campsite varies from 10 to 12 campers at sites where you're the only instructor, to large campsites where five counselors will oversee 60 campers.

You'll be expected to work anywhere from six to 12 weeks. The earliest camps (those in Berlin) begin in mid-June; the last one (in Bavaria) ends in the middle of September. Because no singular campsite runs during the entire summer, you'll be expected to work in a new town almost every week and will often be informed as to where you will be working at short notice. You could begin in Berlin in June, transfer to Hungary in July, move on to Austria in August, and then have a last week in Bavaria in September.

Typically, you'll have no more than one unpaid week off during your internship, and you'll be expected to be available to work for the entire period if necessary, as well as participating in the training week, a workshop on the first weekend after your placement has started, and a final "wrap up" feedback meeting. Training is mandatory for all counselors, even returning ones. Training generally takes place during the first week of your work period and is not paid. (But you'll get room and full board for this week.) Training sessions usually take place in Berlin, Vienna, Munich, Dortmund, or Budapest; ESDC will tell you where your training city is as soon as possible so you can make your travel preparations.

A coordinator is responsible for the camps and counselors in a specific geographical area, supervising the camp and counselors and registration of children and ensuring that necessary materials are at each campsite. Coordinators will also act as resources for counselors about the campsite and available playgrounds and so on. Since a coordinator is not always present at the campsite, counselors are solely responsible for the daily campsite program, as well as their spare time.

You'll probably stay at your camp site in simple, rudimentary facilities and often in shared-living quarters. Accommodations will vary according to the camp venue:

- **Boy Scout Houses:** Rooms usually have a shower and kitchenette.
- **Bed and Breakfast:** Simple short-stay accommodations providing room and breakfast.
- **Youth Hostel:** Some with mixed dorm rooms.
- **Family Homestay:** Lodging with a family of one of your children at camp.

HOW TO APPLY

Download the application at http://www.ccusa. com/PROGRAMS/Global/inquiry.aspx?action=download&programcode=RU and submit online.

Complete the application form and mail it to the preceding address. CCUSA will evaluate your application and may contact you to schedule an interview within 15 days. If your application is successful, you'll get a letter of acceptance and an ESDC contract. When you receive the CCUSA contract, sign and return it with your application. Your final contract will be ready for you at training week. The duration of your work period will be finalized in May but not finally confirmed until your performance evaluation during training week. You'll receive weekly correspondence from ESDC and their coordinators containing more information, general greetings, and an exchange of information among the other counselors. Training weeks begin in March and continue until the end of July.

CAMP COUNSELORS USA—RUSSIA

Camp Counselors USA
2330 Marinship Way, Suite 250
Sausalito, CA 94965
(415) 339-2728; (415) 339-2740; (800) 999-2267
Fax: (415) 339-2744
ccru@ccusa.com
http://www.ccusa.com/PROGRAMS/RU/intro.aspx#

What You Can Earn: Small stipend, plus room and board.
Application Deadlines: Rolling.
Educational Experience: None specified.
Requirements: Experience working with children; adaptability; flexibility.

OVERVIEW

If you're adaptable, adventurous, and thrive on challenges, you may want to consider an internship at a Russian summer youth camp. For 13 years, CCUSA has offered this challenging program for four to eight weeks from June through August.

Just like in the United States, every summer thousands of children head off for camps across Russia, from the shores of Lake Baikal to the beaches of the Black Sea. In many ways, these camps look a lot like those you'd find in the United States and Canada, with their own philosophies and desire to give kids a place to relax while having fun in an outdoor setting. Usually found in rural areas miles away from the nearest town, often by a lake or river, most camps have a large dining hall, crafts and sports buildings, and dormitories and offer swimming, boating, and canoeing. Other activities may include theater, sports, arts, crafts, dance, performing arts, and teaching. Campers usually stay for sessions between 10 to 28 days.

You can choose one of two internship positions in the Russia Program: camp counselor or English/American culture instructor. As a counselor, you'll serve as a teacher, leader, and a friend to a group of children between the ages of 8 and 16. You're also responsible for their safety and well being as you spend most of the day outdoors.

Camp Counselor

Life as a counselor in Russia is not easy. The hours are long and you'll be busy constantly, teaching, eating, answering questions, and even sharing dorms with campers.

Interning in Russia is not for everybody; you'll need to be able to adapt to unfamiliar customs, traditions, and uniquely Russian approaches to the summer-camp model. This program is rigorous; you may experience culture shock and physical stress because of dietary changes, climate, and the location of each camp.

English/Culture Instructor

As an instructor, you'll be teaching English every day to different classes while incorporating lessons about your American culture.

HOW TO APPLY

Download the application at http://www.ccusa.com/PROGRAMS/Global/inquiry.aspx?action=download&programcode=RU and submit online.

CAMP COUNSELORS USA—UNITED KINGDOM

Camp Counselors USA
2330 Marinship Way, Suite 250
Sausalito, CA 94965
(415) 339-2728; (415) 339-2740; (800) 999-2267
Fax: (415) 339-2744
info@ccusa.com
http://www.ccusa.com/PROGRAMS/RU/intro.aspx#

What You Can Earn: £175 pounds a week (about $304), plus room and board.
Application Deadlines: Rolling.
Educational Experience: None specified.
Requirements: Some kind of experience working with children; adaptability; flexibility; must be at least age 18 and able to obtain a U.S. visa.

OVERVIEW

Just like American children, youngsters in the United Kingdom love going to camp; more than 10,000 of them will go to camp each year. The Youth Hostel Association (YHA) provides these camps in rural areas throughout the country, where campers join in activities, sports, and games.

As a camp counselor intern, you'll work for about nine weeks at a camp specifically suited to your personality and interests. You'll begin your internship with a 10-day mandatory training session for all staff at Ambleside in northwest England before campers' arrival at camp in early July. (You'll travel to the training site via free buses leaving from both London and Manchester.)

As a general counselor, you'll work as a leader, a role model, and a friend to children ranging in age from 11 to 17 years. Your duties include planning, leading, and joining in a variety of activities throughout the day and into the evening, acting as an assistant as you move with your campers from activity to activity. At the end of the day, you're responsible for getting the campers to bed, having cabin chats, or providing stories or quiet games as the children drift off to sleep.

Your primary responsibility is to ensure their safety, overall supervision, and well being and to make their camp experience fun and rewarding.

When your camp assignment ends, you can travel on your own in the UK for as long as your visa permits, exploring Scotland, England, Ireland, and Wales. If you're interested in working after camp is over, CCUSA can guarantee you a placement right after camp with one of the many employers it works with in a variety of companies throughout the UK.

HOW TO APPLY

Download the application at http://www.ccusa.com/PROGRAMS/Global/inquiry.aspx?action=download&programcode=RU and submit online.

CANADIAN EMBASSY INTERNSHIP

Intern Coordinator, Canadian Embassy
501 Pennsylvania Avenue, NW
Washington, DC 20001
(202) 682-1740, ext. 7530.
Fax: (202) 682-7791
http://www.canadianembassy.org

What You Can Earn: Unpaid; college credit possible.
Application Deadlines: Rolling.
Educational Experience: College undergraduate or graduate.
Requirements: U.S. or Canadian citizenship.

OVERVIEW

Prominently located on the Main Street of America, Pennsylvania Avenue, the Canadians are the only embassy located between the U.S. Capitol and the White House. An internship with America's close ally and neighbor can provide students with an opportunity to get involved in governmental affairs and gain a general understanding of the Canada–U.S. bilateral relationship. Established in 1927, the embassy is the official chancery of the Canadian ambassador to the United States and is responsible for watching out for Canadian interests in the United States. The embassy provides information about working and traveling in Canada and tries to boost Canadian corporations.

There are several internship positions in the embassy, depending on your particular academic interests, but typically these include public affairs, academic relations, culture, press/media, information services, trade, environment, energy, and Congressional relations.

All interns usually work four-and-a-half days per week. Because the internships are unpaid, you should apply for academic credit from your university.

HOW TO APPLY

You can download an application form at http://www.canadianembassy.org/embassy/internships-en.asp. To apply, fax your application form, resume, an autobiographical sketch stating your goals/interests and why you are applying to the internship, an academic transcript, and three letters of recommendation (academic/employment).

CARNEGIE ENDOWMENT FOR INTERNATIONAL PEACE INTERNSHIP

Carnegie Endowment
1779 Massachusetts Avenue, NW
Washington, DC 20036
(202) 483-7600
info@CarnegieEndowment.org
http://www.carnegieendowment.org/about/
    index.cfm?fa=jrFellows

What You Can Earn: $2,583.00 a month for full-time fellowship, plus a full benefits package.

Application Deadlines: Endowment deadline is January 15; however, most schools set an earlier deadline to receive and review applications. Consult your university for application deadlines and details on the school's application process.
Educational Experience: Graduating college seniors and individuals who have graduated during the past academic year.
Requirements: Individuals who have started graduate school are not eligible.

OVERVIEW

The Carnegie Endowment for International Peace is a private, nonprofit organization dedicated to advancing cooperation between nations and promoting active international engagement by the United States. Founded in 1910, its work is nonpartisan and dedicated to achieving practical results. Through research, publishing, and creating new international networks, endowment associates shape fresh policy approaches. Their interests span geographic regions and the relations among governments, business, international organizations and civil society, focusing on the economic, political, and technological forces driving global change.

Through its Carnegie Moscow Center, the endowment helps develop a tradition of public policy analysis in the states of the former Soviet Union and improve relations between Russia and the United States. The endowment also publishes *Foreign Policy*, one of the world's leading magazines of international politics and economics, which reaches readers in more than 120 countries and several languages.

Each year the endowment offers eight to 10 one-year fellowships from a pool of nominees from 300 colleges across the country. Carnegie Junior Fellows work as research assistants to the endowment's senior associates, providing research assistance to associates working on the Carnegie Endowment's projects such as nonproliferation, democracy building, trade, US leadership, China-related issues, and Russian/Eurasian studies. Junior Fellows have the opportunity to conduct research for books, co-author journal articles and policy papers, participate in meetings with high-level officials, contribute to congressional testimony and organize briefings attended by scholars, activists, journalists, and government officials.

HOW TO APPLY

The Carnegie Endowment relies on participating universities to nominate uniquely qualified students. No applications are accepted directly from students. The Carnegie Endowment accepts applications only through participating universities via designated nominating officials; therefore, if you're interested, you should consult your university on the nomination process. If you graduated during the previous academic year and have not started graduate studies, you may apply through the university from which you graduated. For a list of participating schools, visit this Web site: http://www.carnegieendowment.org/about/universities.htm.

CENTER FOR WORLD INDIGENOUS STUDIES INTERNSHIP

Center for World Indigenous Studies
Fellowship/Internship Program
PMB 214
1001 Cooper Point Road, SW
#140
Olympia, WA 98502-1107

What You Can Earn: Unpaid but college credit may be arranged at both undergraduate and graduate levels.
Application Deadlines: Rolling.
Educational Experience: Undergraduate and graduate students.
Requirements: American citizenship.

OVERVIEW

If you find the Fourth World fascinating, you might be interested in the opportunity to support a diverse group of world leaders, scholars, and activists who live in this area. CWIS offers internships in Olympia, Washington, and Yelapa, Mexico.

Administration

Interns in this area will help with public relations and community outreach, write grant proposals, and help maintain the CWIS George Manuel Memorial Library.

Communications/Media

As an intern here, you might write and distribute press releases on a variety of CWIS events and issues, gather information on current media contacts, and update the database for networking and educational programs.

Mexico Internship

Successful applicants will live and learn in the Comunidad Indigena de Chacala in semitropical western Mexico. Interns are accepted to study in areas such as traditional medicine; ethnobotany; traumatic stress studies; health education; tropical public health; anthropology; somatics; health psychology; Fourth World studies; politics; diplomacy; economics; environmental studies; and tourism and development. In addition, a 15-20 hour a week service project that supports the activities of the Center for World Indigenous Studies in Western Mexico is required.

Interns in Mexico should expect to work between 20 to 25 hours a week in organization, program, and clinical/educational areas, for at least four weeks. If you land an internship here, you'll be eligible to participate in two seminars and receive individual/group supervision.

Olympia Internship

You can choose to work in international relations; policy formulation and economic development; health, spirituality, and traditional medicine; and environmental issues including resource management; biodiversity; geography; or mapping projects. Activities may include records and documents management, documents research, information management, meeting organization, or office support.

Most of the projects and departments are interdisciplinary and offer a broad range of opportunities for learning and practical application. The internships last at least three months for 20-40 hours a week.

Publications

CWIS publishes the Fourth World Journal, as well as occasional papers, books, and online publications. If you intern in this area, you may help to produce both hard-copy and electronic publications, including graphic design, research, editing, and writing. You'll be encouraged to publish the results of your research, and you may serve as primary or secondary authors with CWIS staff.

HOW TO APPLY

To apply, complete an electronic application at http://www.cwis.org/int_app.htm or print this form and mail it to the preceding address, along with the names of two references. After a review of your application, CWIS will e-mail or mail a confirmation of your application.

The Olympia internship requires an application fee of $35. The Mexico internship requires an application fee of $35, plus a $125 internship fee, full-month lodging ($610), seminar lodging and meals ($322), and one seminar tuition ($1,524).

COOPERATIVE CENTER FOR STUDY ABROAD: IRELAND INTERNSHIP

Northern Kentucky University
Cooperative Center for Study Abroad-Ireland
301 Founders Hall

Highland Heights, KY 41099
(800) 319-6015
Fax: (859) 572-6650
ccsa@nku.edu
http://www.ccsa.cc

What You Can Earn: Unpaid but academic credit is possible; tuition fee charged ($3,495).
Application Deadlines: February 28 for summer (early June to early August); Early April for fall (mid-August to mid-October and mid-October to mid-December); early October for spring (mid-January to mid-March and mid-March to mid-May).
Educational Experience: College freshmen through seniors.
Requirements: Must be at least 18 years of age.

OVERVIEW

The Dublin internship allows students to get experience in business, industry, social or government agencies, theatres, museums, or other work environments. As an intern here, you'll be expected to commit to a full-time internship for eight weeks. CCSA will try to tailor your internship to meet your needs based on your academic background, work experience, and interests. Once the application has been received, companies and organizations that may match your skills will be contacted and given your resume to consider. During monthly meetings, students will be able to discuss anything about their internship with their supervisor. When possible, the supervisor will visit the site during your placement and will complete an evaluation form on your performance at the end of your internship.

HOW TO APPLY

Complete the application at: http://www.ccsa.cc/application.html if you are not one of the universities affiliated with the CCSA program, listing your preferred areas of work as clearly as possible.

COSTA RICA INTERNSHIP INSTITUTE

Costa Rica Internship Institute
PO Box 1171
C.P. 2050
San Pedro de Montes de Oca
San Jose, Costa Rica
(011-506) 273-5286
Fax: (011-506) 273-5285
info@costaricainternships.com
http://www.costaricainternships.com

What You Can Earn: Unpaid; fee is required. While participants don't receive academic credit, CRINI will issue a certificate of participation that may enable you to negotiate credit with your college.
Application Deadlines: Rolling.
Educational Experience: Advanced undergraduates and graduate students and all others interested in academic research or hands-on internship work; an adequate knowledge of Spanish is required; you should have at least the equivalent of two years of college Spanish or may study Spanish in Costa Rica before you begin the internship.
Requirements: None specified.

OVERVIEW

The internship program includes professionals, researchers, and individuals who are clearly focused or have specific areas of interest or expertise. The goal of each internship is to benefit both the intern and the host community or organization. Internships are available in national parks, community-development organizations, women's groups, businesses, health clinics, and indigenous reserves and include diverse projects within both natural and social science areas. The program places individuals with organizations that offer specific internship projects. When necessary, internships can be created to match your own specific goals and background. Before arriving in Costa Rica, you should send CRINI information about the type of work you'd like to do, in order to begin the process of selecting and negotiating your internship.

The institute accepts interns at any time of year (except December) for between two and four months. Interested interns and researchers can negotiate a longer stay if required. The specific program schedule depends on the needs of the individual.

No two internships are alike. Some require scientific research, some require hands-on work, and some require your initiative or creativity for designing a project. Some involve a great deal of community contact or interaction with fellow workers; others do not. Each internship, however, will challenge your flexibility and adaptability. Typically, it will take about two or three weeks for you to integrate well into your community and project site and to define or determine the scope and variety of tasks in any given internship.

You'll live with a family (or CRINI will find you appropriate housing for the duration of the internship). If you decide to work within a national park, you'll be placed at the park's biological station.

You're expected to keep a daily record of your work and experiences. This record may help your host develop research or policy agendas. These final reports are to be written in Spanish.

HOW TO APPLY

You can apply electronically for this internship or download an application in PDF format. You'll find the application form at http://www.costaricainternships.com/application.htm.

E-mail the completed application form along with one letter of recommendation to the preceding address.

COUNCIL ON FOREIGN RELATIONS INTERNSHIP

Council on Foreign Relations, New York Office
Human Resources Office
58 East 68th Street

New York, NY 10021
(212) 434-9400
humanresources@cfr.org
http://www.cfr.org

What You Can Earn: Unpaid, but a small stipend is offered upon completion of the internship to defray expenses.

Application Deadlines: Rolling.

Educational Experience: College and grad students majoring in international affairs, political science, regional studies, or economics is preferred. Previous event planning experience also is preferred.

Requirements: Interns should be extremely detail-oriented, be able to work in a pressured environment, have excellent communication skills and research skills.

OVERVIEW

Founded in 1921, the Council on Foreign Relations is an independent, national membership organization and a nonpartisan center for scholars dedicated to producing and disseminating ideas so that individual and corporate members, as well as policymakers, journalists, students, and interested citizens in the United States and other countries, can better understand the world and the foreign policy choices facing the United States and other governments. The council does this by convening meetings where prominent thinkers debate and discuss the major issues of our time; conducting a wide-ranging studies program; publishing Foreign Affairs, the journal covering international affairs and U.S. foreign policy; maintaining a diverse membership; sponsoring independent task forces; and providing up-to-date information about the world and U.S. foreign policy on the Council's Web site.

The Council has two locations—one in New York City located in a landmark townhouse on the Upper East Side of Manhattan, close to Central Park. The newly renovated Washington, D.C., office is located in Dupont Circle, in the middle of the nation's capital.

The Council's National Program brings together an increasingly influential group of Americans involved in international affairs from around the country and the world. The responsibilities of the intern will include helping staff coordinate National Program events, helping staff plan, organize, and coordinate the annual National Conference, which brings together members from around the country to discuss foreign policy issues. Interns also will help with various research projects for the National Conference, as well as provide general administrative support to the department.

HOW TO APPLY

Qualified candidates should e-mail, fax, or mail a resume and cover letter including the internship position you want, and the days and times you're available to work, to the Human Resources department at the above address.

COUNCIL ON HEMISPHERIC AFFAIRS (COHA) INTERNSHIP

Internship Coordinator
Council on Hemispheric Affairs
1250 Connecticut Avenue, NW, Suite 1C
Washington, DC 20036
http://www.coha.org

What You Can Earn: Unpaid.

Application Deadlines: Rolling.

Educational Experience: College students should have some knowledge and/or interest in U.S.-Latin American affairs or international relations and should display impressive research and writing skills. Language ability in Spanish or Portuguese is desired, although a track record in journalism, English, or one of the social sciences may be substituted for the normal background requirements. Candidates who lack these qualifications are at times selected if they exhibit proven research and writing skills.

Requirements: Should be highly motivated with excellent computer literacy. Will be expected to show initiative and a capacity for innovation. Interns are expected to work from 9:00 A.M. to 5:00 P.M. daily, although the office is open long after 5:00 P.M. and on weekends as well. COHA internships last 18 weeks (14 weeks in the summer).

OVERVIEW

For almost 30 years, the Council on Hemispheric Affairs (COHA), a major tax-exempt, nonprofit, and nonpartisan national research and information organization, has offered internships in Washington, D.C., in the fields of U.S., Latin American, and Canadian relations. These internships provide entry-level practical experience in dealing with a variety of hemispheric political, economic, diplomatic, and trade issues. They also provide young scholars with an excellent opportunity to be exposed to the policymaking process. COHA internships are highly respected by the Washington policymaking community for their rigor and the valuable learning experience they provide. Former COHA interns have gained prominent positions in journalism, the Foreign Service, and congressional offices, as well as being admitted to some of the most prestigious professional schools in the country.

Interns quickly become fully integrated into COHA's research activities and also select modest administrative tasks that they are expected to fulfill along with their research and writing assignments. COHA internships, which are available throughout the year, are entirely voluntary and are awarded on a highly competitive basis.

Part of an intern's responsibility is to help keep the office and their work areas neat. Interns pursue research topics of their and the organization's interest. Former interns have had their bylined work published in various COHA publications and in the *Congressional Record*, as well as in the opinion pages of newspapers across the world including the *Christian Science Monitor, New York Times, Atlanta Constitution, Miami Herald, Boston Globe, Oakland*

Tribune, Los Angeles Times, Baltimore Sun, Philadelphia Inquirer, Washington Times, and scores of other dailies.

Some of the many responsibilities of interns (research associate) include conducting research and writing articles for the *Washington Report on the Hemisphere (WRH)*, as well as take turns drafting its irregular "News and Analysis" series of press memorandums. Interns also draft press memoranda as often as two or three times per week; conduct research on a variety of economic, political and social issues; initiate telephone queries with congressional and administrative personnel; publish articles under their own by-lines in major newspapers and newsweeklies; attend a variety of Washington conferences and briefings as a representative of COHA; conduct interviews with policymakers; and prepare research for insertion into the Congressional Record and Library of Congress under their own names. Interns also compose sign Opinion-Editorials and letters to the editor, as well as make research inquiries to legislative and executive agency offices; attend meetings, Congressional hearings, legislative seminars, and substantive discussions on topics relevant to COHA's work. Interns perform telephone and personal interviews with Washington officials concerned with hemispheric affairs and assist in the production and distribution of the *WRH,* press releases, monographs, and promotional mailings. In addition, you'll be expected to help in office administration, producing financial reports, maintaining and fulfilling subscription lists, clipping newspapers, sorting and filing resource information, supervising promotional mailings, servicing mail and telephone inquiries, as well as various other supply and maintenance functions. In general, as an intern you can expect to have two-thirds of your time devoted to research/writing activities and less than one-third to administrative functions.

Many interns have gone on to solid graduate or professional schools, joined the Foreign Service and other U.S. government agencies, become journalists, or entered other challenging careers in the public and private sectors.

HOW TO APPLY

To apply, submit:

- a completed application that you have downloaded from http://www.coha.org/application.php
- an official transcript (photocopies acceptable)
- a resume
- a writing sample, which is important because we want to be certain you are an effective researcher and author
- two letters of recommendation
- cover letter detailing what you hope to obtain from a COHA internship and your familiarity with the hemisphere.

THE ECONOMIST INTERNSHIP

The Economist
25 St James Street
London SW1A 1HG
United Kingdom
http://www.economistgroup.com/Employment/internships.html

What You Can Earn: Nominal.
Application Deadlines: January through February.
Educational Experience: None specified.
Requirements: Must be under age 25.

OVERVIEW

Edited in London since 1843, *The Economist* is a weekly paper of news, ideas, opinions, and analysis that is printed in six countries and published on the Internet. More than 80 percent of its circulation lies outside the United Kingdom. Because of its independent and international editorial perspective, it is read by more of the world's political and business leaders than any other magazine. The paper remains true to the principles of its founder, James Wilson, who championed free trade, internationalism, and minimum interference by government.

The Economist has no formal training program, although it does offer two internship programs: the Richard Casement and Marjorie Dean internships. Otherwise, in the summer, one intern is usually taken in the foreign department and another in the business department. Occasionally, a third is hired to write about Britain.

The Marjorie Deane Financial Journalism Internship

The Marjorie Deane Financial Journalism Foundation offers an internship for a would-be or junior journalist to spend three months at *The Economist* writing about finance. This internship is advertised in the finance section of *The Economist* in March/April.

Richard Casement Internship

This formal internship, advertised in the science section of *The Economist* in February, allows an intern to spend three months writing about science and technology. The paper's aim is more to discover writing talent in a science student than to develop scientific aptitude in a budding journalist. Interns are treated much as members of staff and expected to join in accordingly. The competition is fierce, the pay is nominal, and there is no guarantee of a when the internship comes to an end.

HOW TO APPLY

If you're interested, send a cover letter to the appropriate editor (business affairs, John Peet; Britain, Emma Duncan) with a resume and examples of any writing you think may be relevant.

Marjorie Dean internship: Applicants should write a letter of introduction, along with an article of approximately 600 words suitable for inclusion in the financial section.

Richard Casement internship: Applicants should write a letter of introduction, along with an article of approximately 600 words suitable for inclusion in the science and technology section.

HANSARD SOCIETY SCHOLARS PROGRAM

The Hansard Society
Scholars Program Coordinator
9 Kingsway
London WC2B 6XF
United Kingdom
study@hansard.lse.ac.uk
http://www.hansardsociety.org.uk/programmes/
study_programme/scholars

What You Can Earn: None; fee required.
Application Deadlines: June 1 for spring semester (early January to late April); January 1 for summer semester (mid-May to very late July/August); April 1 for autumn semester (wmid-September to late December); late applications may be considered.
Educational Experience: University undergraduate.
Requirements: GPA of 3.0 or above; personal integrity and commitment. Upon acceptance, you must pay a deposit; the balance of fees must be paid no later than six weeks prior to the start of the internship. The current fees are $11,472.95 per term, which includes board at private apartments in central London, which are usually shared by about six people, with two (occasionally three) students per room. The apartments include kitchen facilities, furniture, and bedlinen; all apartments are cleaned regularly and are located close to shopping and entertainment facilities in central London.

Fees include all tuition, access to LSE student services, IT facilities, events, public lectures, restaurants, and bars; cultural and social events; membership of the British Library of Political and Economic Sciences; self-catering accommodation in central London; a London Transport Travel-card allowing unlimited travel on public transport throughout Zones 1 and 2; an internship in Westminster or other prominent political organization; and all administration and student support services, including pastoral care and access to the LSE medical facilities.

OVERVIEW

If you're an anglophile interested in politics and current affairs, you'll find a summer internship with the Hansard Society Scholars Program an incredible experience. As a Hansard participant, you'd work in the U.K., at the heart of the Parliamentary process, with key decision-makers from Parliament, government, campaign organizations, think tanks, lobbying groups, and the media. The Hansard Society Scholars Program offers an outstanding opportunity for American students to gain academic and practical knowledge of the British political system and current debates in U.K. public policy. Each semester lasts 14 weeks in the autumn and spring or 12 weeks in summer.

As a Hansard Scholar, you'll attend courses in British politics and U.K. public policy at the London School of Economics & Political Science, one of the foremost universities in the world. You'll have lectures with politicians and other senior figures from a variety of organizations and participate in an intensive internship at one of many political organizations in the U.K., including interest groups, campaign organizations, research institutions, lobbying companies, or Parliament.

Accredited Courses

As part of your internship experience, you'll take two lecture courses in addition to pursuing an individual research dissertation. Each lecture course requires you to attend a weekly seminar, produce a six- to eight-page essay, and take a three-hour exam at the end of the semester. All courses are assessed by a current member of the London School of Economics Government Department faculty.

The British Politics & Parliament course examines the constitutional and political process in Britain, including the role of Parliament, the Prime Minister, and the Civil Service, the policy-making process. The U.K. Public Policy course analyzes current policy issues, including the economy, social policy, education, foreign policy, and the role of the media. You're also required to complete a 9,000 to 10,000 word dissertation on some topic that interests you.

In addition, you're required to attend a guest lecture each week, which might include former Conservative and Labour Cabinet ministers, MPs, and peers from each of the main British political parties, political journalists from the BBC and national newspapers, or experienced lobbyists, campaigners, and policy experts.

Internship Placements

The key to the Hansard program is the internship in some segment of the British political system. You may work for a Member of Parliament in the House of Commons or a Peer in the House of Lords, writing speeches, carrying out research, and attending parliamentary meetings. You may work in the parliamentary clerks' office, with access to the behind-the-scenes workings of Parliament. You may intern for the BBC, researching articles and analyzing the work of the government. Or you may work for a campaign group, helping to devise and run media campaigns on key social and political issues. You may work in the national headquarters of a political party or for one of the other many organizations and businesses that drive the policy agenda in the U.K. and beyond.

All placements are individually selected by the Hansard Society to match your interests, expertise, and career hopes. Internships last approximately 250 hours in total. Academic credit is awarded upon successful completion, subject to a performance evaluation.

Past internship placements have included Parliamentary offices of the Labour Party, the Conservative Party, the Liberal Democrats, Plaid Cymru, and the Scottish Nationalist Party; members of the House of Lords; The Cabinet Office; government departments; National Labour Party Headquarters & Conservative Central Office; BBC Westminster; campaign groups such as Amnesty International, Liberty, the CLA, and the Womens' National Commission; lobbying organizations, and various businesses.

At the end of your internship, you'll earn 15 academic credits: three each for British Politics & Parliament, U.K. Public Policy, and the dissertation, and six for your internship. You are responsible for arranging the transfer of credits to your home university.

HOW TO APPLY

The society assumes you have no previous knowledge of British politics or any experience with political internships. Instead, it's more important that you show a genuine interest in politics and public policy and a commitment to working in a high-level political environment. Because you'll often be involved in work of a sensitive nature, personal integrity, in addition to commitment and enthusiasm, is crucial.

You must download and complete the application form (see the preceding Internet address) and return it by post to the preceding address. Along with the form, you should include a short personal statement outlining your reasons for applying, a resume, a sample of written academic work (about 2000 words), two letters of recommendation (at least one academic), copies of transcripts from your current university, or evidence of your completion of a degree.

INTERNATIONAL ATOMIC ENERGY AGENCY INTERNSHIP

IAEA Internship Application
Brookhaven National Laboratory
Building 438
PO Box 5000

Upton, NY 11973-5000
(631) 344-3054
Fax: (631) 344-5832
osiecki@bnl.gov
http://iaeainternship.bnl.gov/Internship/Home

What You Can Earn: Competitive stipend based on the current market, a round-trip air ticket to and from Vienna, and a small allowance for shipment of personal belongings.

Application Deadlines: Rolling.

Educational Experience: College students or graduates between ages 18 and 32; for specific educational requirements, see internship listings below.

Requirements: Capable of independent work, with good communication skills; must be a U.S. citizen or permanent resident of the United States.

OVERVIEW

The International Atomic Energy Agency, a member of the United Nations located in Vienna, is an independent intergovernmental science- and technology-based organization that serves as the global focal point for nuclear cooperation. As of April 2002, 134 countries belong to the IAEA, which is responsible for helping with the development and transfer of peaceful nuclear technology, establishing and maintaining a global nuclear safety regime, and verifying that nuclear material is not being diverted for weapons.

The IAEA Department of Safeguards is responsible for addressing the verification of this mandate; safeguards inspectors visit nuclear facilities around the world, while staffers provide the specialized equipment, training, and analysis to support the inspectors. Currently, more than 1,100 nuclear facilities worldwide contain safeguard material.

This year-long internship program, affiliated with Brookhaven National Laboratory, gives four to 10 interns the chance to live for a year in Vienna and work for the IAEA in computer science, open source information collection, engineering services, and technical writing. Internships typically begin in June or September.

Computer Science

In this area, interns may help develop small applications, support database administration, manage equipment and application installation, and troubleshoot.

Engineering Services

The IAEA uses portable and installed equipment for radiation monitoring, surveillance, and securing inventories and assets. As a result, interns can help develop and manage this equipment, testing new equipment, troubleshooting and maintaining inspection equipment, monitoring performance, preparing equipment, and developing procedures and software for instrumentation.

Candidates should be mechanical, electrical, and nuclear engineering graduates or graduate students.

Open Source Information Collection

The IAEA uses open source information to clarify the declared activities of its member states. Here, you'll help collect, process, and evaluate open source information.

Candidates should be graduate students specializing in nonproliferation, arms control, or international security, with experience in conducting research (particularly on the Internet) to support analytical programs. Candidates should have an educational background in nuclear engineering, physics, and political science, with experience in nonproliferation and information research.

Technical Writing

Interns in this area are needed to help prepare procedures, technical specifications, user documentation, and training materials. Applicants should have a technical education in science or engineering and excellent English writing skills.

HOW TO APPLY

Apply online at http://iaeainternship.bnl.gov/Internship/Login. To complete the application, you will need a resume and two letters of recommendation in an electronic format (files should have one of the following extensions: .pdf, .txt, .rtf, or .doc) or a resume and two e-mail addresses of the people giving you recommendations.

If you cannot apply online or you have trouble with the system, you may apply by sending a resume and two letters of recommendation to the preceding address.

UNICEF GRADUATE STUDENT INTERNSHIPS

United Nations Children's Fund (UNICEF)
3 United Nations Plaza, TA-26A
New York, NY 10017
(212) 326-7000
internships@unicef.org
http://www.unicef.org

What You Can Earn: Unpaid.
Application Deadlines: Rolling. UNICEF country offices usually take summer interns and have the following deadlines: October 1 for spring session (January through May); March 1 for summer session (June through August); July 1 for fall session (September through December).
Educational Experience: A currently enrolled graduate or postgraduate student in a field related to UNICEF's interests, with excellent academic performance; must submit a letter from one of your professors supporting your application.
Requirements: Fluent in English and one other UNICEF working language (French or Spanish); health and life insurance.

OVERVIEW
UNICEF, involving more than 7,000 people working in 157 countries around the world, works to protect the rights of every child. With the global authority to influence decision-makers and the variety of partners at the grassroots level to turn the most innovative ideas into reality, UNICEF advocates girls education, immunization programs, food programs, HIV/AIDS prevention, and emergency care programs.

UNICEF also offers an internship program to qualified students at both its headquarters and country offices for a period of six to 16 weeks, depending on the needs of the office to which you are assigned, your qualifications, and interests. Most interns work on a project or several projects, which will benefit both them and UNICEF, such as research or studies and creating or improving databases and/or Web sites. While most internships are full time, quite a number are not. How long and how often you work in the office depends on the project and office you are assigned to. Sometimes projects can be done on a part-time or even virtual basis.

HOW TO APPLY
To obtain the internship program application (Word) for New York, visit http://www.unicef.org/about/employ/files/Apply-Internship-NYonly.doc. For the application for internships outside of New York, visit http://www.unicef.org/about/employ/files/Apply-internship-except-NewYork.doc.

After completing the forms, if you are applying for the New York internship, you should submit them to the preceding e-mail address. For internships in all other offices in other countries, your application should be sent directly to the head of the given office by checking the list of addresses of UNICEF country offices at this Web site: http://www.unicef.org/about/structure/index_worldcontact.html.

In addition, you should prepare the following documents, which you will need if you are called for an interview and later offered an internship:

- A letter from your university or institution, certifying your enrollment, course of study, and expected date of graduation/degree.
- An original, up-to-date university transcript or equivalent institutional record.
- Two letters of recommendation, one of which should be from the college professor supervising your internship.

UNICEF will contact you if they are able to find you an internship position. If UNICEF doesn't contact you, you may assume that there is no suitable opening for you at this time.

WOMEN'S INTERNATIONAL LEAGUE FOR PEACE AND FREEDOM INTERNSHIP

WILPF Office at the United Nations
777 United Nations Plaza, 6th Floor
New York, NY 10017
(212) 682-1265
(215) 563-7110
flick@igc.apc.org

WILPF National Office
1213 Race Street
Philadelphia, PA 19107

Women's International League for Peace and Freedom
110 Maryland Avenue, NE, Suite 102
Washington, DC 20002
(202) 546-6727
Fax: (202) 544-9613
ggilhool@ix.netcom.com

Director, WILPF International Secretariat
1, rue de Varemb,, CP 28
CH-1211 Geneva 20
Switzerland

What You Can Earn: NY and PA unpaid; Geneva, Switzerland, about $450/month, plus round-trip travel; WILPF pays for round-trip travel from your home to Geneva and provides housing and pays a small stipend to cover basic living expenses.

Application Deadlines: November 15 for the internship lasting January 1 to March 30; April 1 for the June 1 to August 30 session; July 15 for the September 15 to December 15 session; May 15 for the Geneva internship from January to November.

Educational Experience: Female college undergraduate and graduate students interested in the environment, human rights, peace studies, and women's issues; Pennsylvania interns can be high school students or high school graduates.

Requirements: Initiative and desire to enhance skills that you'll need in a social-change organization; details for specific internships are given below.

OVERVIEW

Founded in 1915 during World War I by two women who went on to win Nobel Peace Prizes, the Women's International League for Peace and Freedom (WILPF) is the world's oldest international women's organization and promotes political rather than military solutions to conflicts. Jane Addams was the organization's first president (she was also the first woman to win the Nobel Prize).

WILPF works to achieve through peaceful means world disarmament, full rights for women, racial and economic justice, and an end to all forms of violence. The organization also strives to establish political, social, and psychological conditions that can assure peace, freedom, and justice for all. The group works to create an environment of political, economic, social, and psychological freedom for all members of the human community, so that true peace can be enjoyed by all. Focusing on the impact of disarmament, environmentally sustainable development, racism, and human-rights policies for women, WILPF publishes informational brochures and journals as well as collaborates with a variety of UN agencies, including ECOSOC, UNCTAD, UNESCO, FAO, ILO, and UNICEF.

Internships with WILPF are offered only to women, in recognition of the fact that women typically have been excluded from positions related to foreign policy and international relations. The group's current (2005–2008) program campaigns are Women Challenge U.S. Policy: Building Peace on Justice in the Middle East and Save the Water. Currently, the group operates sections in 37 countries and 80 groups and branches in the United States.

Interns in New York and Geneva, Switzerland, monitor UN meetings and briefings, prepare oral and written reports, and help with administrative tasks. The internships last for three months in New York throughout the year (except for July and August); for 10-15 weeks in Pennsylvania throughout the year; and for 11 months in Geneva, starting in January.

Interns are welcome to attend WILPF press conferences and United Nations and NGO meetings.

Geneva, Switzerland, Interns

Since 1981, WILPF has been sending an American intern to its offices in Geneva, Switzerland, to learn about lobbying and participating in U.N. conferences. You can choose an internship from one of three concentrations: disarmament, development, or human rights.

Development

This program focuses on the work of the UN, related agencies, WILPF, and other nongovernmental organizations interested in development and political relations. As an intern here, you'll attend the meetings of the UN, in particular those of the UN conference on trade and development and other meetings concerned with issues of development and environment. You'll report on new developments, alert WILPF to events and new publications, and propose actions for WILPF to take. You'll also take part in and help organize the activities of WILPF and those organized jointly by nongovernmental organizations.

Disarmament

This program focuses on the work of the UN and nongovernmental organizations in promoting and strengthening efforts for disarmament and the peaceful settlement of conflict. You'll track the conference on disarmament and other disarmament-related activities of the United Nations and nongovernmental organizations, reporting on developments, alerting WILPF to events and new publications, and proposing actions for WILPF to take. You'll also take part in and help organize the activities of WILPF and those organized jointly by nongovernmental groups.

Human Rights

If you're interested in advancing human rights in economic, social, cultural, civil, and political spheres, this internship is for you. You'll follow the annual session of the UN Commission on Human Rights and its subcommission on prevention of discrimination and protection of minorities, as well as the meetings of working groups and committees dealing with specific aspects of human rights. You'll report on new developments, alert WILPF to events and new publications, and propose actions for WILPF to take. You'll also help organize the activities of WILPF and those organized jointly by nongovernmental organizations.

Jane Addams Interns

Pennsylvania interns work with publications as editorial assistants and also in the areas of fundraising, membership, and resources. As an intern in this office, you'll work in an open, supportive environment with a staff of all women, using a participatory, feminist type of decision making. The internship involves a minimum of 15 hours a week, ranging from 10 weeks to one year, based on availability, project length, and your performance. Typically, though, the term is 12 weeks. Stipends are occasionally offered for this position.

You'll focus on one area of organizing for in-depth experience: the Dean Reed program, leadership/outreach, development, or Internet communications.

Dean Reed Program

As an intern here, you'll help develop and implement national programs, focusing primarily on four national campaigns. You'll work with WILPF branches around the country, track legislation, use online resources, and enhance skills that you'll need for organizing work: communication and diplomacy, writing, time management, and so on.

You'll also learn a great deal about particular issues on which WILPF focuses.

Candidates should be committed to WILPF's goals, have excellent verbal and interpersonal skills, excellent research and writing ability, initiative, flexibility, responsibility, imagination, patience, a sense of humor, and the ability to see a job through to completion.

Development

Here you'll help work to fund WILPF's national political campaigns. You can choose projects involving coordinating national board members' fund-raising, appeal letters, major donors, foundation grants, or planned giving efforts.

Candidates should be creative, responsible, committed to WILPF's goals, have good writing skills, and initiative.

Internet Communications

As an intern in this department, you'll help develop and maintain the Web site, including becoming familiar with WILPF operations, issues, and resources and gathering materials and resource leads from staff, members, and allied organizations. You'll also recommend materials to be posted and removed, process documents for uploading, update the site weekly, archive obsolete materials, and coordinate Web site maintenance with WILPF listserv postings and membership and branch e-mail alerts and with structure and information of International WILPF's new Web site. You'll also survey other sites and recommend improvements to make the WILPF Web site more dynamic and attractive, solicit reciprocal links to the WILPF site, and monitor search engines to improve WILPF Web siteexposure. Finally, you'll help plan, design, and produce a Washington Internet Starter kit, including a CD or disk and manual for conducting intergenerational workshops for WILPF members and other senior activists throughout the country to increase their use of the Internet as a resource and organizing tool and to improve the WILPF's communication system.

Candidates should have excellent communication, interpersonal, and computer skills, Internet research experience, and knowledge of HTML. Web site maintenance experience is a plus, and an information-sciences background is preferred. An active interest in peace and economic and social justice or gender issues is necessary.

Leadership/Outreach

As a membership intern, you'll be involved in every phase of the membership department. You'll keep records, answer phone inquiries and correspondence, and work with database and word processing programs. You'll also help figure out how to attract new members by working with the young women's caucus.

Candidates should have good organizing and communications skills as well as a commitment to social change.

Jeannette Rankin Internship Program

The legislative office of WILPF in Washington, D.C., provides information, educational materials, and organizing connections for the grassroots work of WILPF's 10,000 members across the United States. The organization works with other organizations interested in disarmament, women's human rights, and racial and economic justice to translate women's experience and vision into new policies to promote peace and justice.

As a Rankin intern, you'll help research issues; track legislation; attend coalition meetings, briefings, and hearings; write short articles, updates, and alerts; keep e-mail list postings current; produce resource materials; fill requests for information; and perform general office duties.

Candidates should have excellent communication, interpersonal, and computer skills; academic work in international affairs, politics, or women's studies; work experience or a demonstrated interest in peace, economic justice, or gender issues; and the ability to work independently. Organizing experience, strong Internet skills, and database proficiency are helpful.

United Nations Intern

Interns in this area work in the UN office in New York, founded in 1985. This internship is a good option if you're interested in international affairs, you're committed to social and economic change, and you're dedicated to working for peace and justice. You'll get the chance to work within the UN system. A willingness to work as part of a team, sensitivity to women's issues, and a strong commitment to world peace are essential.

At this time, there is no stipend attached to the internship. A term may vary in length from three to eight months. Although hours are flexible, you must work at least 12 hours during the week. As an intern in New York, you'll be expected to attend UN meetings, briefings, conferences, and nongovernmental organization committee meetings; prepare written and oral reports; and perform some administrative assistant work, such as correspondence, typing, filing, and answering phone calls.

Candidates should have excellent writing and listening skills, a sense of order, and initiative. Knowledge of Macintosh is useful.

HOW TO APPLY

All applications for the following positions should be sent to the preceding respective addresses. In addition, an office interview is preferred (although phone interviews are possible); an interview will be set up after the group receives your application.

Jane Addams Internship

Send a resume, writing sample, your internship goals, date available, and your preferred internship placement to the Philadelphia preceding address.

Jeannette Rankin Internship Program

Mail, fax, or e-mail a letter of interest, resume, and short writing sample to the legislative organizer at the Washington, D.C., preceding address.

UN Internship in New York

Your application should include a cover letter indicating your interests and expectations, a resume or CV, two written letters of recommendation, and a sample of your writing: an essay, article, a "letter to the editor" you have written, and so on.

Submit the materials to the preceding New York address.

Geneva Internship

Send the following materials to the Geneva preceding address:

- your resume, indicating education, relevant activities, and experience.
- a 1,500- to 2,000-word essay explaining why you want to be an intern in Geneva and how you think the experience would be useful for future work.
- your area of interest (disarmament, development, or human rights).
- your plans after the internship.
- two recommendations from nonfamily members (people writing recommendations should indicate their relationship to you and discuss your ability to take initiative in developing activities, your skills in written and oral communication, and your fluency in English; your long-term commitment to working for peace and justice; and your maturity in dealing with others.

WORK CANADA

Work Canada—BUNAC
PO Box 430
Southbury, CT 06488
(203) 264-0901 or 1-800-GO-BUNAC
info@bunacusa.org
http://www.bunac.org/usa/workcanada/#
What You Can Earn: Varies. The program fee is $250 plus the mandatory travel insurance. This covers administration in America and Canada, overnight courier fees, program handbook and use of SWAP hosting centers in Toronto, Vancouver and Montreal (summer only) for job and accommodation listings and program support.
Application Deadlines: Rolling.

Educational Experience: You must be a full-time student taking at least eight credit hours and enrolled for either the fall or spring after your Canada work experience at an accredited college or university. Proof of student status must be either an official transcript or a signed letter on official stationery from your school.

Requirements: You must be a U.S. citizen with a passport, between ages 18 and 30. You must enter Canada with at least $700. While in Canada under this program, you cannot attend any educational institutions and take any courses in Canada other than English or French as a second language. If you plan to work in agriculture, childcare, health services or teaching, you are required to undergo medical clearance before entering Canada.

OVERVIEW

Work Canada is a program authorized by the Canadian government to allow U.S. university students to work and travel in Canada. With Work Canada, you can spend up to six months living, working and traveling in Canada. You could choose to work in one of Canada's excellent ski areas in the winter, or experience big city life in Toronto, Vancouver or Montreal. Noncity summer options include working in a Canadian coastal, mountain or lakeside resort.

The Canadian sponsor is the Student Work Abroad Programs (SWAP); while you're in Canada, which provides on-the-spot backup and support, including a special phonecard featuring voicemail and fax facilities for 24-hour emergency assistance from SWAP.

BUNAC (the organization that sponsors this program) will issue you a SWAP certificate of participation. When you get to the Canadian border, you present this certificate to Canadian immigration authorities along with acceptable identification (preferably a U.S. passport). You'll then be given your Canadian work visa, called an Open Employment Authorization document, which is valid for six months. (You must have the Certificate of Participation from BUNAC in your hand before you enter Canada.) An Open Employment Work Authorization allows you to be legally employed in Canada for up to six months, anywhere, by any employer. Most participants find casual employment in stores, bars, restaurants, hotels, and ski resorts, but it's also possible to find career-related work. Most participants look for work once they have arrived in Canada, taking on average seven days to get a job. However, there's no reason why you can't start your job hunt before you go, arranging for a job ahead of time.

You can choose the date you want to enter Canada within your eligibility period and book your own travel accordingly. BUNAC strongly recommends that you attend an arrival orientation at SWAP offices in Toronto, Vancouver, and Montreal (although orientations in Montreal are limited to one a week from September to May only). The orientation includes helpful tips such as advice on bank accounts, tax, and applying for an SIN (Social Insurance Number), as well as practical information on job and house hunting. You should budget carefully for the first few weeks of your stay. Unless you have friends or relatives to stay with, you will typically need to pay in advance for your accommodation (plus a security deposit). Also bear in mind it may be two to four weeks before you receive your first paycheck. On average, a room in a shared house costs approximately $342 to $513 (U.S.) per month with general living costs about $85.50 extra per week. The program requires that you have a minimum amount of $700 (U.S.) personal support funds available at the time of application. Some employers provide accommodation, but if yours doesn't, you'll need somewhere temporary to stay until you sort out something more permanent. Youth hostels, student dorms or tourist homes are your best bet when you first arrive in a town to start your job or look for work.

HOW TO APPLY

For a listing of campuses that BUNAC representatives will attend, visit: http://www.bunac.org/usa/events.

To apply, first download the Work Abroad Application Form at http://www.bunac.org/usa/brochure/downloads.aspx.

Complete the form and mail with a money order or certified check to cover your program fee of $250 plus insurance premium. You'll also need to provide proof of $700 (either a copy of a bank statement showing name, date, and balance, or a copy of your parent's statement with a statement from them that funds will be available to you on request). With this, you should include proof of student status (either an unofficial transcript or a signed letter on official stationery from your school), and a signed Travel Insurance Declaration Form. Once BUNAC receives the documents, they will normally process an application within two working days and send your SWAP Certificate of Participation to you via courier.

MEDIA

ABC *GOOD MORNING AMERICA* INTERNSHIP

Good Morning America Internship Director
147 Columbus Avenue, 6th Floor
New York, NY 10023

What You Can Earn: Unpaid.
Application Deadlines: November 15 for spring I semester (mid-January to mid-April); February 1 for spring II semester (early April to early June); April 1 for summer semester (early June to mid-August); July 1 for fall semester (early September to mid-December); October 1 for winter semester (early December to mid-January)
Educational Experience: Should have some journalism experience in print or broadcast or internship experience.
Requirements: Good written and verbal communications skills; must receive academic credit for participation; must have initiative, grasp concepts quickly, mix well with others, be efficient, reliable, and able to juggle several tasks at one time.

OVERVIEW

Good Morning America, hosted by Diane Sawyer and Charles Gibson, is broadcast weekdays on ABC-TV in New York City. Internships are offered year-round, in eight- to 12-week sessions (both part time and full time).

If you land an internship here, you'll perform a variety of duties, helping to manage the enormous flow of information every day. Interns are included in some editorial meetings and in all phases of TV production.

HOW TO APPLY

Send a one-page resume, cover letter, two written recommendations, and an academic transcript to the preceding address. In addition, provide a notice of credit approval from your school. You'll be informed of your acceptance four to six weeks before the internship start date.

ABC JOHN STOSSEL SPECIALS INTERNSHIP

ABC News Recruitment Coordinator
47 W. 66th Street, 6th Floor
New York, NY 10023
http://abcnews.go.com/Reference/
    story?id=141275&page=1

What You Can Earn: Unpaid.
Application Deadlines: March 15 for summer internships.
Educational Experience: Must be at least a junior in an undergraduate college program and be interested in a journalism career.
Requirements: Must receive academic credit in return for the internship.

OVERVIEW

ABC News offers a summer internship with John Stossel's one-hour ABC specials. Your main responsibility is to support the producers through both clerical and research-related tasks. The Stossel Unit is fairly small, so talented interns are heavily relied upon and gain a hands-on learning experience in multiple facets of production.

HOW TO APPLY

Interested students should forward a resume and cover letter to the preceding address.

ABC NEWS INTERNSHIP

ABC News Recruitment Coordinator
Nissa Walton Booker
47 W. 66th Street, 6th Floor
New York, NY 10023
nissa.walton-booker@abc.com
http://abcnews.go.com/Reference/
    story?id=141275&page=1

What You Can Earn: Unpaid.

Application Deadlines: March 15 for summer internships.

Educational Experience: Must be at least a junior in an undergraduate college program and be interested in a journalism career.

Requirements: Must be willing to learn, have a good attitude, good phone manner, a general curiosity about the world, and a good grasp on current events and public figures. Must receive academic credit in return for the internship.

OVERVIEW

ABC News offers a variety of internships in different areas to qualified students interested in pursuing a career in broadcast journalism. Interns will be placed on ABC News programs and in departments in the New York City or Washington, D.C., bureaus, where they will be exposed to all aspects of network news. ABC's various units that take interns include the ABC News Operations Group, the graphics department, the Long-Form unit, the ABC film and tape library, the law and justice unit, the affiliate feed (NewsOne), news production, ABCNEWS.com, Brian Ross Investigative Unit; rights, clearance and permissions; advertisement and promotion; and ABC News videosource.

ABC News Advertising and Promotion

This department is the marketing arm for the ABC News brand. Creatively, the staff produces award-winning campaigns using technologically advanced editing and graphic tools. The ABC News brand is then strategically presented in various markets, promoting to an already faithful audience and expanding its reach to new viewers. An internship in this area would expand your knowledge of the broadcast business as you work closely with the producers and interact with various news programs. Here you'll learn the process of gathering footage, choosing eye-catching shots, and copy writing. You must be energetic and organized with a strong interest in creative production to apply for this internship.

ABCNEWS.com

At this 24-hour operation of ABC News, staffers produce text news stories and audio and video and interactive components while covering breaking news and reporting original features. Web site staffers also work with TV correspondents to produce network content for the Web site. Departments within ABCNEWS.com include editorial (including national and international news, business, science and technology, and entertainment sections), graphics, broadband video, photo and graphics, and technical production.

ABC News Operations Group

This news group serves as a liaison with all news shows, departments, and bureaus and the information systems division of the ABC network (computer applications development, engineering, and implementation). If you intern here, you'll help schedule and track the acquisition and installation of computer equipment and software through the entire ABC News Division. You'll also research new communications technologies and focus on those that could be tested and implemented. You also may be able to research story proposals for some network news correspondents and provide general help to the ABC News' Polling Unit. To apply to this unit, you should be interested in technology, new media, and TV production.

ABC News Videosource

This is the stock-footage sales arm of ABC News, providing commercial producers with licensable content from the vast holdings of ABC News and other represented collections to producers for cable and public TV, movie studios, educators, and corporate and advertising clients. You'll be exposed to all aspects of the operation and will chiefly help in library database research, videotape ordering and screening, filing, and other administrative tasks. To intern here, you should be interested in current affairs and be able to work well under deadline pressure and with a wide range of people.

Brian Ross Investigative Unit

This is ABC News' investigative team, which is looking for hardworking, bright college students who are passionate about investigative journalism. The 10-member Brian Ross Unit produces award-winning pieces for *20/20*, *World News Tonight*, *Primetime*, *Good Morning America*, and *Nightline*. You should have basic research and office skills if you want to apply here; although you'll do administrative work, you'll also conduct extensive research for national and international stories, screen tape, and learn about TV news.

Film/Tape Library

Interns at the film and tape library will work with the air histories department, mainly in screening and dubbing of show tapes, clip reel making in *World News Tonight* edit rooms, database entry, general administrative support, expediting, filing, and other general office duties.

Graphics

ABC News Graphics interns will help art directors and artists from several ABC shows, including *World News Tonight*, *20/20*, and *Primetime*. In that capacity, you'll be able to learn about the design process, the technology, and how to meet deadlines. You'll be able to see how software you've learned about in class is used in a professional environment. In addition, you'll work on breaking news items, learning how the editorial information from news events is turned into visual images to help tell the story. You'll help gather information and images and organize them for use on the air.

Law and Justice Unit

This unit includes a group of former attorneys and award-winning producers who report and produce major legal stories for several of the network's news programs: *World News Tonight*, *Good Morning America*, *Primetime*, and *Nightline*. The unit works on subjects ranging from crime mysteries to U.S. Supreme Court rulings, juvenile justice, or terrorism-related trials. As a division of the Investigative Projects Unit, the Law & Justice Unit has also contributed to the networks' coverage of September 11 and its aftermath. Being a small group, the unit relies on interns not only for basic research but also for reporting. Interns will have the opportunity to work on pieces with ABC News' senior legal correspondent Cynthia McFadden.

Long-Form Unit

This unit specializes in documentary specials for ABC Network, such as *Hopkins 24/7*, *Boston 24/7*, *State v.* and *Vanished*. Your responsibilities would include topical and investigative research, contributing toward series concepts, logging tape, animation, and other duties.

NewsOne

This is the ABC affiliate news-feed service of ABC News, responsible for gathering and producing news material for ABC affiliates and other clients in the United States and around the world. The internship at NewsOne will expose you to various areas, such as the news desk, satellite operations, the Northeast bureau, digital services, and client services. You'll also be exposed to the editorial side of NewsOne, so you'll accompany producers and crews on shoots and help with writing and editing.

News Production

This unit develops and produces a wide variety of programming for a number of cable TV networks, including most *Biography* programs that air on A&E. The unit also produces documentaries for the Discovery Channel such as *Army Psychological Operations Unit*, *Ghengis Khan's Tomb*, and *For the Defense*. Recent shows in production include *Biographies* of James Beard, John Ritter, and George Lucas. If you intern here, you'll do the same sorts of jobs as would a production assistant, with whom you'll primarily work. You'll be informally assigned to a team of producer, associate producer, and one or more production assistants. You'll then support all facets of the production of a cable documentary, including: library research, ABC news database research, video tape ordering, logging and dubbing, and many other tasks.

Rights, Clearances, and Permissions

The permissions department negotiates with outside sources and evaluates the permissibility of a request to use ABC News material for educational, political, and commercial endeavors. They also serve as a liaison between the legal department and producers for the ABC newsmagazine shows. If you're thinking of interning here, you should be interested in TV broadcasting and news and/or legal affairs and be highly motivated, organized, and responsible. You'll be responsible for providing general administrative support, dubbing tapes, filing, and doing other office tasks.

HOW TO APPLY

If you're interested in interning in any of these areas, forward a resume and cover letter to the preceding address.

ABC NEWS *PRIMETIME LIVE* INTERNSHIP

PrimeTime Live Internship Program
ABC News
147 Columbus Avenue, 4th Floor
New York, NY 10023
(212) 456-1600
http://abcnews.go.com/Reference/
    story?id=141275&page=1

What You Can Earn: Unpaid.
Application Deadlines: March 15 for summer internships.
Educational Experience: Must be at least a junior in an undergraduate college program and be interested in a journalism career; however, this internship is not limited to journalism students.
Requirements: Must receive academic credit in return for the internship.

OVERVIEW

If you like news magazine shows, you may be interested in interning for ABC's *Primetime*, where you'll learn about what goes on behind the scenes in a news magazine shows. ABC News' *PrimeTime Live* is an Emmy award–winning news magazine show anchored by Sam Donaldson and Diane Sawyer. Since 1989 it has concentrated on investigative news pieces using hidden cameras, as well as profiles of newsmakers. Six to 10 interns per quarter work in all areas of the organization: research, production, and editing. You'll receive on-the-job training with some of the best producers, directors, writers, editors, and correspondents in the television news business.

As an intern here, you'll learn what's involved in several aspects of production, from editing to reporting to story development, by participating with and observing professional reporters and producers in action. You'll also benefit from organized intern seminars hosted by in-house ABC professionals, producers, editors, and on-air reporters.

HOW TO APPLY

Interested students should send a resume and cover letter to the preceding address.

ABC NEWS RADIO INTERNSHIP

ABC News Recruitment Coordinator
Nissa Walton Booker
47 W. 66th Street, 6th Floor
New York, NY 10023
nissa.walton-booker@abc.com
http://abcnews.go.com/Reference/
    story?id=141275&page=1

What You Can Earn: Unpaid.
Application Deadlines: March 15 for summer internships.
Educational Experience: Must be at least a junior in an undergraduate college program and be interested in a journalism career.
Requirements: Must receive academic credit in return for the internship.

OVERVIEW

If you want a career in the radio news business, you may be interested in checking out the ABC News Radio fall, spring, or summer internships. Here you'll learn about covering news for a network of 4,500 radio stations. You'll learn how to create a newscast for radio, featuring writing, voicing, and research. You'll work with producers and correspondents who have years of experience.

HOW TO APPLY

Interested students should send a resume and cover letter to the preceding address.

ABC NEWS SPECIAL EVENTS INTERNSHIP

ABC News Recruitment Coordinator
Nissa Walton Booker
47 W. 66th Street, 6th Floor
New York, NY 10023
nissa.walton-booker@abc.com
http://abcnews.go.com/Reference/
    story?id=141275&page=1

What You Can Earn: Unpaid.
Application Deadlines: March 15 for summer internships.

Educational Experience: Must be at least a junior in an undergraduate college program and be interested in a journalism career.
Requirements: Must be interested in journalism; TV news production; willing to learn; have a good attitude; good phone manner; ability to work under deadline pressure and a grasp on current events and public figures. You must receive academic credit in return for the internship.

OVERVIEW

ABC News Special Events produces special reports that pre-empt regularly scheduled programs with breaking news. These events also include election coverage and other nonscheduled programming. As an intern here, you'll do research, screen video, and handle other aspects of TV news production. You'll also help producers in videotape, graphics, and control rooms and have an opportunity to research story proposals.

HOW TO APPLY

Interested students should send a resume and cover letter to the preceding address.

ABC NEWS WASHINGTON BUREAU INTERNSHIP

ABC News Washington Bureau Internships
1717 DeSales Street, NW
Washington, D.C. 20036
ABCTV.News.DC.Interns@abc.com

What You Can Earn: Unpaid.
Application Deadlines: March 15 for summer internships.
Educational Experience: Must be at least a junior in an undergraduate college program and have a serious interest in broadcast journalism.

Requirements: Must be interested in journalism, TV news production, willing to learn, have a good attitude, good phone manner, the ability to multi-task, ability to work under deadline pressure, and a grasp on current events and public figures. You must receive academic credit in return for the internship. Above all, initiative is a strong component of a successful internship. Journalism experience is helpful.

OVERVIEW

The Washington bureau of ABC News offers internships with *Good Morning America*, *Nightline*, the political unit, news graphics, ABC News Radio, *This Week with George Stephanopoulos*, and *World News Tonight*.

HOW TO APPLY

Interested students should forward a resume and cover letter to the preceding address. No phone calls.

ABC-TV (CHANNEL 7) LOS ANGELES INTERNSHIP

ABC 7, Diversity Programs & Community Relations
500 Circle Seven Drive
Glendale, CA 91201
(818) 863-7231
http://www.abc7.com

What You Can Earn: Unpaid.
Application Deadlines: Six months prior to the desired semester.
Educational Experience: Journalism, English, or broadcast engineering majors preferred.
Requirements: Basic computer skills and working knowledge of Windows; students must receive college credit for the internship to be considered.

OVERVIEW

ABC 7 in Los Angeles is an ABC-owned TV station responsible for producing 33 hours of local news a week, as well as weekly public affairs programs, specials, and a number of public service announcements. Internships are available for the fall, spring, and summer semesters.

Internships are available for both graduates and undergraduates to do editing, reporting, sales, research, production, community affairs, programming, and computer work. A variety of intern opportunities are offered in the following departments:

- general news
- information systems
- entertainment
- health
- sports
- weather
- creative services
- public affairs
- early morning news
- production
- programming

HOW TO APPLY

To apply for an internship, send a cover letter with your resume and an application form to the preceding address. You can obtain an application by calling (818) 863-7230. This station does not accept faxed applications.

ABC *WEEKEND NEWS* INTERNSHIP

ABC News Recruitment Coordinator
47 W. 66th Street, 6th Floor
New York, NY 10023

http://abcnews.go.com/Reference/story?id
=141275&page=1

What You Can Earn: Unpaid.
Application Deadlines: March 15 for summer internships.
Educational Experience: Must be at least a junior in an undergraduate college program and display a serious interest in journalism and a sincere desire to learn more about the business. Although a major in communications is not a requirement, previous journalism-related internships and either print or broadcast curriculum are strongly suggested.
Requirements: Must receive academic credit in return for the internship; should demonstrate strong written and verbal communication skills as well as an interest in national and international affairs.

OVERVIEW

Weekend News is ABC's weekend news program, anchored by Terry Moran and Bob Woodruff, who bring viewers all of the latest news on Saturday and Sunday evenings. As an intern here, you'll play an essential role in producing the evening news program on Saturdays and Sundays. You'll be responsible for managing the flow of information between correspondents and producers, so you must remain levelheaded and ingenious. You'll have the most success here if you can mix well with others, juggle several tasks at once, be efficient, and act with integrity. Initiative, both through your approach to tasks and to playing a role in the development of the program, is not only highly respected but is expected as a member of the show.

You'll be included in some editorial meetings and in all aspects of TV production. *Weekend News* provides interns with valuable behind-the-scenes exposure to the making of a network news program.

HOW TO APPLY

Interested students should forward a resume and cover letter to the preceding address.

ABC *WORLD NEWS TONIGHT* INTERNSHIP

ABC News Recruitment Coordinator
47 W. 66th Street, 6th Floor
New York, NY 10023
http://abcnews.go.com/Reference/
story?id=141275&page=1

What You Can Earn: Unpaid.
Application Deadlines: March 15 for summer internships.
Educational Experience: Must be at least a junior in an undergraduate college program and be interested in a journalism career.
Requirements: Must receive academic credit in return for the internship.

OVERVIEW

For this show, you'll work primarily on site, although you'll also have the opportunity to participate in field assignments. The summer will be divided into multiweek sections during which you'll work with staff at all levels, in both production and editorial departments. Hour-to-hour and day-to-day duties may change, but typically your duties will include research, materials search and retrieval, and administrative support. You'll shadow producers, and you may work off site depending on your ability and the producer. You also may get the chance to participate in story pitching and development, as well as help to coordinate and attend interviews.

HOW TO APPLY

Interested students should send a resume and cover letter to the preceding address.

THE AD CLUB (BOSTON) INTERNSHIP

The Ad Club
Attn: Internship Program
38 Newbury Street, 5th Floor
Boston, MA 02116
http://www.adclub.org/internship.2005.html

What You Can Earn: $3200 summer stipend.
Application Deadlines: Rolling.
Educational Experience: Major in advertising.
Requirements: Minority students, juniors, seniors, or graduate students who plan to pursue a career in the ad industry and who have a 3.5 or higher GPA. U.S. citizenship (or permanent residency status) is required.

OVERVIEW

Minority students in New England with an interest in checking out the advertising scene in Boston from June through August may be interested in this internship by the Ad Club. During the 10-week program, interns will work about 40 hours a week (which may vary based on company work schedules) in an advertising agency, a marketing department in a large organization, or in the ad department of a radio station, TV station, magazine, or newspaper.

Interns will also attend Friday Forum advancement sessions to hear presentations from industry professionals and have the chance to explore major companies in the Boston area. Interns will also work with program mentors and participate in an Intern Community Service Day. At the start of the summer, you'll meet with your matched mentor to get to know each other. Your mentor will arrange one informational interview based on the mentor's contacts and will serve as your resource throughout the summer.

This program provides minority students with the opportunity to break into the advertising/communications industry, the opportunity to meet ad professionals, and the opportunity to network with peers. Interns are recruited from top schools across the country, with a focus on those living in New England. In 2004, the program included 23 interns from schools including Harvard, Brown, Boston College, and Amherst.

The summer internship is a cornerstone program of the Ad Club, which hopes to expose minority students to opportunities within the Boston advertising and communications industry and to help increase the level of diversity within the industry. Each year, the Ad Club signs on a number of different companies as worksite sponsors; the number of internships available varies each summer based on the number of positions available.

The Ad Club runs the program, reviewing applications, scheduling interviews, and placing accepted students at the varied worksites. Once the program begins in June, the intern's main contact will be the worksite supervisor, who remains the contact for the entire 10-week program.

HOW TO APPLY

Complete the application available at the club's Web site (see preceding section) and submit it along with your current resume, a current official transcript, two letters of recommendations from a faculty member, advisor, counselor, or employer, and an answer to the essay question listed in the application.

After the application is submitted, the interview process will include an initial screening followed by interviews by work-sites in February and March.

ADVERTISING CLUB INTERNSHIP

The Advertising Club
235 Park Avenue South
New York, NY 10003

Attention: Internship Coordinator
(212) 533-8080
http://www.theadvertisingclub.org

What You Can Earn: $300 stipend.
Application Deadlines: Last day of February; applicants selected for a phone interview will be notified by April 1.
Educational Experience: Major or minor in advertising, journalism, or communications helpful.
Requirements: Students must be college junior or seniors.

OVERVIEW

If you dream of creating instantly-recognizable ads and producing mind-blowing ad campaigns, you'll be interested in this internship at the Advertising Club, which offers internships at some of the largest ad agencies in New York City. As an Ad Club intern, you'll see firsthand what it takes to create an ad campaign, learn the intricacies of developing a brand strategy, map out a media plan, research a product category, or create a collateral package.

The Advertising Club's summer internship program places about 30 students from across the country in New York City ad agencies, marketing, and publishing companies and acts as a mentor during the program, providing weekly seminars to help you learn about different facets of the industry and the opportunity to network.

The popular 10-week program also encourages you to attend the Advertising Club's programs and events, where you'll be able to interact with other members and hear about current and future trends. Areas of possible internships include account management, creative, media, publishing, and account planning. Many ad interns are eventually offered jobs upon graduation in the agencies where they work.

HOW TO APPLY

Download an internship application at the Ad Club's Web site, http://www.theadvertisingclub.

org/prog_internships.html, or write for an application at the preceding address.

AKRON BEACON JOURNAL INTERNSHIP

Akron Beacon Journal Internship Coordinator
PO Box 640
44 E. Exchange Street
Akron, OH 44309-0640
bbolden@thebeaconjournal.com
(330) 996-3730
http://www.ohio.com

What You Can Earn: $425 a week for fall and summer sessions; unpaid internships are available year round.
Application Deadlines: March 31 for fall session (photography only); November 30 for summer session (copyediting, reporting, graphics).
Educational Experience: College and graduate school students eligible.
Requirements: A car and driver's license are required. Prior internship is preferred, but not required.

OVERVIEW

This Knight-Ridder newspaper is located 35 miles south of Cleveland. Photography internships are available in the fall session; summer internships are available in the reporting, graphics, and copyediting departments.

HOW TO APPLY

Send resume, cover letter, and clips to the address above.

AMERICAN RED CROSS MEDIA INTERNSHIP

American Red Cross
Internship Coordinator
8111 Gatehouse Road, Second Floor
Falls Church, VA 22042
carnoj@usa.redcross.org
http://www.redcross.org/services/
    youth/0,1082,0_416_,00.html

What You Can Earn: Paid and unpaid.
Application Deadlines: Rolling.
Educational Experience: High school, college, and graduate school students eligible.
Requirements: U.S. citizenship.

OVERVIEW

The American Red Cross employees, interns, and volunteers help keep the public prepared to respond to disasters and personal emergencies. The Red Cross provides training in lifesaving skills such as CPR and first aid, collects and distributes half the nation's blood supply, and helps victims of more than 67,000 disasters annually. Internships are available at the national office of the American Red Cross in Washington, D.C., (see below) and in many of the 1,100 chapters across the country (call your local ARC chapter to check on area internships).

While most internships are available only to college students, the American Red Cross offers paid and nonpaid internship positions for high school students as well as undergraduate and graduate students. These internship positions offer students the opportunity to gain career-related work experience related to their academic programs.

If you participate in the American Red Cross internship programs, you'll be working on professional projects, assignments, and activities during your tenure with a staffer. All work assignments are designed to provide student interns with stimulat-ing and challenging work that will help both you and the ARC.

Communication and Marketing: Online Media

In this Washington, D.C., internship, you'll help maintain and enhance the public Web site as well as a secure Internet site for employees and volunteers. You'll code and post material, make corrections and other changes, and provide graphic support by helping design new content that meets style guidelines. You'll also monitor the inbox for requested changes and carry out daily postings, enforce style and graphics rules, and help develop new features for site. You must know HTML coding, HomeSite, Photoshop, and WS FTP. Experience with Flash is preferred, and understanding Spanish is a plus.

Communication and Marketing: Program Communication

In this Washington, D.C., internship, you'll obtain media clips, identify news articles of organizational interest and forward them to appropriate personnel, and conduct research related to media lists. You also may research and write articles for external and internal communications. You should know Microsoft Word and Excel and have Web site capabilities. Spanish is a plus.

Communication and Marketing: Public Relations

In this Washington, D.C., internship, you'll research media outlets, develop pitches for the Red Cross president and the organization, and pitch the Red Cross to the media. You'll write press releases, craft talking points for the Red Cross president and other senior spokespeople, and write stories for redcross.org and CrossNet. You also may help the disaster operations center in times of crisis.

HOW TO APPLY

You should e-mail for applications and a list of current available internships at the preceding address.

AMERICAN SOCIETY OF MAGAZINE EDITORS INTERNSHIP

American Society of Magazine Editors
Internship Program
919 Third Avenue
New York, NY 10022
(212) 872-3700
http://www.magazine.org/Editorial/Internships

What You Can Earn: $325 weekly (minimum). You'll be a temporary employee of the magazine to which you're assigned and will be paid a minimum stipend of $325 a week. However, your stipend may not cover all your expenses, and you're responsible for your own travel, housing, food, and personal expenses. ASME will help make dormitory arrangements in New York and Washington, D.C.; students who come from the area may live at home. Most interns in New York stay in a New York University dormitory.
Application Deadlines: November 15.
Educational Experience: Must have completed junior year of college by June and be entering senior year in the fall; journalism majors should have taken some courses in reporting, writing, and editing.
Requirements: Liberal arts majors *must* have held a senior position on the campus magazine, newspaper, or yearbook and have had at least one summer job or internship in journalism.

OVERVIEW

The American Society of Magazine Editors sponsors an editorial internship program each summer for college juniors who are journalism majors or deeply involved in campus journalism, offering a 10-week summer session that provides the opportunity to work in the editorial offices of consumer magazines and business publications.

Many journalism schools and career-placement offices are asked to review applications from their students and submit the application of the one candidate who most closely meets the requirements of the program. Although applications are accepted from individual students, preference is given to candidates submitted by their schools. Therefore, you should check with your dean, department head, or career services office before sending an application on your own.

The internship program is intended for editorially oriented students, and the emphasis is on editing magazines; other tasks may include handling reader mail, evaluating unsolicited manuscripts, researching articles, checking facts, proofreading, copyediting, interviewing, covering press conferences, and attending editorial meetings. At a number of magazines, there may also be reporting and writing opportunities and even a few bylines. Some interns have the opportunity to see how the circulation, advertising, and other business departments of a magazine function.

The program begins with a two-and-a-half-day orientation in New York, during which you'll get to know other interns, hear from top editors and other magazine executives about magazine editing and publishing, and meet alumni of the program who talk about magazine jobs and living in and enjoying the city. A brief orientation meeting is also held in Washington, D.C., for interns assigned there.

During the program, there are weekly luncheons where interns meet and visit a varied group of editors and other magazine people. Each intern is asked to submit a written report by the final day of the internship on specific work experience, suggestions for the program, and comments on journalism education.

Students are selected for the magazine internship program on the basis of their complete application package. Strong consideration is given to heavy involvement in journalism and interest in magazine work.

Students accepted to the program are assigned to publications based on their skills and the preferences of participating editors. It may not be possible to assign a magazine according to an applicant's preferences. If an applicant refuses the assignment, ASME will offer the spot to another applicant. Because of the diversity and specialization of the magazine publishing business, internships will be offered by some magazines not well known to the applicants.

The list of participating magazines may change, but they have included: *AARP The Magazine; BusinessWeek; The Chronicle of Higher Education; Essence; Family Circle; Field & Stream; Food & Wine; Glamour; Guideposts; In Style; Kiplinger's Personal Finance; Ladies' Home Journal; Money; More; National Geographic; National Geographic Traveler; Newsweek; Parenting; Parents; People; Popular Science; Reader's Digest; Real Simple; Self; Seventeen; SmartMoney; Smithsonian; Teen People; Travel and Leisure; U.S. News & World Report;* and *YM*.

HOW TO APPLY

The application form may be filled out online by visiting http://www.magazine.org/editorial/internships/Requirements_and_Application.

However, applications can't be submitted online; you must print the completed application form and mail everything to the preceding address. This includes an application form, signed by you and a dean or department head, along with a cover letter discussing activities or experience in campus journalism, internships or summer jobs in journalism, courses taken or planned, previous summer activity, extracurricular activity, magazines regularly read (such as business, science, entertainment, fashion, alternative press), whether or not you can accept an assignment in Washington, D.C., and why you want to be an intern and what you hope to contribute to the assigned magazine. Your attitude toward magazines as expressed in your letters and your willingness to work hard as a full-time employee are essential to a successful internship.

In addition, you should send a supporting letter from a dean, department head, or professor who personally knows your journalistic experience and academic ability, along with examples of your writing, such as clips from your college magazine or newspaper. You also can include a letter from a former ASME intern indicating your qualifications.

You should send a recent portrait photograph no smaller than 2 1/2" x 3 1/2" and no larger than 3 1/2" x 5 1/2" (such as a passport photo), which will be used in a promotional folder; it is not used in the selection process. You should add a processing fee of $25.

An application with glaring grammar, spelling, punctuation, or syntax errors, or that is incomplete, will not be considered.

ANCHORAGE DAILY NEWS INTERNSHIP

Anchorage Daily News
1001 Northway Drive
Anchorage, AK 99508

What You Can Earn: $9.50 an hour plus mileage (when on assignment).
Application Deadlines: Reporters must apply by December 31; photographers must apply by February 1.
Educational Experience: For reporters, at least two years of journalism education.
Requirements: Reporter applicants should have published work from school or other publications and should have been trained in the basics of journalism.

OVERVIEW

Internships are about 40 hours a week for 12 weeks. Reliable transportation is needed, and mileage is paid when the intern is on assignment.

Photography Interns
The *Anchorage Daily News* offers one photography internship each summer for a three-month period

beginning as early as May and ending as late as October. This full-time position includes a variety of office and field duties, ranging from clerical and darkroom responsibilities to general assignment photographic duties.

You'll be expected to pitch in as a member of the photographic staff, sharing in most of the responsibilities. You'll be expected to provide your own basic photo equipment, but the paper also owns its own Nikon, Canon, and digital equipment. You'll be expected to go on assignment and bring back photos that can run in the paper each day and produce at least one picture story during the summer.

Reporter Interns

The *Daily News* offers two reporting internships, one in news, and one in feature writing; you should specify which area interests you most. Reporting interns are considered to be general-assignment reporters, covering stories in a variety of subject areas. Although some stories will be assigned, you'll also be expected to develop your own ideas.

HOW TO APPLY

You should mail a letter and resume (do not fax or e-mail internship applications) to the attention of either the Reporter Internship Coordinator or the Photo Editor. Reporter applicants should include at least six samples of your best articles; photographer applicants should include 20 photo samples in any form (tearsheets, prints, slides, CD, zip, or disc) that represent work appropriate for newspaper publication. If you send your work digitally, make sure it can be displayed on Macintosh computers.

ASSOCIATED PRESS INTERNSHIP

The Associated Press Headquarters
450 W. 33rd Street
New York, NY 10001

(212) 621-1500
http://www.ap.org/apjobs/internship.html

What You Can Earn: Stipend available.
Application Deadlines: November 15 for the next summer's internship.
Educational Experience: A full-time junior, senior, or graduate student at an American college or university. Graphics interns must have two years in basic drawing or computer illustration classes, with proficiency in operating a vector drawing tool.
Requirements: Graphics interns must have two years of basic photo manipulation skills in Photoshop, good writing skills, and the ability to read and recognize grammatical and factual error in English or Spanish.

OVERVIEW

The Associated Press is one of the world's best-known news cooperatives that provide multimedia news coverage, offering fast, aggressive, and distinctive journalism that meets the deadline and media format needs of a range of members and customers. It's been the backbone of the news and information industry since its creation in 1848. Today, it has transformed itself from a wire service to an interactive news network that integrates text, photographs, graphics, sound, and video for distribution to newspapers, broadcasters, Web sites, and commercial customers worldwide.

As the essential global news network, AP hires more journalists than any other news organization who are dedicated to the highest standards of fairness, balance and accuracy, and sharply focused on gathering the facts, presenting the news with authority and clarity, and delivering it fast. The AP has news bureaus in every state and many countries around the world. Because the AP provides content to newspapers, broadcasters, and Web sites all over the globe, there are no formal deadlines; every minute of each day is a deadline. As a result, AP journalists often write more every day than daily journalists in their quest to "get it fast, get it first, and get it right."

The AP offers a highly selective, 12-week, individually tailored training program for up to 22 aspiring print, photo, graphics, broadcast, and multimedia journalists. If you're selected, you'll get to work in an AP bureau under the supervision of a designated trainer, which may include covering breaking news that may be featured in many media outlets.

Interns on the metro desk intern will assist the Metro Washington, D.C. news desk by making beat calls, monitoring newscasts, and going out to assist in coverage of stories for both the broadcast-style and print-style wires. The intern will also train as an in-house writer and reporter for AP's radio services.

Graphics interns get to create breaking and advance graphics for national, international, sports and business fields. You will also get to hone your research and interviewing techniques, and learn to manipulate data and create meta-data oriented graphics. You also get to learn vector rendering, 3-D rendering and rendering styles for graphics.

Start dates may be between mid-May and mid-June, depending on your schedule.

HOW TO APPLY

If you're interested in an AP internship, inform your nearest AP bureau that you want to apply for the AP Internship Program. Submit a completed employment application, a timed newswriting test, and a 300-word autobiographical essay on this topic: "The Associated Press seeks to recruit and retain a workforce that embodies a wide range of talents, experiences, achievements and journalistic skills. Please describe the qualities and accomplishments you would bring to the company."

You also should include a resume, with five to seven clips; two letters of reference from professors or employers; and have an interview with an AP chief of bureau. You'll also need to take a timed newswriting test.

Photography interns also should submit a portfolio of work. Submissions should be a collection of jpeg images with captions on a CD. You should forego programs that include music or special transitions. A link to a Web site may be offered as a substitute for a CD.

In addition to the above items, applicants for the graphics internship should include a portfolio of their work.

In addition to the above items, applicants for the metro desk should also submit three writing samples that can be any combination of the following, but requiring at least one broadcast writing sample:

- a news writing assignment completed for a journalism class
- a clip of a story written for a college newspaper
- a script written for a radio or TV newscast
- a script or story written for an internship at a newspaper or broadcast station

ASSOCIATED PRESS BROADCAST NEWS INTERNSHIP

The Associated Press Headquarters
450 W. 33rd Street
New York, NY 10001
(212) 621-1500
http://www.ap.org/apjobs/internship.html

What You Can Earn: Basic stipend.
Application Deadlines: November 15 for the next summer internship.
Educational Experience: Full-time juniors, seniors, and graduate students at American colleges and universities; any major is accepted.
Requirements: None specified.

OVERVIEW

The Associated Press Broadcast News Center (BNC) in Washington, D.C., offers two summer news internships. If you're chosen, you'll help the Metro Washington, D.C., news desk by making beat calls, monitoring newscasts, and going out to help cover stories for both the broadcast-style and print-style wires. You'll also train as an in-house writer and reporter for AP's radio services. Start dates may be anytime in June, depending on your schedule, and last 12 weeks.

HOW TO APPLY

Send a completed employment application and a 300-word autobiographical essay on this topic: "The Associated Press seeks to recruit and retain a workforce that embodies a wide range of talents, experiences, achievements and journalistic skills. Please describe the qualities and accomplishments you would bring to the company." You also should include a resume, including your college or university e-mail address; two reference letters in sealed envelopes; and three to five writing samples that can be any combination of the following samples, but requiring at least one broadcast writing sample.

- a copy of a news writing assignment completed to meet the requirements of a class
- clips of stories written for a college newspaper
- a script written for a radio or TV newscast
- scripts or stories written during internships at newspapers or broadcast stations

After you've assembled all the requirements for application, e-mail Clyde Blassengale at cblassengale@ap.org; you will take a broadcast internship writing test at your nearest AP bureau, where you can submit your materials. All your application materials, including your test, will be forwarded from the bureau to BNC for evaluation. Intern applicants in the Washington, D.C.-area will bring all their application materials to and test at the Broadcast News Center. You'll also need to schedule an interview with AP Broadcast's recruiter.

ATLANTA JOURNAL CONSTITUTION INTERNSHIP

News Personnel Manager
The Atlanta Journal and Constitution
72 Marietta St. NW
Atlanta, GA 30303
(404) 526-5151
http://www.ajc.com

What You Can Earn: $550 a week.
Application Deadlines: December 31.
Educational Experience: Full-time college juniors, seniors, or graduate students or people who have graduated within six months of the start of the internship.
Requirements: Must have professional daily-deadline experience; newspaper experience preferred. Must have worked on a campus newspaper or other publications. Must have driver's license. Internship offers are contingent upon passing a company-required drug test. Interns are responsible for locating their own housing, but the newspaper offers suggestions and generally has several staffers willing to rent out space in their homes to interns for the summer. A car isn't a requirement; there are a limited number of staff cars available and public transportation is very limited in Atlanta's suburban areas.

OVERVIEW

The *Atlanta Journal and Constitution* is offering 10-week internships for the winter and summer to college students interested in pursuing a career as a reporter, photographer, page designer, copy editor, on-line editor, or graphic artist. Interns are treated as full-time professional journalists and every attempt is made to place you in departments that match your area of interest or specialization.

As an intern here, you'll be assigned a supervisor in the department you're assigned to work in, who will be responsible for your work schedule, assignments, and five-week and final performance evaluations. You'll also be assigned a nonsupervisor mentor, who will act as your support system. The number of stories you write varies by department. In general, you'll be kept very busy with a variety of reporting and writing challenges.

Summer interns generally start the second week of June, but the start date is flexible. Winter interns generally start the second week in January. Occasionally, a fall internship is offered, but the paper does not encourage students to take a semester off from school to complete a fall internship.

HOW TO APPLY

Send a 500-word essay explaining why you want to be a journalist and how an internship at the *Atlanta Journal* and *Constitution* will help you pursue your goal, along with copies of five to 10 news clips or samples of your photos, graphics or headlines, a resume, and references. Specify which of the following areas you wish to apply to: reporting, photography, copyediting, or graphic art.

ATLANTIC MONTHLY INTERNSHIP

The Atlantic Monthly
77 North Washington Street
Boston, MA 02114
http://www.theatlantic.com

What You Can Earn: Unpaid; Boston subway system passes available; college credit given.

Application Deadlines: June deadline for fall session (September through December); November deadline for winter/spring session (January through May); February deadline for summer session (June through August); deadlines may be moved up if there are a large number of applications, so let the magazine know of your interest as early as you can.

Educational Experience: College juniors and seniors and recent graduates of all ages.

Requirements: Ability to work a consistent 16-20 hours a week, although the magazine is flexible regarding school and part-time work requirements.

OVERVIEW

The *Atlantic Monthly* magazine began in Boston, following a meeting with some of the brightest literary stars of the day, including Ralph Waldo Emerson, Henry Wadsworth Longfellow, James Russell Lowell, and Oliver Wendell Holmes. Soon the new magazine acquired an editor, James Russell Lowell, and the first issue of *The Atlantic Monthly* appeared in November 1857. It billed itself as a journal of literature, politics, science, and the arts and within two years was being read by more than 30,000 Americans. Today the number of readers is estimated to be at least 1.2 million.

If you're interested in interning here, you'll find yourself reading submissions as a "first reader" and maintaining files of correspondence between authors and editors as part of the magazine's archives. Each intern is also assigned to a staff editor/fact-checker to help with library research and fact-checking and will serve as backup for switchboard operators. You also may be asked to send faxes and photocopies of articles requested by the public and the media.

But you'll also get an education. During each session, editors, writers and members of the production and art departments give informal seminars for all the *Atlantic Monthly* interns, along with a unique opportunity to be involved in many aspects of the magazine's editorial procedures.

Three intern sessions a year offer positions for a maximum of seven interns per session.

HOW TO APPLY

If you're interested in interning here, send a resume and cover letter to the preceding address. The *Atlantic Monthly* will then send you a short story to comment on, which lets the editors assess your ability to read and report on a piece of fiction. This also introduces the primary task of the job. Interns uphold a tradition established by the magazine's founding editors: Every manuscript submitted receives the attention of a first reader. The magazine does not accept applications by fax or e-mail.

ATLANTIC MONTHLY WEB SITE CONTENT INTERNSHIP

The Atlantic Monthly
77 North Washington Street
Boston, MA 02114
http://www.theatlantic.com

What You Can Earn: Unpaid; Boston subway system passes available; one-year subscription to the magazine; college credit given.
Application Deadlines: July deadline for fall session (September through December); December 1 deadline for spring session (January through May); March 15 deadline for summer session (June through August); deadlines may be moved up if there are a large number of applications, so let the magazine know of your interest as early as you can.

Educational Experience: College juniors and seniors and recent graduates of all ages.
Requirements: Ability to work a consistent 16 hours a week.

OVERVIEW

The *Atlantic Monthly's* Web site internship offers a broad introduction to the publishing industry. As an intern here, you'll work closely with the Web site staff in producing *The Atlantic Online*. Editors, writers, and members of the production and art departments also will occasionally give informal seminars.

The standard responsibilities in the Web site internship are to research, compile, and write an introduction for a "Flashbacks" feature for online publication. You'll also help code magazine articles in HTML in preparation for publishing articles on the Web site and help editors fact-check, proofread, and complete research projects. You'll also help analyze the Web site and construct creative ideas for new features and prepare mailings to promote selected features in online editions to members of the media. Finally, you may be asked to perform office-support tasks such as faxing, filing, answering phones, and helping with monthly billings.

HOW TO APPLY

To apply, please send a resume and cover letter to the preceding address. The magazine does not accept applications by fax or e-mail.

AUDUBON INTERNSHIP

Audubon
700 Broadway
New York, NY 10003
kkloor@audubon.org
http://magazine.audubon.org/jobs/applications/
    editorial.html

What You Can Earn: $800 for two-day a week fall and spring sessions; $1600 stipend for four-day week session in summer.
Application Deadlines: December 31.
Educational Experience: Upper-level college undergraduate or graduate students.
Requirements: Some reporting and writing experience and a demonstrated interest in journalism and the environment.

OVERVIEW

Audubon, the magazine of the National Audubon Society, is a bimonthly publication with a circulation of nearly 500,000 dedicated to helping readers appreciate, understand, and protect the natural world, with a particular focus on birds, other wildlife, and their habitats.

Audubon uses interns throughout the year in one of three 13 week-sessions. If you're chosen as an intern, you'll get the chance to work with several departments while learning about magazine publishing and the environment. In addition to some clerical duties (opening and sorting mail, copying, filing, and so on), you may be involved with copyediting and copy flow, inputting copy and research changes, creating and circulating galleys, and general editorial work such as responding to reader or writer queries, responding to manuscript submissions, or researching story ideas for writers. You also may get a chance to write for the *Audubon in Action* department of the magazine.

For the fall (September through December) and spring (January through April) sessions, you'll be required to work at least two days a week for 13 weeks; during the summer session (late May through August), you must work four days a week.

HOW TO APPLY

If you're interested in this internship, send a cover letter, clips, application, and resume to the preceding address.

AUSTIN AMERICAN-STATESMAN INTERNSHIP

Austin American-Statesman Internship Coordinator
305 South Congress Avenue
Austin, TX 78704
512-445-3661
dmarcks@statesman.com
http://www.statesman.com

What You Can Earn: $437 a week plus apartment-style housing at the local St. Edward's University.
Application Deadlines: November 4 for summer session.
Educational Experience: You should be a college junior or senior. You don't have to be a journalism major, but college newspaper experience or a previous internship is a plus, as is a good academic record.
Requirements: Car and driver's license are required. You should have a strong desire to be a newspaper journalist, and work samples that show talent and promise.

OVERVIEW

The *American-Statesman* is an award-winning daily in the capital of Texas, serving a metro area of more than 1.2 million people. The paper strives to provide a comprehensive newspaper with a focus on issues that affect Austin and central Texas.

Eight internships are available in copyediting, reporting, graphics, online, and photography. These interns do news reporting, feature writing, copyediting, online content, photography, graphics, page design, and editorial page writing. Interns do the same work as full-time journalists.

HOW TO APPLY

Send to the above address a resume, a two- or three-page autobiography talking about you and your interest in newspaper journalism, and a cover letter. You also should include an appropriate sampling of your work (clips, headline samples, photo slides, copies of graphics or pages you've designed); and the names of at least two references with phone numbers.

BALTIMORE SUN TWO-YEAR INTERNSHIP

Internship Coordinator
The Baltimore Sun
501 N. Calvert Street
Baltimore, MD 21278
http://www.sunspot.net

What You Can Earn: $631 a week in first year; $781 a week in second year; group medical, dental, and life insurance coverage; vacations, holidays, and sick pay.
Application Deadlines: November 30.
Educational Experience: Senior journalism, English, or writing students who will complete undergraduate degrees by the spring.
Requirements: Candidates must be committed to a career in print journalism. Most finalists have already completed two internships at daily newspapers.

OVERVIEW

The *Baltimore Sun* is Maryland's most trusted daily newspaper, with a more than 160-year history of serving its readers and a circulation of almost 500,000 readers.

This unusual entry-level program offers full benefits for journalism interns, along with feedback from supervisors and the editors of the newspaper, advice from graduates who have joined the staff, and a mentor to help you navigate your first year.

HOW TO APPLY

To apply, send a cover letter, resume, names, and telephone numbers of three references and up to 12 work samples to the preceding address.

BANGOR DAILY NEWS INTERNSHIP

Bangor Daily News
491 Main Street
PO Box 1329
Bangor ME 04402-1329
(207) 990-8000
http://www.bangornews.com

What You Can Earn: $9.75 an hour.
Application Deadlines: December 31.
Educational Experience: Undergraduate or graduate students in English, journalism, or communications.
Requirements: None specified. The University of Maine Student Service Office may be able to help you find accommodations.

OVERVIEW

The *Bangor Daily News* offers a summer college internship program that provides realistic experience in news gathering and writing. You'll get a chance to work directly with assignment editors, cover spot news and features, and research and find your own feature stories.

The *Bangor Daily News* area ranges from mid-coast Maine towns as far south as Damariscotta and north to the Canadian border. Bureaus in Fort Kent, Madawaska, Presque Isle, Calais, Machias, Ellsworth, Augusta, Pittsfield, Fairfield, Belfast, and Rockland bring local news of business, the arts, community, and politics. In particular, interns often cover features on anything from symphony orchestras, ballet, or visual-art exhibits in the scores of art galleries along the Maine coast and in central Maine. Located near the University of Maine Orono campus, the paper is also within easy driving distance to Camden and Rockport, where community theaters and other art groups are very active.

HOW TO APPLY

Send a resume and cover letter to the preceding address.

BLETHEN MAINE NEWSPAPERS MINORITY SUMMER INTERNSHIP

Blethen Maine Newspapers Minority Summer Internship Program
c/o Eric Blom
Portland Press Herald
390 Congress St.
Portland, ME 04101

What You Can Earn: Undisclosed stipend.
Application Deadlines: Early March.
Educational Experience: Bachelor or graduate-level college students, as well as recent college graduates.
Requirements: Must be an entry-level journalist of minority ethnic or racial descent in any discipline; writers, copy editors, photographers, graphic artists, and other journalists may apply.

OVERVIEW

Blethen Maine Newspapers, which is part of the Seattle Times Co., is the largest newspaper company in Maine. This 12-week program gives entry-level journalists of minority ethnic or racial descent some valuable daily newsroom experience

at Maine's largest newspaper. Intern work as members of the staff, only with more coaching.

HOW TO APPLY

Send a resume, cover letter, and a half-dozen samples of your work to the preceding address.

BOSTON GLOBE INTERNSHIP

The Boston Globe, Newsroom
PO Box 55819
Boston, MA 02205
(617) 929-3212
http://www.bostonglobe.com/newsintern

What You Can Earn: $580 a week.
Application Deadlines: November 1.
Educational Experience: Not limited to journalism majors, but interns should have an interest in newspapers.
Requirements: A driver's license and typing speed of at least 30 words a minute.

OVERVIEW

The largest newspaper in New England, the *Boston Globe* offers an editorial summer internship program for college students interested in journalism. The internship began more than 45 years ago as an opportunity for college students interested in journalism to gain practical experience on a major newspaper.

A number of interns work as general-assignment reporters on the metropolitan staff; others are assigned to sports, living/arts, business, and the Washington bureau. Intern positions also are available in the photography and graphics departments and on the copy desk. A health/science position is provided through the Kaiser Foundation.

An aptitude for newspaper work is the most important qualification for the internship; although interns don't have to be journalism majors, most interns have worked on a student newspaper and have had at least one previous internship at a daily newspaper.

Summer interns work as full-time employees for 12 weeks, between Memorial Day and Labor Day. An intern supervisor serves as a writing coach, and there are weekly meetings with editors and staff members on a range of issues and topics pertaining to journalism.

Members of minority groups and candidates with unusual cultural backgrounds are strongly encouraged to apply.

HOW TO APPLY

Download an application at the preceding address; submit this with a resume, clips, and cover letter explaining how your background and experience qualifies you for the program. Finalists will be asked to come to the *Globe* for an interview.

CBS NEWS INTERNSHIP

Director, Internship Program
CBS News
524 West 57th Street
New York, NY 10019
internships@cbsnews.com
http://www.cbsnews.com/stories/2004/04/26/
broadcasts/main613839.shtml

What You Can Earn: Unpaid but college credit is given.
Application Deadlines: February 28 for the summer internship.
Educational Experience: Must currently be attending an accredited college and entering your junior or senior year. Eligible majors include journalism, broadcasting, communications, public relations, marketing, advertising, English, history, international studies, political science, and computer science.
Requirements: Basic computer skills; excellent written and oral communication skills; minimum 3.0 GPA; must receive college credit for internship. See specific requirements for specific positions listed below.

OVERVIEW

Internships are available in New York, Washington, D.C., Los Angeles, London, and Tokyo for the following shows: "CBS Evening News," "60 Minutes; 60 Minutes II," "48 Hours Investigates," "The Early Show," "The Saturday Early Show," "Sunday Morning," "Face the Nation," "BET Nightly News," and "Up to the Minute." Internships are also available in news and production companies, radio news, press office, advertising/promotions, broadcast marketing, and the political unit.

Internships on CBS Shows
BET Nightly News
This newscast addresses topics that are important to people of color. "BET Nightly News" is produced by CBS News and has an editorial responsibility to Black Entertainment Television. There is a diverse staff that produces a 30-minute weeknight newscast whose mission is for the show to cover "our world, our culture, and our issues." Although the "BET Nightly News" is targeted to people of color, the objective is to give a real sense of the news of the day and news from an African-American perspective to all viewers who tune into the broadcast.

Interns should have a strong sense of social commitment, with a sense of "community" and who want to learn how to produce a niche broadcast while bringing a broad base of journalistic excellence into the product. Intern should have strong written and oral communication skills. Research and computer skills are a must.

CBS Evening News
This broadcast covers news reports, features, and interviews by CBS News correspondents cover-

ing events throughout the world. "CBS Evening News" includes "CBS Evening News with Bob Schieffer," "CBS Evening News," "Saturday Edition," and "CBS Evening News with John Roberts." Weekday evenings, interim anchor Bob Schieffer heads the team of correspondents. Schieffer has covered Washington for CBS News for more than 30 years. He also serves as anchor and moderator of "Face The Nation," the CBS News Sunday public affairs broadcast. The team of "CBS Evening News" correspondents are John Roberts at the White House; Jim Stewart covering the Justice Department; David Martin, who covers national security; and Anthony Mason and Byron Pitts in New York. "Saturday Edition" is co-anchored by Russ Mitchell and Thalia Assuras. "CBS Evening News with John Roberts" continues on Sundays with daily coverage of events by CBS News correspondents. Each week, the "Sunday Cover" segment takes an in-depth look at an issue of national importance. John Roberts became the anchor of the broadcast in 1995. He also is the chief White House correspondent for CBS News.

Interns must have strong research and computer skills and knowledge of Lexis-Nexis. They also must be able to work the phone with contacts and sources, make affiliate calls, and do light clerical work.

CBS Evening News Weekend Editions

This broadcast features reports and interviews by CBS News correspondents covering events, trends, and issues around the world.

Interns must have a strong self-motivated desire to be part of that news team and be willing to contribute to the final product. After demonstrating their journalistic talents, interns will be given a chance to co-produce stories for the broadcast. Common sense is required, as are strong research and phone skills.

The Early Show

This is a hard-news daily broadcast with breaking news reports and regular feature segments that cover business and personal finance, con-

sumer affairs, entertainment, home improvement, lifestyle, and health. Anchors for *The Early Show* include Julie Chen, Harry Smith, Hannah Storm, and Renee Styler.

Interns must be organized and have strong interpersonal skills. Computer skills are helpful.

Face the Nation

One of the longest-running news programs in the history of television, this show premiered on CBS on November 7, 1954. Each Sunday, CBS News Chief Washington Correspondent Bob Schieffer interviews newsmakers on the latest issues. The program broadcasts Sunday mornings from Washington, D.C., where Schieffer has spent more than 25 years covering government and politics.

Guests include government leaders, politicians, and international figures in the news. CBS News correspondents engage the guests in a lively round-table discussion focusing on current topics.

The intern assists with gathering research and videotape and works with producers in the control room on the day of air. Candidates should be well organized, efficient, and have good editorial judgment.

48 Hours Investigates

This CBS News magazine goes behind the headlines to investigate baffling crimes, heartless scams, and compelling real-life dramas. In its unique approach, "48 Hours" delves into a single subject, examining it from multiple angles with saturation coverage and action-driven style. The broadcast has received 19 Emmy awards, a George Foster Peabody Award, and an Ohio State Award.

Interns must be organized, efficient with their time, and aggressive. Computer skills and proficiency with Lexis-Nexis are required, and strong interpersonal skills recommended.

The Saturday Early Show

This live Saturday morning program of news and features made its debut as the CBS News "Saturday Morning" in September 1997. "The Saturday Early Show" broadcasts from the GM building on

New York's Fifth Avenue, right across the street from Central Park, covering breaking news and the news of the week. The show also presents special reports from well-known experts on a wide range of subjects from consumer and health issues to personal finance. Anchors are Russ Mitchell and Tracy Smith.

Interns must be organized and have strong interpersonal skills. Computer skills are helpful.

60 Minutes

The flagship CBS News magazine provides a blend of investigative reports, interviews, feature segments and profiles of people in the news. The most successful broadcast in television history, it's been rated the number one program five times and finished in Nielsen's top 10 programs 23 consecutive seasons—something no other program has ever done. It still remains among Nielsen's top 20 programs and finished the 2004–05 season as the number one–rated news magazine. Correspondents include Ed Bradley, Steve Kroft, Lara Logan, Scott Pelley, Andy Rooney, Morley Safer, Bob Simon, Lesley Stahl, Dan Rather, and Mike Wallace. Since the program was created in 1968, "60 Minutes" has won more Emmy Awards than any other news program—a total of 77, including the Lifetime Achievement Emmy given to Hewitt and the correspondents in 2003. The program has also won virtually every other broadcast journalism award, plus 11 Peabody Awards for exceptional television broadcasting.

Interns here must have strong research skills, with knowledge in computers and Lexis-Nexis a must.

Sunday Morning

This special news broadcast show reviews events of the preceding week, celebrating human accomplishments and achievements and journeying through the world of fine art, music, nature, sports, science, and Americana. This special feature program on Sunday mornings is anchored by Charles Osgood, who has held the position since 1994.

Interns should be organized, have strong interpersonal skills, and basic computer knowledge.

Up to the Minute

CBS's overnight news broadcast offers very late workers, very early workers, insomniacs, and anyone else in the growing Monday-through-Friday overnight audience a unique combination of hard news, news features, interviews, weather, sports, business, and commentary. The show draws from the full resources of CBS News, including the "CBS Evening News," affiliate stations, the CBS Radio Network, CBS "Marketwatch," and Reuters Television.

Internships in CBS Departments and Production Companies

Advertising and Promotion

This unit produces the advertising and promotions for all news broadcasts, which includes television, radio, and print promos, as well as affiliate sales tapes.

Interns should be interested in television and film production and have some technical background. Computer skills are helpful.

Broadcast Marketing

This unit deals with all of the CBS News' broadcasts and acts as a liaison between CBS News and all CBS affiliates.

An intern assigned to this unit must have a great phone manner and be able to juggle several projects at one time. The ideal candidate must be interested in marketing and production and have some sales ability. Depending on skills, an intern will have an opportunity to learn how to book and produce satellite tours and edit excerpts and promos for affiliate use. At the same time, the candidate must be a self-starter, patient, capable of handling various clerical assignments, and must enjoy being a team player. There is a certain amount of typing, research, and photocopying. The Intern should have skills in marketing, enjoy writing, and not be averse to pitching in where needed.

Los Angeles, London, and Tokyo Bureaus

Interns for the Los Angeles bureau are hired as needed. The London and Tokyo bureaus hire only one to two students per semester. Students interested in the Tokyo bureau must be fluent in Japanese.

Interns in these bureaus help the staff with the daily duties and functions of the particular bureau. Intern must have strong written and oral communication skills, computer knowledge, and excellent research skills.

News Productions

This is the production company within CBS News that creates and distributes a diverse mix of original nonfiction and reality-style programming for domestic and international markets, including network and cable television, home video, DVD, audio books and in-flight, as well as schools and libraries. CBS News Productions and CBS Eye Too Productions produce programs across a wide spectrum of genres, from history to science to entertainment.

Interns in this department should understand how to log tapes and have research experience and general administrative duties. Interns must have computer skills as well as strong interpersonal skills.

Newspath

This unit is responsible for feeding footage to CBS stations and affiliates. This 24-hour-a-day news service feeds national and international news, weather, sports, medicine and health reports, business and consumer news and a broad range of feature stories from around the world.

Interns in this department should have strong written and oral communication skills.

Political Unit

Based in Washington, D.C., this department contributes political stories to CBS News broadcasts. Interns must have computer skills, excellent phone manners and oral skills, and must be up-to-date on current political news.

Press Office

The press office serves as the liaison between CBS News broadcasts/talent and the media. The department is responsible for publicizing each of the national news broadcasts. An internship with the press office is an opportunity to experience public relations in a fast-paced, professional environment.

Interns here must be well organized and have excellent written and oral communication skills. Computer experience is a must.

Radio News

CBS Radio serves radio stations with hourly newscasts, instant coverage of breaking stories, special reports, updates, features, customized reports, and news feed material.

Interns here should be interested in broadcast journalism (especially radio), and should have basic knowledge of computers. Interns should also be self-starters with a fundamental concept of reporting and research.

Web Site

This department is responsible for producing the CBSNews.com Web site. Students should have an interest in either online journalism, Web design, or Web development. HTML, news writing, and/or Adobe Photoshop experience is a plus. Journalism students will help write and produce stories; design students will assist in graphic design for the site.

HOW TO APPLY

If you're interested in this internship, mail the following materials to internships@cbsnews.com:

- resume
- two letters of recommendation
- a letter from your university guaranteeing you credit for this internship
- a school transcript
- a two-page essay on a topic of your choice

CBS will review all applications and will contact qualified applicants for an interview. CBS will not respond to questions about application status.

CHARLOTTE OBSERVER INTERNSHIP

Intern Coordinator, The Charlotte Observer
PO Box 30308
Charlotte, NC 28230
(704) 358-5048
http://www.charlotteobserver.com

What You Can Earn: $500 a week; reporting and photography interns receive an auto allowance.
Application Deadlines: December 1.
Educational Experience: Seniors, although occasionally recent graduates are chosen; a journalism major is not required.
Requirements: A reliable car is mandatory for reporters and photographers; experience working for a college newspaper; at least one previous newspaper internship. Must also pass a drug test.

OVERVIEW

The *Observer* is the largest newspaper in the Carolinas, whose staff includes 260 newsroom positions and whose internship salaries are competitive with other medium-sized newspapers in the Southeast. If you land an internship here, you'll be assigned to one of the following departments: city desk, features, photography, business news, or a regional news bureau.

As part of the intern program, you'll be expected to participate in weekly seminars, where experienced reporters and editors talk about such topics as interviewing, writing techniques, graphics, libel law, and researching public documents. The editors expect you to function as beginning professionals, going out on stories or photo assignments that can be published immediately.

HOW TO APPLY

To apply, submit a cover letter, resume, five clips, and a one-page autobiography. Decisions are made by February.

CHICAGO SUN-TIMES MINORITY SCHOLARSHIP AND INTERNSHIP PROGRAM

Chicago Sun-Times
401 N. Wabash Ave.
Chicago, IL 60611

What You Can Earn: $1500 scholarship paid to your college, plus stipend.
Application Deadlines: December 15; notification is May 15.
Educational Experience: Must have an interest in newspaper reporting, editing, graphics, or photography.
Requirements: Minority college students and recent college graduates who graduated from a Chicago-area high school or have been a resident of the Chicago area for the past five years.

OVERVIEW

Selected applicants receive a 12-week paid summer internship and a $1,500 scholarship payable to their schools.

HOW TO APPLY

To apply, send a comprehensive resume (include name, social security number, phone numbers, address, education information, extracurricular activities/interests, honors, and job history), two letters of recommendations, a 500-word biographical essay on why you want to become a journalist, and writing, editing, or photography samples to the preceding address.

CHICAGO TRIBUNE INTERNSHIP

Senior Editor for Recruitment
Chicago Tribune
435 N. Michigan Avenue
Chicago, IL 60611
http://www.chicagotribune.com

What You Can Earn: $567 a week.
Application Deadlines: November 1.
Educational Experience: College juniors, seniors, and graduate students.
Requirements: Tough, aggressive, professional reporting abilities.

OVERVIEW

The legendary *Chicago Tribune*, founded in 1847, was led for most of its first 50 years by the outstanding journalist and publisher Joseph Medill. The Tribune Company began to expand its operations into other media in the 20th century, launching its first radio venture in 1924 and entering television in 1948. Today, the Tribune Company has a TV station in nearly every major market. On the print side, its newspapers include the *Baltimore Sun*, the *Hartford Courant*, and New York's *Newsday*.

Internships are vital for journalism students who might one day want to work full time at the *Tribune*, a job that can require anywhere from three to seven years of minimum previous work experience. If you're a recent college graduate, and you apply for a job as a reporter via the company's human resources department, you'll probably get a rejection letter in a few days. Insiders at the *Chicago Tribune* say no one in editorial

is hired straight out of college. Instead, having a couple of internships under your belt is the way to go. After interning at the *Tribune*, interns have access to jobs posted in-house and can use their contacts to network and find out about potential openings.

The 12-week internship program seeks students who thrive in a "sink or swim" professional atmosphere where the emphasis is on doing, not teaching. Applicants must have at least one previous internship at a daily newspaper other than college. We set the same high performance standards for interns as we do for our regular staff members. Make-work, trivial intern assignments do not exist here. *Tribune* interns must be able to cover major stories their first few days on the job.

HOW TO APPLY

You should send a cover letter, resume, 15 to 20 clips, and the names of at least two professional and one school reference to the preceding address.

CHRONICLE OF HIGHER EDUCATION INTERNSHIP

Senior Editor for Copy
The Chronicle of Higher Education
1255 23rd Street, N.W.
Washington, D.C. 20037
(202) 466-1017
Fax: (202) 452-1033
http://chronicle.com/help/staff/intern.htm

What You Can Earn: $475 a week, plus academic credit.
Application Deadlines: Mid-March.
Educational Experience: None specified.
Requirements: Strong reporting and writing skills and the ability to work independently; must have experience writing for publication, whether at a student newspaper or professional publication.

OVERVIEW

The *Chronicle* is an award-winning, independent, weekly national newspaper with a Web site updated daily. Full-time editorial internships in the Washington, D.C., office last from winter through spring, running from January to May. Here, you'll be involved in reporting, writing, research, fact-checking, and proofreading, with the opportunity to produce plenty of bylined articles. Your primary responsibilities are reporting and writing brief features for the "Short Subjects" section and daily news articles for the Web site (which usually appear subsequently in print). Other opportunities include writing short features for the various sections of the paper and doing research for special projects. There is some grunt work, but not much. If you prove yourself as a reporter and writer, you'll often be asked to write full-length features.

The Chronicle places a premium on reporting that is accurate and writing that shines. All writing, including that done by staff reporters, is carefully edited. Interns typically leave with a set of strong, varied clips.

HOW TO APPLY

If you're interested in this internship, send a resume, cover letter, and five impressive clips to the preceding address. (No phone calls.)

CLEVELAND PLAIN DEALER INTERNSHIP

Recruitment and Development Editor
The Plain Dealer
1801 Superior Avenue
Cleveland, OH 44114
(216) 999-4800
http://www.cleveland.com

What You Can Earn: $675 a week.
Application Deadlines: December 1.

Educational Experience: College juniors, seniors, and graduate students, including May graduates.
Requirements: Vigor, intelligence, ambition, curiosity.

OVERVIEW

The *Plain Dealer,* Ohio's largest newspaper, typically hires 16 interns each summer to work in the newsroom. An enthusiastic supporter of the internship program, the *Plain Dealer* offers internships in every corner of the newsroom: metro, features, business, sports, photo, graphics, and the copy desk. If you're good and want to get better, if you want to work alongside and learn from some of the best journalists in the country, gather up your best clips or artwork and apply for one of these positions.

Plain Dealer interns are treated like professionals, earning a wide range of assignments, with lots of opportunities to cover significant stories and get your work on the front page. What's more, you're paid like a professional, earning the entry-level Guild scale.

Although you'll be treated like an entering professional, the *Plain Dealer* also realizes you're there to learn, so you'll be assigned a personal mentor, and staff members throughout the newsroom are instructed to share their knowledge and experience with you.

HOW TO APPLY

To apply for an internship, submit a copy of your resume (including three references), a one-page autobiography, and 10 samples of your work to the preceding address.

CNN NEWS INTERNSHIP

CNN News Producer
637 Washington Street
Suite 208
Brookline, MA 02446
(617) 264-9905

CNN News Internship Coordinator
435 N. Michigan Avenue, Suite 715
Chicago, IL 60611
(312) 645-8555

CNN News Internship Coordinator, Human Resources
6430 Sunset Boulevard
Suite 300
Los Angeles, California 90028
(323) 993-5256
Fax: (323) 993-5256

CNN News Internship Coordinator
12000 Biscayne Boulevard
Suite 101
North Miami, Florida 33181
(305) 892-5155

CNN News Coordinator
1 Time Warner Center
4th Floor
New York, NY 10019-8012
(212) 275-7877

CNN News Internship Coordinator
50 California Street, Suite 950
San Francisco, California 94111
(415) 438-5000
http://www.cnnsf.com/sfbureau/internships/
internships.html

CNN News Human Resources
820 First Street, NE
Washington, DC 20002
(202) 898-7900
dcinternships@cnn.com

What You Can Earn: Unpaid; public transit passes may be provided.
Application Deadlines: Apply online from November 1 to December 31 for winter internship (January through May); apply online from February 14 to May 20 for summer internship (June through August); apply online from April 4 to July 29 for fall internship (August through December).

Educational Experience: College junior, senior, or graduate students (students must still be enrolled in school during the time of the internships).
Requirements: Strong academic record, good character, and course credit.

OVERVIEW
As a CNN intern, you'll be exposed to how a worldwide news network operates, helping with story planning, script writing, editing, live shots, and satellite feeds. Although an internship with CNN is not an assurance of placement with CNN, many CNN interns have progressed to positions in the broadcast news industry. CNN interns are involved in virtually every aspect of the news-gathering process, scanning wire services, newspapers, incoming mail, and telephone calls; making calls; developing information for stories; sometimes conducting interviews for camera; and helping reporters and producers with background information. Interns also help with office work, screening calls, story and script filing. Interns occasionally accompany reporters and camera crews on breaking news and feature stories.

HOW TO APPLY
To apply for an internship in the Atlanta office, you should create a candidate profile on http://turnerjobs.com and submit your resume by clicking on the "Search for Jobs" logo. You'll be directed to the "Time Warner careers" Web site; select "Turner Broadcasting System" as the Time Warner division and "Intern" as the position type to view intern opportunities.

You may submit your resume and cover letter online, along with a list of three references with contact information.

CNN cannot respond to application-status inquires. You will be contacted for an interview if you are being considered for a position in the internship program.

To apply for CNN internships outside Atlanta, send a resume and cover letter directly to the bureau contact listed previously.

COLUMBIA JOURNALISM REVIEW INTERNSHIP

Columbia Journalism Review
Internship Coordinator
Columbia University
207 Journalism Building
2950 Broadway
New York, New York 10027
http://www.cjr.org/internship

What You Can Earn: $8 an hour.
Application Deadlines: March 1.
Educational Experience: Undergraduates and recent graduates.
Requirements: An interest in magazine journalism generally and media criticism in particular.

OVERVIEW

The Columbia Journalism Review, affiliated with Columbia University's Graduate School of Journalism, is the country's foremost journal of media criticism. The magazine offers a summer internship from May through August for college students and graduate students interested in journalism.

On this magazine, your duties would include reporting, research, fact-checking, some writing, and administrative tasks. Ideally, interns will be able to work 20 hours a week at the office on the campus of Columbia University.

The internship program, which began in 1981, has graduated a number of well-known journalists, including Laurence Zuckerman, business writer for *The New York Times*, and Andy Court, editor of *American Lawyer*.

HOW TO APPLY

If you're interested, send your resume with a cover letter, the names and numbers of two references, and three writing samples (clips preferred) to the preceding address. For more information, call (212) 854-9768

C-SPAN TV (WASHINGTON, D.C.) INTERNSHIP

C-SPAN
Human Resources Senior Specialist
400 North Capitol Street, NW-Suite 650
Washington, DC 20001
Phone: 202-626-4868
http://www.c-span.org

What You Can Earn: Unpaid.
Application Deadlines: Rolling.
Educational Experience: Journalism, English, broadcast engineering, or photography preferred, but any major is considered.
Requirements: Must receive college credit for this intern experience.

OVERVIEW

C-SPAN (the Cable Satellite Public Affairs Network) provides live, gavel-to-gavel coverage of the U.S. Senate and House of Representatives. C-SPAN's programming also includes in-depth coverage of the federal government's executive and judicial branches, campaigns, and elections, and so on. C-SPAN offers internships for 15 undergraduate students during the fall, spring, and summer semesters.

C-SPAN interns arrive from colleges and universities all over the world, with majors ranging from political science and communications to marketing and American studies. Between one to four student interns work per department, providing an opportunity for a hands-on, real-life experience. Interns also have an opportunity to interact with interns from other departments.

The C-SPAN internship program tries to use the talents and education of students interested in communications and politics. During your internship, you'll become familiar with the workings of a cable television network and you'll get to watch the political process.

You'll help research, write, and help with production for a specific unit or department, which may include learning aspects of print and video production; technical, promotional, and public relations techniques; or program production. Depending on your interests, you can go to Capital Hill to do research; learn camera and technical requirements for field production; help in public relations and advertising; or help develop a daily schedule and coordinate elements for on-air production. Interns can learn about business and sales trends in the cable industry and take part in community outreach programs. Interns also can get involved in the development of online technology.

The departments that offer internships include marketing, programming, programming operations, new media, and C-SPAN Radio 90, tape library, and human resources.

C-SPAN Radio 90
Broadcasts a mix of daily programs similar in style to those found on the C-SPAN TV networks, including congressional hearings, speeches, debates, and forum discussions.

Engineering
Responsible for the overall technical quality of C-SPAN's products; works with other departments to purchase and repair technical equipment; tracks new technologies and recommends ways C-SPAN can use these technologies to improve its product.

Marketing
The marketing department consists of four units:

- Affiliate relations, which maintains carriage of C-SPAN networks among cable affiliates through affiliate promotions and relationships with cable contacts at the corporate level.
- Marketing communications, which targets key audiences with promotional and marketing efforts to extend the C-SPAN message, develops and promotes C-SPAN products, and conducts market research.
- Community relations, which helps secure carriage of C-SPAN networks by establishing and maintaining relationships.

- Media relations, responsible for providing C-SPAN programming and special-projects information to national local news outlets.

New Media
Develops and implements strategies in online services, audio products, and other developing technologies.

Programming
C-SPAN's Programming department researches, shoots, and produces the programming for the networks:

- **Book TV:** Every weekend, BOOK TV on C-SPAN2 explores the world of nonfiction books, including recently published biographies and historical works; older books that have had an impact on history, politics, or culture; books about current events or public policy issues; and historical fiction and nonfiction for young adults and children.
- **Field producers:** Develop programming ideas by researching specific areas of government, its history, and its processes, as well as coordinate logistical aspects required in production.
- **Program producers:** Develop specific live and taped public affairs programs that air on C-SPAN and C-SPAN2, including Washington Journal, America and the Courts, and campaigns and debates during an election year.

Programming Operations
This department is responsible for getting C-SPAN's product on the air and includes editorial and technical staff members who work closely together to ensure quality, balanced programming.

- **Editorial:** Develops the daily schedule, tracks House and Senate floor debate, and coordinates elements for the final programming that airs on C-SPAN. Script writing, voice overs, and program scheduling breaks are some of the responsibilities of this unit.

- **Technical:** Works around the clock to handle the technical aspects of getting C-SPAN and C-SPAN2 on air 24 hours a day, including program direction, master control, camera operation, lighting and sound, editing, and on-air promotions.

HOW TO APPLY

If you're interested in media and politics and you're able to work at least 16 hours a week, send your resume and cover letter, stating which department(s) interests you, and specifying the spring, summer, or fall semester. Because cover letters and resumes are processed as the station receives them, you should plan ahead and submit your materials at the earliest possible date.

To apply, send a cover letter with your resume and details on the area and semester in which you're interested. Students can apply online at http://www.c-span.org. Click "About C-SPAN" and "Job Opportunities." For a list of current internship openings, visit http://www.recruitingcenter.net/clients/cspan/publicjobs/.

DALLAS MORNING NEWS INTERNSHIP

Deputy Managing Editor
The Dallas Morning News, Communications Center
PO Box 655237
Dallas, TX 75265
Telephone: (800) 431-0010

What You Can Earn: $535 a week; college credit is possible.
Application Deadlines: November 1; photography applications must be postmarked by January.

Educational Experience: Must be enrolled in college and working toward a degree or may have graduated six months before your start date.
Requirements: Previous daily newspaper experience is desirable. Dallas is extremely hot during the summer, with temperatures often above 100 degrees. Interns should have a car equipped with a working air conditioner. You'll need to pay for parking.

OVERVIEW

The *Dallas Morning News*, which published its first edition on October 1, 1885, is the nation's 10th-largest newspaper with a daily circulation of more than 500,000 and a Sunday circulation of more than 750,000. The paper is owned by Belo, a Dallas-based media company with holdings in newspaper, TV, cable TV, and interactive media industries.

With more than 2,000 employees and a network of foreign and domestic news bureaus, the paper has won journalism's highest honor — the Pulitzer Prize — in 1986, 1989, 1991, 1992, 1993, 1994, and 2004 for national reporting, explanatory journalism, feature photography, investigative reporting, spot news photography, international reporting, and breaking news photography, respectively.

The *Dallas Morning News* offers full-time internships for 10 to 12 weeks in summer, in a variety of areas, including the news, copyediting, business, features, and sports departments. Additional internships are available for photography, graphic arts, editorial writers, and the reference department.

Once you're accepted as an intern, every attempt will be made to give you assignments that match your skill level. You'll be expected to work in and for the departments to which you've been assigned unless you have prior approval from a supervisor to do otherwise. If you're selected, you will become part of the regular staff, with a standard newsroom workload, and your work will be judged by the same standards, including adhering to standard journalistic principles as well as professional decorum in areas of dress, promptness, and courtesy.

HOW TO APPLY

All applicants must send a cover letter, resume, one-page autobiography, and three telephone references. In addition to these, the following materials should be sent for specific positions:

- **Reporters:** Send seven to 10 newspaper clips, which must be photocopied onto 8 x 11 or 11 x 14 paper. Clips may be reduced but must be legible.
- **Copy Editors:** Send seven to 10 headline and editing samples. Clips should include notes explaining applicant's role in shaping the story for publication.
- **Photographers/Photo Editors:** Send a tightly edited portfolio showing a diversity of work (slides or CDs acceptable). Return of the original work cannot be guaranteed.
- **Graphic artists/Designers:** Send slides and photocopies of 10 to 20 work samples; samples may be reduced but must be legible. Return of original work can't be guaranteed.
- **Editorial writers:** Send seven to 10 newspaper clips. Editorial writing is preferred, but news stories and columns are accepted.

You'll be notified of your acceptance by telephone and/or letter by March.

DENVER POST REPORTING/ PHOTOGRAPHY INTERNSHIP

Internship Recruiter
The Denver Post
1560 Broadway
Denver, CO 80202
http://www.denverpost.com

What You Can Earn: $500 a week.
Application Deadlines: October 29.
Educational Experience: Rising college seniors and graduate students at an accredited college or university.
Requirements: Demonstrated interest in journalism (clips or portfolio) and previous internships and/or work on a college newspaper.

OVERVIEW

The No. 1 newspaper in the Rocky Mountain region, The *Denver Post* offers a full-time, 10-week internship for the summer in any part of the newsroom—as reporters, graphic designers, or photographers. The paper is looking for talented young people who want to make a difference. The paper also works with the Dow Jones Newspaper Fund to identify candidates for copyediting and a minority business reporting internship. However, you should apply directly to the Dow Jones Newspaper Fund for these positions.

HOW TO APPLY

If you're interested in an internship, send a cover letter outlining which position interests you most, a resume, and three references. If you're interested in reporting, include no more than five clips. Photography applicants should add a portfolio submitted on a CD encased in a CD envelope, rather than a plastic jewel case. Include a self-addressed, stamped envelope for return of the CD. Graphic artists may send portfolios of 8-1/2 x 11 photocopied designs, nonreturnable tearsheets, or CDs.

DES MOINES REGISTER INTERNSHIP

Des Moines Register Internship Coordinator
PO Box 957
Des Moines, IA 50304

515-284-8590
http://www.desmoinesregister.com

What You Can Earn: $440 a week.
Application Deadlines: November 15 for the summer session.
Educational Experience: College undergraduates (journalism major helpful).
Requirements: A car and a driver's license are required. While a previous internship is not required, it's a distinct advantage.

OVERVIEW

The *Des Moines Register,* published since 1849, employs about 1,100 people responsible for reporting and delivering the newspaper 365 days a year. Part of the Gannett Company, the paper offers internship opportunities in copyediting, reporting, and photography.

HOW TO APPLY

Send a resume, a cover letter and eight to 10 appropriate work samples for the position you seek.

DETROIT FREE PRESS INTERNSHIP

Recruiting & Development Editor
Detroit Free Press
600 W. Fort Street
Detroit, MI 48226
grimm@freepress.com
http://www.freep.com/jobspage/interns/fpintern.htm

What You Can Earn: $541 a week.
Application Deadlines: December 1.
Educational Experience: College undergraduates (journalism major helpful).
Requirements: None specified.

OVERVIEW

Free Press internships offers students a chance to work side by side with professional journalists, taking progressively more ambitious assignments while being supported by editors and professional partners. This two-week summer internship offers positions in copyediting, design, photography, sports writing, business writing, features and local news reporting, and editorial writing.

HOW TO APPLY

You must submit a resume, six clips (for writers, artists, designers) or 20 images (for photographers), along with a cover letter explaining how a *Free Press* internship can benefit you, a two-page professional essay describing your interest in journalism (including key influences and your plans) and the names of three references.

DOW JONES NEWSPAPER FUND MINORITY SUMMER INTERNSHIP

Dow Jones Newspaper Fund
PO Box 300
Princeton, NJ 08543-0300;
(609) 452-2820
Fax: (609) 520-5804
newsfund@wsj.dowjones.com
http://DJNewspaperFund.dowjones.com/fund/cs_internships.asp

What You Can Earn: $350 weekly stipend for a minimum of 10 weeks; interns who return to college full time the following fall will receive $1,000 scholarships.
Application Deadlines: November 1 for next summer's program; undergraduate and gradu-

ate students who will be enrolled in a fall semester are eligible to apply for the next summer's internships

Educational Experience: Professional and former professional journalists, even though attending college or graduate school, are not eligible for these programs.

Requirements: Must be a minority college sophomore or junior.

OVERVIEW

The Dow Jones Newspaper Fund offers annual summer internships for minority students in business reporting, newspaper copyediting, and sports copyediting, including free preinternship training seminars on college campuses.

Participating news organizations include the *Wall Street Journal*; the *Associated Press*; *Reno Gazette-Journal*; the *Star Tribune*; the *Columbus Dispatch*; the *Tennessean*; the *Denver Post*; *Houston Chronicle*, *Erie Times-News*; *San Jose Mercury News*; the *Rochester Democrat & Chronicle*; the *New York Times*; the *Washington Post*; *Detroit Free Press*; *Philadelphia Inquirer*; the *Hartford Courant*; *and* the *Standard-Times*.

If you land this internship, you'll cover business and consumer news at one of these daily newspapers or news services and attend a one-week training seminar at New York University's Department of Journalism and Mass Communication in Manhattan.

The fund also offers a Newspaper Copyediting Program for juniors, seniors, and graduate students who choose to work as news copy editors at daily newspapers. Those selected as newspaper editors attend the Centers for Editing Excellence at Temple University, Philadelphia, Pa.; Florida Southern College; Lakeland; University of Missouri; Columbia; San Jose State University; Pennsylvania State University; University of North Carolina at Chapel Hill; and University of Texas at Austin. Sports Copyediting Program interns, who will work on sports copy desks at daily newspapers, attend training

at the University of Nebraska at Lincoln. These seminars last two weeks.

HOW TO APPLY

You may apply for either or both programs, submitting an application, a resume, three to five recently published clips, a list of courses with grades, and a 500-word essay. A business reporting test should be completed no later than December 1. You should designate a professor to receive and administer the test on the application form. You also must take a one-hour copyediting exam, which will be mailed directly to a professor who will act as a monitor on your campus.

ENTERTAINMENT WEEKLY INTERNSHIP

Annabel Bentley, Director of Research Services
Entertainment Weekly
1675 Broadway
New York, NY 10019
(212) 522-1864
http://www.ew.com

What You Can Earn: $10 an hour.
Application Deadlines: Deadline February 15 for summer session (June through Aug); deadline June 1 for fall session (September through December); deadline October 15 for spring session (January through May).
Educational Experience: The summer program is open to rising junior and senior undergraduates, but because the commitment is full time, the fall and spring programs are open to students who have graduated within the past year only. Applicants are not required to study journalism or to have their school's endorsement.

Requirements: Strong writing skills, as well as interest and experience in writing about entertainment, are preferred.

OVERVIEW

Entertainment Weekly is owned by Time Inc. This weekly magazine is written for readers looking for the latest news, reviews, and updates in the entertainment world. It has a circulation of 1.6 million.

If you intern here, you'll do the usual beginner stuff: answer phones, make copies, send faxes, and so on. You'll also maintain databases of forthcoming events, answer reader mail, and do research for upcoming articles. If you're talented and assertive, you'll also probably snag opportunities to report and write stories.

You can expect to spend 35 hours a week for three months in the summer, four months in the fall, and five months in the spring.

HOW TO APPLY

To apply, send a cover letter, resume, and four or five clips or writing samples to the preceding address.

EUREKALERT! WEB SITE INTERNSHIP

EurekAlert! Project Director
American Association for the Advancement of
  Science
1200 New York Avenue NW
Washington, DC 20005
(202) 326-6213
Fax: (202) 898-0391
comalley@aaas.org
http://www.aaas.org/careercenter/internships/
  eurekalert.shtml

What You Can Earn: Modest stipend.
Application Deadlines: Rolling.
Educational Experience: Science, journalism, communications, or a related field.
Requirements: Strong computer skills, including familiarity with word processing programs and the Internet; excellent oral and written communication skills; knowledge of HTML preferred (not required, but applicants unfamiliar with HTML must be willing to learn).

OVERVIEW

This unique science writing internship is a Web-based project designed to link the scientific community with the media, sponsored by the office of public programs at the American Association for the Advancement of Science (AAAS). Since 1996, EurekAlert! (http://www.eurekalert.org) has provided scientific organizations with an effective way to distribute research news to reporters while giving journalists a central location in which to find news-story ideas. The Web site also archives these press releases and makes them available to the public in an easily retrievable system. As an online news service, EurekAlert! provides an inexpensive and effective way for subscribing organizations to distribute science-related press releases to the news media and the public. Subscribers include research institutions, universities, medical centers, government and private agencies, public relations firms, and corporations engaged in scientific research.

EurekAlert! is not a medical information Web site nor an online magazine. Like its sponsoring organization AAAS, it is devoted to the promotion of all sciences.

If you're selected as an EurekAlert! intern, you'll help with site maintenance and operations, formatting and posting press releases on the Web site, helping customers, performing general office tasks, helping proofread Web site articles, and helping with special projects. This four- to five-month internship includes flexible hours totaling between 30 to 40 hours per week.

HOW TO APPLY

To apply, send a cover letter and resume to the preceding address (through e-mail or regular mail).

FRESNO BEE INTERNSHIP

Senior Editor
The Fresno Bee
1626 E Street
Fresno, CA 93786
http://www.fresnobee.com

What You Can Earn: $450 a week.
Application Deadlines: December 1.
Educational Experience: Seniors in college, recent graduates, or students in master's programs.
Requirements: Daily journalism experience, either with a university publication or with a daily newspaper; Spanish-speaking skills are a plus.

OVERVIEW

The *Fresno Bee,* Central California's leading newspaper, typically has openings for four 12-week summer internships in news, business, features, and sports reporting, as well as photography and graphics.

The *Fresno Bee* was first published in 1922, and today it is Central California's leading newspaper, serving Fresno, Kings, Madera, Tulare, Mariposa, and Merced counties.

The *Bee,* which employs more than 800 people, tries to reflect the region's diversity in staff and coverage; the area is home to large populations of people of Hmong, Cambodian, Laotian, and Latin American heritage.

The *Bee* is owned by the McClatchy Company, which also owns newspapers in California (Atwater, Chowchilla, Clovis, Livingston, Los Banos, Merced, Modesto, Oakhurst and Sacramento),

Washington, Alaska, Minneapolis, Minnesota, and in North and South Carolina.

HOW TO APPLY

If you're interested in an internship, submit a resume to the preceding address. In addition, reporter candidates should submit clips; photography and graphics candidates should submit a portfolio.

HARPER'S INTERNSHIP

Ben Austen, Associate Editor
Harper's Magazine
666 Broadway, 11th Floor
New York, NY, 10012
austen@harpers.org

What You Can Earn: Unpaid.
Application Deadlines: February 15 for summer, June 15 for fall, and October 15 for spring.
Educational Experience: College graduates or graduate students; some use the program as an introduction to publishing after having pursued careers elsewhere. Work experience matters far less than how well you know *Harper's* and how much you have to contribute to the making of the magazine each month.
Requirements: None specified.

OVERVIEW

Harper's is an American journal of literature, politics, culture, and the arts, published continuously from 1850 and made famous by its sophistication and high-quality writing. Interns work here in the editorial department on a full-time basis for three to five months and receive practical experience in critical reading and analysis, research, factchecking, and the general workings of a national magazine. Each intern works closely with an editor on one section of the magazine, takes part in the creation of the *Harper's Index*, and is encouraged to read widely, generate ideas, and approach problems creatively.

You'll be assigned to help particular editors while participating in the more general tasks shared by all interns, such as researching the *Harper's Index* and reading unsolicited manuscripts. The range of responsibilities and level of challenge depend largely on your initiative and self-motivation. You're always welcome to suggest ideas and to generate material for any section of the magazine.

You'll be expected to work from 10:00 A.M. to 6:00 P.M. with an hour off for lunch. Some flexibility is possible and can be discussed in individual cases.

HOW TO APPLY

Applicants must complete a complex application prepared by *Harper's,* which requires strong familiarity with the magazine and gives prospective interns a sense of the actual duties involved in this placement. The application process weeds out all but very literate, culturally aware individuals with a passionate interest in publishing and an outstanding ability to express themselves in writing. Ability to generate ideas and sources for Harper's Index is critical.

If you're interested in this highly competitive program, you are invited to download the application as an RTF file, a format readable by most word processors, at http://www.harpers.org/Harpers Internships.html. You may also request that an application be mailed to you by calling (212) 420-5720.

HBO INTERNSHIP

Internship Program; Home Box Office
  H3-37A
1100 Sixth Avenue H3-33A
New York, NY 10036
(212) 512-1000

What You Can Earn: $500 stipend.
Application Deadlines: March 1 for summer, June 1 for fall, and November 1 for spring.
Educational Experience: College freshmen through seniors majoring in film or TV.
Requirements: Check requirements for individual HBO department internships.

OVERVIEW

Home Box Office (HBO) is America's oldest and most successful premium TV network. It is the largest pay-TV company, reaching more than 38.8 million subscribers with programming ranging from theatrical blockbusters, HBO Films presentations, innovative original series, provocative documentaries, concert events, and championship boxing. From its prestigious documentary division, HBO aired the Academy Award–winning Chernobyl Heart, examining the continuing impact of the worst nuclear accident in history. HBO's subscription video-on-demand products HBO On Demand and Cinemax On Demand expanded their reach in 2003 to a combined eight million subscribers.

At HBO, internships are available in a variety of departments, including original programming, marketing, production, media relations, finance, accounting, human resources, and film programming.

Creative Services (HBO Pictures, HBO NYC, Theatrical Movies)

In this department, you'll screen HBO movies, theatrical movies, press kits, trailers, clip reels, and so on, while you take extensive notes. In addition, you'll edit all of the preceding items for online and offline editing purposes. You may help book talent, studios, editing facilities, submit contracts, tape requests, and handle invoices and purchase orders for any/all projects in this group. You'll also handle responsibilities for doing print, library, and magazine research and other production-assistant responsibilities. Night work may be necessary at HBO studios.

Requirements include familiarity with Macintosh, Excel, typing, fax, e-mail, extensive longhand notes, duplicating video cassettes, preparing dubs, and operating in-house audio and video equipment for office use only.

East Coast Production

For this department, interns will help the production department make production arrangements for events such as World Championship Boxing or Wimbledon. Interns will work with many aspects of production and scheduling, answer phones, file, follow up on scheduling, invoicing, and so on. Interns also will have chances to go on studio shoots and local remotes. Introductory TV classes would be helpful but aren't required; interns do need good computer, letter writing, and communication skills.

Film Programming

In this department, you'll prepare Microsoft Excel charts of availabilities for international territories and research key title statistics including cast, director, genre, box office, and ratings. You'll also screen titles, write evaluations, recommend selections for further evaluation, and research and write special reports about product sources, programming models, and so on. Requirements include ability to use Microsoft Word and Microsoft Excel (preferred) for Macintosh.

HBO en Espanol

You'll help in the administrative area, screening products, editing, and shooting. If you are capable, you'll be given the chance to handle independent and unsupervised projects. Requirements include the ability to read and write Spanish and English.

HBO NYC

Interns will assist in answering telephones for production executives and will deliver dailies and documents to various HBO departments. The intern will develop an active knowledge of the inner workings of production from a "studio" point

of view. Interns must be familiar with Microsoft Word, Excel, and Now up to Date for Macintosh; any other calendar-making software knowledge is a big plus.

HBO Sports

Interns will help in all phases of production of Inside the NFL, Wimbledon Tennis, World Championship Boxing, and other sports specials and documentaries. Interns will screen and log footage of all ENG shoots, researching and locating footage, assembling production books, and completing filling and other related production work. There will be an opportunity to observe edit sessions, audio sweetening, paintbox, chyron and infinit sessions. This internship is geared primarily toward college juniors, but sophomores are encouraged to apply also. This internship requires some TV production experience either at a local TV affiliate or college TV station. Knowledge of sports and an interest in TV sports production is preferable. Working knowledge of Macintosh would be helpful but is not mandatory.

Hobnobber

The intern will be doing research for long-running projects, writing features and brief articles and helping with limited clerical tasks. The ideal candidate will be interested in journalism and have strong writing skills; interest in Web site construction helpful. This internship requires experience in journalistic, expository, and professional writing. Intern must have some interviewing skills; some Microsoft Word, Quark, and Photoshop would be helpful but is not necessary.

Home Video

Interns will provide all types of support in two areas: kids/nature and video and special market/direct sales. This will involve both analytic and creative talents and will provide opportunity to learn video marketing from soup to nuts. Interns are required to have Macintosh, Word, and Excel computer skills. Sales experience of any kind a is plus.

Media Relations

Intern responsibilities include maintaining a library of newspaper clips and putting together a daily press digest for the media relations staff. Interns also will participate in departmental brainstorming sessions, staff meetings, and screenings.

For this job, interns need to have a strong interest in media and Macintosh/Word. Other interns in the media relations department will assemble press kits and clips for HBO sports events, coordinate conference calls and press conferences, and handle media inquiries. Intern also will work on all New York City-based press events. For this sports-related internship, students need good writing and phone skills, lots of sports knowledge, flexible hours, and familiarity with Macintosh.

Original Programming

In this department, interns will screen, write summaries of, and evaluate various taped documentary and news programs (such as "20/20" or "Sixty Minutes") each week. Interns also will screen, write summaries of, and evaluate documentaries submitted to HBO for possible acquisition. For this internship, students need good word-processing and writing skills, along with some experience in TV, film, and documentaries. Other interns in this department will help with research, filing, typing dubbing tapes, answering phones, and so on. Interns need to be familiar with Macintosh and be able to do a library search.

Special Projects

In this department, interns will help coordinate corporate contributions, maintain the awards display case, and schedule and set up Bryant Park Summer Film Festivals. Requirements include experience with Mac/Filemaker Pro and excellent writing and interpersonal skills.

HOW TO APPLY

If you're interested in an internship in any of these departments, send in only one copy of your cover letter and resume to the preceding address. Be sure to indicate in your cover letter all of the departments for which you'd be interested in interning, along with information about yourself, your education, relevant experience, and other information you think would be interesting.

KAISER MEDIA MINORITY INTERNSHIPS IN URBAN HEALTH REPORTING

Kaiser Media Fellowships Program
Kaiser Family Foundation
2400 Sand Hill Road
Menlo Park, CA 94025
Phone: (650) 854-9400
Fax: (650) 854-4800
pduckham@kff.org
http://www.kff.org

What You Can Earn: Travel to and from Washington, D.C., your internship city, and Boston. All training and accommodation expenses in D.C. and Boston are paid by the Kaiser Family Foundation. The foundation also provides a minimum $500 weekly stipend, but you are responsible for housing and other expenses during the 10 weeks spent working at your news organization.
Application Deadlines: Early December for print applications; early January for broadcast applications (check Web site for exact deadlines).
Educational Experience: Journalism or communications major.
Requirements: U.S. citizenship.

OVERVIEW

If the rising asthma rates among young inner-city youths or the risk of heart disease in black urban women concern you, you might be interested in the Kaiser Media Internships, a program established in 1994 offering an intensive 12-week summer internship for young minority journalists interested in specializing in urban public health reporting. In the program, 12 summer internships are offered by 11 major metropolitan newspapers and three TV stations to young minority journalists or journalism graduates interested in reporting on urban public health issues.

If you're one of the interns selected by the papers and TV stations, you'll attend a one-week briefing on urban public health issues and health reporting at the National Press Foundation in Washington, D.C., before beginning the internships. Briefing topics include major public health concerns such as AIDS, diabetes prevention, violence, smoking, healthcare provisions, and paying for healthcare. During the week, you'll meet a wide range of health policy experts, health providers, and senior health reporters and editors. Briefings and discussions focus on journalistic concerns and reporting techniques, with emphasis given to city-specific information about the different internship locations (for example, children's health programs in Chicago).

Then it's off for 10 weeks to your sponsoring newspaper or TV station, typically under the direction of the health or metro editor or news director, where you report on health issues. The program ends with a three-day meeting and site visits in Boston. Most interns, after 10 weeks, have a significant number of published clips or a professional tape with their own reporting on a wide range of public health topics.

This work is pooled, and in the final week you'll get together with other interns in Boston for more briefings and an intensive clip/tape critique session with leading health journalists.

HOW TO APPLY

There is no application form. Instead, you should submit a detailed letter describing your reasons for applying, including information about previous internships or newsroom work experience, any previous health reporting experience and/or college course work in health/science-related issues, along with expected graduation date and degree, and a contact mail or e-mail address. You should indicate if you wish to apply to a particular news organization and also include a resume, examples of recent work, and one or more letters of support.

Print applicants should send original clips or photocopies mounted on 8.5"x11" or 11"x17" paper. If clips are reduced in size to fit the page, they should be legible. For oversize work or series, you may submit an original in addition to the mounted copy. TV applicants should send transcripts, not tapes.

KFSK-SOUTHEAST ALASKA PUBLIC RADIO INTERNSHIP

KFSK-Southeast Alaska Public Radio
(907) 772-3808
kfsknews@pobox.alaska.net
http://www.kfsk.org

What You Can Earn: $100/week stipend, plus housing and roundtrip airfare from California to Petersburg, AK.

Application Deadlines: March 31.

Educational Experience: Experience or training as a public radio reporter/producer is a definite plus, as is live, on-air experience and knowledge of digital editing and broadcast software such as Cooledit and AudioVault.

Requirements: Excitement about being a reporter; an interest in Alaska; willingness to learn on the job; the ability to work independently; and strong interest in producing accurate, well-written stories on a regular basis. The applicant needs to work well with the public and genuinely care about how his or her work affects people.

OVERVIEW

KFSK Public Radio, a member of the CoastAlaska and Alaska Public Radio Networks, is seeking applicants for a two- to three-month summer internship at the radio station in Petersburg, AK. About 3200 people live in Petersburg, one of Alaska's major fishing ports. The community is located on Mitkof Island in the heart of the 17 million acre Tongass National Forest, about 100 miles south of Juneau. If you're the outdoorsy sort, interning in Petersburg could be a great experience for you, with its opportunities for hiking, watching whales and other wildlife, kayaking, and fishing, in one of the most beautiful environments on Earth.

As an intern here, you'll work full time as a reporter/producer, and you'll also host local news, weather, community announcements, and station breaks during NPR's morning edition. You'll cover a variety of topics, including regional and statewide natural resource issues such as fishing and logging; local, regional, and statewide politics; economics; cultural and social issues; education; crime and courts; healthcare; arts; and local/regional events. There are plenty of opportunities for features and natural sound pieces.

Intern stories may air regionally or statewide as well as on local news, since the news department is a frequent contributor to the Alaska Public Radio Network's statewide news programs as well as local news shows on other APRN and CoastAlaska stations in Juneau, Ketchikan, Wrangell, Sitka, and other communities. The station has two reporters (including the news director) who each work full time nine months of the year. Typically, just one is working in the summer, making the intern a critical part of the team.

HOW TO APPLY

E-mail a cover letter and resume to the preceding address. Indicate "Internship Applicant" in the subject line. References and Internet links to audio samples of your work are welcome but not required, unless you're contacted for an interview. Do not send audio attachments with your resume. You're welcome to e-mail or call with any questions (Matt Lichtenstein, Joe Viechnicki, or Tom Abbott) at the preceding address. They also can put you in touch with former interns if you're interested in asking them about the experience.

KNIGHT RIDDER INTERNSHIPS FOR NATIVE AMERICAN JOURNALISTS

Knight Ridder Native American Internship Coordinator
St. Paul Pioneer Press
345 Cedar Street
St. Paul, MN 55101
(651) 228-5454

What You Can Earn: $5,000 stipend.
Application Deadlines: Early January.
Educational Experience: Journalism or communications majors
Requirements: Internships open only to Native American college students.

OVERVIEW

Native American journalists are invited to apply for 10- to 12-week internships. Interns are placed in paid positions at Knight Ridder newspapers in the Midwest to pursue their career interests in reporting, writing, copyediting, design, and photography. Successful interns may be invited to return to a Knight Ridder newspaper for additional internships and may be considered for future employment. Participating newspapers are the *Aberdeen American News, Boulder Daily Camera, Duluth News-Tribune, Grand Forks Herald, St. Paul Pioneer Press,* and *Wichita Eagle.*

HOW TO APPLY

Submit an application to the preceding address.

KOCE PUBLIC TV (HUNTINGTON BEACH, CALIF.) INTERNSHIP

KOCE Public Television
Internship Coordinator
PO Box 2476
Huntington Beach, CA 92647-0476
(714) 895-5623
http://www.koce.org

What You Can Earn: Varies.
Application Deadlines: Open all three semesters.
Educational Experience: Journalism, English, broadcast engineering, and teaching/education.
Requirements: None specified.

OVERVIEW

KOCE is a nonprofit public TV station serving Orange County and Los Angeles and offers internships for undergraduate and graduate university students. At least five interns each semester are informally placed by division managers according to the station's needs and the particular skills of the applicant. Positions are available during fall, spring, and summer semesters in the following departments: on-air promotion, news reporting, production, programming, business, and engineering.

HOW TO APPLY

To apply for an internship, call the contact person in each division and get his or her e-mail address. You'll need to send a resume, cover letter, and references.

KPNX-TV (PHOENIX) INTERNSHIP

KPNX-TV
1101 North Central Avenue
Phoenix, AZ 85004
(602) 257-6508

What You Can Earn: Unpaid.
Application Deadlines: July for the fall semester, November for the spring semester, and April for the summer semester.
Educational Experience: College journalism majors preferred.
Requirements: Students must receive college credit for their experience.

OVERVIEW

KPNX-TV is a Gannett-owned, NBC-affiliated station that offers unpaid internships during fall, spring, and summer semesters for undergraduates and graduate students. Five interns work a season in three different areas at the station: promotions, community affairs, and the assignment desk.

HOW TO APPLY

To apply for an internship, send a cover letter, resume, references, and proof that you'll be able to receive college credit to the human resources manager at the preceding address.

KTTV-TV LOS ANGELES INTERNSHIP

Fox Television Stations Inc.
Human Resources Manager
KTTV Fox 11
1999 South Bundy Drive
Los Angeles, CA 90025
(310) 584-2280
acoll382@fox.com

What You Can Earn: Unpaid.
Application Deadlines: Rolling.
Educational Experience: Journalism, English, or broadcast engineering. Intern experience is preferred but not required; preference will be given to college juniors and seniors.
Requirements: For credit only, with authorization of your school.

OVERVIEW
KTTV Fox 11 is a local news station that offers 10 internships each semester for undergraduates or graduate students majoring in some type of journalism and interested in pursuing a career in the television industry, encouraging hands-on training as well as providing mentoring and feedback. The internship offers experiences in news, sports, promotions, research, community affairs, programming, human resources, and engineering.

Most internships require a 12- to 15-hour commitment per week; weekend hours are available for news and sports areas only.

HOW TO APPLY
To apply for an internship, send a cover letter, resume, and an application form to the station's human resources manager at the preceding address. Resumes will be reviewed as they are received, and eligible candidates will be contacted by phone to set up interview appointments.

LOS ANGELES TIMES INTERNSHIP

Los Angeles Times
Editorial Internship Director
202 W. 1st Street
Los Angeles, CA 90012.
(800) 283-NEWS, ext. 77992
randy.hagihara@latimes.com

What You Can Earn: $480 weekly.
Application Deadlines: December 1 for summer, June 1 for fall, and October 1 for spring.
Educational Experience: Undergraduates with journalism experience; recent graduates are eligible if they've finished school within six months of the start of the internship.
Requirements: A valid driver's license and access to a car in good working condition; interns must not have worked professionally as staff reporters.

OVERVIEW
If you've got a yen to cover the news in one of the country's most exciting cities, you may be interested in one of the *LA Times*' internships. Spots are available in one of the following areas: reporting, copyediting, photojournalism, graphics, and online systems. The program offers hands-on experience with little training provided, and business, sports, features, and arts/entertainment reporting internships are generally available. Positions are usually in the *LA Times*' daily news editions (Los Angeles, Orange County, Valley, and Ventura County) and the Washington, D.C., bureau.

HOW TO APPLY
To apply, submit a cover letter indicating that you're interested in the summer internship and which section of the paper you prefer, along with a one-page autobiography, a resume, a dozen pho-

tocopies of your work samples (all must be on 8 1/2 x 11 paper) and three references.

MARVEL COMICS INTERNSHIP

Marvel Enterprises Inc.
Internship Program Coordinator
10 East 40th Street
New York, NY 10016
internship@marvel.com

What You Can Earn: Unpaid.
Application Deadlines: Rolling.
Educational Experience: Must receive college credit for this internship.
Requirements: For specific requirements, see individual internships below.

OVERVIEW

With a library of over 4,700 proprietary characters, Marvel Enterprises Inc. is one of the world's most prominent character-based entertainment companies whose operations are focused in four areas: entertainment (Marvel Studios), licensing, publishing, and toys (Toy Biz).

Marvel's main job is to create entertainment projects, including feature films, DVD/home video, video games, and TV based on its characters, and it also licenses its characters for use in a wide range of consumer products and services including apparel, toys, collectibles, snack foods, and promotions.

Internships at Marvel run year-round on a semester-to-semester basis, in a variety of departments, including art returns; editorial; production; marvel interactive; creative services; sales and marketing; legal; accounting; manufacturing; scanning intern; Marvel Studios; or human resources.

Accounting

Interns are responsible for data entry, general filing, creating Excel spreadsheets for special projects, basic accounting, and verifying proper backup for travel and entertainment expenses.

Art Returns

In this department, you'll help organize and process the original artwork that needs to be returned to the artists and also do filing, mailings and deal with extensive paperwork. You'll also work in the Bound Book Room and digital archives, organizing comic books and CD archives and doing occasional research for the editorial staff or the toy department. Candidates should know how to use Excel and Word.

Creative Services

In this internship, you'll help maintain a vast character database, scanning and retouching artwork and tracking files. You should be a graphics or illustration major, and you must have a basic knowledge of Photoshop, along with a general knowledge of Marvel characters and comic books.

Editorial

Here you'll help in the editorial process, including the transmittal and receipt of artwork, plots, and scripts.

Human Resources

Interns in this department should have a business-related or liberal arts major and the ability to devote two days a week to the internship. Ideally, this intern would be interested in working for Marvel in the human resources department after graduation.

Legal

Here, you'll help in the legal department with day-to-day operations, including drafting and editing contracts, project development, office administration, and helping with the licensing and promotions operations.

Manufacturing

In this area, you'll help to compile comic books, gaining hands-on experience with several computer programs such as Adobe Photoshop, and Quark.

Marvel Interactive

As a Web intern, you'll work on Marvel.com and a wide range of other on-line initiatives at the company. Applications for this internship are accepted from both students of design/fine arts, or computer sciences/information technology. Duties include scanning, graphics selection, preparation and optimization, trafficking of editorial content, and HTML/PHP/MYSQL development.

For this job, you'll need to be smart, with initiative and enthusiasm; a working knowledge of the Adobe suite of graphics applications is preferred and experience with Flash, HTML, and/or PHP/mySQL is a big plus.

Marvel Studios

Development interns in this area will handle script coverage, project research, filing, faxing, photocopying, and other basic office duties in the Los Angeles facilities. You must be eager and work well with others, but no formal experience is required.

Production (the "Bullpen")

In this department, you'll format disks containing comic-book interiors and lettering and help organize the reference library, giving you firsthand knowledge about how to produce a comic book.

Sales & Marketing

In this department, you'll be involved in sales analysis and tracking, helping to prepare marketing materials and gaining a basic understanding of the distribution process.

Scanning Intern

In this internship, you'll organize and scan various office files, in addition to ad-hoc data entry assignments. The ability to work with a PC is a must, but you will be trained to use the scanning equipment. Organization skills are also very important, and you should be able to work with potentially sensitive/confidential material, as files will range in content from art encyclopedias to legal and financial files.

HOW TO APPLY

For the Marvel Studios internship, you should fax resumes to (310) 234-8481.

To apply as an intern for Marvel Interactive, go online at http://www.marvel.com/company/webinterns.htm.

For all other internships, send your resume and a cover letter stating your area of interest (no phone calls) to the preceding address.

MIAMI HERALD INTERNSHIP

Miami Herald
Internship Director
1 Herald Plaza
Miami, FL 33132
(305) 376-2287
http://www.miami.com/mld/miamiherald

What You Can Earn: $520 a week.
Application Deadlines: October 31 for spring and summer internships.
Educational Experience: College juniors, seniors, and graduate students.
Requirements: None specified.

OVERVIEW

The *Miami Herald* is an internationally recognized, prize-winning newspaper serving one of the most vibrant, diverse regions in America; it has published the International Edition for readers in the Caribbean and Latin America since 1946 and in Mexico starting in 2002. Serving a million readers each day in South Florida, the Caribbean, and Latin America, *The Miami Herald* is produced each day in an 800,000-square-foot plant on the edge of Biscayne Bay at the northeast fringe of downtown Miami.

Launched in 1903 as the *Evening Record* and rechristened in 1910 as the *Miami Herald,* it is South Florida's oldest newspaper. Now one of the nation's largest daily newspapers, The Herald endured the Florida boom and subsequent bust in the early 1920s, the devastating 1926 hurricane and the Great Depression.

Today, it remains one of the nation's great metropolitan daily newspapers, winning 16 Pulitzer Prizes. The Herald is owned by Knight-Ridder, an international communications company.

The paper offers an intensive 12-week journalism internship in metro, business or sports reporting, features writing, design, or photo or copyediting.

HOW TO APPLY

Send a cover letter, clips, and the names of at least three references to the preceding address.

MODESTO BEE INTERNSHIP

Modesto Bee
Internship Coordinator
PO Box 5256
Modesto, CA 95352-5256
dpeterson@modbee.com
http://www.modbee.com

What You Can Earn: $450 a week plus overtime for work over 7.5 hours in a day and/or 37.5 hours in a week.
Application Deadlines: November 1.
Educational Experience: Seniors in college, recent graduates, or students in master's programs.
Requirements: Daily journalism experience, either with a university publication or with a daily newspaper; Spanish-speaking skills are a plus.

OVERVIEW

You can choose an internship as the *Bee's* reporter or photographer, working on deadlines as a copy editor, or creating informative, attractive graphics as a graphics designer intern.

Modesto, with a population of 185,000, is located in the heart of the San Joaquin Valley, 70 miles east of the Bay Area. The *Modesto Bee* has a daily circulation of 84,000 on weekdays and 94,000 on Sunday, with about 105 newsroom employees. Coverage isn't limited to Modesto and its population of about 190,000 people, however. The newspaper also covers six counties spread over a wide geographic area ranging from Merced on the south to Manteca on the north, Interstate 5 to the west and Yosemite National Park and the Sierra to the east. Owned by McClatchy Newspapers Inc., the *Sacramento* and *Fresno Bees* are sister newspapers in a fleet that also includes daily newspapers in Sacramento, Fresno, Minneapolis (*Minneapolis Star Tribune*), Raleigh (*News & Observer*), Anchorage (*Anchorage Daily News*), and Tacoma (*Tacoma News Tribune*).

If you land an internship here, you'll do a rotation through the newsroom that will probably begin in late spring or early summer. (Interns in the sports department, however, begin in winter, usually February.) As an intern reporter, you'll cover breaking news: crime, courts, politics, education, and health. You might also spend some weeks in the Work and Money section, which covers business-related issues, and some time in the Life section, where you'll create feature stories.

Interns compete for front-page stories from the first day on the job, because the editors at the *Bee* want to get you onto the street and into real reporting situations right away. You won't spend your internship rewriting press releases, although that might happen from time to time, as it does with full-time staff.

Although you'll have a designated editor at each step of your internship, you'll be encouraged to approach any editor if you have a question and your designated editor isn't on duty. Full-time reporters also are asked to mentor interns, offering advice and guidance throughout the program.

HOW TO APPLY

If you're interested in this internship, send a resume, cover letter, and from five to seven writing samples sent to the attention of the internship coordinator at the preceding address.

MOTHER JONES INTERNSHIP

Mother Jones Magazine
Dave Gilson, Research Editor
222 Sutter Street, Suite 600
San Francisco, CA 94108
internships@motherjones.com
http://www.motherjones.com/about/admin/jobs.html

What You Can Earn: $100/month travel stipend, plus a five-vacation allowance; those who qualify may obtain a scholarship stipend to offset the cost of living. Download a scholarship application at http://www.motherjones.com/about/admin/internships.html. Fellows receive a $1,380/month stipend.
Application Deadlines: Two months prior to start date.
Educational Experience: None specified.
Requirements: Organized, detail oriented, and well informed; ready to track down hard-to-find information, juggle several deadlines at once, and take on a variety of journalistic challenges.

OVERVIEW

Mother Jones editorial interns receive training and hands-on experience in fact-checking, research, and reporting, in addition to a firsthand look at the production of an award-winning national magazine. Interns' primary focus is fact-checking articles and doing research for upcoming issues. Fact-checking involves calling sources, locating primary documents, evaluating information, and working closely with the research editor, story editors, and writers.

Internships are full time, five days a week, generally from 10:00 A.M. to 5:30 P.M. unless otherwise arranged with the assistant editor. Cycles begin during the first week of February, June, and October.

Over the course of a four-month internship, interns participate in the production of two issues, working closely with the research editor, story editors, and writers to verify everything that goes in the magazine. When the production cycle is over, interns are expected to pitch ideas and write short pieces for the magazine and Web site.

If you're chosen as an intern, you'll conduct research in support of articles and special projects published on the site; report, research, and write two significant feature stories; occasionally pitch story ideas and write shorter pieces, including sidebars and boxes for the magazine and short features for the Web site; fact-check feature stories as assigned; and proof/copyedit as assigned. You'll also work on HTML stories for Web exclusives and the magazine archive, compile letters to the editor, and produce the weekly e-mail newsletter. You'll also be expected to attend editorial and Web meetings as well as trainings and seminars on various topics and handle other projects as assigned by the research editor.

Interns who distinguish themselves in their editorial duties are eligible to become fellows, but keep in mind that promotion to fellow after completing your four-month internship is not automatic. The fellowship requires an additional four-month commitment. In return, fellows receive a $1,380/month stipend. Fellows have the same duties as interns but also have more freedom to pursue their own story ideas and work on larger projects.

HOW TO APPLY

Download an application at http://www.motherjones.com/about/admin/intern_app.pdf. Submit it along with a cover letter, resume, two references (with names and numbers), and two clips or writing samples. Decisions will be announced one month prior to the internship start date. No phone calls.

MSNBC INTERNSHIP

MSNBC
Human Resources
Internship Coordinator
One MSNBC Plaza
Secaucus, NJ 07094
Fax: (201) 583-5819
internships@msnbc.com
http://msnbc.msn.com/id/3080682

What You Can Earn: Unpaid.
Application Deadlines: Rolling.
Educational Experience: Sophomores or above enrolled at an accredited four or five-year university, able to provide proof of credit from college before starting assignment, and on track to receive a bachelor's or advanced degree.
Requirements: Committed to a career in media/broadcasting through experiences in your major, college clubs, or organizations; prior media-based internships or prior media work experience. GPA, community service, and leadership experience are also important.

OVERVIEW

MSNBC is a partnership between NBC and Microsoft that includes a 24-hour cable news network and an Internet news service. With an MSNBC internship, you'll have the chance to take that first step into the broadcasting industry. This is a unique opportunity to be a real part of a cable news network, and you'll earn the kind of experience that will give you an edge in a competitive industry. You may work during the fall, spring, or summer college semesters, either full or part time (but for at least three days a week), based on your schedule and MSNBC's needs. All internships are located in Secaucus, NJ, unless otherwise stated.

There are a range of different internships in various departments, including the newsroom; "Primetime;" "Imus in the Morning" show; marketing; production; audio post-production; strate-gic operations; human resources; media relations; on-air graphics; or technical operations.

Audio Post Production Internship

As a post-production intern, you'll help with the daily tracking of voice-over announcers, music searches, editing music for length, music dubbing, post production, sound-to-picture (effects), and sweetening. You'll have primary use of Pro Tools music editing system, scenaria mixing console, beta decks, and data recorders, and you'll need to plan on spending at least three days per week on the internship.

Human Resources Internship

In this department, you'll help a team of human resources recruiters and managers bring in and maintain top talent at MSNBC cable. You'll help recruiters with research, job postings, and screening candidates, as well as help with the everyday functions of the office. To be considered for this internship, you must be proficient in Microsoft Office and have excellent interpersonal and writing skills.

Imus in the Morning Internship

During this hands-on internship, you'll help in the preproduction of the Imus program and log live programs and pieces. You should be dedicated and willing to work early morning hours (from 5:30 A.M. to noon). In return, you can expect to get lots of experience in live TV production, remote cameras, and video editing.

Marketing Intern

If you're chosen for this internship, you'll help in marketing, research, copyediting, scheduling, and listings. You'll work with the vice president of marketing, advertising, and promotions in developing marketing strategies and third-party partnerships for the network. This position will give you valuable insight and marketing skills related to on-air as well as off-channel advertising. You'll need to spend a minimum of three days a week here. Marketing majors are preferred.

Media Relations Internship

Duties for this internship include screening tapes, updating and creating press lists, answering phones, distributing press clips, filing, and helping to research upcoming MSNBC programs for releases. To be considered, you should have an interest in media relations, good writing skills, an outgoing personality, and experience in a professional environment. During this internship, you'll learn a lot about how a media relations department works, including the ability to write a press release, edit information, and field calls from the press.

Newsroom Internship

Here, you'll be part of a team, working closely with production assistants in completing tasks assigned by the senior producer. You'll perform various production-assistant tasks, such as answering phones, logging tape, researching story ideas, printing scripts, retrieving tapes, and working within the tape department. For this position, you must know a lot about politics, history, and current events. If you intern here, you'll end up with a solid understanding of how a live newscast works, from start to finish.

On-Air Graphics Internship

During this internship, you'll help research and create graphics for all MSNBC programs and help artists and researchers by finding graphic elements for future use. To be considered, you should have basic computer skills; Photoshop and Internet experience is a plus. You also should have an interest in electronic graphics, news, and current events. During this internship, you'll get hands-on experience with the latest graphics equipment and software as you help create graphics that will be used on-air. Day and weekend shifts are available.

Primetime Intern

If you're selected for this internship, you'll work on research and help with production elements for live talk-oriented programming. You'll work with production assistants to produce key elements of the show such as graphics, tape-cuts, and scripts.

Control room experience will let you learn factual knowledge, so some TV experience is an asset. This would be an ideal position if you're a detail-oriented, quick learner who can handle pressure and juggle lots of tasks at the same time.

Production Intern

If you prefer the behind-the-scenes work, this internship is for you. Here, you'll help producers, production assistants, and coordinators research, screen, and log tapes. You'll get hands-on experience and learn all about the components of creating on-air promotion, including writing, research, editing, and audio. You'll need to spend a minimum of three days a week on this internship. Communications majors with TV coursework are preferred.

Strategic Operations Internship

If you're chosen for this internship, you'll help with audience research, TV Web research, and content production for MSNBC. Your duties will include compiling Nielsen audience data and Web research data for MSNBC and its competitors; analysis of e-mail viewer feedback; and copyediting and updating TV and special programming content on MSNBC's Web site. The ideal candidate should be a self-starter and a quick learner, as well as organized and detail oriented. You also should have excellent interpersonal and writing skills and an interest in the business side of TV. Knowledge of Microsoft Office products (including Excel, Word, and PowerPoint) are required, and Internet experience is a plus. A background in mathematics or statistics is helpful.

Technical Operations Internship

There are various opportunities for students to work and learn the behind-the-scenes aspects of live TV news production at the MSNBC Secaucus, New Jersey, facility. Selected interns will be able to customize their own internship to focus on one or several of the following areas:

- Editing (cuts-only, avid, online, and non-linear)

- Studio Operations (camera, stage managing, TelePrompTer, and studio lighting).
- Control Room Operations (technical director, audio, video, playback, and electronic graphics).
- Remote Operations (Live shot coordination, satellite/fiber feeds, and field logistics).

To be considered, you should have taken production courses in related areas of interest or relevant experience. MSNBC interns will receive hands-on instruction with staff supervision.

HOW TO APPLY

If you're interested in applying for an internship at MSNBC, you should mail, fax, or e-mail a resume and cover letter specifying which internship you are interested in to the preceding address.

MSNBC MULTIMEDIA INTERNSHIP

Director of Multimedia, MSNBC.com
One Microsoft Way
Building 25/2N
Redmond, WA 98052
http://www.msnbc.com

What You Can Earn: Paid.
Application Deadlines: March 29.
Educational Experience: None specified.
Requirements: Journalism experience, the ability to adapt quickly to the evolving medium, the ability to edit effectively on tight deadlines, and the ability to work creatively.

OVERVIEW

MSNBC is a partnership between NBC and Microsoft that includes a 24-hour cable news network and an Internet news service. MSNBC.com boasts more than 1.5 million users each day.

For this special multimedia internship based in Redmond, Washington, interns will edit photographs, audio, and video for stories and special packages. In addition to covering the daily news desk, multimedia interns have the opportunity to work on special projects such as:

- twip
- Picture Stories http://msnbc.com/picturestories
- Video News http://video.msnbc.com
- Live Video http://livevideo.msnbc.com
- Broadband http://highspeed.msnbc.com

HOW TO APPLY

To apply, send a cover letter, resume, references, a portfolio, your Web address, or a demo tape to the director of multimedia at MSNBC.com, at the preceding address.

NATIONAL ASSOCIATION OF BLACK JOURNALISTS SUMMER JOURNALISM INTERNSHIP

NABJ, Student Services Associate
8701-A Adelphi Road
Adelphi, MD 20783
warren@nabj.org
(301) 445-7100, ext. 108
Fax: (301) 445-7101
http://www.nabj.org

What You Can Earn: $400 to $600 weekly for 10 weeks. You are responsible for your own living expenses.

Application Deadlines: November 1.

Educational Experience: Journalism majors or those planning a journalism career.

Requirements: African-American undergraduate sophomores and juniors enrolled in an accredited four-year college or university; must be a student NABJ member.

OVERVIEW

The National Association of Black Journalists (NABJ) is an association of 3,000 journalists, media professionals, and students dedicated to expanding job opportunities for African American journalists and students and improving the media's coverage of the African American community and experience. NABJ annually awards 10-week summer internships to students committed to journalism careers, in paid print, broadcast, or online positions at news organizations around the country, ranging from small black-owned weekly newspapers to major-market dailies and broadcast outlets.

If you're selected, you'll get hands-on reporting, editing, shooting, and design experience in professional settings in either print (reporting, business reporting, health reporting, copyediting, graphic design); broadcast (radio and TV); online journalism; sports journalism (a multicultural program sponsored by the Associated Press Sports Editors); or photojournalism.

To obtain a print internship, you must have experience at your college paper or with professional media that allowed you to write basic news stories for publication or do basic copyediting, graphic design, or photojournalism in print, broadcast, or online media for publication.

Most NABJ internships are at print outlets, which include small weekly newspapers in small cities as well as magazines and major newspapers in large urban areas. Typically, NABJ internships at major magazines and newspapers are for students with at least two semesters of extensive campus print media experience and at least one prior print internship involving reporting, editing, shoot-

ing, or designing under tight deadlines. If you're interested in a broadcast internship, you would be expected to have had prior broadcast internships or student broadcast media experience.

Interns have worked at news outlets such as the Associated Press, the *Seattle Times,* the *Raleigh News & Observer*, CBS-TV, National Public Radio, and the *Atlanta Journal-Constitution*.

HOW TO APPLY

You can download an application at http://www.nabj.org/programs/internships/index.html and submit it to the preceding address, along with additional materials listed below (depending on your specialty). To have the best chance of being selected, proofread your application carefully and make sure that it thoroughly describes your journalism skills and college or professional journalism experience. Submit your application on time; late applicants will be placed only if there are unfilled internships after the other applicants have been placed.

Print and online applicants must submit a minimum of six samples of published work focusing on reporting or graphic design. Print photographers must submit six mounted samples of published work.

Selected broadcast interns are required to attend the NABJ Broadcast Short Course. Broadcast applicants must send a resume tape (VHS or audio cassette), which begins with the following identifying information: name, academic year, college, address, phone, and e-mail.

TV on-air applicants must submit three to five stand-ups or anchor sequences and at least two reporter packages; tape should be no longer than 10 minutes.

TV off-air applicants (producers, directors, and broadcast photographers) must submit at least two stories or an edited version of a newscast or program produced, directed, shot, or edited by you; tape should be no longer than 10 minutes.

Broadcast photojournalists should send a five- to 10-minute tape with three to five stories you've shot.

Radio applicants should submit at least three on-air reports, stories, interviews, and/or newscasts or an edited version of a program that you've written, broadcast, directed, or produced. Tape should be no longer than 10 minutes.

Sports journalism interns are required to attend the annual convention of the Associated Press Sports Editors (transportation and hotel accommodations are included).

NBC INTERNSHIP

NBC Internships
http://www.nbcjobs.com/Internship_Program. html

What You Can Earn: Unpaid.
Application Deadlines: For fall: Resumes accepted May through August; interviews scheduled June through August; For spring: Resumes accepted September, November, December; interviews scheduled November and December; For summer: Resumes accepted January through March; interviews scheduled February, March, and May.
Educational Experience: Sophomore or above; committed to a media/broadcasting career.
Requirements: Enrollment at an accredited four or five-year college or university; able to provide proof of credit from your university before starting; on track to receive an undergraduate or advanced college degree; good GPA.

OVERVIEW

The NBC internship program gives you real-world TV news experience and lets you become familiar with NBC's organization and work style. NBC works with interns to provide them the opportunity to apply coursework from the classroom to practice in the workplace. Students are placed in TV broadcast/production areas, business operations, and NBC interactive positions related to their major and career goals.

You may work during the fall, spring, or summer semesters full time or part time (minimum three days a week) based on your schedule and the department or show's needs. You may work at NBC offices in New York City; Burbank, California; the 14 NBC-owned and operated TV stations; MSNBC; CNBC; Telemundo; or mun2.

HOW TO APPLY

Because opportunities are limited and competition is high, for full consideration you should apply early. GPA, community service, and leadership skills are all important considerations in landing an NBC internship.

To apply, you should submit a cover letter and resume by clicking the link found at the preceding Internet address. In the cover letter, indicate the semester and type of internship desired in the body of the e-mail; resume files must be in MS Word 97 or compatible.

NEWSWEEK INTERNSHIP

Newsweek Internship Program
251 West 57th Street
New York, N.Y. 10019
(800) 631-1040; (212) 445-4000
http://www.newsweek.com

What You Can Earn: Paid.
Application Deadlines: December 15.
Educational Experience: College seniors, graduate students, and professionals with a few years of experience in journalism.
Requirements: Experience reporting and writing for college newspapers, in previous internships or at other publications.

OVERVIEW

Founded by Thomas J.C. Martyn, a former foreign editor at *Time* magazine, *Newsweek* was first published on February 17, 1933 as *News-Week*, which featured seven photographs from the week's news on the cover. At 10 cents a copy, it had a circulation of 50,000. In 1961, *Newsweek* was bought by *The Washington Post* Company.

Today, *Newsweek* has a worldwide circulation of more than 4 million and a total readership of more than 21 million and has earned more National Magazine Awards than any other newsweekly. It offers comprehensive coverage of world events with a global network of correspondents, reporters, and editors covering national and international affairs; business, science, and technology; and society, arts, and entertainment.

Newsweek has a paid, 13-week summer internship program working at company headquarters in New York, where you'll do reporting, research, and fact-checking and help with the weekly close of the magazine. In addition, if you're interested in public relations work, you can be assigned to the communications department.

HOW TO APPLY

If you're interested in this internship, submit a one-page letter stating your qualifications and aspirations, a detailed resume, five samples of published articles (including name and date of publication), and the names and phone numbers of two references to the preceding address.

NEW YORK DAILY NEWS GRAPHICS DESIGNER INTERNSHIP

Daily News
450 West 33rd Street
New York, NY 10001
(212) 210-2318
Fax: (212) 643-7842

akotler@nydailynews.com
http://www.nydailynews.com

What You Can Earn: Unpaid; receive college credit.
Application Deadlines: February.
Educational Experience: Junior or senior college students.
Requirements: Extensive knowledge of Adobe InDesign, Photoshop, Illustrator, as well as a working knowledge of Quark.

OVERVIEW

The *New York Daily News,* called "New York's picture newspaper," hosts graphics design interns each summer. If you're chosen as a graphics design intern, you'll be responsible for the design of advertisements, posters, brochures, and flyers, as well as assisting with work flow and production in the art services department. Points will not be lost for excessive enthusiasm.

HOW TO APPLY

E-mail your resume to akotler@nydailynews.com and be ready to present your portfolio.

NEW YORK DAILY NEWS INTERNSHIP

Daily News Internship
450 West 33rd Street
New York, NY 10001
(212) 210-2318
Fax: (212) 643-7842
http://www.nydailynews.com

What You Can Earn: Unpaid; receive college credit.
Application Deadlines: February.
Educational Experience: Junior or senior journalism, English, communications, or history majors.

Requirements: Writing experience, preferably at a daily paper.

OVERVIEW

The *New York Daily News* was the first successful tabloid newspaper in the United States. It was founded in 1919 as the *Illustrated Daily News* by Joseph Medill Patterson and was a subsidiary of the Tribune Company of Chicago.

Reporter interns at this daily picture-heavy newspaper will be responsible for a variety of tasks, including reporting, writing, research, fact-checking, and proofreading.

HOW TO APPLY

Send a resume, six to 10 clips, and a cover letter describing your journalism ambitions and reporting interests to the preceding address. Photo intern candidates should send samples. (Indicate whether you would like your materials returned. Do not send anything that you will need returned in a short time; this can be a long process.)

NEW YORK TIMES COPYEDITING INTERNSHIP

Senior Manager, Reporter Recruiting
The New York Times
229 West 43rd Street
New York, NY 10036
newsfund@wsj.dowjones.com

What You Can Earn: $800 a week, plus a housing allowance for out-of-area interns and a $1,000 Newspaper Fund scholarship.
Application Deadlines: November 1.

Educational Experience: College juniors, seniors, and graduate students.
Requirements: Newspaper experience and academic excellence.

OVERVIEW

A copyediting intern for the *New York Times* is chosen each year by the Dow Jones Newspaper Fund through its national selection process. If you land this internship, before coming to the *Times* for the summer, you'll participate in a two-week seminar sponsored by the Newspaper Fund, discussing libel law, journalistic ethics, page layout, headline writing, copyediting, grammar, punctuation, style and the finer points of newsroom protocol.

During the 10-week internship at the *Times*, you'll be assigned to a major desk in the news department and—under the guidance of the copy desk chief and an assigned mentor—edit copy and write headlines. The intern also participates in workshops with ranking editors and reporters. After completing the internship successfully and returning to school, you'll be given a $1,000 Newspaper Fund scholarship.

HOUSING

Housing is available on the New York University campus for interns who live outside New York area, for about $40 a night (offset in part by a housing allowance).

HOW TO APPLY

Send your completed application, essay, and editing test to the preceding address. Applications are available through placement offices, campus newspapers, by calling (609) 452-2820, or by visiting http://djnewspaperfund.dowjones.com. Selection is based on experience (such as work on campus publications, reporting internships, or work as a stringer) academic excellence, an essay, and an editing test that all applicants must pass before being considered for the program.

NEW YORK TIMES GRAPHICS, DESIGN, AND PHOTOGRAPHY INTERNSHIP

Senior Manager, Reporter Recruiting
The New York Times
229 West 43rd Street
New York, NY 10036

What You Can Earn: $800 a week, plus a housing allowance for out-of-area interns; eligibility for one $1,500 intern prize.
Application Deadlines: November 15.
Educational Experience: College juniors or seniors; in recognition of the school Morgan attended, students from the University of Missouri at Columbia will be given preference for one of the internships each year.
Requirements: Newspaper experience.

OVERVIEW

The *New York Times* offers 10-week summer internships to college students who have decided on careers in journalism. In its first 17 years, it was aimed at members of minority groups who, because of race or ethnicity, had been historically excluded from opportunities in America's newspaper industry. While internships are now open to all applicants, the program remains an integral part of the *Times'* enduring commitment to recruit and hire as diverse and as highly qualified a staff as possible.

The Tom Morgan Graphics Internship includes an internship in each of these categories: graphics, design, and photography. The internship was named for Tom Morgan, a reporter, editor, and manager at the *Times* and a role model in every assignment he has undertaken. A past president of the National Association of Black Journalists, the largest organization of minority journalists in the country, he has

received lifetime achievement awards from NABJ and the University of Missouri, his alma mater. He won a Nieman Fellowship in 1989.

If you're selected for this internship, you'll be given assignments for publication in various sections of the *Times* and credit lines where applicable. As a Morgan intern, you'll participate in workshops with ranking editors, graphics and design specialists, and reporters. At the end of the summer, one Morgan intern will be awarded $1,500—on the basis of performance—the Thomas Morgan Outstanding Summer Intern Prize.

The first week of the internship is an orientation program to New York City and the newsroom. Beginning with the second week, interns work in their respective areas.

Design

Working closely with art directors, as a design intern you'll help design and produce pages and process art and photographs. You'll attend editorial meetings and learn the Atex and Macintosh systems used at the *Times*. The goals of the program are to introduce you to newspaper design and to identify future designers for the *Times*.

Graphics

As a graphics intern, you'll work with the graphics editors, developing the skills to organize and present the news visually through charts, graphs, and diagrams. Using Macintosh computers, you'll design and execute graphics for publication in various sections of the *Times*. The goals are to help you develop fresh, to-the-point informational graphics and to identify future graphics specialists for the *Times*.

Photography

If you're selected as the picture desk intern, you'll work with *Times* photographers and editors, shooting assignments for every section of the newspaper. The goal is to give you a taste of news, feature, and sports photography, as well as the opportunity to learn lighting techniques from professionals. You'll also be expected to initiate projects apart from your daily assignments. An editor serves as mentor and works with you every day, reviewing contact sheets and providing guidance on work in the field.

HOUSING

Housing is available on the New York University campus for interns who live outside New York area, for about $40 a night (offset in part by a housing allowance).

HOW TO APPLY

Photography applicants should send a resume and portfolio reflecting a cross-section of their best work (portraits, features, sports, and hard news). Graphics applicants should send a resume and samples of writing and graphic design work. Design applicants should submit a portfolio that includes layouts, dummies, and typography. All applications should be sent to the preceding address.

NEW YORK TIMES REPORTING FELLOWSHIP

Senior Manager, Reporter Recruiting
The New York Times
229 West 43rd Street
New York, NY 10036

What You Can Earn: $800 a week, plus a housing allowance for out-of-area interns.
Application Deadlines: November 15.
Educational Experience: College students.
Requirements: None specified.

OVERVIEW

The *New York Times* offers 10-week summer internship to college students who have decided on careers in journalism. The *Times* began the program in 1984. In its first 17 years, it was aimed at members of minority groups who, because of race or ethnicity, had been historically excluded from opportunities in America's newspaper industry. While the internships are now open to all applicants, the program remains an integral part of the *Times'* enduring commitment to recruit and hire as diverse and as highly qualified a staff as possible.

James Reston (called Scotty by virtually everyone who knew him) was a columnist, Washington correspondent, and executive editor in his 50-year association with the *Times*. Perhaps the most influential journalist of his generation, he won two Pulitzer Prizes. He was also a talent scout of prodigious capacity, hiring and training some of the *Times'* best-known journalists. He died in 1995 at the age of 86.

The James Reston Reporting Fellowship offers regular reporting assignments and bylines, four days in Washington on a behind-the-scenes tour of the nation's capital, and eligibility for an extended internship of six months, which could lead to a staff reporting position.

HOUSING

Housing is available on the New York University campus for interns who live outside the New York area, for about $40 a night (offset in part by a housing allowance).

HOW TO APPLY

Applicants for the reporting fellowships should send a resume and eight to 10 newswriting samples from daily newspapers to the preceding address.

NIGHTLINE INTERNSHIP

ABC News Nightline
Internship Coordinator
1717 DeSales Street NW
Washington, DC 20036
http://abcnews.go.com/Nightline/
    ABCNEWSSpecial/story?id=173272

What You Can Earn: Unpaid; interns must receive academic credit for participation in the program.
Application Deadlines: Deadline is November 15 for spring I internship (mid-January to mid-April); deadline is February 1 for spring II (early April to early June); deadline is March 15 for summer internship (early June to mid/late August); deadline is July 1 for fall session (early September to mid/late December); deadline is October 1 for winter session (early/mid-December to mid/late January).
Educational Experience: College juniors and seniors in good academic standing in any major; no journalism experience is required.
Requirements: Initiative, curiosity, and a solid work ethic; the ability to grasp concepts quickly, work well with others, and be efficient, reliable, and able to juggle several tasks at once. Applicants should have good communication skills and a serious interest in broadcast journalism.

OVERVIEW

Nightline, a late-night news program, is broadcast weeknights on ABC from Washington, D.C., where 95 percent of the show is produced. Full and part-time internship positions are available year round, during sessions lasting eight to 12 weeks. The show was introduced in 1980 as TV's first late-night network news program.

If you land a *Nightline* internship, you'll perform a variety of duties, managing the enormous flow of daily information (from phones to faxes, viewer mail to Web site content). In exchange, you're exposed to all aspects of story development and production. You'll be encouraged to take part in editorial conferences, and you'll be able to experience what life in a national newsroom is like.

HOW TO APPLY

In you're interested in this internship, request an application form by e-mailing niteline@abc.com, writing "INTERNSHIP APPLICATION REQUEST" in the subject line. To apply, send this complicated application form to the address below, along with a one-page resume, a cover letter, two written recommendations (preferably one academic and one professional), an academic transcript, and a notice that your college will grant you college credit for this internship.

You'll receive notice of acceptance by December 1 for the spring I session; by March 1 for the spring II session; by April 15 for the summer session; by August 1 for the fall session; and by November 1 for the winter session.

ORLANDO SENTINEL INTERNSHIP

Orlando Sentinel
North Orange Avenue
Orlando, FL 32801
(407) 420-5427
deagles@orlandosentinel.com
http://www.orlandosentinel.com

What You Can Earn: $525 a week.
Application Deadlines: October 15 for winter session; November 15 for summer session.
Educational Experience: Juniors, seniors, recent graduates, or graduate students.
Requirements: A previous internship is required, and a car and a driver's license is required.

OVERVIEW

The *Sentinel* has won three Pulitzer Prizes and many other national awards for newspaper journalism as the paper's writers and editors deliver information not just in print, but online, on radio and on TV, in both English and Spanish, through innovative partnerships with network affiliates and a 24-hour cable news channel.

The paper reaches much of central Florida—an increasingly diverse community that is one of the nation's fastest-growing metropolitan areas as well as one of the world's top tourist destinations. The newspaper covers six counties, with 10 bureaus in its principal coverage area and offices in Miami, Tallahassee, Washington, D.C., and San Juan, Puerto Rico. There are seven internships available in copyediting, reporting, graphics, and photography are available. Sports reporting is only available in the winter.

HOW TO APPLY

Apply to the above address with a letter, resume, references, and at least five samples of published work related to the type of internship you're seeking.

PHILADELPHIA INQUIRER MINORITY INTERNSHIP

For Art Peters minority reporting or copyediting, contact:
Internship Coordinator
Philadelphia Inquirer
PO Box 8263
Philadelphia, PA 19101
(215) 854-4975
Fax: (215) 854-2578
amoore@phillynews.com

For photojournalism, contact
Director of Photography
Philadelphia Inquirer
PO Box 8263
Philadelphia, PA 19101
ehille@phillynews.com

For graphic arts, contact
AME/Recruiting
The Philadelphia Inquirer
PO Box 8263
Philadelphia, PA 19101
showard@phillynews.com

What You Can Earn: $633 a week; summer housing is available at the intern's expense at the University of Pennsylvania campus.

Application Deadlines: November.
Educational Experience: Juniors, seniors, recent graduates, or graduate students.
Requirements: Minority students with at least one prior newspaper internship.

OVERVIEW

Founded June 1, 1829, by John Norvell and John R. Walker at 5 Bank Alley, the *Philadelphia Inquirer* is America's third-oldest surviving daily newspaper. It is now owned (along with the *Philadelphia Daily News*) by Knight-Ridder Newspapers Inc. Over the years, the *Philadelphia Inquirer's* tradition of aggressive enterprise, explanatory reporting, and stylish writing has earned 18 Pulitzer Prizes. Today, the paper has bureaus in Moscow; London; Berlin; Johannesburg; Cairo; Manila; Washington D.C.; New York; Chicago; Los Angeles; Houston; New Orleans; Boston; Pittsburgh; Harrisburg; Trenton; and Atlantic City. Since 1982, the *Inquirer* has added nine "Neighbors" sections, tabloid sections aimed at particular areas of suburbia and the northeast section of the city. There are five in the Pennsylvania suburbs, three in the New Jersey suburbs, and one in northeast Philadelphia.

The *Inquirer* offers seven 10-week summer internships (four for copy editors and three for reporters, one for graphics, and one for photojournalism). Like all the internships available at this newspaper, these positions are very much hands-on, professional, and tough assignments. Interns typically emerge at the end of the session very tired but with lots of good bylines, photos, or graphics. Interns are assigned mentors and evaluated twice during the summer.

HOW TO APPLY

For the Art Peters minority reporting or copyediting position, you should submit five to seven clips, a resume and cover letter, and references to Acel Moore at the preceding address.

For photojournalism internships, you should submit 20 to 40 images in any form of news, features, sports, environmental portraits, or a photo story and a resume, cover letter, and references to Ed Hille at the preceding address.

For the graphic arts internship, you should submit five to seven samples of your work (published or unpublished).

PHILADELPHIA INQUIRER NONMINORITY COPYEDITING AND GRAPHICS ARTS INTERNSHIP

Philadelphia Inquirer
PO Box 8263
Philadelphia, PA 19101
(215) 854-4975
Fax: (215) 854-2578
recruiting@phillynews.com (for questions only)

What You Can Earn: $633 a week.
Application Deadlines: November.
Educational Experience: Juniors, seniors, recent graduates, or graduate students at Ball State University (graphics), Pennsylvania State University (copyediting), University of Kansas (copyediting), and Howard University (copyediting).
Requirements: Students with at least one prior newspaper internship.

OVERVIEW

Founded June 1, 1829, by John Norvell and John R. Walker at 5 Bank Alley, the *Philadelphia Inquirer* is America's third-oldest surviving daily newspaper. It is now owned (along with the *Philadelphia Daily News*) by Knight-Ridder Newspapers Inc. Over the years, the *Philadelphia Inquirer's* tradition of aggressive enterprise, explanatory reporting, and stylish writing has earned 18 Pulitzer Prizes. Today, the paper has bureaus in Moscow; London;

Berlin; Johannesburg; Cairo; Manila; Washington, D.C., New York; Chicago; Los Angeles; Houston; New Orleans; Boston; Pittsburgh; Harrisburg; Trenton; and Atlantic City. Since 1982, the *Inquirer* has added nine "Neighbors" sections, tabloid sections aimed at particular areas of suburbia and the northeast section of the city. There are five in the Pennsylvania suburbs, three in the New Jersey suburbs, and one in northeast Philadelphia.

The *Inquirer* offers nonminority summer internship programs with Ball State University (graphics), Pennsylvania State University (copyediting), University of Kansas (copyediting), and Howard University (copyediting). Interns are chosen through campus visits.

Like all the internships available at this newspaper, these positions are very much hands-on, professional, and tough assignments. Interns typically emerge at the end of the session very tired but with lots of good bylines, photos, or graphics. Interns are assigned mentors and evaluated twice during the summer.

HOUSING

Summer housing is available at the intern's expense at the University of Pennsylvania campus.

HOW TO APPLY

For the copyediting position, you should submit five to seven clips, a resume and cover letter, and references to the preceding address. For the graphic arts internship, you should submit five to seven samples of your work (published or unpublished), a resume, cover letter, and references to Acel Moore at the preceding address.

REUTERS INTERNSHIP

Summer Internship Program
Reuters America Inc.
1333 H Street, NW
Washington, DC 20005

What You Can Earn: Paid.
Application Deadlines: December 1.
Educational Experience: Juniors, seniors, or graduate students enrolled in a degree program with excellent journalism skills and an interest in business/financial reporting.
Requirements: Previous internships or other professional experience in journalism.

OVERVIEW

Reuters is a global information company providing information tailored for professionals in the financial services, media, and corporate markets, with a reputation for speed, accuracy, and freedom from bias. The company is best known as the world's largest international multimedia news agency, supplying news (text, graphics, video, and pictures) to media organizations and Web sites around the world. The company also provides news to businesses outside financial services. Founded in London in 1851, Reuters today is the world's largest international multimedia news agency, with 2,300 editorial staffers, journalists, photographers, and camera operators in 197 bureaus serving 130 countries. Reuters publishes about eight million words daily in 19 languages and is among the most read news source on the Internet, reaching millions each day.

Reuters typically hires 10 summer reporting interns in Washington, D.C., New York, Chicago, Miami, and Los Angeles. Internships are also available for students interested in online publishing, photography, and TV. But make no mistake; an internship here is not easy to land. Typically, about 3000 students apply for the 65 internships in all the departments at Reuters.

As a Reuters intern, you will not only be showered with endless opportunities if you're willing to take the initiative, but you'll also work in a fun, diverse, and challenging environment. Reuters interns are given real responsibility from day one and are a vital part of the Reuters community. In fact, one of the greatest assets of being a Reuters intern is the unique experience you can gain from working at such an immense multinational company.

HOW TO APPLY

If you're interested, submit a resume including your e-mail address, a cover letter indicating preference of location, two letters of recommendation, and three to five clips. Final candidates will be required to take a short e-mailed writing test.

Photography applicants must send sample slides, in addition to the preceding requirements; TV candidates should provide a tape.

ROCKY MOUNTAIN PBS-TV STUDIO AND PRODUCTION INTERNSHIP

Internship Coordinator
Rocky Mountain PBS
1089 Bannock Street
Denver, CO 80204
(303) 620-5729
http://www.rmpbs.org

What You Can Earn: Unpaid.
Application Deadlines: Deadline for the fall is September 1; spring deadline is December 1; summer deadline is March 1.
Educational Experience: Journalism and English majors preferred.
Requirements: None.

OVERVIEW

KRMA-TV is Colorado's first PBS station, now a network with stations in Pueblo (KTSC) and Grand Junction (KRMJ). Each fall, spring, and summer semester, the station offers four non-news internships for undergraduates and graduate students in studio and field productions and development/marketing productions. During the internship, students may obtain experience in editing, promotions, or production.

HOW TO APPLY

To apply for one of these internships, send a cover letter with your resume to the internship coordinator at the preceding address. To receive a brochure, e-mail the internship coordinator at Sally_M_Reed@KRMA.PBS.org.

SACRAMENTO BEE INTERNSHIP

The Sacramento Bee
PO Box 15779
Sacramento, CA 95852
(916) 321-1224

What You Can Earn: $475 a week.
Application Deadlines: November 1.
Educational Experience: Must be working toward a college degree or be a recent college graduate.
Requirements: Must pass a drug test and physical examination.

OVERVIEW

The award-winning *Sacramento Bee,* one of the oldest, largest, and best-known companies in the Sacramento region, offers full-time, 12-week internship positions from June through August in reporting, photography, copyediting, or graphics design.

Reporting interns may do rotations in the metro, regional, business, and features departments. Sports interns generally spend time writing and working on the sports copy desk. Copyediting, photo, and graphics interns take regular shifts in those departments.

HOW TO APPLY

For more information on any of the internships, contact the internship director by phone at the preceding number or via e-mail. If you are looking for an internship as a reporter or copy editor, you should send a cover letter, a resume with three references, and up to eight clips demonstrating a range of work (including headlines for copy editors) to the internship director at the preceding address.

Those interested in a graphic artist internship should send a cover letter, resume, three references and copies of 10 to 20 work samples to thegraphics director at the preceding address. Samples will not be returned unless specifically requested.

Aspiring photography interns should send a cover letter, resume, and 10 to 20 work samples to the director of photography at the preceding address. Samples will not be returned unless specifically requested.

SAN FRANCISCO CHRONICLE SUMMER INTERNSHIP

Summer Internship Program
Director of Editorial Hiring and Development
San Francisco Chronicle
901 Mission Street
San Francisco, CA 94103-2988
http://www.sfgate.com

What You Can Earn: $554 a week.
Application Deadlines: November 15.
Educational Experience: College students and recent college graduates.
Requirements: None specified.

OVERVIEW

The *San Francisco Chronicle* offers 12-week summer internships for copy editor, reporter, photographer, and graphic artist positions. After a brief orientation period, you'll become part of the regular staff of journalists, and your work is generally judged by the same standards as staff work.

The Daily Dramatic Chronicle was first produced on January 16, 1865, as "a daily record of affairs—local, critical and theatrical," by Charles and Michael deYoung. The teenaged brothers borrowed a $20 gold piece from their landlord, bought an old desk, several fonts of used type and some newsprint, established themselves in the corner of the landlord's printing shop on Clay Street, and published their first four-page newspaper. Within a month, circulation reached 2,000.

Three months later, the theater paper published its first "extra," reporting the assassination of President Abraham Lincoln. By 1868, the newspaper's aggressive, competitive reputation had flourished, and the deYoungs decided to sell subscriptions to the new *Morning Chronicle*. With the help of local writers including Mark Twain and Bret Harte, who wrote short pieces in return for desk space, the *Chronicle* boasted the largest circulation west of the Mississippi.

In the more than 130 years since then, the *Chronicle* has become a pioneer in changing newspaper writing, readability, and design, while adhering to the deYoungs original vision of bold, independent coverage. Every morning, more than 1,175,000 people read the *Chronicle*, making it the eleventh-largest newspaper in the United States. Owned and operated by the deYoung family for most of its existence, in 2000 The Hearst Corporation bought the *Chronicle* and merged it with the *Examiner,* with the staffs of both papers merging into a new Hearst-owned *Chronicle*.

HOW TO APPLY

To apply, send an autobiographical cover letter, a resume, references, and work samples. State specifically what position you would like (reporter, photographer, artist, and so on). Include three references (with names, addresses, and telephone numbers) who may be journalism or other academic advisers or employers.

In addition to the preceding materials, you must submit certain items depending on the internship in which you're interested.

Copy Editors

Submit as many as 10 clippings of published headlines you have written, pages you have laid out, or articles you have written. Photocopies are acceptable. Clips will not be returned.

Reporters

Submit as many as 10 clippings of published articles you have written. Photocopies are acceptable. Clips will not be returned.

Photographers

Submit a portfolio of 20 to 60 slides, including news, features, and sports photos. Do not send oversized slide presentation boards, original clips, prints, tearsheets, yearbooks, or transparencies. However, you should include caption information, and label each slide with your name. Slides will be returned.

Graphic Artist

Submit as many as 10 slides or photocopies of your work, such as illustrations, infographics, and page designs. Do not submit original work. Slides will be returned.

SAN FRANCISCO CHRONICLE TWO-YEAR INTERNSHIP

San Francisco Chronicle
Two-Year Internship Program
Attn: Leslie Guevarra, Director of Editorial Hiring
    and Development
901 Mission Street
San Francisco, CA 94103-2988
http://www.sfgate.com

What You Can Earn: $35,000 the first year; $40,000 the second year; second-year interns are eligible for comprehensive health benefits after three months.

Application Deadlines: December 31.

Educational Experience: Recent college graduates (those who have been out of school no longer than one year prior to the start of the internship).

Requirements: None specified.

OVERVIEW

After a brief orientation period, interns become part of the regular staff of journalists. Their work is generally judged by the same standards as staff work. The *Chronicle* makes no promises about landing a staff position following an internship. Competition for jobs is extremely fierce, and the paper generally requires at least three years of experience at a daily newspaper. However, outstanding interns may be considered for staff openings at the end of their internships.

HOW TO APPLY

To apply, send a cover letter describing yourself; the work you have done, what you would like to accomplish in journalism and why you would like to work at the *Chronicle*. State specifically what position you would like to attain (reporter, photographer, artist, and so on). Also include your resume, which details your experience, educational background, and skills. Include three references (with names, addresses, and telephone numbers) who may be journalism or other academic advisers or employers.

In addition to the preceding materials, you must submit certain items depending on the internship in which you're interested.

Artists

Submit as many as 10 slides or photocopies of your work, such as illustrations, infographics, and page designs. Do not submit original work. Slides will be returned.

Copy Editors

Submit as many as 10 clippings of published headlines you have written, pages you have laid out, or articles you have written. Photocopies are acceptable. Clips will not be returned.

Photographers

Submit a portfolio of 20 to 60 slides, including news, features, and sports photos. Do not send oversized slide presentation boards, original clips, prints, tearsheets, yearbooks, or transparencies. However, you should include caption information, and label each slide with your name. Slides will be returned.

Reporters

Submit as many as 10 clippings of published articles you have written. Photocopies are acceptable. Clips will not be returned.

SCIENCE MAGAZINE INTERNSHIP

American Association for the Advancement of Science
Senior Human Resources Officer
Science Intern Program
1200 New York Avenue, NW #102
Washington, DC 20005
hrtemp@aaas.org
http://www.aaas.org/careercenter/internships/science.shtml

What You Can Earn: "Modest" salary.

Application Deadlines: November 1 for winter-spring internship (January through June) and April 1 for summer-fall internship (July through December).

Educational Experience: A scientific background is advantageous but is not required, with science writing experience; should be prepared to report, research, write, and edit under weekly deadlines.

Requirements: Must be a college graduate or senior in college when you apply.

OVERVIEW

Science is the largest circulating weekly magazine dedicated to basic research, founded in 1880 by Thomas Alva Edison and published by the American Association for the Advancement of Science (AAAS*). Science* covers a variety of topical issues just like other newspapers and news magazines, but its writers also analyze technical subjects on the research frontier.

As a *Science* intern, you'll join the regular news staff in Washington, D.C., and devote most of your time to contributing to the magazine and to ScienceNow, the magazine's daily online news service. In addition, you'll research and write other news stories, help in production, fill in for absent staffers, and provide help as needed to staff writers and editors.

HOW TO APPLY

Send your resume with published writing samples and references to the preceding address. You may be asked to complete a short writing or editing assignment, which (along with experience and submitted pieces) will provide a basis for evaluation by news editors. Editors make a final selection of the January intern in the middle of November and of the July intern in the middle of April.

SCIENCE NEWS INTERNSHIP

Science News Internship
1719 N Street, N.W.
Washington, DC 20036
(202) 785-2255

scinews@sciserv.org
http://www.sciencenews.org/pages/internships. asp

What You Can Earn: $1800 a month.
Application Deadlines: October 15 for spring session; February 1 for summer session; June 15 for fall session.
Educational Experience: College graduates planning careers in science writing; preference is given to students completing an advanced degree in journalism with an emphasis in science writing; skilled writers working toward an advanced degree in science are also considered.
Requirements: None specified.

OVERVIEW

Science News is an award-winning weekly magazine covering all fields of science for a general readership whose 16 pages include short articles that appeal to both general readers and scientists. Published since 1922, the magazine now has more than one million readers.

The weekly magazine debuted on March 13, 1922 as the *Science News-Letter,* as a way to supply newspapers with timely reports on scientific and technical developments. It quickly grew into a primary source of science news; over the years, the *Science News-Letter* reported a wide range of scientific developments from the beginning of atomic energy to modern genetics. The magazine became *Science News* with the March 12, 1966 issue and remains the only U.S. science weekly newsmagazine.

As an intern, you'll work as a full-time science writer for three months under the guidance of editors and writers in Washington, D.C. You'll come up with many of your own story ideas, reporting and writing one or two articles a week, including news stories and longer features. One applicant is chosen for spring (January through April); summer (May through August) and fall (September through December).

HOW TO APPLY

Send a cover letter indicating the period for which you're applying, a resume, references with contact information, and at least three journalistic science-writing samples to the preceding address.

SEATTLE TIMES INTERNSHIP

**Danyelle Lesch, Coordinator/Hiring & Staff
 Development**
The Seattle Times
PO Box 70
Seattle, WA 98111
newsinternships@seattletimes.com
http://seattletimes.com/internships

What You Can Earn: Internship is paid.
Application Deadlines: Rolling.
Educational Experience: Sophomores, juniors, seniors, and graduate students attending a four-year college or university. Applicants must be journalism majors or have a demonstrated commitment to print journalism. Internship experience on a daily newspaper is a plus.
Requirements: Must have a car.

OVERVIEW

The Pulitzer Prize-winning *Seattle Times*, founded in 1896, is one of the best newspapers in the Pacific Northwest and offers paid summer internships to outstanding students pursuing a journalism career. For 12 weeks, interns attend weekly training sessions and staff meetings with other employees and work on a variety of assignments. Each intern also receives a skill-development plan and guidance from a staff mentor and works as a general-assignment reporters at the city desk and in suburban bureaus. You could also choose to work as a business reporter, copy desk editor, photographer, artist/page designer, and sports reporter.

HOW TO APPLY

Send a cover letter, resume, work samples, names of three references familiar with your work, and a one-page essay on why you're interested in journalism as a career to the coordinator/hiring & staff development, at the preceding address. Include several samples of reporting, editing, photos, or page designs. For further information, e-mail newsinternships@seattletimes.com.

SIERRA MAGAZINE INTERNSHIP

Associate Editor, Sierra
85 Second Street, 2nd Floor
San Francisco, CA 94105
Fax: (415) 977-5794
jennifer.hattam@sierraclub.org
http://www.sierraclub.org/jobs/edintern.htm

What You Can Earn: $600 per season.
Application Deadlines: Winter/spring (January through April): November 1; summer (May through August): March 1; fall (September through December): July 1.
Educational Experience: Journalism experience helpful.
Requirements: Ability to work 20 hours a week; strong editorial skills and a well-rounded awareness of environmental issues.

OVERVIEW

Sierra is the award-winning national magazine of the Sierra Club, which acts as a guide to its more than one million readers to help them reflect their passion to explore, enjoy, and protect the planet. Expertly written and strikingly photographed, each issue celebrates the wonders of the natural world, combining analysis with outdoor adventure and travel features.

Editorial internships at *Sierra* give students an overview of the process of selecting and preparing manuscripts for publication in a national magazine.

As a *Sierra* intern, you'll sit in on all editorial meetings and perform a variety of research and fact-checking tasks for editors in any of three four-month internships.

HOW TO APPLY

To apply for a *Sierra* internship, send a letter describing your qualifications and interests, which internship period you prefer, and a resume and a brief writing sample to the preceding address. The most helpful writing samples are not research papers or essays but newspaper or magazine articles that illustrate your ability to research facts, organize information, and interview a variety of sources.

ST. PETERSBURG TIMES SUMMER INTERNSHIP

St. Petersburg Times
PO Box 1121
St. Petersburg, FL 33731-1121
(727) 893-8780
Fax: (727) 892-2257
waclawek@sptimes.com
http://www.sptimes.com/internship

What You Can Earn: $450 a week (no benefits); returning full-time students are eligible to apply for scholarships worth $3,500 for undergraduates and $1,500 for graduate students.
Application Deadlines: December 1 for news; February 15 for all others.

Educational Experience: Sophomores, juniors, seniors, and graduate students interested in careers in the newspaper industry.
Requirements: Experience at a college publication and at least one professional internship; car and valid driver's license.

OVERVIEW

The *St. Petersburg Times'* internship program introduces college students to careers in the newspaper industry. Interns work in departments throughout the company, gaining valuable hands-on experience. Each year, the *Times* offers about 20 internships in news, advertising, circulation, marketing, production, and Web publishing. Interns work in the downtown St. Petersburg office, the newspaper's headquarters, and in several bureaus in the paper's five-county circulation area in West Central Florida.

Internships are for a full-time workweek, Monday through Friday. The newspaper has won six Pulitzer Prizes for reporting and was named one of the country's top 10 newspapers for color reproduction in 2002. It has been ranked consistently as one of the best newspapers in the nation, according to *Time* magazine; in 1999 the *Columbia Journalism Review* ranked the *Times* No. 9 on its list of the 21 top newspapers for the 21st century.

Perks for interns include a Poynter Institute seminar on ethics; tour of the printing plant; tour of the bureaus; workshops on job interviews and the business side of the newspaper; a Devil Rays baseball game; and an end-of-summer luncheon.

HOW TO APPLY

Send a cover letter with an application (you can download one at http://www2.sptimes.com/pdfs/intern2004.pdf), a resume, and three references to the preceding address. News intern applicants should include five or six clips that show the range of your work.

For advertising internships in classified, retail, and Web sales, contact Joanne Horst, Advertising, at the preceding address.

For photography internships, contact Sherman Zent at the preceding address.

For an online product internship (multimedia reporter and page designer), contact Christine Montgomery, Director of Electronic Publishing.

ST. PETERSBURG TIMES YEARLONG NEWSROOM INTERNSHIP

St. Petersburg Times
PO Box 1121
St. Petersburg, FL 33731-1121
(727) 893-8780
Fax: (727) 892-2257
http://www.sptimes.com/internship

What You Can Earn: $625 a week with benefits.
Application Deadlines: February 1.
Educational Experience: College graduates.
Requirements: Experience at a college publication and at least one professional internship; car and valid driver's license.

OVERVIEW

The *St. Petersburg Times'* year-long news internship program begins September 1 through August 31 as a more in-depth introduction to professional print journalism. Interns work in departments throughout the company, gaining valuable hands-on experience. Each year, the *Times* offers about 20 internships in news, advertising, circulation, marketing, production and Web publishing. Interns work in the downtown St. Petersburg office, the newspaper's headquarters, and in several bureaus in the paper's five-county circulation area in West Central Florida.

Internships are for a full-time workweek, Monday through Friday. The newspaper has won six Pulitzer Prizes for reporting and was named one of the country's top 10 newspapers for color reproduction in 2002. It has been ranked consistently as one of the best newspapers in the nation, according to *Time* magazine; in 1999 the *Columbia Journalism Review* ranked the *Times* No. 9 on its list of the 21 top newspapers for the 21st century.

Perks for interns include a Poynter Institute seminar on ethics; tour of the printing plant; tour of the bureaus; workshops on job interviews and the business side of the newspaper; Devil Rays baseball game; and end-of-summer luncheon.

HOW TO APPLY

Send a cover letter, a copy of your resume, 10 or 12 clips that show the range of your work, and three references to the deputy managing editor Rob Hooker at the preceding address.

TAMPA TRIBUNE INTERNSHIP

Tampa Tribune
200 S. Parker Street
Tampa, FL 33606
(813) 259-7633
bdominick@tampatrib.com
http://www.tampatrib.com

What You Can Earn: $480 a week with benefits.
Application Deadlines: December 1 for summer session.
Educational Experience:
Requirements: Experience at least one professional internship; car and valid driver's license.

OVERVIEW

Internships are available in copyediting, reporting, graphics, and photography. The internship program is competitive—the paper solicits applications from across the country. The staff also interview students on a dozen or so campuses each fall. However, a personal interview isn't a prerequisite to being selected—every year some interns are invited to Tampa solely on the basis of their resumes, work samples, and recommendations. At the paper, you'll work beside talented staffers, competing with them to get the best play for your stories. Every summer at least some interns see their byline on Page 1, but all of them write stories for virtually every section of the newspaper. But at least you won't be making coffee, distributing faxes, or answering the telephone! It's not unusual for Tribune interns to write 30 to 50 bylined stories during their 10 weeks in the newsroom.

Although there's no typical intern experience at the *Tribune,* most interns spend part of the summer in one of the metropolitan bureaus, each of which has an editor and three to six reporters. Bureau interns are responsible for producing local zoned sections once or twice a week which concentrate on broad issues and profiles plus the minutiae of homeowners meetings and zoning boards. Bureau reporters also cover breaking news in their area for the daily newspaper. Interns are given the opportunity to request a new assignment midway through the summer. That means you might start in a bureau and then transfer to county government; or start in business and then transfer to a bureau. Transfers are not mandatory and some interns opt to stay with one editor for the full internship.

Your assignment depends on your interests and what is needed in your bureau. You might fill in for a vacationing cops or city hall reporter. You might be asked to develop a little-covered topic. You might be given a general assignment beat, the point person on whatever story develops each day. The editors value enterprise, so you should expect that 50 to 60 percent of the stories you write will be your own ideas. You'll be treated like other reporters in the office, with allowances for your experience level. That means if the bureau staff takes turns answering the telephones, you'll have a stint answering telephones. But you will not be the only person in the office assigned that duty.

HOW TO APPLY

To download an application, visit this Web site http://recruiting.tampatrib.com/recruiting/internships/internapplication.doc. Fill out the application and send it, along with your resume along with six clips, a 500-word essay, and a completed application form to the address above. To fill out the online application, visit this Web site http://recruiting.tampatrib.com/recruiting/internships/internapplication.htm.

Working on your campus newspaper, stringing for your hometown daily, and being able to write on a variety of topics all improve your chances of being selected.

TEEN PEOPLE SUMMER INTERNSHIP

Teen People
Attn: Kimberly Beder
Time/Life Building, Room 35-58B
1271 Avenue of the Americas
New York, NY 10020
http://www.teenpeople.com

What You Can Earn: $5.15 an hour.
Application Deadlines: Early February for summer session (mid-June to early September); July 1 for fall session (early September to December 31); early November for spring session (early January to mid-July).
Educational Experience: College students majoring journalism or possessing a serious interest in journalism.
Requirements: None specified.

OVERVIEW

Teen People is an entertaining, inspiring monthly version of *People* magazine for teens. This takeoff of the popular weekly gossip magazine says it takes teens seriously and talks about the issues that matter most to them.

Each trimester, the magazine selects four bright, energetic journalism students to intern. If you're chosen, you'll get a firsthand look at the inner workings of a monthly magazine while helping assist the staff in a number of capacities. In the past, interns have read and responded to readers' letters, fact-checked features, and created clip files to help writers with their stories. Some interns have pitched their own ideas to the editors. The magazine is flexible and will work with you to develop a schedule around your classes and other work commitments.

HOW TO APPLY

To apply for this internship, send a cover letter explaining your interest in *Teen People's* internship program, a copy of your current resume, and at least one writing sample (preferably a journalistic piece that appeared in either a newspaper or magazine, but an essay will suffice). Do not send fiction or poetry. If you want your work to be returned, be sure to include a self-addressed stamped envelope.

Summer interns will be notified of acceptance by April 15; fall interns will be notified by early August; spring interns will be notified by early December.

TIME INC. SUMMER INTERNSHIP

College Relations Manager
Time Inc.
1271 Avenue of the Americas, 40-10
New York, NY 10020
linda_reals@timeinc.com
http://www.timeinc.com

What You Can Earn: Varies, ranging from $5.15/hour to $16/hour.
Application Deadlines: December 1 for summer internship.
Educational Experience: Undergraduates who will be between their junior and senior years during the internship or students pursuing a master's degree in journalism; minority and disabled students are encouraged to apply.
Requirements: None specified.

OVERVIEW

The *Time* summer editorial internship is a nine-week program for qualified students seeking experience in magazine and book publishing as reporters, writers, photographers or graphic designers. Interns work on the staff of one of Time Inc.'s magazines: *Time; Life; Money; People; People En Español; Teen People; Sports Illustrated; SI For Kids; Fortune; Entertainment Weekly; InStyle; Your Company*; and *Time Digital*.

As an editorial intern here, you'll do research, check facts, copyedit, and help with events, shoots, and interviews. You'll also participate in social events and career development and networking seminars scheduled specifically for interns. Although you'll probably not be writing finished copy for publication, students with exceptional writing skills have a better chance of writing for the magazines. Applicants for photo editing and graphic design internships are also encouraged to apply.

Most internships are available in New York, although a few are available in other offices, including Washington, D.C., Los Angeles, San Francisco, Atlanta, Chicago, Austin, Dallas, and Miami.

HOW TO APPLY

Your application must include an academic transcript, a resume, a 300-word statement of your background (school, jobs, activities, interests, and recent reading) and why you want to become a Time Inc. summer intern. Also send letter-size copies of two or three unstapled writing samples (published work preferred but not required). When you apply, rank your top-three magazine choices for assignment.

USA TODAY SUMMER INTERNSHIP

Internship Coordinator
USA TODAY
7950 Jones Branch Drive
McLean, VA 22108
(703) 854-3683
http://www.usatoday.com

What You Can Earn: Unpaid; college credit available.
Application Deadlines: December.
Educational Experience: College sophomores, juniors, seniors, and graduates students.
Requirements: Hard-working, ambitious students with outstanding journalistic skills and good academic records. Candidates should have completed at least one internship or have experience working for a school publication or other type of publication.

OVERVIEW
USA Today is the nation's largest-selling daily newspaper, with a circulation of approximately 2.3 million. Owned by Gannett, *USA Today* is available in 60 countries worldwide. Its newsmagazine weekend edition (*USA Weekend*) has a circulation of 22.7 million and is included in more than 600 newspapers each week.

USA Today offers several internships as reporters, copy editors, editorial page assistants, graphic artists, or photographers available each semester (spring, summer, fall, and winter) in its new facility in Tysons Corner, MD.

As an intern here, you'll be responsible for helping assignment editors with research for graphics and stories and learning online publishing techniques. Hours are flexible, but the daily paper needs you at least two days a week. They promise you a rare inside view of the nation's newspaper and an opportunity to learn from the best.

HOW TO APPLY
To apply, send your resume, cover letter, and six clips (if you have them), writing samples, or examples of your photo or design work to the preceding address. The application package also should include the names and phone numbers of three persons who can serve as references.

U.S. NEWS & WORLD REPORT INTERNSHIP

Intern Coordinator, U.S. News & World Report
1050 Thomas Jefferson Street NW
Washington, DC 20007
interns@usnews.com
http://www.usnews.com
http://www.usnews.com/usnews/usinfo/webjobs.
   htm#editintern

What You Can Earn: $12 an hour.
Application Deadlines: December 15 for a summer internship.
Educational Experience: College juniors, seniors, and recent graduates.
Requirements: Newspaper or magazine experience.

OVERVIEW
U.S. News & World Report is a weekly news magazine with a circulation of 2 million and was founded in 1948 by a journalistic merger of a weekly newspaper called the *United States News* and a weekly magazine called *World Report*. From 1962 to 1984, *U.S. News* was employee-owned; it was subsequently bought by publisher and real

estate developer Mortimer B. Zuckerman, who was also chair and co-publisher of the *New York Daily News.*

In 1983, *U.S. News* began its annual rankings of American colleges and universities. The fall of 1987 marked the first publication of the newsstand book, *America's Best Colleges.* It was joined by *America's Best Graduate Schools* in 1994. *U.S. News* began its Internet ventures in 1993, with a two-year stint as a content provider to the CompuServe Information Service. *U.S. News Online* (www.usnews.com), the magazine's Web site, went online in 1995. All articles from the print edition of *U.S. News* also appear on *U.S. News Online.*

If you're selected as an intern for *U.S. News,* you'll work at the headquarters in Washington, D.C., from June to August. As an intern, you'll be treated like a junior reporter and assigned to one of the magazine's six sections (although you'll also have ample opportunity to work in other sections). In addition to researching and reporting for other staffers, you'll write and report stories of your own. Interns nearly always leave with bylined clips; the quantity, length, and significance of the clips depend on many factors, but creativity, talent, and drive don't hurt.

HOW TO APPLY

If you're interested in this internship, send a cover letter, resume, five to 10 published clips, contact information for two references, and anything else you think might be interesting to the preceding address.

WALL STREET JOURNAL INTERNSHIP

Assistant Managing Editor
The Wall Street Journal
PO Box 300
Princeton, NJ 08543-0300

(609) 520-7004
http://www.wsj.com

What You Can Earn: $600 a week.
Application Deadlines: November 1 for summer internship.
Educational Experience: College students (either undergraduate or graduate school).
Requirements: Most interns have had prior internships with other newspapers as well as extensive experience on a campus newspaper.

OVERVIEW

Dow Jones & co. publishes the *Wall Street Journal,* the world's leading business publication, and its international and online editions, the *Wall Street Journal Europe* and the *Asian Wall Street Journal.* Their other publications include *Barron's,* the *Wall Street Journal Sunday,* the *Wall Street Journal Special Editions,* and the *Wall Street Journal Classroom Edition.* Founded in 1889, the *Wall Street Journal* reaches the nation's top business and political leaders, as well as investors across the country. Earning at last count 29 Pulitzer Prizes for outstanding journalism, the *Journal* seeks to help its readers succeed by providing essential and relevant information, presented fairly and accurately, from a dependable and trusted source.

Ten-week internships at this newspaper begin in June and end in August. About 18 student journalists are selected each year during a highly competitive process.

HOW TO APPLY

There is no application form. If you'd like to be considered, send a cover letter, resume, and a dozen of your best by-lined clips to the preceding address. Your clips should be clear, unbound photocopies on letter- or legal-sized paper. PDF and Web-based clips submitted by e-mail are also acceptable. The screening process puts heavy emphasis on clips and journalistic experience. Only applicants selected for final consideration are interviewed, but all applicants, accepted or not, will be notified of a decision by the end of February.

WASHINGTONIAN ADVERTISING INTERNSHIP

The Washingtonian
Media Manager
1828 L Street, NW, Suite 200
Washington, DC 20036
(202) 296-1246

What You Can Earn: $6.15 an hour.
Application Deadlines: June for the fall session (September through December); December for the spring session (January through May); May for the summer session (June through August).
Educational Experience: All undergraduates eligible for academic credit.
Requirements: Must have proof that you are receiving class credit from your university; newspaper/magazine or marketing/sales experience is preferred but not required.

OVERVIEW

The *Washingtonian* is a monthly lifestyle magazine for the Washington area, located in downtown D.C., and offers two or three part-time internships in advertising in three different sessions. As an advertising intern on the *Washingtonian,* you'll spend three to five months contacting prospective advertisers and drafting direct marketing and copywriting letters for each monthly issue. You'll also serve as real estate and travel department sales support. PC and Mac computer data systems are used to update and research advertising files (File Manager, Act, Word, and Excel). This part-time position is typically about 20 hours a week and a flexible schedule can be arranged.

HOW TO APPLY

If you're interested in advertising, submit a cover letter and resume to the media manager at the preceding address. Do not send applications via fax or e-mail. For more information, call the preceding number.

WASHINGTONIAN ART DEPARTMENT INTERNSHIP

The Washingtonian
Design Assistant
1828 L Street, NW, Suite 200
Washington, DC 20036
(202)296-1246

What You Can Earn: School credit only.
Application Deadlines: June 1 for the fall session (September through December); October 1 for the spring session (January through May); April 1 for the summer session (June through August).
Educational Experience: Any undergraduates eligible for academic credit.
Requirements: Knowledge of the Macintosh computer system is essential, especially QuarkXPress and Adobe Photoshop.

OVERVIEW

The *Washingtonian* is a monthly lifestyle magazine for the Washington area, located in downtown D.C., and offers two part-time internships in art each semester to college students interested in publication design and the production process. The internships are for school credit only, so interns must be enrolled in college. As an art intern, you'll help with production, scanning photos, designing in-house ads, designing promotional pieces, calling for stock photos, and contacting and filing incoming illustrator and photography samples. Qualified interns also will be given magazine layout assignments. Twenty hours a week is required and a flexible schedule can be arranged.

HOW TO APPLY

If you're interested in art, submit a send a cover letter specifying the term for which you're applying (spring, summer, or fall), along with a resume and nonreturnable samples of your print design, to the design assistant at the preceding address. E-mailed applications are not accepted. You should be prepared to attend an interview and present a portfolio. The portfolio should consist of work created in QuarkXpress and Adobe Photoshop.

WASHINGTONIAN EDITORIAL INTERNSHIP

The Washingtonian
1828 L Street, NW, Suite 200
Washington, DC 20036
What You Can Earn: $6.15 an hour.
Application Deadlines: July for the fall session (September through December); November for the spring session (January through May); March for the summer session (June through August).
Educational Experience: College students and recent graduates.
Requirements: Intelligence; good research, reporting, and writing skills; independence.

OVERVIEW

Editorial internships are 40 hours a week for four months in the fall, five months in the spring, and three months in the summer. The *Washingtonian* offers an experience that's "low on grunt work and high on opportunity." Duties include fact-checking, research, and some writing.

During each session, editors, writers, and the heads of the advertising, promotion, production, circulation, art, and photography departments will meet with you once or twice a week to discuss their own roles at the magazine and careers in journalism. Graduates of the internship program have gone on to publications such as *Vanity Fair, People, Entertainment Weekly, National Geographic, Allure,* and *USA Today.*

HOW TO APPLY

Send a cover letter, resume, three clips, and a list of references to the preceding address. Do not send applications via fax or e-mail.

WASHINGTON POST INTERNSHIP

The Washington Post
Attn: Newsroom Summer Internship Program
1150 15th Street, NW
Washington, DC 20071

For more information, contact
Newsroom Personnel Administrator
(202) 334-6765

What You Can Earn: $825 a week.
Application Deadlines: November 1.
Educational Experience: College junior, senior, or graduate student enrolled in a degree program the winter before the summer internship.
Requirements: Previous internships and/or experience on a college newspaper are preferred. It is very helpful if reporting interns have a car available for their use during the internship. All interns must provide their own transportation to and from work.

OVERVIEW

The *Washington Post* offers 12-week, paid reporting internships on the metro, financial, sports, and style desks; copyediting internships on the financial, foreign, national and metro desks; page and graphic design internships on the news desk and in news art; a photography internship on the photo desk; and a writing internship in the editorial department. Interns write articles, edit copy, take photographs, design pages and produce graphics, and are treated as staff members during their 12 weeks of employment.

During the first week, the paper offers a welcome lunch to introduce interns to senior editors, a daylong bus tour of the Washington, D.C., metropolitan area, and computer training. The *Post* also hosts seminars on on various topics. Weekly lunches with senior editors and reporters as guest speakers enhance understanding of the *Washington*

Post and the industry. In recent summers, lunch speakers have included *Washington Post* company chairman Donald Graham; publisher Bo Jones, former executive editor Ben Bradlee; executive editor Len Downie; and assistant managing editor Bob Woodward.

The internship program is competitive, with more than 480 applications received for the 2005 summer program. Most of the summer interns have had previous internships at noncampus daily newspapers, in addition to working on their college publications.

HOW TO APPLY

Download an application form at http://www.washpost.com/xnet/washpost/requests.nsf/frmInternshipApp?OpenForm. You must submit your application packet by mail. Do not send your packet in a notebook, presentation cover, clear plastic pages or other fancy packaging. The packaging will be discarded before your application is evaluated. The packet must include, in this order:

- checklist (download at: http://www.washpost.com/news_ed/summer_internships/pdf/checklist.pdf

- signed application
- typed autobiographical essay of at least 500 words
- resume
- work samples (on 8 ½ x 11 paper); don't staple materials together
- reporters, copy editors and Editorial Page candidates: 6 to 8 clips, preferably photocopies, on 8 1/2 x 11 paper.
- photographers: portfolio of 20 to 40 shots that include sports/action, features, portraits and a picture story; prints (preferred), CD or slides
- graphic artists and news editors/page designers: portfolio of 10 to 20 samples on 8 1/2 x 11 photocopies, slides, prints or PDF files on CD
- two letters of recommendation (Use the greeting "To whom it may concern:")
- college transcript (Note: Although the paper prefers they be included in your application packet, some colleges and/or references may want to send transcripts and letters of recommendation directly to the *Washington Post*.)

NATURE

AMERICAN FARMLAND TRUST INTERNSHIP

American Farmland Trust Internship
1200 18th Street, NW, Suite 800
Washington, D.C. 20036
(202) 331-7300
Fax: (202) 659-8339
kluck@farmland.org
http://www.farmland.org

What You Can Earn: $500-$750 depending on number of hours worked for three-four months; college credit is possible.
Application Deadlines: Rolling.
Educational Experience: College junior or senior.
Requirements: Organized; self-motivated; flexible; and interested in nonprofits, fundraising, land conservation, and/or the environment. Attention to detail is very important.

OVERVIEW

American Farmland Trust (AFT) is a national nonprofit organization working with communities and individuals to protect the best land, plan for growth, and keep the land healthy. As the leading advocate for farm and ranchland conservation, since its founding in 1980 AFT has helped win permanent protection for over a million acres of American farmland. AFT has three strategies for saving America's farmland: protecting the best land through publicly funded agricultural conservation easement programs; planning for growth through effective community planning and growth management; and keeping the land healthy for farmland through encouraging stewardship and conservations practices.

Internships (both part time and full time) are available in the development department (major gifts, foundations, and events). You can work either 10 to 20 hours or 20 to 30 hours a week for the summer (beginning and ending dates are flexible).

While at AFT, you'll be able to work on projects for the entire department and will learn about multiple facets of nonprofit fund-raising, from events to individual and corporate fund-raising to prospect research. The position is highly administrative, helping behind the scenes to cultivate donors. You may be involved in correspondence to funders; mailings; planning for events; identifying and researching prospective donors; and so on. Responsibilities will be based on performance.

HOW TO APPLY

To apply, e-mail your resume and cover letter to the preceding address. No phone calls.

AMERICAN FORESTS INTERNSHIP

American Forests
734 15th Street, NW, Suite 800
Washington, DC 20005
Fax: (202) 955-4588

What You Can Earn: A small stipend (typically $50 a week) or academic credit.
Application Deadlines: Rolling.
Educational Experience: Interns should have completed their first year of studies at a college or university; see specific internship requirements below.
Requirements: See specific internship requirements below.

OVERVIEW

American Forests is the nation's oldest nonprofit citizen conservation organization. Internships at American Forests are a great way to get on-the-job experience, whether you're interested in a conservation career, trees and forests, or simply want to learn more about communications, development, marketing, policy, or research. American Forests offers opportunities for internships in the following areas: communications, development and marketing, forest policy, global ReLeaf, and urban forestry.

In general, interns may help research and write articles and press releases and assist with event coordination; research and develop materials on the value of urban forests; develop tree-planting partnerships with community groups or corporations; and help plan policy initiatives and workshops. Interns may work 20 to 40 hours a week. Exact hours will be discussed during the selection process. Internships normally last three to six months.

Communications Intern

In this department, you'll write, research, and edit for *American Forests Magazine*, newsletters, and brochures; draft press releases; learn printing and production processes; communicate with authors and photographers; help with media outreach; and help with administrative tasks as needed. The intern will work half time with publications and half time with media relations.

Candidates should be English or communications majors and have an interest in conservation issues and possess good writing and editing skills, a desire to learn, organizational skills, flexibility, and creativity. Knowledge of Microsoft Word for Macintosh and familiarity with QuarkXpress are pluses.

Development and Marketing Intern

This intern will help with corporate-outreach efforts, prospect for new clients, and help maintain corporate files and databases. Other duties will include researching potential foundation supporters, calling foundations for preliminary discussions of interest, drafting letters, proofreading grant proposals, and visiting local trust-management offices to review annual reports.

Forest Policy

Forest policy interns will work on American Forests' community-based ecosystem management program, which helps build the capacity of citizens to participate in policy issues and, ultimately, implement projects on the ground. The intern will attend congressional hearings and report to community partners nationwide, meet the public and within the organization, help set up and manage the database, redesign and update publications, redesign and update Web pages, participate in program and strategy development, and work on special projects.

Candidates should have excellent communication and organizational skills, creativity, a sense of humor, and the ability to work independently and as part of a team. Solid writing skills are essential. You must be computer literate and familiar with the Internet and interested in forestry/natural resources issues that relate to communities. Study in environmental studies/forestry, political science, or sociology or related interdisciplinary experience is required.

Global ReLeaf

In this area, interns will play an integral role in restoring forests ecosystems across the United States and abroad by creating and fostering good relationships with organizations to plant trees and promoting and facilitating the planting, caring, and understanding of rural and urban trees through community grants, shared expertise, and public education.

Candidates should have strong oral and written communications skills; strong organizational skills; knowledge of Microsoft Word and/or Word Perfect, Excel, and database programs; knowledge of HTML helpful; interest in forestry and environment; and must be creative and flexible.

Urban Forestry

Urban forestry interns will help with local and regional analyses of the economic benefits of trees and forests. Interns will help perform analyses, develop presentations, and help develop new versions of CITYgreen, an ArcView extension designed to quantify the benefits of trees and forests. Other geographic information systems (GIS) research or administrative tasks may also be assigned.

Candidates should have experience with ArcView software; experience with ERDAS Imagine and remote sensing, ArcInfo, or Avenue is helpful.

HOW TO APPLY

Email or mail a resume and one-page writing sample, along with a cover letter indicating the internship for which you're applying and reasons for your interest in American Forests, to the preceding address. If you're applying for the communications internship, your writing sample should consist of clips.

AMERICAN RIVERS INTERNSHIP

Internship Coordinator
American Rivers
1025 Vermont Avenue, NW, Suite 720
Washington, DC 20005
Fax: (202) 347-9242

What You Can Earn: Unpaid.
Application Deadlines: Rolling.
Educational Experience: Undergraduate and graduate students interested in river conservation, public policy, communications, and community development.
Requirements: None specified.

OVERVIEW

Founded in 1973, this group is the leader of a nationwide river conservation movement that seeks to protect and restore rivers and the variety of life they sustain. Headquartered in Washington, D.C., the group also operates northwest regional offices in Seattle and Portland and eight field offices across the country that work with local communities and river activists.

Interns work with members of the conservation staff in one of the campaign or program areas, including legislative research, grassroots organizing, working on various conservation programs, responding to requests from river activists, researching conservation issues, and various long-term projects.

If you intern here, you'll do much more than answer phones or make copies; staffers will rely on you to do substantive work, such as writing articles for the membership newsletter, doing research for a report, or working on the American Rivers Web site. In addition, the organization regularly hires former interns as full-time staffers. Other former American Rivers interns currently work in other aspects of environmental policy and communications, both in D.C. and around the country.

American Rivers internships are 25 hours per week; most interns work three full days a week and get a paid part-time job besides.

Communications

This department at American Rivers oversees the development and implementation of the organization's media affairs; publications; Web site and online community development; the organization's annual report on the nation's most endangered rivers; and a full-sized traveling museum exhibit. Working in Washington, D.C., gives interns valuable firsthand experience in national conservation, policy, and communications efforts.

Typically, there are two internships in this area: general communications and Web site/online community development. In these internships, you'll work with communications and conservation staff to promote the goals, accomplishments, and actions of American Rivers' campaigns.

In general communications, the summer communications intern will work on a number of projects, writing stories for the membership newsletter and Web site, researching and acquiring photography for publications, proofreading and copyediting documents and publications, calling reporters to pitch stories, maintaining the department's press clippings system, and assisting in the general day-to-day operations of the department. You'll also have a chance to research a project that interests you.

In Web site development, you'll continually develop and support an online community of River friends and activists as a Web assistant helping the director of Internet strategies with daily maintenance of the American Rivers Web page (http://www.AmericanRivers.org), including basic coding, design, content development, management of community members, and brainstorming about new and innovative ways to use the Internet to communicate American Rivers' message.

Conservation/Policy Internships
Community Rivers Campaign
This campaign works to identify and implement how U.S. communities can best use water. You'll research information related to water-scarcity efforts, including researching community innovators in sustainable water-management practices, preparing information on these innovators for a Web report, preparing an expanded drought and water conservation media tool kit, and conducting research for media pitches in the southeastern and Great Lakes states on water-scarcity issues.

Corps Reform Campaign
American Rivers is one of the leaders of a national effort to reform the U.S. Army Corps of Engineers, a 225-year-old federal agency that helps build and maintain the nation's infrastructure for navigation, flood control, and other water projects. You'll help with legislative/public policy duties, outreach to grassroots organizations, maintain and develop Web-related information/activist toolkits, and research issues to support the reform campaign.

Legislative/Public Policy Campaign
The government affairs department interacts with members of Congress, the administration, federal agencies, and other conservation groups to monitor public policy related to rivers. You'll work with the director of government affairs and conservation staff to develop resource conservation legislation, craft strategies for working with Congress and the administration to protect rivers, and educate key members of Congress and their staffs. You'll also research specific river-conservation issues and legislation, help develop strategies for protecting and restoring rivers, write position papers, and create briefing materials for Capitol Hill.

Outreach Campaign
You may help produce the River Budget, an annual publication that brings together hundreds of conservation groups across the country to advocate federal funding for river protection and conservation.

You may help write sections of the report, identify important river conservation programs and the level at which they should be funded, contact conservation groups for their endorsement of the report, do photo research, and perform administrative tasks. You also may work on content development and/or outreach for the River Agenda, a collaborative initiative involving national, regional, and local river conservation organizations working together to create a common agenda for the river community. The outreach internships provide an excellent opportunity for students to develop expertise in the area of river conservation and gain direct experience working with local, regional, and national environmental groups across the country.

Rivers Unplugged Campaign
This campaign helps facilitate the removal of dams that no longer make sense. You'll help draft resource materials for the dam removal toolkit, implement policy initiatives at the state-agency level, and help on individual removal projects. Duties will also include managing the distribution of the dam removal toolkit resource materials and reorganizing the information-collection system. The ideal candidate will have strong writing and research skills, demonstrable initiative, and passion for the environment.

HOW TO APPLY
Download an application at http://www.amrivers. org/doc_repository/Jobs/Internship%20Brochure %201103.pdf.

Submit the application form with a cover letter, resume, three references, and a brief writing sample to the preceding address.

THE ANTARCTICA PROJECT INTERNSHIP

The Antarctica Project
1630 Connecticut Avenue, NW, Third Floor
Washington, D.C. 20009
(202) 234-2480
 http://www2.asoc.org/support_volunteer.htm

What You Can Earn: Unpaid.
Application Deadlines: Rolling.
Educational Experience: International studies and law students are encouraged to apply; a strong interest in environmental protection is helpful.
Requirements: College junior or senior with at least a 3.0 GPA.

OVERVIEW
If your heart yearns for wild, open spaces and saving the environment, the Antarctica project could be a terrific internship opportunity for you. As the only nonprofit environmental group in the United States that deals solely with the protection of Antarctica and the southern oceans, current issues include the implementation of the Environmental Protocol to the Antarctic Treaty, the protection of the southern ocean marine ecosystem, which includes the southern ocean whale sanctuary.

The Antarctica Project is part of the Antarctic and Southern Ocean Coalition (ASOC), which contains nearly 230 organizations in 49 countries and leads the national and international campaigns to protect the biological diversity and pristine wilderness of Antarctica, including its oceans and marine life. The group works for passage of strong measures that protect the marine ecosystem from the harmful effects of overfishing and works to ensure that the integrity of the southern ocean whale sanctuary is maintained and internationally respected. The organization works closely with the key users of Antarctica, including scientists, tourists, and governments to ensure that activities have minimal environmental impact. The organization conducts legal and policy research and analysis and produces educational materials.

The Antarctica folks cope with small quarters in their Washington, D.C., office, so they are looking for two to five interns a year who can work independently and take on a lot of responsibility. Interns are usually assigned a major project to complete and must be willing to assist in an administrative capacity. You can earn academic credit for this 12 to 16 week internship in fall, spring, or summer.

HOW TO APPLY
Send a resume, cover letter, and a short writing sample to the preceding address.

ARNOLD ARBORETUM OF HARVARD UNIVERSITY INTERNSHIP

The Arnold Arboretum of Harvard University
Isabella Welles Hunnewell Internship Program
125 Arborway
Jamaica Plain, MA 02130-3500
(617) 524-1718
Fax: (617) 524-1418
Email: aaintern@arnarb.harvard.edu
http://www.arboretum.harvard.edu/programs/
   intern.html

What You Can Earn: $8.25 an hour.
Application Deadlines: Mid-February.

Educational Experience: Some experience or training in horticulture or botany or other plant-related studies.

Requirements: Maturity, self-motivation, and flexibility.

OVERVIEW

The arboretum internship combines practical hands-on training in horticulture with educational courses for 14 interns accepted for 12- to 24-week appointments. Ten interns will work with the grounds maintenance department, two in the Dana Greenhouses, and two in the curation department.

As part of the training program, interns are required to take three courses (multiple sessions) in woody plant identification, cultural maintenance of woody plant materials, and plant propagation. Additional lectures and field trips to gardens and historical landscapes are also required. Interns are eligible to audit courses in the arboretum's adult education program on a space-available basis.

Grounds Maintenance

In this internship, you'll be working with mature shrubs and trees planted over large expanses of grass and meadow. Working with the permanent grounds maintenance staff, you'll weed, mulch, mow, plant, prune, and perform other horticultural tasks and participate in renovation and/or hardscape projects as needed.

Dana Greenhouses

In this internship, you'll be working where all arboretum plant material is propagated and maintained until planted on the grounds. You'll help water, weed, mulch, pot, and propagate softwood cuttings. You should have experience in woody plant propagation and/or greenhouse operations.

Plant Records

Curation of the living collections is a fundamental part of the arboretum's mission; in fact, detailed plant records have been kept since 1872. You'll help the curatorial associates in the daily tasks required to maintain these records, such as field-checking plants, labeling, mapping, and collecting herbarium specimens. You should be familiar with woody plants, preferably through formal coursework, and have experience with computers.

HOW TO APPLY

Download the application at the preceding Web address and submit it. Preference will be given to candidates who have one or more years of education in horticulture, botany, landscape design, or other plant-related fields at college or technical high school; related work experience in a nursery, greenhouse, garden center, park, arboretum, or botanical garden; and interest in horticulture, botany, or another plant-related field. You should be healthy, since you'll be expected to work productively in all weather conditions (heat, humidity, and rain) and have some flexibility in start dates (the latest acceptable start date is the end of May, and interns are expected to work through mid-August).

ASPEN CENTER FOR ENVIRONMENTAL STUDIES INTERNSHIP

Aspen Center for Environmental Studies
100 Puppy Street
Aspen, CO 81611
(970) 925-5756
Fax: (970) 925-4819
aces@aspennature.org
http://www.aspennature.org

What You Can Earn: $125 per week stipend, plus housing provided. Tuition-free participation in one or more of ACES' Naturalist Field School courses is offered.

Application Deadlines: March 1.

Educational Experience: Educational background in the natural sciences, environmental education, or related fields.

Requirements: Interested and enthusiastic about environmental education; self-motivated with a sincere interest in the environment; experience working with the public. First aid and CPR certification is necessary.

OVERVIEW

The Aspen Center for Environmental Studies (ACES) is a nonprofit environmental education center with two locations: 25 acre nature preserve at Hallam Lake in Aspen and 113-acre wildlife preserve at Rock Bottom Ranch in Basalt. ACES is open year-round and provides a variety of natural science programs for people of all ages and interests, dedicated to inspiring life-long commitment to the earth by teaching environmental responsibility, conserving and restoring the balance of natural communities, and advancing the idea that the earth must be respected and nurtured.

Elizabeth Paepcke formed ACES in 1969 and donated the 22-acre property behind her West End home, which included Hallam Lake, for the development of an environmental center and preserve.

Although many organizations provide outdoor education, only very few have significant direct involvement in natural science education of elementary and secondary school students. ACES is one of the few that maintain an involvement with children from an early age, conducting about 180 field-study programs each school year at Hallam Lake, Rock Bottom Ranch, and various other outdoor sites serving students from public and private schools.

In addition, the Aspen Center conducts an intensive summer naturalist internship program that trains and employs 12 naturalists each year, from early June through early September. As an intern here, you'll receive valuable education, training, and experience while you conduct environmental education programs and natural history interpretive tours at Hallam Lake Nature Preserve, Aspen Mountain, Snowmass, and at the Maroon Bells.

As an intern, you'll help manage the visitor center and 25-acre nature preserve, teach environmental education programs for children, and lead interpretive nature walks at Aspen Mountain, Snowmass, and the Maroon Bells in the White River National Forest. You'll also conduct birds of prey programs with ACES' resident injured birds of prey (including a golden eagle, peregrine falcon, and red tail hawk) and get involved in special projects including caring for the resident birds of prey, caring for the indoor plants and live animals, upkeep of the indoor trout stream and rearing troughs, and development and maintenance of the self-guided trails.

After serving in the summer internship, you'll have the opportunity to apply as a winter naturalist and educator. Since 1996, more than 80 percent of all winter naturalists and educators came to Aspen through the summer naturalist internship. While most of the hiring for these advanced positions is done in-house, applicants whose background includes experience equivalent to ACES' summer naturalist internship will be considered.

HOW TO APPLY

Download an online application at http://www.aspennature.org/Images/ACES_intern_form.pdf. Fax or mail the completed application form along with three references to the preceding address.

AULLWOOD AUDUBON CENTER AND FARM INTERNSHIP

Intern Coordinator
Aullwood Audubon Center and Farm
1000 Aullwood Road
Dayton, OH 45414

937-890-7360
aacf4@gemair.com
http://www.audubon.org/nas/hr/internship/
   aullwood.html

What You Can Earn: $120 a week plus housing (when available).
Application Deadlines: Rolling. Internships are available in winter/spring (January to May), summer (June through August), and fall (September through December).
Educational Experience: Completion of two years of college-level coursework in environmental studies, education, or a related field. Some teaching experience and/or curriculum development is necessary, as is a strong natural history background.
Requirements: Excellent communication skills, enthusiasm, physical fitness, self-motivation, and a desire to learn; willing to work 40 hours a week, including weekends.

OVERVIEW

The National Audubon Society's mission is to conserve and restore natural ecosystems, focusing on birds, other wildlife, and their habitats for the benefit of humanity and the Earth's biological diversity. The Aullwood Audubon Center and Farm is located 10 miles north of Dayton, Ohio, along a river valley featuring the Stillwater River. The 350 acres of natural areas and organic farm provide outstanding learning opportunities in a diverse and beautiful setting. The land includes flat farmland and leads down through woods, prairie, pond, and meadow to the level of the river.

Internships have been a part of this program for more than 30 years. An Aullwood internship is a full-time responsibility that lasts anywhere from 10 weeks to one year. You'll be working mostly on weekdays but also on some weekends and evenings, to develop and teach programs to school groups, from pre-school through high school. You'll plan and conduct programs for the general public and assist with special events and off-site exhibits. You'll also care for resident animals at the center and livestock at the farm, and complete an approved project around a chosen field of interest. You'll also be expected to serve in other capacities as needed to assist with day-to-day operations.

HOW TO APPLY

For more information and an application, contact the intern coordinator at the address above.

BAY NATURE MAGAZINE INTERNSHIP

Intern Coordinator
Bay Nature
1328 Sixth Street, Suite 2
Berkeley, CA 94710
Intern@baynature.com
http://www.baynature.com

What You Can Earn: Unpaid, but you may be considered for a paid internship after four months.
Application Deadlines: December 31.
Educational Experience: Unspecified.
Requirements: Strong interest (and ideally some prior experience) in journalism, environment, marketing, fund-raising, or office administration. Intern should be mature and self-motivated; able to work independently once a project is assigned; have a commitment to experiencing and protecting the natural environment; basic computer skills (Macintosh), including Word, Excel, Filemaker, Internet. Expertise in design, photography, natural history, computers (software or hardware), accounting, and so on, are highly desirable.

OVERVIEW

Bay Nature is a full-color quarterly magazine that explores the Bay Area natural world—

uniting artistic, scientific, conservation, literary, and recreational perspectives to celebrate, understand, and protect the environment. This two-year-old nonprofit magazine is based in West Berkeley, and affiliated with Heyday Books.

As an intern here, you'll get a chance to discover how a small magazine works while making substantive contributions; you'll be exposed to many aspects of the business, such as editorial, photo research, advertising sales, circulation, newsstand sales, marketing, community outreach, special events, foundation grants, and administration. While not every project will tax your intellect to its limits, there are ample opportunities to learn, exercise your creativity, and help build a successful magazine. At the same time, you'll help keep the office functioning as you answer phones, ship magazines, and so on, which is crucial to the magazine's day-to-day survival.

You will be matched with a staff member, who will help manage your workflow and make sure you have a good experience.

HOW TO APPLY

Send cover letter and resume to the address above.

CALLAWAY GARDENS INTERNSHIP

Callaway Gardens, Internship Coordinator
PO Box 2000
Pine Mountain, GA 31822-2000
1-800-CALLAWAY (225-5292); (706) 663-2281
Fax: (706) 663-6812
http://www.callawaygardens.com

What You Can Earn: $7.26 an hour.
Application Deadlines: January 15 for spring session; February 1 for summer session.
Educational Experience: Unspecified.
Requirements: Unspecified.

OVERVIEW

This award-winning, 14,000-acre gardens, resort, and preserve lies in the southernmost foothills of the Appalachian Mountains in Pine Mountain, Georgia, where year-round programs provide guests opportunities to explore the environment and learn more about the world around them. The Callaway Education Department presents workshops on many different horticultural, wildlife, and environmental topics.

Callaway is a manmade landscape in a unique natural setting created by businessman Cason J. Callaway and his wife, Virginia Hand Callaway, to provide a wholesome family environment of beauty, relaxation, and inspiration.

During the summer, college students from throughout the country are selected to intern at Callaway in horticulture and education. The internship program exposes students to challenges and opportunities in the field to give them a well-rounded experience to enhance their classroom education.

HOW TO APPLY

Write to the preceding address or call to request an application.

CHINCOTEAGUE NATIONAL WILDLIFE REFUGE INTERNSHIP

Volunteer Coordinator, Chincoteague National Wildlife Refuge
PO Box 62
Chincoteague, VA 23336
http://www.fws.gov/northeast/chinco/internships.htm

What You Can Earn: $125 a week plus free housing.

Application Deadlines: For interpretive internships: January 15 for spring (mid-March to mid-June); March 15 for summer (late May to early September); July 15 for fall (late August to early December); for environmental education internships: January 1 for spring (mid-March to early June); for field research assistant/wildlife management internships: March 1 for summer (mid-May to mid-August), August 1 for fall (early September to late November).

Educational Experience: A background in biology, wildlife management, recreation education, interpretation, or a related field; see individual internships below for more specific information.

Requirements: Applicants must have experience speaking in front of groups, knowledge of animal and plant identification (especially birds), and the ability to communicate well in writing. You must agree to spend 12 weeks at the internship. See individual internships below for more specific information.

OVERVIEW

Chincoteague National Wildlife Refuge includes more than 14,000 acres of beach, dunes, marsh, and maritime forest located mostly on the Virginia end of Assateague Island. The refuge's location along the Atlantic Flyway makes it a vital resting and feeding spot for a large number and diversity of birds. Within a workday's access to millions of people, Chincoteague Refuge is one of the most visited refuges in the United States, providing visitors with outstanding opportunities to learn about and enjoy wildlands and wildlife.

Chincoteague Refuge, originally established in 1943 to provide habitat for migratory birds (with an emphasis on conserving greater snow geese), today provides habitat for waterfowl, wading birds, shorebirds, and song birds, as well as other species of wildlife and plants. Refuge staff manages this barrier-island habitat to allow many species of wildlife to co-exist, each establishing its own place in the environment. Refuge management programs restore threatened and endangered species and conserve local wildlife and plants. The refuge also provides environmental education and wildlife-dependent recreational opportunities such as fishing, hunting, wildlife observation, interpretation, and wildlife photography.

A number of internships are available at the refuge center, in interpretation, environmental education, and field research and wildlife management.

Environmental Education Internships

Interns work directly with the refuge's education staff to present curriculum-based environmental education programs for school and youth groups, develop teaching aids, and assist with teacher workshops.

Applicants should have experience working with young people in an outdoor setting, with good oral and written communication skills.

Field Research Assistant/Wildlife Management Internships

The refuge offers field research assistant internships during the summer and fall, allowing interns an array of biological activities, including collecting data and monitoring a population of the threatened piping plover. Duties include weekly population surveys, nest searches, behavioral observations, nest monitoring, ghost crab and predator monitoring, vegetation transects, waterfowl surveys, and data collection at the deer check station.

Applicants should be recent graduates or undergraduates in wildlife biology, ecology, environmental biology, general biology, natural resource management, or related fields. Communication skills, writing skills, the desire to work with people, good observational and recording skills, and a valid driver's license are required. Experience working with shorebirds, waterfowl, and wading birds or a background in ornithology/general biology and knowledge of computers are desirable.

Interpretive Internships

Spring, summer, and fall interpretive interns staff the Refuge Visitor Center and develop and conduct interpretive programs as well as other informational material. These duties provide interns with the opportunity to reach diverse groups of people with a knowledge and appreciation of the environment and the National Wildlife Refuge System.

Applicants must understand animal and plant identification (especially birds) and have the ability to communicate well in writing.

HOW TO APPLY

To apply, send a resume and cover letter to the preceding address, specifying in which internship you're interested.

FRIENDS OF THE EARTH INTERNSHIP

Friends of the Earth
1717 Massachusetts Avenue, NW, Suite 600
Washington, DC 20036-2002
http://www.foe.org

What You Can Earn: Unpaid.
Application Deadlines: Rolling.
Educational Experience: Bachelor's degree (although upperclassmen with demonstrated interest and experience in the environment will be considered); see specific internships for details.
Requirements: Experience or interest in environmental issues and politics; superb oral and written communication skills, including the ability to translate complex issues into layman's terms; flexibility and willingness to work long hours if needed; and computer skills; see specific internships for more details.

OVERVIEW

Friends of the Earth (FoE) is a nonprofit organization and a leading national environmental group dedicated to protecting the planet from environmental degradation; preserving biological, cultural and ethnic diversity; and giving citizens an influential voice in decisions affecting the quality of their environment.

Economics for the Earth Intern

This three-month internship (20 hours a week) promotes sustainable transportation and energy, green fiscal and tax policy, and protection of public lands. Interns will work directly with FoE staff to research and write policy papers and conduct outreach to grassroots groups.

Candidates should have a degree in, or strong interest in, public health; environmental economics; ecology; energy and climate change; transportation; community planning; economic and social justice; grassroots organizing; or preferably some combination of the above. You'll also need strong analytical and communication skills, the desire and ability to work as part of a team, and experience with spreadsheet and/or database programs.

Government Affairs Internship

FoE offers summer internships in government affairs, to help advance the group's agenda on Capitol Hill and work on issues including energy policy, public lands, the federal budget, and international trade. As an intern here, you'll help provide support on a variety of legislative activities including monitoring bills and attending hearings and markups; researching and writing fact sheets and other materials for distribution on Capitol Hill; and helping with lobbying by making whip calls to congressional offices, representing FoE at meetings, and directly lobbying members of Congress. You'll also help write action alerts, draft "letters to the editor," and assist with other grassroots organizing on key votes; and maintain the congressional database and help out with administrative tasks.

Grassroots Intern—D.C. Environmental Network

The D.C. Environmental Network (DCEN), spearheaded by Friends of the Earth, seeks a volunteer grassroots intern to assist with the activities and campaigns of DCEN. The intern will work with DCEN's grassroots coordinator and director to carry out local campaigns and events contributing to the growth of DCEN and leading to improvements in quality of life for all D.C. residents.

As an intern here, you'll conduct outreach to nonprofits and community groups to expand membership of the network; help organize volunteer opportunities and events including monthly luncheon highlighting local environmental issues; conduct outreach to D.C.-area colleges and universities, establishing a connection to relevant professors and campus groups and involving them in local efforts; and help develop DCEN campaign materials, including pamphlets, display materials, and so on. You'll also serve as an additional contact for community members and network member groups.

You must be at least a college sophomore and have good communication and interpersonal skills; experience working with diverse groups of people; the ability to write clearly and succinctly; and the ability to do outreach (that may require public speaking) and to work independently. Good computer skills are a bonus, and knowledge of D.C. neighborhoods and city politics and basic knowledge about particularly urban environmental and environmental-justice issues are major pluses.

Public Lands Advocacy Internship

The public lands of the American West present rugged and remarkable landscapes that FoE is working to conserve by protecting entire ecosystems and archaeological communities, not merely small, isolated tracts surrounded by development.

With this internship, you can protect the environment while learning to work effectively with the grassroots; research and write practical policy papers; develop proactive Internet and electronic outreach efforts; and reach out to the media, Congress, and the states.

You'll have the opportunity to organize and build a national campaign to increase funding and protections for our public lands; track news coverage and write materials to influence it; monitor legislative and regulatory developments and perform outreach around them; research and write brief reports or other materials on lands, environmental economics, and ethics in government;

and develop campaign Web sites, e-mail listservs, databases, and other tools that can help to build a strong grassroots movement to protect the country's national treasures.

Candidates should have a passion for protecting the environment, human health, and the public interest; education, background, or demonstrated interest in public health; political science/policy; environmental economics; ecology; energy and climate change; economic and social justice; or preferably some combination of the above; strong analytical, computer, and communication skills, including the ability to write clearly and succinctly for a variety of audiences; an eagerness to learn; and the desire and ability to work as part of a team. Experience in activism, advocacy, and issue campaign work, including as a volunteer, is especially helpful.

This internship requires a 20-hour weekly commitment for between three to six months.

HOW TO APPLY

To apply, e-mail a letter, resume, and brief writing sample to

- szdeb@foe.org for the government internship
- khartwich@foe.org for the public lands advocacy internship
- jobs@foe.org for the economics for the earth and grassroots internship

HAWK MOUNTAIN SANCTUARY INTERNSHIP

Hawk Mountain Sanctuary Acopian Center for Conservation Learning
410 Summer Valley Road
Orwigsburg, PA 17961
(570) 943-3411, ext. 108
Fax: (570) 943-2284

What You Can Earn: Free housing at the sanctuary, plus a $500 monthly stipend; you may receive academic credit.

Application Deadlines: Rolling.

Educational Experience: Undergraduate and graduate students, college graduates, and others interested in careers in conservation; must have at least two years of college coursework.

Requirements: A willingness and ability to interact with the public.

OVERVIEW

Hawk Mountain Sanctuary Association is a private, nonprofit organization founded in 1934, whose mission is to foster the conservation of birds of prey worldwide and Appalachian environments locally. The sanctuary is one of the oldest conservation associations for raptors and features an internship program that has trained more than 230 interns from 30 countries all over the world since 1976. Internships, which are offered twice a year, once in the spring and once in the autumn, are designed to provide training and support for those interested in contributing to raptor conservation programs in their own countries or abroad. The internships draw together education and research programs to give interns a broad view of how global raptor conservation can be achieved.

You can apply for an internship in science education, ecological research, or biological survey and monitoring. Interns work with professionals in the field and gain hands-on experience in their chosen areas of conservation. The spring/summer session runs from April to July; the fall session runs from mid-August to mid-December. Other times are by special arrangement.

Biological Survey And Monitoring

As a monitoring intern, you'll learn about long-term monitoring programs for migrant raptors, songbirds, and other flora and fauna. Emphasis is on data management and analyses and report writing. You'll also participate in the interpretive activities for sanctuary visitors and design and complete a final project report.

Ecological Research

As a research intern, you'll learn how the sanctuary studies migrating raptors, worldwide, and Appalachian mountain fauna and flora, with an emphasis on designing field protocols, capturing and banding birds, studying hawk migration, conducting library research, managing databases, and writing results for publication. You'll also participate in interpretive activities for sanctuary visitors and design a research project and complete a proposal or paper for publication.

Science Education

As an education intern, you'll learn fundamental principles and concepts of nature interpretation, including the use of migrating raptors in teaching nature conservation to school groups and the general public. Emphasis is on the development of science-based education programs and on refining presentation techniques. You'll also learn about the care and use of captive live raptors in education programs.

As an important part of your internship, you'll design and complete a project that may include the development of new programs or teaching materials both on the sanctuary and at other conservation centers.

HOW TO APPLY

Download an online application at http://www.kjb211.org/application/apply.asp. Complete the application and send it to the preceding address, along with a two-page resume indicating all college-level courses applicable to the internship program, positions held and job responsibilities, and certifications (such as first aid, CPR, raptor care, and so on). Include type of certification and expiration date. Also provide the names, addresses, and phone numbers of three references.

Also, attach a two-page writing sample that answers the following:

- How will an internship at Hawk Mountain help you achieve your educational and conservation career goals?

- How have your experiences prepared you for an internship at Hawk Mountain?
- What are your career plans after the internship?
- What are your skills, hobbies, pursuits or interests?
- What are your greatest strengths and weaknesses?
- Discuss your most rewarding nonacademic experience. (This could include travel, a hobby, cultural activity, employment, community service, and so on.)

JANE GOODALL INSTITUTE INTERNSHIP

Jane Goodall Institute
8700 Georgia Avenue, Suite 500
Silver Spring, MD 20910-3606
(240) 645-4000
(301) 565-3188
ngandelman@janegoodall.org
http://www.janegoodall.org

What You Can Earn: $1,000 stipend (unless otherwise noted below).
Application Deadlines: Rolling.
Educational Experience: See specific internships for details.
Requirements: Strong computer skills, a pleasant telephone manner, and excellent organizational skills.

OVERVIEW

Grounded in Dr. Jane Goodall's pioneering study of chimpanzee behavior in Gombe National Park, Tanzania, more than 40 years ago, the Jane Goodall Institute emphasizes the power of the individual to make a difference for all living things. Since 1977, the institute's research, conservation, and education programs have created a worldwide network of individuals joined in their commitment to improving life on earth. With Dr. Goodall's words and examples as guiding principles, the Jane Goodall Institute inspires hope for a brighter future.

Several internships are available at the institute, including Web development, communications, development, Roots & Shoots, and chimp research.

Africa Programs Intern

This internship, which requires at least a three-month commitment and pays a modest stipend, involves work on the Goodall creative team to conserve wildlife in Tanzania and the Congo Basin. Interns here will carry out small library and Internet research projects, handle office administration and organization, public outreach projects, and the processing information requests.

Applicants must have a B.A. or equivalent degree, and preference will be given to individuals with knowledge of African primate conservation, environmental education, community conservation/sustainable development programs, and the commercial bushmeat trade. Requirements include strong communication skills, excellent writing ability, and computer knowledge. French translation and writing skills are helpful.

ChimpanZoo Intern

The ChimpanZoo program consists of professionals and volunteers who conduct behavioral research on captive chimpanzees and strive to improve chimpanzees' living conditions. A limited number of internship positions for college students are available at the ChimpanZoo office in Tucson. Although funding is not available for ChimpanZoo interns, academic credit can be arranged for students who wish to study chimpanzee behavior while taking part in a research project. Only individuals interested in chimpanzee research are accepted.

Communications Department

The Jane Goodall Institute Communications Department is seeking two summer interns beginning July 1. One intern should have strong writing skills and the other experience in digital images and photo-editing software. Both interns will help with a wide variety of duties, including writing press releases and news items for the Web site, maintaining and updating the electronic photo library, providing Web site updates, performing general office administrative support, and participating in other ongoing projects. The internships require at least a four-month commitment.

Development Intern

If fundraising interests you, the Jane Goodall Institute offers a three-month internship to help with various fund-raising initiatives. Tasks vary from general administrative support and office organization to Internet research, responding to information requests, and assisting with other projects as required.

Candidates should be detail orientated and computer literate, with excellent organization and communication abilities and a desire to work for the Jane Goodall Institute.

Roots & Shoots Administrative and Education Internship

Roots & Shoots, the Jane Goodall Institute's global environmental and humanitarian program designed to engage and inspire youth of all ages through service-learning projects, will sponsor two full-time, six-month internships at its West Coast office in Berkeley, CA. Here, you'll gain experience in various aspects of program management and development. All Roots & Shoots groups plan and implement service projects showing care and concern in three areas: people, animals, and the environment. Candidates must have a B.A. or equivalent degree or be currently enrolled in college. You also should have computer experience, experience in an environmental or educational field, good communication and organizational skills, and an interest in helping young people learn about and take responsibility for their environment and community.

Roots & Shoots Membership and Outreach Intern

The Membership and Outreach interns will help the Special Projects Coordinator and Member-

ship Manager with the day-to-day administration of the Roots & Shoots program, including member services, marketing, and outreach. While many of the interns' duties are administrative, these positions offer a unique behind-the-scenes look at a small, fast-growing non-profit organization and the opportunity to effect lasting change on an evolving program.

As an intern here, you'll help handle general program information requests by phone, mail, e-mail, and fax; enter and acknowledge activity reports received from Roots & Shoots groups; interact with the general public and representing the program at events; and help with member mailings. You'll also administer and write content for program listserv, respond to and track letters from children, help design and implement the program's membership plan, write articles for *Roots & Shoots Newsletter* and eNewsletter, handle phones on a rotating basis with the receptionist, and complete one or two long-term projects based on your interests and staff needs.

Successful applicants will want to help kids make a positive difference and have a bachelor's or equivalent degree or be currently enrolled in a college program. You also should have experience working with young people or in education, have office and/or business experience, strong computer skills (Microsoft Office and prior database experience preferred), a courteous and professional phone manner, exceptional writing skills and prior journalism experience, and be able to be flexible in a fast-paced and constantly changing working environment. You should be able to work independently and have some foreign language ability (Spanish, French, German, and Kiswahili are especially useful).

The internship requires a minimum three-month commitment (four to six months preferred) and pays a $1000 monthly stipend. Hours are full time from 9:00 A.M. to 5:30 P.M. Monday through Friday (with some flexibility). Work will be based out of the Arlington, Virginia, office.

Web Development Intern

The Web Development intern will help the director of Web development and the communications director maintain and develop the Jane Goodall Institute family of Web sites and INSITE, the institute's employee extranet. Immediate responsibilities will include editing previously created code as well as creating new pages. This position will be geared toward polishing coding skills as well as developing Dreamweaver, Web usability, information architecture, and project-management skills to a professional level. The Web intern also will assist as needed with other communication department daily tasks, working with the communications coordinator and manager.

Candidates should be proficient using Dreamweaver for HTML, ASP, and VBScript coding, with a basic understanding of databases, CSS, and ODBC. You must have working knowledge of HTML and ASP/VBScript, experience using Macromedia DreamWeaver and Microsoft Access, basic knowledge of Cascading Style Sheets (CSS), experience with Photoshop, and knowledge of Web usability and accessibility guidelines. Experience with content-management systems is a plus. The internship requires a three-month commitment.

HOW TO APPLY
Send a copy of your resume and a cover letter to:

- Bryce Tugwell at the address above for the Web development internship
- Stacy Stryjewski at: sstryjewski@jane-goodall.org or the address above for the communications internships
- Diane Skinner at the address above, or e-mail at dskinner@janegoodall.org for the development internship
- Dr. Virginia Landau at: info@chimpan-zoo.org for the ChimpanZoo internship. The cover letter should detail your proposed research project; applications will be judged on the merit of the proposed research project
- Hans Cole at hcole@janegoodall.org for the Roots & Shoots administrative/education internship

- Elan Wang, Roots & Shoots Membership Manager, at ewang@janegoodall.org or fax to 301-565-3188 for the Roots and Shoots membership and outreach internship
- Lisa Pharaoah to the address above. Include a writing sample

LONGWOOD GARDENS INTERNSHIP

Longwood Gardens
Student Programming
PO Box 501
Kennett Square, PA 19348
(610) 388-1000, ext. 508
Email: studentprograms@longwoodgardens.org
General Web site: http://www.longwoodgardens.org
Application: http://www.longwoodgardens.org/Education/student%20programs/College%20Internship/CollegeInternship1.htm

What You Can Earn: $6.50 an hour plus free housing and garden space
Application Deadlines: February 1 for internships starting in June; May 1 for September; November 1 for January or March.
Educational Experience: Current college students and individuals who have graduated within the past year and are legally able to work in the United States.
Requirements: You must have a valid driver's license and be able to lift 50 pounds.

OVERVIEW
Interning at Longwood Gardens offers excellent opportunities for you to gain practical experience, learn career skills, and study amid the world's premier horticulture display. Internships last three to 12 months, and you specialize in one work area. These include arboriculture; nursery; continuing

education; indoor horticulture display; curatorial; outdoor horticulture display; greenhouse; production; performing arts; groundskeeping, horticulture research; integrated pest management; student programs; landscape design display; visitor education; and library science.

In addition to their regular tasks, Longwood interns participate in student activities one afternoon a week, together with occasional all-day activities, to learn about local and regional horticulture. These activities will give you the opportunity to explore the diversity of the horticulture field. During these activities, you'll go behind the scenes at Longwood Gardens, visit private estates, and tour orchards, public gardens, and nurseries. You'll be paid for your regular work hours while participating in student activities.

College interns are paid $6.50 an hour for a 40-hour week. If you wish, you may live rent free (a taxable benefit) on the grounds of the former estate of industrialist Pierre S. du Pont. The student houses are furnished and include nearby garden space and are located on Red Lion Row. Each house has three or four bedrooms. At any given time, there are 20 to 40 students are living on The Row.

Red Lion Row was originally built around the turn of the century by Pierre S. du Pont to house his employees and their families. The Row is within easy walking distance of Longwood Gardens. To see pictures of what the houses look like, visit the Web site http://www.longwoodgardens.org/Education/student%20programs/Housing%20and%20Activities/Housing/Housing.htm.

Directly south of the student houses is the student garden space, where you may have garden space. You're responsible for the upkeep of your garden, and you must return the plot to its original condition before leaving. Communal tools are available, as well as mulch, potting soil, and leaf mold. A greenhouse and head house are provided for the professional gardeners' class work; any space they aren't using in the greenhouse may be used by interns.

After work, from May through October, you may go on weekly plant walks, guided garden walks to nearby private and public gardens, where you can meet the gardeners and see some amazing landscapes.

Longwood internships start four times a year: January, March, June, and September. Typically, you will start your orientation the first Monday of the month. For information on availability and start dates for specific internships, you can check the internship availability age at http://www.longwoodgardens.org/Education/student%20programs/College%20Internship/internship_availability.htm.

Arboriculture

If you intern in this area, you'll learn tree-care skills, involving tree climbing and pruning as well as the use of hand tools, chain saws, chippers, and bucket trucks. Duties may include tree trimming and cabling, bracing, taking down trees, hedge pruning, and tree-health evaluation. A fall internship involves several months of Christmas-light installation and maintenance. Previous arboriculture or urban-forestry training or experience is preferred. This internship is a one-year position designed to teach the practical aspects of tree care through hands-on training in a safety-oriented environment.

You are required to be elevated in a bucket truck, learn how to operate a chain saw, and work in adverse weather conditions.

Continuing Education

In this internship, you'll gain exposure to an extensive lifelong learning program and help plan and implement this program. Ongoing responsibilities include preparation, setup, and assistance for courses, workshops, and lectures, including the operation of audiovisual equipment, plant material collection for horticulture and botanical art courses, floral-design preparation, development of self-guided study walks, course manual preparation, writing of press releases and publicity, and Web site updates. You'll also help with plant society flower shows. This one-year position involves some evening and weekend hours and starts in June. You must be willing to work weekends and evenings.

Curatorial

This internship provides exposure to a wide variety of plants in all parts of the garden and is designed to teach you methods and techniques used in curating a plant collection in a public garden. You'll work closely with the curatorial staff on diverse projects including plant acquisition, identification, labeling, inventory, mapping, and plant trials data collecting. You'll also help with field trips and preparation for courses and lectures given by the curatorial staff. This one-year position begins in June. During this internship, you'll develop a thorough understanding of the principles of plant nomenclature, with special emphasis on cultivated plants; become familiar with a wide range of cultivated plants and become proficient in utilization of plant identification keys; learn and practice all aspects of plant-records management, including name verification, accessioning, database maintenance, inventories, and labeling; learn techniques of field mapping by triangulation utilizing grid markers, measuring tapes, and electronic measuring devices; and contribute to plant-evaluation trials by collecting data in the field, entering data into a computer, writing reports, and coordinating help from other students.

You'll also become proficient in personal computer applications, including database use, word processing, image scanning, e-mail, intranet, and Internet use; and become familiar with a wide variety of publications and other informational resources, including on-line databases.

You must have basic computer skills and familiarity with plant nomenclature and be willing to work alone in adverse weather conditions.

Display Design

In this internship, you'll work closely with the display specialist on design projects in an effort to learn the process of implementing permanent and seasonal displays from concept to construction. Your duties will include evaluating the effectiveness of current displays and helping with drafting projects, presentation drawings, field-note taking, and site measuring. You'll need to take a leadership role with individual design projects as well as active roles in the staging and installation of indoor and outdoor designs. You'll evaluate the effectiveness of current displays, help with research for design and display development, play an active role in the staging and installation of major outdoor designs, take part in presentations to various committees, and help with Christmas-display design and implementation.

You should have a strong desire to learn and a high degree of self motivation. This nine- to 12-month position is ideal for a student in landscape architecture, landscape design, or architecture who has a strong interest in horticulture. You also must be enrolled in, or recently graduated from, a landscape architecture, landscape design, or landscape construction program.

You must have excellent hand-drafting skills and interest or experience in horticulture, garden design, and/or fine art. Excellent written and communication skills are important; experience with surveying is helpful but not necessary.

Also, experience with AutoCAD and/or GIS and experience with MS Office are good but not necessary. A portfolio of five samples of your creative work must accompany your application.

Greenhouse Production

This internship offers practical experience in growing flowering plants in a controlled greenhouse environment, so you can learn about the systems and horticultural skills needed to manage a state-of-the-art container production greenhouse through hands-on involvement in the daily operations of a production facility. You'll sow, seed, and handle seedlings; propagate by cuttings; transplant, pot, and repot; and stake, tie, groom, water, fertilize, and transport potted plants. You'll also help in the upkeep and cleaning of the greenhouse and other work areas, help install the larger displays and any special garden-wide projects, and perform primary plant care in the absence of full-time staff. This experience could be useful if you intend to grow plants for a display garden or for commercial purposes. Opportunities range from three to 12 months.

You must be willing to work independently doing repetitive tasks and willing to work some weekends.

Groundskeeping

This internship is designed to help you learn proper turfgrass management techniques through hands-on involvement in the day-to-day management of the turf within Longwood Gardens. You'll cut turf, weed and edge beds, prune shrubs and trees, prepare soil and compost, and help in other maintenance projects important to outdoor-display horticulture. You'll also maintain lawns, including mowing and string trimming; weed and edge beds; perform turf repair, renovation, and fertilization; and help remove leaves in fall; Winter internships involve woods-cleanup work and removing woody invasives and snow.

This internship is a six-month to one-year position. You must be willing to participate in student activities and field trips as scheduled, be willing to work independently and at repetitive tasks, and be willing to work in adverse weather conditions.

Indoor Display

If you select this internship, you'll learn about the special nature of gardening in conservatories through hands-on involvement in the day-to-day process of installing and maintaining greenhouse displays and collections. You'll have the opportunity to work in one of several areas in the conservatory, including seasonal changing displays in the main conservatory; a rotation through permanent displays including palms, aquatics, orchids, bananas, roses, ferns, and the Mediterranean, Silver, or Cascade Gardens; or assignment to the children's garden, bonsai, and espaliered fruit houses. Duties include grooming, planting, and maintaining plant displays.

A general knowledge of greenhouse environments and plant culture is preferred for this three- to 12-month internship. You also must be able to lift 30 pounds and be willing to perform repetitive tasks, work independently, work some weekends, and work in adverse weather conditions.

Landscape Design

This internship offers interdepartmental exposure to planning and design in a world-class public-display garden and is designed to introduce the intern to the relationship between design and horticulture. You'll work with design and engineering staff on projects related to master planning, computer graphics, teaching, display horticulture, and a variety of design projects. You'll help with garden, architectural, display, and graphic design at different stages and scales, from conceptual to detail design. Projects also may include the design and development of interpretive signs and exhibits associated with projects and displays. You'll also help design plantings ranging from landscape buffers to plantings for seasonal displays and present designs to staff groups and committees using effective and creative verbal, written, and graphic communication skills. You'll also interact with consulting architects, artists, artisans, landscape architects, engineers, and designers and help with construction issues related to the aesthetic and interpretive intent of various projects. In addition, you'll help teach various design courses offered through continuing education and the professional gardener training program, preparing material for class, helping with studio critiques, and taking notes for the instructor.

To qualify for this internship, you must be pursuing a design degree at the university level and must have basic knowledge of ornamental plants along with competence in basic graphics, hand-drafting, and proficiency in AutoCad, Microsoft Word, and Excel. A portfolio of five samples of your creative work must accompany your application.

You also must have strong skills in written and verbal communication and be able to work independently as well as part of multidisciplinary teams. You also should have a strong desire to learn, a high degree of self-motivation, and a basic knowledge of plants and horticulture. This one-year position is ideal for a student in landscape architecture, landscape design, or architecture with a strong interest in horticulture. (Note: the internship will not provide time creditable to licensure requirements.)

Integrated Pest Management (IPM)

This internship prepares you to practice essential pest management and plant health diagnostic skills, such as proper pest scouting and identification techniques and the recognition of common plant disease/pest infestation symptoms on plants. You'll learn these skills while working on a wide variety of crops grown in greenhouse, conservatory, landscape, and natural environments.

You'll release beneficial insects throughout Longwood Gardens, mainly in certain conservatory areas, and perform outreach and educational activities such as discovery carts and pest walks. You'll also learn proper pesticide-application techniques and apply chemical pest control materials (usually only for internships longer than six months). In addition, you'll study proper pest management decision-making through discussion and observation.

You'll help the IPM coordinator diagnose pest problems throughout the gardens, indoors, and outdoors, performing applied research projects, designing and implementing pest sampling and monitoring programs, and developing lectures and displays concerning IPM. You'll learn about beneficial insect releases, cultural control methods, and least-toxic chemical controls often utilized in Longwood's display settings and help to evaluate the effectiveness of these treatments. Opportunities range from three to 12 months.

You must be willing to work in adverse weather conditions, to perform repetitive tasks, and to work independently.

Library

This internship will allow you to learn about the workings of a horticultural library through hands-on involvement in the day-to-day operation of Longwood Gardens' library. You'll check in new publications and check circulated items back in; help patrons perform searches in Sydney Plus, OCLC, Agricola, and so on; compile daily statistics and shelve and organize library materials; and type, file, sort mail, and answer phones as needed. You'll also prepare materials for archives; learn copyright requirements; pull books on bibliographies; help prepare new bibliographies; help in collation and binding; perform basic book repairs; help patrons with AV equipment, copier, fax, and microform

equipment; and cover the responsibilities of head librarian as needed. You must be willing to work independently do repetitive work.

Nursery

This internship involves propagation, potting, labeling, record-keeping, pruning, transplanting, and other duties related to the day-to-day operation of Longwood's nursery. You'll prune and maintain woody and herbaceous material at Longwood's nursery; prepare plants for potting; and transplant and install plants in display gardens by hand-digging, ball and burlapping, or using a tree spade. You'll also help with labeling and record-keeping; conduct general nursery maintenance including controlling weeds and mulching; and cover all the responsibilities of a full-time gardener as needed. You'll also evaluate woody plant material for potential use in Longwood's displays. The internship runs March through December.

You must be willing to work in adverse weather conditions, do repetitive work, and work independently.

Outdoor Display

In this internship, you'll learn a variety of horticultural skills through hands-on work in the outdoor display gardens, working in all sections of the gardens helping with garden tasks such as planting, weeding, mulching, pruning, deadheading, staking, and general garden maintenance. Additionally, you may help with plant labeling and other projects. You'll be exposed to a wide range of plant material, from spectacular displays of annuals, groundcovers, vegetables, roses, and formal topiary to a vast variety of trees, shrubs, and native plants.

Your interaction with staff gardeners provides you with excellent opportunities to learn proper techniques and cultural requirements while working in some of Longwood's most intensively cultivated areas. Opportunities range from three to 12 months.

You must be willing to work in adverse weather conditions, to work independently, and to do repetitive tasks.

Research

Research at Longwood focuses upon applied, practical studies to enhance the indoor and outdoor horticultural displays. In addition to an on-going evaluation of new plants, current trials include camellia hardiness, boxwoods, and shrubs. You'll work with extraordinary hardy and nonhardy plants, performing relatively mundane horticultural tasks in research plots at the nursery and in the research greenhouses, performing weeding, watering, soil preparation, planting and transplanting, labeling, and data collection.

The internship is designed to teach you about the daily tasks involved in operating a horticultural research facility through hands-on involvement with the research team. You'll work with a research physiologist, research employees, professional gardener students, and international students to maintain trial plants in the field and greenhouse including weeding, mulching, watering, fertilizing, and pruning; plant in field and greenhouse; and prepare soils and apply pesticides. You'll also help evaluate and develop new ornamental plants; collect data on seed germination, bloom periods, and hybridization results; and propagate plants by seed, cuttings, grafting/budding, and tissue culture. Additionally, you'll use the plant records database for plant inventory management and help with laboratory procedures for soil testing, virus testing, and plant tissue culture.

Attention to detail is important. This three- to 12-month internship is ideal for students eager to learn about a wide range of plants. You must be willing to work independently, do repetitive tasks, work in adverse weather conditions, and work some weekends.

Student Programs

This internship is ideal for those interested in helping to coordinate resident student programs in a public garden. You'll learn to plan, implement, and manage various student programs through hands-on involvement in the daily operation of the five student programs run by the student programs office. You'll help revise student information; evaluate programs; conduct orientations and student meetings; organize field trips; write press releases; and work on special projects. You'll also help coordinate the high school internship program and the groundskeeping apprenticeship program.

You'll also arrange weekly field trips/learning opportunities for intern, international, and high school students and evaluate the effectiveness of those activities; answer questions from the public about student programs; help with requests for student involvement in special tours, community events, and other public relations activities; prepare a quarterly summary of activities; and help in the coordination, instruction, and day-to-day logistics of the high school groundskeeping apprenticeship program, summer internship program, and discover program as well as the middle school "after the bell" program.

Personable individuals with writing, computer, and communication skills are idea for this one-year internship, which involves working with all levels of staff within the organization. You must be willing to work independently and be organized and attentive to detail.

Visitor Education

These interns become an integral part of the visitor-education team, sharing responsibilities for program development and implementation. You'll develop programs and activities for children and adults; write interpretive materials about plants and garden displays; train, schedule, and manage volunteers; create and post daily activity schedules and event signs; research and respond to visitor inquiries; act as intern editor for Longwood's in-house newsletter; and assist with the development and implementation of special displays and events, such as Arbor Day, Plant Experts, Pot-a-Plant, GardenFest, Chrysanthemum Festival, and the Christmas Display.

You'll need good organizational, communication, and people skills, as well as an interest in horticulture and working with children. Knowledge of word processing and graphics programs is a plus. There are two one-year positions available; both positions involve flexible hours including some weekends. Knowledge of Microsoft Office and QuarkXPress is helpful.

HOW TO APPLY

The internship application is available online in PDF format, downloadable at the Web site provided previously. To receive an application by mail, send a letter of request to the preceding address.

MORRIS ARBORETUM OF THE UNIVERSITY OF PENNSYLVANIA INTERNSHIP

Internship Coordinator, Morris Arboretum
9414 Meadowbrook Ave.
Philadelphia, PA 19118
(215) 247-5777

What You Can Earn: As full-time employees of the university, interns earn $8.32 an hour; health, dental, and vacation benefits from the University of Pennsylvania; college credit; and an administrative vacation for all staff and interns is provided between Christmas and New Year's Day. Interns also become eligible to receive tuition benefits from Penn, Chestnut Hill College, or Temple University's Ambler Campus. Arboretum staff assists interns in finding housing by providing a list of nearby moderately priced possibilities. Occasionally, there are opportunities for interns to live with hosts and exchange work around the home of their hosts for reduced rent.

Application Deadlines: February 15 for all sessions.

Educational Experience: Individuals who have already obtained or are working toward an undergraduate degree in horticulture, landscape architecture, or a related area.

Requirements: Interns must commit themselves to a full-year internship and be able and willing to communicate with arboretum visitors, work independently and as part of a team, work in all weather conditions, and be able to lift at least 25 pounds. See additional individual requirements below.

OVERVIEW

The Morris Arboretum of the University of Pennsylvania is an interdisciplinary center that integrates art, science, and the humanities. Thousands of rare and beautiful woody plants, including many of Philadelphia's oldest, rarest, and largest trees, are set in a romantic 92-acre Victorian landscape garden of winding paths, streams, flowers, and special garden areas.

In the early 1900s, John and Lydia Morris envisioned that one day their estate would become a world-class educational institution. John said he imagined the arboretum would be "a school where young men, and possibly young women, may be taught practical gardening and horticulture." The internship program marked its 25th anniversary in 2004, where students can come for a one-year internship to study botany, biology, propagation, arboriculture, landscape design, landscape architecture, and education. This year-long, paid internship program starts in mid-June and focuses on providing practical training as well as the development of a wide range of management skills. Graduates of the program have gone on to administrative careers in the horticulture industry and in botanic gardens, arboreta, and government as well as positions in research, education, and extension service.

While at the arboretum, you can sign up to take free arboretum classes and arboretum-sponsored conferences and symposia.

The Arboriculture Intern

Here, you'll work alongside the chief arborist in maintaining and caring for the trees on the Morris Arboretum's 167 acres. You'll participate in all aspects of tree-care management, including tree pruning, hazard inspection, tree-support systems, and integrated pest management. You'll learn to teach climbing techniques and basic arboriculture concepts by assisting with arborist training for tree-care professionals and climbing enthusiasts. The arboriculture internship is physically demanding and involves climbing and working in trees at heights in excess 60 to 80 feet. Safety-conscious techniques are emphasized, and recent innovations in climbing and rigging are demonstrated and put into practice. Other opportunities include attendance at the International Society of Arboriculture Conference and outreach activities including workshops and off-site consulting.

Applicants should have an academic background in forestry, horticulture, landscaping, or a related field; basic tree climbing ability; good written and verbal communication skills; and working knowledge of Word, Excel, and PowerPoint. A valid driver's license is required.

Education Internship

As an intern here, you'll be an integral part of the education team, which develops and delivers educational programs for professionals, adults, families, and children. You'll work with staff to direct the activities of volunteer guides, including training and workshop planning, and provide committee leadership and education program support. You'll meet regularly with volunteer guides and other professionals to plan, coordinate, and evaluate programs. You'll also have the chance to communicate with the public through newsletter articles, course-brochure descriptions, and a monthly volunteer publication. Although you'll spend most days indoors, you'll have ample opportunity to be outside in good weather. The position involves regular field trips with guides as well as the opportunity to attend at least one professional conference. You'll also have an excellent opportunity to meet others in the field of informal education and to work as part of a team to develop hands-on, curriculum-based educational programs.

Candidates should have good communication and interpersonal skills; a working knowledge of Word, Excel, and Publisher; and be adaptable and flexible.

Flora of Pennsylvania Internship

This is a joint program between the Morris Arboretum and the Academy of Natural Sciences. As an intern here, you'll receive training and work experience in all aspects of managing collections in a major herbarium, along with an opportunity to do a research project on some aspect of the flora of Pennsylvania. You'll gain hands-on experience to increase your skills as a professional botanist as you divide your time between the botany departments at the Morris Arboretum and the Academy of Natural Sciences of Philadelphia.

The Academy of Natural Sciences in Center City Philadelphia houses the oldest natural history museum in the United States, including an herbarium of more than 1.5 million specimens of plants, fungi, and algae.

Candidates should have an undergraduate degree in botany or biology with coursework in botany and be self-motivated and reliable.

Horticulture Intern

The horticulture internship is a hands-on program in which interns help care for the arboretum's extensive collection of plants. As an intern here, you'll get hands-on training in all phases of garden development and care of the living collection, with emphasis on refining practical horticultural skills. You'll help direct the activities of volunteers and part-time staff as you develop integrated pest management (IPM) skills, arboriculture techniques, and the operation and maintenance of garden machinery. Special projects will be assigned to develop individual skills in garden planning and management. The horticulture intern helps manage various specialty gardens throughout the arboretum, rotating through all areas of the garden. The intern also helps manage and coordinate the horticultural volunteer group.

Candidates should have a strong academic background in horticulture or a closely related field. A valid driver's license is required.

Plant Propagation Internship

This internship covers the whole range of traditional plant-propagation skills and production schemes. You'll get hands-on training in managing the field nursery and the arboretum's state-of-the art greenhouses and maintenance of the Victorian fernery. Emphasis is placed on the refinement of skills and developing the protocols for the propagation of a wide range of plants, with a concentration on woody plants. On a typical day, you'll begin by checking environmental data reports on the computer, watering in the glasshouses and outdoor areas, and preparing for the volunteers. The propagation and management calendars are consulted for scheduled activities such as covering outside hoop houses with plastic for the winter, grafting witchhazels, planting in the nursery, taking holly cuttings, weeding pots, researching protocol for the seed propagation of newly wild-collected seed, or releasing beneficial insects as part of the IPM program.

Candidates should have a strong academic background in horticulture, especially woody landscape plants, with coursework in physiology, botany, and propagation.

Plant Protection Internship

As an intern here, you'll work with the arboretum's senior botanist and plant pathologist to monitor plant pest and disease problems affecting the living collection. You'll spend time each day out of doors or in the greenhouses observing plants in the collection for pest and disease problems. In addition, laboratory facilities are provided for researching, diagnosing, and culturing pest and disease organisms. You'll also be responsible for scheduling and coordinating other interns' participation in staffing the plant clinic. Interacting with plant-clinic users, either in person or by telephone, is another important role. Follow-up may include drawing on the expertise of other arboretum staff members or conducting research via the Internet or more traditional avenues to answer specific questions.

Candidates should have a good working knowledge of the ornamental flora, coursework in plant pathology and entomology, good communication skills, the ability to relate to the public both in person and on the telephone and to work well with peers, keen powers of observation, and curiosity.

Rose and Flower Garden Internship

This intern helps the Rosarian in garden development, management, and care of the collections. Specialty gardens include: formal rose garden with rock wall; cottage; hardy fern; herb, hosta, and meadow gardens; mixed border; and crabapple orchard. You'll have the chance to refine your horticulture skills, including techniques in formal garden maintenance. At the end of this internship, you'll have mastered the skills used in the culture of modern and antique roses and their garden companions. You'll be encouraged to attend workshops, classes, and conferences, such as the Woody Plant Conference in July and the Perennial Plant Conference in October, both at Swarthmore College, and the Philadelphia Rose Society meetings and the Rose Show in June. You'll spend about four days a week working outdoors in the rose garden section, which will provide a great opportunity for hands-on training in an array of specialty gardens.

Candidates should have a strong academic background in horticulture or a closely related field, with coursework or a very strong interest in herbaceous and woody landscape plants.

Urban Forestry Internship

As an intern in this area, you'll work in urban forestry and learn natural resource management practices, assessments, programs, and planning for public gardens, government agencies, and educational and community organizations. You'll also learn and teach stewardship concepts and practical applications through natural land restoration and urban tree management projects, as well as developing community partnerships, vegetation analysis, and management-planning skills. In addition to urban forestry, you'll spend time helping the natural areas manager with land management in the Paper Mill Run Restoration Project, the Wetland Project, and the forest restoration of the Thomas Mill Ravine.

Candidates should have an academic background in urban forestry, ecology, horticulture, arboriculture, landscape design, or a related field. Landscape design, ecology, or woody plant experience is desirable. Experience in publication production or report writing is useful, and a range of computer experience is important, including a working knowledge of MS Word, Excel, and PowerPoint, as well as AutoCAD and ArcView.

HOW TO APPLY

Interested applicants should first download an online application at https://jobs.hr.upenn.edu/applicants/jsp/shared/frameset/Frameset.jsp?time=1116199944924 and proceed with the online application process. Alternatively, you may send the application with a letter indicting the internship position desired and how it will help the organization in achieving its goals, along with a resume, academic transcripts, and three letters of recommendation, including one academic and one work reference, to the preceding address.

NATIONAL PARK FOUNDATION INTERNSHIP

Intern Coordinator, National Park Foundation
11 Dupont Circle, NW, Suite 600
Washington, DC 20036
(202) 238-4200
Fax: (202) 234-3103

What You Can Earn: $1,300 a month, plus one personal day and one sick leave day a month, for working five days a week from 8:30 A.M. to 5:30 P.M.
Application Deadlines: Rolling.
Educational Experience: Recent college graduates who are highly motivated.
Requirements: Strong written and oral communication skills, demonstrated organizational and research skills, high energy and enthusiasm, the ability to juggle multiple tasks, and a keen interest in the National Park System.

OVERVIEW

The National Park Foundation (NPF) is the congressionally chartered nonprofit partner of America's National Parks. The NPF strengthens the enduring connection between the American people and their national parks by raising private funds, making strategic grants, creating innovative partnerships and increasing public awareness. A variety of internships are available in different areas, including profit management, marketing/communications, development, grants/programs, and graphics.

Internships are six months in duration. Each department of NPF has a dedicated intern. NPF interns work on a variety of tasks including research/development, publications, promotions, and special events. Interns will also spend some of their time with administrative duties, including file maintenance, phone inquiries, and donor and financial database upkeep.

Interns are encouraged to share ideas and approaches to improve current systems and to actively get involved with other departments in addition to their own.

The Nonprofit Management intern will work closely with the NPF's president, executive vice president, senior vice president of marketing and communications, senior director of finance, and associate for government relations to understand the day-to-day management of a Washington, D.C., nonprofit organization. The intern will also work closely with the director and manager of special events to help learn about board, donor, and in-house events for the National Park Foundation. This internship will have an emphasis on communication and relationships with key constituencies: members of Congress, the presidential administration, the National Park Service, the Department of the Interior, and so on. Intern responsibilities and focus vary depending on the department to which you are assigned. Responsibilities may include working on publications, events, research, development, data management, and promotions.

The Nonprofit Management intern will gain experience in the following areas by assisting staff with day-to-day duties:

- participate in monthly and quarterly NPF budget reviews
- writing, editing, and publishing of the Hill Update, the National Leadership Council Update, and Finance communications
- organize and participate in meetings with members of Congress and their staff in relation to legislative initiatives
- research on future events to support site selections, contract negotiations, and so on
- provide assistance on event preparations immediately prior to events (day-of support for in-town or in-house events)
- participate in other various meetings or events as needed to help understand the day-to-day workings of a Washington, D.C., nonprofit

On a rotation basis, interns are responsible for maintaining the office environment, including the kitchen area and mailroom, and providing (back-up) coverage for the front desk. Required knowledge, skills, and abilities:

- highly motivated individuals with written and oral communications skills.
- demonstrated research and organizational capabilities.
- high energy and enthusiasm
- the ability to juggle multiple tasks and demands
- a keen interest in management and the National Park System.

HOW TO APPLY

Please send cover letter, resume, references and writing sample to the intern coordinator at the above address.

STUDENT CLIMATE OUTREACH INTERNSHIP

Grassroots Coordinator, Chesapeake Climate Action Network
PO Box 11136
Takoma Park, MD 20912
(301) 891-6726
josh@chesapeakeclimate.org
http://www.chesapeakeclimate.org

What You Can Earn: $1,000 a month.
Application Deadlines: Rolling.
Educational Experience: None specified.
Requirements: Someone who learns quickly, takes responsibility, has a good grasp of environmental issues and some ideas on how to expand the movement; interest and experience specifically with climate change or energy policy; experience with some form of organizing, including media work, research, advocacy, and lobbying; ability to work independently and carry a task from start to finish.

OVERVIEW

The Chesapeake Climate Action Network (CCAN) is the first grassroots, nonprofit organization dedicated exclusively to fighting global warming in Maryland, Virginia, and Washington, D.C. Its mission is to educate and mobilize citizens of this area to foster a quick switch to clean, efficient energy, slowing the dangerous trend of global warming. CCAN has been instrumental in passing landmark renewable energy bills in D.C. and Maryland over the past three years.

The student outreach intern will work 40 hours a week with the grassroots coordinator to design an outreach campaign. The intern will build coalitions with existing student climate groups, design campaign materials, and conduct early outreach with summer contacts. In addition, the intern will aid CCAN in designing its grassroots strategy for renewable energy in Virginia. The intern will research student environmental organizations in

D.C., Virginia, and Maryland; conduct outreach to existing organizations to set the grounds for a Maryland, Virginia, and D.C. climate coalition; help plan a summer-outreach event in Maryland to raise awareness about the importance of clean cars; and help with general CCAN activities.

HOW TO APPLY

Send a resume, cover letter, and references (professors, advisors, or friends) to Josh Tulkin at josh@chesapeakeclimate.org. The subject line should read "summer internship application."

STUDENT CONSERVATION ASSOCIATION INTERNSHIP

Student Conservation Association
   Recruitment Department
PO Box 550
Charlestown, NH 03603
(603) 543-1700
Fax: (603) 543-1828
Realinternships@thesca.org
http://www.thesca.org

What You Can Earn: Conservation internships across the country: biweekly stipend and paid travel to the site, free housing, free or low-cost health insurance, loan deferment on qualified student loans, possible student loan forbearance and AmeriCorps Education awards of $1,000 to $4,725 (only some positions qualify); Houston-area internships include a $125/week and possible AmeriCorps Education Award worth $1,000.
Application Deadlines: Rolling.
Educational Experience: See specific internships below.
Requirements: See specific internships below.

OVERVIEW

The Student Conservation Association (SCA) is a national nonprofit organization dedicated to changing lives through service to nature. From the Rocky Mountain terrains of the Northwest and the arid deserts of the Southwest across the Great Plains to the Appalachian Mountains, SCA positions span the entire United States. From environmental education and historical interpretation to botany and fisheries management, SCA offers internships in more than 50 disciplines and in all 50 states for individuals ages 18 and up.

SCA is the nation's leading provider of high-school and college-aged volunteers for the conservation of public lands. This organization's mission is to build the next generation of conservation leaders and inspire lifelong stewardship of the environment and communities.

Conservation Internships

Conservation internships are available throughout the United States. Internship positions vary from 12 weeks to 12 months and offer valuable training and certifications and possible academic credit.

Fire Education Corps Internship

With this internship, you'll experience the heritage and culture of America's Native Americans when you live and work on a reservation as part of SCA's Fire Education Corps. As a team member, you'll participate in an education project to provide tribal communities with education and information designed to reduce the impact of wildland fires. You'll help specialists conduct a variety of essential fire-management activities. (For more information, visit http://www.thesca.org/pdfs/fireflyer.pdf.) Teams will be located across the United States. Tribal partners include the Oklahoma Bureau of Indian Affairs, The Confederated Tribes of the Salish Kootenai (MT), Nez Perce (ID), Menominee Reservation (WI), Southern Pueblos Agency (NM), White Mountain Apache (AZ), and the Mescalero Apache (NM).

Your responsibilities include starting grassroots fire-education initiatives; attending community events and meetings; conducting home-risk evaluations; and planning and staffing youth-education days and school presentations. You'll also help implement fuels-reduction projects.

Site-specific projects are developed with guidance from the project staff leader and tailored to meet local tribal needs. Interns will participate in training conducted in Boise, ID, before traveling to specific sites; this training may include fire ecology and history; fire behavior; Wildland Firefighter/Red Card certification; defensible space concepts; team building; community education and outreach techniques; driver training; risk management; and extra onsite trainings.

Candidates should have excellent organizational and communication skills; experience living with and working in a group environment; the ability to take initiative and work both independently and as part of a team; the ability/willingness to learn to drive a 4WD vehicle; and the ability/willingness to learn to use various field equipment and tools. You also should have a valid driver's license, first aid/CPR certification, and interest/experience in one or more of the following areas: community outreach, public speaking, GPS, basic computer programs, fire behavior, tutoring/teaching, and communication/media skills.

Houston-Area Conservation Internships

Several internships in the Houston area are available in environmental education, youth development, conservation, and interpretation.

Environmental Education at Sheldon Lake State Park

This summer internship takes place at Sheldon Lake, a 2,800-acre outdoor education and recreation facility located in northeast Houston. The park is home to a self-guiding nature trail that winds over 20 naturalized ponds with alligators and other wildlife. As an intern, you'll help with educational programs for schools and other children's groups, conduct a control program for invasive species, canoe on Sheldon Lake as nec-

essary for invasive plant location, and plan new educational curricula. You'll need a car.

Botany/Horticulture/Environmental Education at Katy Prairie Conservancy

This summer-long internship is available at Katy Prairie, a protected nature sanctuary 30 miles west of Houston. Interns will help with botany and horticulture projects and conduct environmental education for young visitors, including creating new field trip activities.

Environmental Education/Wetlands Conservation at San Jacinto State Historic Site

This summer internship takes place at the San Jacinto State Historic Site, home to the Battleship TEXAS and a five-mile Marsh Trail located east of Houston in LaPorte, TX. As a San Jacinto intern, you'll conduct environmental education, provide visitor services and interpretation of the San Jacinto site and Marsh Trail for children's groups and other visitors, and help with wetlands conservation by monitoring water quality.

GIS at Trees for Houston

Trees for Houston utilizes GIS for urban forestry and planning applications. As an intern, you'll add to current data collection systems and develop new data-collection techniques and processes. This 12-week position requires good knowledge of GIS.

Wildland Fire Internships

In this internship, you'll work in teams of three to gather forest inventory and fire hazard risk assessment data for tribal lands using GPS and GIS to record and display fuel data. Site-specific projects are developed with guidance from the SCA project staff leader and agency fire fuels coordinator and tailored to meet local tribal needs. Teams will be located across the United States. Tribal partners include: The Oklahoma Bureau of Indian Affairs (OK), The Confederated Tribes of the Salish Kootenai (MT), Nez Perce (ID), Great Lakes Agency (WI), Bemidji Agency (MN), Southern Pueblos Agency (NM), and Mescalero Apache (NM).

You'll travel by truck and hike up to six miles a day to locations throughout the tribal lands to collect and record vegetation and landscape data, manage data and build fuel data layers for reservation GIS maps, and present project information and results in organized formats for reservation and National Interagency Fire Center.

Candidates should have experience with GPS hardware such as Trimble Recon; GIS familiarity including the ability to use software such as ESRI ArcView, ArcPad, and ArcGIS 8.3; a valid driver's license; the ability or willingness to learn to drive a 4WD vehicle; first aid/CPR certification; desire to work with people of various backgrounds; self-motivation and willingness to take initiative; ability to work independently and as part of a team; experience living and working outdoors; and the ability to hike over rough terrain.

You should have college coursework in GPS, GIS, botany, forestry, fire/resource management, geography, fire ecology, environmental studies, or related fields; presentation skills; experience collecting field data and performing data entry; the ability to work outdoors in all weather conditions and the ability to navigate using topographic maps; and knowledge of basic computer programs and fire behavior.

You also must be 21 years of age and able to pass a driver's background check and training.

HOW TO APPLY

- For the conservation internships, e-mail your resume and cover letter to: Realinternships@thesca.org.
- For the fire education corps internship, submit a letter of interest, along with a resume and contact information for three references to: makecontact@thesca.org.
- For the Houston internships, send a resume and cover letter indicating your interest, skills, and availability (spring, summer, part time or full time) to Sheryl Wallin, SCA Texas Program Coordinator, at swallin@thesca.org.
- For the Wildland Fire internships, send a cover letter, resume, and contact information to SCA at: gis@thesca.org.

SCIENCE

AMERICAN ASSOCIATION FOR THE ADVANCEMENT OF SCIENCE INTERNSHIP

American Association for the Advancement of Science (AAAS)
Human Resources Department
1200 New York Avenue, NW, Suite #100
Washington, DC 20005
Fax: (202) 682-1630
Hrtemp@aaas.org
http://www.aaas.org/careercenter/internships

What You Can Earn: Varying stipends; some positions are paid, but some are unpaid.
Application Deadlines: Rolling (check with individual areas).
Educational Experience: Science background helpful.
Requirements: Applicants must be graduate or undergraduate students.

OVERVIEW

Volunteer internships at AAAS exist to make use of the abilities of undergraduate and graduate students in developing special projects or studies for the organization. Students can relate their education and training to particular subject areas in providing services. Volunteer internships can be full time or part time, and students can earn college credit depending on the requirements of the college or university.

Paid internships at AAAS provide actual or practical work experience and can be full or part time; they are granted for a period of less than six months.

A variety of science and policy program internships are available, including the Center for Science, Technology and Security Policy (CSTSP); Scientific Freedom, Responsibility, and Law Program; Science & Human Rights Program; Science & Technology Policy Fellowship Programs; and Program of Dialogue on Science, Ethics, and Religion (DoSER).

The Center for Science, Technology and Security Policy (CSTSP)

This center was established by AAAS with a grant from the MacArthur Foundation to encourage the integration of science and public policy for enhanced national and international security. The center facilitates communication among academic centers, policy institutes, and policymakers. This internship allows a part-time undergraduate or graduate student intern interested in the fields of science and public policy to work at the center for about three to four months (with an extension possible). Scheduling is flexible, but an intern is expected to work 20 hours per week and will receive course credit from his or her university. If selected, you'll have the opportunity to be trained in numerous aspects of monitoring science, technology, and security policy issues. You'll help monitor legislation; conduct science, technology and policy research; attend Congressional hearings and meetings and report back to the center; and help draft policy briefs. The ideal candidate will have strong research and writing skills and an interest in national and international security issues.

Science and Human Rights Program

This program was established in 1976 to help scientists assist their colleagues around the world whose human rights are threatened or violated. The program is concerned with violations of scientific freedom and the professional rights of scientists; violations of the human rights of scientists in their capacity as ordinary citizens; and participation by scientists in practices that infringe on the rights of others. If this sounds interesting to you, you might find yourself as an intern researching topics important for science and human rights, helping with publications and activities, and providing support for other activities. Internships are unpaid part-time positions of up to six months, usually based on spring, summer, and fall semesters. You should have a strong interest in human rights and how they interact with science, excellent written and oral communication skills, and a strong academic background. All majors will be considered, but computer experience is necessary and research experience is desirable.

Scientific Freedom, Responsibility, and Law Program

This AAAS program provides opportunities for undergraduate and graduate students to experience how issues in science, ethics, and law are handled within a policy setting. Interns work closely with AAAS staff to prepare proposals, organize meetings, contribute to publications, manage computer databases, obtain resource materials, participate in research, and attend conferences and meetings in Washington, D.C. Scheduling is flexible, but interns are expected to work at least four days per week. Internships are unpaid, but you can receive course credit from your university. Further information is available at http://www.aaas.org/spp/sfrl/.

HOW TO APPLY

To apply for one of the AAAS internships, send a resume along with a cover letter indicating the type of internship (volunteer or paid) and the department/program sponsoring the internship, via e-mail, fax, or regular mail to the preceding contact address.

AMERICAN ASSOCIATION FOR THE ADVANCEMENT OF SCIENCE ENTRY POINT INTERNSHIP

AAAS Project on Science, Technology and Disability
1200 New York Avenue, NW
Washington, DC 20005-3920
(202) 326-6649 (Voice/TDD)

Fax: (202) 371-9849
lsummers@aaas.org
http://ehrweb.aaas.org/entrypoint/index.html

What You Can Earn: Stipend varies according to internship; travel funds included.
Application Deadlines: Rolling.
Educational Experience: Full-time undergraduate or graduate students majoring in a science or engineering field (some fields of business also considered) with at least a B average.
Requirements: Internships available only to students with disabilities and who are U.S. citizens or who have a right-to-work permit.

OVERVIEW
ACCESS

This program (Achieving Competence in Computing, Engineering, and Space Science) is a joint effort by AAAS and NASA managed by Entry Point that offers a summer internship program for students with disabilities. The application process is identical for both ACCESS and Entry Point.

Entry Point

Entry Point is a program of the American Association for the Advancement of Science (AAAS), which offers internships in science, engineering, mathematics, computer science, and some areas of business to students with disabilities who have demonstrated motivation, persistence, and achievement in academic areas. Internships are available at research labs and centers throughout the United States, where you'll work with mentors who advise you on future undergraduate coursework, plans for graduate study, and jobs.

As part of the Entry Point program, AAAS locates opportunities for students in all parts of the country and helps negotiate any accommodations you might need or any geographic limitations you might have. In fact, one benefit of this internship is the chance to spread your wings and work in an area far from your university or hometown. AAAS works with a variety of national corporations, including IBM, NASA, Texas Instruments, and JPMorganChase to screen students with disabilities. In addition to offering competitive salary stipends, the companies and agencies provide assistive technology and other accommodations, such as TDDs, screen readers, and magnifying software, that allow students with disabilities to be productive members of an R&D team.

HOW TO APPLY

To apply for an Entry Point or ACCESS internship, first fill out and submit the online preliminary application (also available in PDF format; see below) at http://ehrweb.aaas.org/entrypoint/application.cfm. Next, submit a full application package:

- letter of introduction including field(s) of interest
- current resume
- official transcript
- two letters of recommendation (one of which must be from faculty)
- statement of disability, plus assistive technology needs

Or, if you prefer, you can download and print the application form in PDF format at http://ehrweb.aaas.org/entrypoint/application.pdf and mail it in with your other information to the preceding address. Acceptances will be announced in late April.

AMERICAN GEOGRAPHICAL SOCIETY INTERNSHIP

American Geographical Society
120 Wall Street, Suite 100
New York, NY 10005-3904
(212) 422-5456

Fax: (212) 422-5480
AGS@amergeog.org
http://www.amergeog.org/organization.htm

What You Can Earn: Unpaid but recommendations for graduate school are possible.
Application Deadlines: Rolling.
Educational Experience: College students, recent college graduates, and graduate students.
Requirements: Interest in geography, environment/nature studies, or animal rights.

OVERVIEW

The oldest nationwide geographical organization in the United States, the American Geographical Society is an international organization interested in geographical research and education, whose members are professional geographers and others interested in the field. The society sponsors expeditions and travel programs; presents lectures, conferences, and symposia; awards honors to scholars and explorers; and conducts research on a wide range of geographical topics. In addition, the society performs geographical research and specialized cartography under contract for many branches of the United States government, the National Science Foundation, the Center for Disease Control and Prevention, American universities, and corporations. Its publications include the *Geographical Review* and *FOCUS on Geography*.

Interns play an important part in activities at the AGS, working either part time or full time for at least 10 weeks. As an intern here, you might find yourself researching Web sites, looking for travel information that could be used by participants in the AGS travel program. You might conduct biographical research of the signers of the Fliers' and Explorers' globe or construct a database of all American institutions offering courses or a major in geography. You might find yourself preparing letters and mailings to individuals who have just earned a Ph.D. in geography, completing various research tasks on the Internet, and creating an e-mail database of all AGS media contacts. You might edit the American Geographical Society

Information Booklet or sift through the AGS archives and create records of the holdings. Most assignments are for work in the AGS office in New York on Wall Street, but a few projects could be carried out elsewhere.

HOW TO APPLY
Send a current resume to the preceding address.

AMERICAN SOCIETY FOR MICROBIOLOGY RESEARCH INTERNSHIP

ASM Minority Undergraduate Research Fellowship
Education Board
American Society for Microbiology
1752 North Street, NW
Washington, DC 20036
(202) 942-9283
Fax: (202) 942-9329
http://www.asm.org/Education/index.
   asp?bid=4322

What You Can Earn: Up to $5840 for minority undergraduate research fellows and $5,000 for undergraduate research fellows.

Application Deadlines: February 1.

Educational Experience: Must be either a freshman with college-level research experience or a sophomore, junior, or senior who will not graduate before the completion date of the summer program; have taken introductory courses in biology, chemistry, and preferably microbiology prior to submission of the application; have a strong interest in obtaining a Ph.D. or M.D./Ph.D. in the microbiological sciences; and have lab research experience.

Requirements: Must be a U.S. citizen or hold permanent visa status. For minority undergraduate research fellows, students must be Black/African American, Mexican American, Native American, Puerto Rican, Alaskan Native American, or Pacific Islander.

OVERVIEW
The American Society for Microbiology is the oldest and largest life-science membership organization in the world, representing 25 disciplines of microbiological specialization plus a division for microbiology educators. Microbiologists study microbes (bacteria, viruses, rickettsiae, mycoplasma, fungi, algae, and protozoa) some of which cause diseases but many of which contribute to the balance of nature or are otherwise beneficial. Some of the world's leading scientists (Pasteur, Koch, Fleming, Leeuwenhoek, Lister, Jenner, and Salk) have been microbiologists. Eligibility to become a member of the society is open to anyone interested in microbiology who holds at least a bachelor's degree or equivalent experience in microbiology or a related field. Microbiology students can become student members.

The society accepts both undergraduate and minority undergraduate research fellows and encourages students to pursue careers in the biological and microbiological sciences by offering opportunities to participate in research projects and to present their results at regional or national meetings. Microbiological research focuses on learning more about infectious diseases, recombinant DNA technology, alternative methods of energy production and waste recycling, new sources of food, new drug development, and the etiology of sexually transmitted diseases, among other areas. Microbiology is also concerned with environmental problems and industrial processes.

The goal of the Microbiology Undergraduate Research Fellowship program (MURF) is to increase the number of underrepresented undergraduate students who want to pursue graduate careers in microbiology. During this program, you'll have the chance to conduct full-time summer research and present research results at the next ASM general meeting.

Community Based Program
Here, five to eight fellows are placed at the same institution to conduct basic science research for 10 to 12

weeks. Fellows will participate in a weekly seminar series, journal club, GRE preparatory course, graduate admission counseling, and career counseling.

Minority Undergraduate Research Fellows

These interns will work either through a New York School of Medicine organized program or individual laboratories nationwide. Applicants should be African American, Mexican American, Native American, Puerto Rican, Alaskan Native American, or Pacific Islander and be U.S. citizens or hold permanent visa status.

You'll be allowed to choose the institution, research area, and level of activity for the summer. Based on your interests, independence, and ability, you can choose the model that best meets your needs. The ASM MURF host institution program offers two models for students to choose from: traditional and community based.

Traditional Program

In this program, you'll have the choice of remaining at your home institution or request to be placed at a host U.S. institution of your choice to conduct basic science research. From a list provided on the application, if you're interested in conducting research at a host institution, you'll choose three where you'd like to conduct your summer research. In most cases, you'll be the only ASM fellow at that institution, and you'll become a participant of a larger summer program already in existence at the institution. You'll also have the chance to participate in poster presentations, journal clubs, social activities, and so on. Summer activities vary at each institution.

Undergraduate Research Fellows

These interns will work at their home institution in collaboration with an American Society for Microbiology faculty mentor and present research results at the ASM general meeting the following year.

The program requires a joint application from both the student and his or her corresponding faculty mentor. The ASM Undergraduate Research Fellowship (URF) is aimed at highly competitive students who wish to pursue graduate careers in microbiology.

HOW TO APPLY

This program requires a joint application from both the student and a faculty mentor; applications are available online: http://www.asm.org/Education/index.asp?bid=4322.

BETTIS ATOMIC POWER LAB INTERNSHIP

Internship Coordinator, Bettis Atomic Power Lab
PO Box 79
West Mifflin, PA 15122
Fax: (412) 476-5363
interns@bettis.gov
http://www.bettislab.com/internprogram.html

What You Can Earn: Stipends vary according to placement.
Application Deadlines: September 30.
Educational Experience: Rising college juniors or seniors and graduate students majoring in metallurgical, electrical, mechanical, chemical, or nuclear engineering; computer science; material science; numerical analysis; chemistry; physics; mathematics; welding engineering; or environmental science; high academic achievement (at least a 3.2 GPA).
Requirements: U.S. citizenship; applicants selected will be subject to a federal background investigation and must meet eligibility requirements for access to classified material.

OVERVIEW

Bettis is a lab that plays a key role in all aspects of the Naval Nuclear Propulsion Program by focusing on fundamental research in a range of areas, developing superior materials, chemistry controlled environments, and components for better nuclear propulsion technology.

Bettis scientists design new reactor and propulsion systems and components that will be installed on new or existing navy surface ships and submarines. Researchers at Bettis also work on the design of new reactor and propulsion systems and components that will be installed on new or existing navy surface ships and submarines and provide technical expertise during new construction, periodic maintenance, and refueling of surface ships and submarines. The lab also trains enlisted and officer propulsion-plant operators at its Charleston facility and operates a reactor core examination facility at its Idaho Falls, Idaho, location.

Each year, Bettis hires about 30 summer interns, which can provide you with a unique opportunity to participate in research at the lab. Interns at Bettis participate in the all of the projects at Bettis.

HOW TO APPLY
Bettis Laboratory sends recruiters to many different universities around the United States; check this Web site for the most recent recruiting schedule: http://www.bettislab.com/campusinterviews. html.

Interested candidates should fax or send a copy of their resumes, unofficial transcripts, and cover letters to the preceding address. Interviews are conducted in late November and early December for internships lasting from May/June through August/September (start and end dates are flexible).

CALIFORNIA ACADEMY OF SCIENCE A. CRAWFORD COOLEY INTERNSHIP IN CALIFORNIA BOTANY

A. Crawford Cooley Internship
c/o Research Division
California Academy of Sciences

875 Howard Street
San Francisco, CA 94103-3009
http://www.calacademy.org/research/internship/
    crawford_cooley_internship.html

What You Can Earn: $3,500 for the internship period. In addition, some travel costs (up to $450) to San Francisco will be reimbursed, and a $1,500 housing allowance is given (some housing may be available)
Application Deadlines: Mid-February
Educational Experience: Junior and senior undergraduates with a B average or better
Requirements: U.S. citizenship

OVERVIEW
The California Academy of Sciences is a comprehensive natural history museum supporting research and collection activities in anthropology, botany, diatom research, entomology, geology, herpetology, ichthyology, invertebrate zoology, ornithology, and mammalogy. Founded in 1853 as the first scientific institution in the western United States, the academy is dedicated to exploring, explaining, and protecting the natural world. With eight scientific research departments, the academy's natural history collections are used by scientists from around the world. The collections provide essential tools for comparative studies in biodiversity and are ranked among the world's largest.

Each summer the academy offers an internship in California botany, in which you'll work with an academy scientist to revise text, rewrite taxonomic keys, identify collections, and work with published literature about the plants of Marin County. The internship begins in late June and runs through mid-August.

HOW TO APPLY
The application can be downloaded at http://www. calacademy.org/research/internship/ssi/appform. htm. Send a letter of interest, a completed internship application, a summary of experience and/

or coursework in the natural sciences, a letter of recommendation from a science professor, and one set of official transcripts to the preceding address.

CALIFORNIA ACADEMY OF SCIENCE INTERNSHIP IN BIOLOGICAL ILLUSTRATION

Biological Illustration Internship
c/o Research Division
California Academy of Sciences
875 Howard Street
San Francisco, CA 94103-3009
http://www.calacademy.org/research/internship/
   biological_illustration_internship.html

What You Can Earn: $3,500 for the internship period. In addition, some travel costs (up to $450) to San Francisco will be reimbursed, and a $1,500 housing allowance is available (some housing may be available).
Application Deadlines: Mid-February
Educational Experience: Currently enrolled undergraduate or graduate students interested in developing illustration techniques related to biological specimens.
Requirements: U.S. citizenship.

OVERVIEW

The California Academy of Sciences is a comprehensive natural history museum supporting research and collection activities in anthropology, botany, diatom research, entomology, geology, herpetology, ichthyology, invertebrate zoology, ornithology, and mammalogy. Founded in 1853 as the first scientific institution in the western United States, the academy is dedicated to exploring, explaining, and protecting the natural world. With eight scientific research departments, the academy's natural history collections are used by scientists from around the world. The collections provide essential tools for comparative studies in biodiversity and are ranked among the world's largest.

As part of the internship in biological illustration, the intern will work with one or more academy scientists to develop illustrations that may be used in scientific publications.

HOW TO APPLY

To apply, send to the preceding address a letter of interest, an internship application, a resume, two letters of recommendation from faculty members, an official set of transcripts, and a sample of your work (original materials, including slides; no e-mailed images, CDs, or floppy disks can be accepted). Your samples will be returned to you after the applications are reviewed. The application form can be downloaded at http://www.calacademy.org/research/internship/ssi/appform.htm.

CALIFORNIA ACADEMY OF SCIENCE ROBERT T. WALLACE UNDERGRADUATE RESEARCH INTERNSHIP

Robert T. Wallace Research Intern
c/o Research Division
California Academy of Sciences
875 Howard Street
San Francisco, CA 94103-3009
http://www.calacademy.org/research/internship/
   robert_wallace_internship.html

What You Can Earn: $3,500 for the internship period. In addition, some travel costs (up to $450) to San Francisco will be reimbursed and a $1,500 housing allowance is given (some housing may be available).

Application Deadlines: Mid-February.

Educational Experience: Junior and senior undergraduates (graduating seniors are not eligible) with a B average or better and participation in a wide range of campus activities.

Requirements: U.S. citizenship.

OVERVIEW

The California Academy of Sciences is one of the 10 largest natural history museums in the world. Like its sister institutions, the Smithsonian Institution, the American Museum of Natural History in New York, and the Field Museum in Chicago, the California Academy of Sciences is devoted to the study, display, and interpretation of scientific collections that inspire people of all ages to explore the rich variety of life on Earth.

Founded in 1853 as the first scientific institution in the western United States, the academy is dedicated to exploring, explaining, and protecting the natural world. With eight scientific research departments, the academy's natural history collections are used by scientists from around the world. The collections provide essential tools for comparative studies in biodiversity and are ranked among the world's largest.

As the museum's valuable collections of natural history specimens have grown, so have its public exhibits. A variety of classes, lectures, and trips also are offered for adults, children, and teachers.

The California Academy of Sciences offers an eight-week Robert T. Wallace undergraduate research summer internship that matches a student with an academy scientist working on a specific research project.

As a Wallace intern, you'll have the chance to learn about a specific group of organisms, be involved in original scientific research, and learn more about the how a natural history museum is involved in research and education. The research project may include laboratory and field-expedition components, and you'll take part in all activities offered by the institute.

HOW TO APPLY

You can find the application form at http://www.calacademy.org/research/internship/ssi/appform.htm. To apply, send:

- a statement of interest in working at the academy
- a completed application form
- an adviser and project
- two letters of recommendation (at least one must be from a science professor)
- one set of official transcripts

All application materials should be sent to the preceding address. Decisions will be made in mid-March.

CENTER FOR SCIENCE IN THE PUBLIC INTEREST INTERNSHIP

Center for Science in the Public Interest
Internships
1875 Connecticut Avenue, NW, #300
Washington, DC 20009
http://www.cspinet.org/about/jobs_internship_2005_2006.html

What You Can Earn: $6/an hour ($7 an hour for graduate students).

Application Deadlines: Rolling.

Educational Experience: Undergraduate and graduate students; specific requirements for CSPI programs are listed below.

Requirements: None specified.

OVERVIEW

The Center for Science in the Public Interest is a national consumer organization that focuses on health and nutrition issues. CSPI offers internships for a small number of qualified students in undergraduate, graduate, law, and medical schools each summer and during the school year.

CSPI was started in 1971 by three scientists who recognized the need for an organization to evaluate the effects of science and technology on society and to promote national policies linked to consumers' interests. CSPI focuses primarily on health and nutrition issues, disclosing deceptive marketing practices, dangerous food additives or contaminants, and flawed science propagated by profits. Findings are communicated in interviews and in reports, books, posters, software, videos, and the center's Nutrition Action Healthletter.

CSPI has a number of programs in which an intern can play an important role.

Alcohol and Public Policy

CSPI has taken the lead in advocating public health-oriented policies on alcohol. Through coalition-building, media attention, and information campaigns directed at legislators, the project campaigns to reduce the health and social consequences of alcohol use and abuse and to counter the industry view that alcohol is a necessary part of the good life. Interns in this program will help with publicizing tighter restrictions on marketing strategies aimed at minorities and youths, warning-label legislation, and increases in alcohol excise taxes. Applicants should be senior undergraduates or graduate students.

Biotechnology

The CSPI biotechnology project is concerned with government policies and corporate practices related to genetically engineered plants, animals, and other organisms. The program is currently working on advocating a mandatory approval process at the U.S. Food and Drug Administration for all genetically engineered foods, strengthening the environmental regulation of biotechnology products at the Environmental Protection Agency and the U.S. Department of Agriculture, publicizing the benefits and risks of biotechnology, and ensuring that developing countries have access to biotechnology.

Applicants should have some background in the biological sciences.

Communications

Through public-information campaigns, media attention, and its Web site, CSPI advocates a variety of progressive public health policies including honest food labeling, healthier foods, safer food additives, sensible alcohol policies, and sustainable agriculture.

As an intern in the communications department, you'll help with many different assignments, such as conducting research using newspapers, magazines, LEXIS/NEXIS, and online sources; preparing reports, press releases, press kits, and fact sheets; and updating the media database.

Excellent computer skills and knowledge of nutrition or food- safety issues are important. Preference will be given to students who have completed coursework in public relations or communications.

Eating Green Project

The goal of the Eating Green project is to get people to eat less meat as a way of improving human health and the environment. CSPI believes that intensive animal agriculture production and their feed grains are affecting air, water, soil, and objects to the fact that industrial farming methods use more than twice the amount of antibiotics as do humans, which could affect the usefulness of these essential medicines. CSPI wants to lessen meat consumption because the center believes eating meat has been linked to numerous cancers, obesity, heart disease, stroke, diabetes, and a shortened life expectancy. As an intern with this project, you may be involved in research, data analysis, Web design, and writing.

Food Safety

This project covers a broad array of topics, divided into the production and inspection of meat, poultry, and seafood; sustainable organic agriculture; food additives; and pesticide safety.

Applicants in this area must have a strong background in either toxicology, biochemistry, biological sciences, law, or public health, plus strong writing and computer skills.

Foundation Fund-raising

This department identifies foundation funding sources for all of CSPI's work. As an intern here, you'll help the director of foundation development research foundation prospects, asking for information from foundations and researching other organizations' funding sources. You'll also help draft foundation fund-raising correspondence (such as acknowledgments and updates), proposals, and reports and assemble materials for grant proposals and update databases and files.

Applicants should be upper level undergraduate students with an interest in fund-raising.

Integrity in Science

This project investigates and publicizes the influence of corporate interests on scientific research and promotes policies for the ethical conduct and oversight of science in an effort to prevent conflicts of interests that color research findings, news stories, and public-policy decisions. Target audiences for the project include academic researchers, journalists, environmental and public health organizations, policymakers in Congress, and federal agencies such as the EPA and the FDA.

Candidates should have strong research and writing skills and an interest in public policy.

Legal Affairs Office

CSPI's attorneys work with project directors and scientists to develop strategies for legislation and regulatory action. As an intern here, you'll help prepare legal documents and research issues involving food and drug law and consumer protection.

Second- and third-year law students who have completed administrative law are eligible to apply. Preference will be given to students who have completed coursework in food and drug law and/or

consumer protection. A science background is useful but not required.

Litigation Project

In 2005, CSPI decided to add litigation to its agenda and is working to join or offer helpful insights to existing lawsuits around the country in the areas of private consumer fraud, products liability, and personal injury. In addition, CSPI is developing its own advocacy lawsuits with private lawyers. As a result, at least one law student intern will be needed to work either in Washington, D.C., or Dallas, where the litigation project is based.

Marketing

CSPI solicits new members through a variety of venues, including direct mail campaigns and inserting preprinted advertising in newspapers throughout the country. Projects for interns primarily focus on reviewing and analyzing demographic data, coordinating and tracking the placement of acquisition packages in newspapers, and analyzing and tracking the results of advertisements.

Candidates should be undergraduate students with an interest in marketing and strong organizational, phone, and computer skills. Experience with WordPerfect 6.1 and LOTUS 1-2-3 is also required.

Nutrition Action Healthletter

The Healthletter is read by the organizations' 800,000+ members, as well as by the press and members of Congress. Interns can help with many aspects of the publication of this newsletter, including research for future articles.

Nutrition and Public Policy

This program covers a broad area of topics related to nutrition and health policies. Current issues include nutrition education, healthcare reform, food additives, restaurant foods, vitamins, saturated fats, synthetic foods, pesticides, and microbial contamination of foods. As an intern here, you may get involved in research for policy analysis and development, op-ed pieces, reports, tracking legislation and regulations, and assisting in policy advocacy.

Applicants should have a strong college-level science, public policy, or law background and must submit a writing sample.

Technology

This department keeps all the company computers running. As an intern here, you'll help with software training and support, hardware troubleshooting and support, and basic programming.

Applicants should be upper-level undergraduate computer science students with extensive computer knowledge. Familiarity with Novell networks is helpful.

HOW TO APPLY

To the preceding address, send a cover letter indicating your issues of interest, future plans, and dates of availability; your resume (experience with advocacy groups is helpful); and a writing sample, if required by the specific project (a popularly written piece is preferred over a technical report).

You should also include two letters of recommendation from instructors or employers that address your academic/work ability and character and an official transcript of courses and grades.

COLD SPRING HARBOR LAB SUMMER INTERNSHIP

Undergraduate Research Program
Watson School of Biological Sciences
Cold Spring Harbor Laboratory
One Bungtown Road
Cold Spring Harbor, NY 11724
(516) 367-8460
urpadmin@cshl.org

http://www.unc.edu/pmabs/northeast/
coldspring.htm

What You Can Earn: $3000 stipend, plus free room and board; health insurance provided if needed.
Application Deadlines: February 1.
Educational Experience: Women and minority sophomore or juniors with good academic standing especially are encouraged to apply.
Requirements: None specified.

OVERVIEW

Located 35 miles from Manhattan on a secluded inlet off Long Island Sound, Cold Spring Harbor Laboratory has for 100 years served as an intellectual watering hole for some of the finest minds in biology. This educational institution specializes in research programs focusing on cancer, neurobiology, plant genetics, genomics, and bioinformatics. It also has a broad educational mission, including the recently established Watson School of Biological Sciences.

The undergraduate research program at Cold Spring Harbor Laboratory provides one of the few places in the world where as a college student you can learn techniques of molecular biology while joining a vibrant scientific community. The fundamental principle of the internship program is to present students with opportunities to conduct research, to help them understand what kind of training they'll need to biological research, and to learn about what research is currently under investigation in the biomedical and life sciences.

Independent research projects may focus on areas such as cancer biology, neurobiology, plant biology, cell biology, genetics, molecular and structural biology, or bioinformatics. Each intern works in a different laboratory directly under the supervision of a senior member of that research group. In addition to research and participation in many social activities, a series of seminars and special events are presented specifically for interns by members of the faculty. Also, as an intern at the lab, you're eligible to attend advanced training postdoc courses taught by visiting eminent scientists during the summer. In these courses, you'll have the chance to learn the latest experimental techniques and to seek advice about future schooling and research. Interns also are invited to all lab social activities, such as Broadway plays or New York City concerts, pool parties, or visiting Long Island beaches.

Internships typically last for about 10 weeks over the summer.

HOUSING

Interns live in new cabins on the lab's campus. Each cabin provides single-gender housing for eight individuals with two per room and two full bathrooms. All linens and towels are provided, along with full housekeeping services. Lamps, desks, dressers, and small refrigerators will be available in each cabin. One phone with voicemail option is available per cabin, and all cabins are air conditioned.

Meals are served seven days a week in the dining hall.

HOW TO APPLY

All applicants must complete an URP application with a personal statement; you may download an application at http://www.cshl.edu/URP. A PDF version of the application is available here: http://www.cshl.edu/URP/urp2005_application.pdf.

Documents should be mailed to the preceding address. Faxes or e-mailed applications will not be accepted. In addition to the application, you should include a transcript (official transcripts are not required) and two letters of recommendation. Letters should be signed and submitted in a sealed envelope, with the referee's signature across the seal and attached to your application. Letters of recommendation may not be sent to the program office separately from the application. Applications that are incomplete will not be accepted by the program office.

The lab will acknowledge the receipt of your application via e-mail, so be sure to include a valid e-mail address. Selection is made by a committee of scientists at the lab.

CORNELL UNIVERSITY MATERIALS SCIENCE RESEARCH INTERNSHIP

Special Programs Coordinator
Cornell Center for Materials Research
621 Clark Hall of Science
Cornell University
Ithaca, NY 14853
(607) 255-0633
Fax: (607) 255-3957
reu@ccmr.cornell.edu
http://www.ccmr.cornell.edu/education/reu

What You Can Earn: $3,750 plus housing and travel expenses.
Application Deadlines: April 30.
Educational Experience: Undergraduate chemistry, physics, and engineering majors; minority and female candidates are strongly encouraged to apply.
Requirements: U.S. citizenship or permanent residents.

OVERVIEW

At Cornell, materials research includes everything from theoretical physics to synthetic chemistry to the design and fabrication of new magnetic, photonic, and microelectronic devices.

The Cornell Center for Materials Research is offering a special summer research program for students who will work with Cornell faculty on interdisciplinary materials research projects involving chemistry, physics, materials science, and engineering disciplines. Research projects for all sorts of materials research interests will be offered, and students will be assisted in choosing a project that matches their interests. Interns will live in one of Cornell's on-campus dorms during the 10-week period. In addition, interns will participate in an organized program of lectures, minicourses, laboratory visits, and a variety of recreational activities.

Samples of typical projects with which interns might get involved include the migration of additives in polymers; imaging nanomaterials; molecular tetris; engineering DNA into a generic material; water in glass; characterization of silica biomaterials from vascular plants; synthesis of polymers; bioinspired drugs; and solid state nitrides.

HOW TO APPLY

Submit an application that you can download at http://www.ccmr.cornell.edu/education/reu/application.html and accompanying materials to the preceding address.

CORNELL UNIVERSITY PLANT GENOME RESEARCH PROGRAM INTERNSHIP

Outreach Coordinator
Boyce Thompson Institute
Tower Road
Ithaca, NY 14853
(607) 254-6732
nph5@cornell.edu
http://outreach-pgrp.cornell.edu/program/
     program_index.asp

What You Can Earn: $320/week plus housing and some travel.
Application Deadlines: Mid-February.
Educational Experience: Qualified high school and undergraduate students interested in plant genome research.
Requirements: None specified.

OVERVIEW

The rapid advances in biological discovery have important consequences in medicine, agriculture, and law, and it is therefore vital that the public be informed in order to better understand these scientific findings. Cornell University has recently developed outreach programs designed to bring together research scientists and public educators. In particular, scientists have begun to address topics related to plant genomics, establishing the Plant Genome Research Program. The programs are designed to provide high school teachers with training in plant genome science and to introduce high school and undergraduate students to laboratory and field research in plant science.

If you're chosen as a summer intern in this program, you'll be placed in one of 16 participating labs according to preference and availability for the internship lasting 40 hours a week for eight to 12 weeks (undergraduates) and six to eight weeks (high school students). You'll work with a graduate student or postdoctoral associate on a project related to plant genomics, learning the latest in molecular biology techniques and perhaps participating in fieldwork. You'll also attend lab meetings, read and discuss recent literature related to your project, and present your research to other students, principal investigators, and mentors at student symposia.

The summer internship culminates in a student symposium called the Colonel's Cup Challenge. This full-day event allows students either to give a presentation or create a poster communicating what they have learned and accomplished during the summer. The posters and presentations are judged by a panel that determines the winner of the Colonel's Cup.

HOW TO APPLY

To apply online, visit http://outreach-pgrp.cornell.edu/program/program_index.asp and fill out separate applications for the high school and college-level internships. Mail them to the preceding address.

DUKE UNIVERSITY NEUROSCIENCES SUMMER RESEARCH PROGRAM IN MECHANISMS OF BEHAVIOR

Duke Undergraduate Neurosciences Program
9 Flowers Drive
Department of Psychology
Duke University, Box 90086
Durham, NC 90086
(919) 660-5765

What You Can Earn: $2,500 for the 10-week program. Students will also be provided with housing at no cost and given a food allowance. Students are expected to cover their own travel expenses.
Application Deadlines: Early April.
Educational Experience: Qualified college students interested in behavior and neurobiology who are considering a career in basic scientific research. Strong preference will be given to sophomores, although awards may be made to exceptionally qualified juniors who have not had previous research opportunities. Women and members of minority groups are particularly encouraged to apply.
Requirements: U.S. citizens or permanent residents.

OVERVIEW

The Duke University Undergraduate Neurosciences Program, with support of the National Science Foundation, offers a summer research program for undergraduates to conduct supervised independent research in behavior and neurobiology.

During this 10-week program, you'll work with a participating faculty mentor at Duke University studying integrative neurobiology, systems neurobiology, or animal behavior. You'll also participate in a two-day orientation conference at the outset of the program and will meet several times each week thereafter for seminars by participating faculty and for tutorials and workshops covering topics such as experimental design and analysis, science writing and oral presentation, science ethics, career paths in science, and applying to graduate school.

At the conclusion of the program, you'll report on your work at an undergraduate research conference held jointly with other summer research programs.

HOW TO APPLY

First, download the application: http://www.duke.edu/neurosci/research/mobappl.doc. Fill out the online application and submit it, along with two recommendations, an essay addressing how your participation in the program will fit into your academic and career interests, a transcript, and a choice of faculty mentors, to the preceding address.

DUPONT ENGINEERING INTERNSHIP

DuPont
1007 Market Street
Wilmington, DE 19898
http://ca.dupont.com/dupontglobal/corp/careers/univ_internships.html

What You Can Earn: Guidelines based on education and experience.
Application Deadlines: Rolling.
Educational Experience: Currently enrolled in an ABET accredited chemical, mechanical, or electrical engineering undergraduate program with a minimum GPA of 3.0.
Requirements: Ability to work in the United States without restriction; strong written, verbal, analytical, and interpersonal skills; resourcefulness in challenging work environments; motivation to drive projects to completion.

OVERVIEW

Operating in more than 70 countries, DuPont offers a wide range of innovative products and services for markets including agriculture; nutrition; electronics; communications; safety and protection; home and construction; transportation; and apparel. The company began in 1802 by producing explosives but evolved over the next 100 years, broadening its focus to include chemicals, materials, and energy. Today, the company delivers science-based solutions in food and nutrition, healthcare, apparel, safety and security, construction, electronics, and transportation. If you look closely at the things around your home and workplace, chances are you'll find dozens of items made with DuPont materials.

DuPont looks for bright, talented students majoring in engineering and chemistry with the leadership capabilities and determination to create new technologies. DuPont offers a wide range of engineering intern opportunities to B.S./M.S. engineering students at sites throughout the United States.

As an intern, you'll integrate classroom theory with practical work as you perform meaningful assignments. DuPont offers assignments in the following disciplines.

Chemical Engineering

In this area, interns typically learn more about various processes such as extrusion, compounding, distillation, compression, and pumping/piping/fluid flow. Interns will apply this knowledge to specific areas such as improved control strategies, process improvements, or new technology scale-up. In addition, knowledge of areas such as reaction analysis, heat transfer, or material balances would be applied to various developments. In the manufacturing process, assignments might involve statistical analysis of data, quality and process improvement, project justification and implementation, and assistance to operations. Duties might include technical computing and running computer simulations with modeling software such as ASPEN or TMODS.

Chemistry

Interns in this area will be assigned to handle chemistry tasks that may include understanding various chemical operations, chemical synthesis, process development, and support to various processes.

Mechanical Engineering

In these assignments, interns typically learn and understand processes such as extrusion, compounding, distillation, compression, and pumping/piping/fluid flow. Students apply this knowledge and solve problems related to mechanical development; new processes and equipment design; project justification and implementation; process optimization; troubleshooting mechanical equipment failures; reliability testing on existing equipment; installation and startup of new systems; and process refinement and improvement.

HOW TO APPLY

To apply online, visit http://www1.dupont.com/dupontglobal/corp/careers/univ_internships.html.

GENENTECH INTERNSHIP

Genentech
Attn: Summer Internship Program
1 DNA Way MS 39A
South San Francisco, CA 94080

What You Can Earn: Competitive monthly stipend, plus membership at a health club.
Application Deadlines: February 10.
Educational Experience: Students must have completed their sophomore year at an accredited college or university and must have plans to return to school in the following term. If you have already graduated, you are not eligible for internship positions. Although interns are hired in many areas of study, most internship opportunities are for students who major in the life or physical sciences or

chemical engineering. You must have completed one year of college algebra, college chemistry, and biology.

Requirements: None specified.

OVERVIEW

Genentech is a leading biotechnology company that discovers, develops, manufactures and commercializes biotherapeutics for significant unmet medical needs. The Genentech Internship Program is an intensive 10- to 12-week program during the summer. Interns participate as members of project teams in research and development that complement their college curricula with relevant hands-on experience. Working side by side with some of the most talented people in biotechnology, the networking and mentoring provide an excellent environment for academic and career growth.

Each year, Genentech hosts approximately 165 interns. Of the available internships, generally 35 percent are in research or development. Research projects vary from year to year and from department to department; however, all internships have interesting and valuable assignments. Most likely you will be working on a small piece of a big project or independently exploring an idea. Research projects in the past have included screening for molecules involved in cell differentiation and regeneration; building tools to analyze the shapes if bioactive small molecules; and developing and performing assays on different clones to determine the roles they play.

Nearly every department in Genentech hosts summer interns, and many host interns year-round. As an intern, you might be a member of one of the following teams: analytical chemistry, antibody technology, assay and automation technology, automation engineering, bioanalytical methods development, bioorganic chemistry, bioinformatics, biostatistics, cell biology and technology, cell culture and fermentation r&d, endocrinology, environmental health and safety, fermentation, immunology, manufacturing sciences, molecular biology, molecular oncology, pathology, pharmacokinetics and metabolism, protein engineering, small molecule pharmacology, thrombolytics research, or toxicology.

HOW TO APPLY

To apply you must submit a resume to the address above. Genentech does not require completion of a formal application to apply.

GLAXOSMITHKLINE INTERNSHIP

GlaxoSmithKline
http://www.gsk.com/careers/us-university/university_us_employment.htm

What You Can Earn: Intern salaries are paid hourly and are competitive with the pharmaceutical industry.

Application Deadlines: Mid-March, but the process opens in January and the earlier you submit, the better.

Educational Experience: College students currently enrolled in an undergraduate, graduate, or Ph.D. level degree program. To be eligible, students must have at a minimum completed their sophomore year of undergraduate studies.

Requirements: None specified.

OVERVIEW

GlaxoSmithKline is the result of the merger of the Glaxo Wellcome and SmithKline Beecham drug companies, resulting in one of the largest pharmaceutical companies in the world. The company offers summer internships in research and development and pharmaceuticals.

The company has more than 16,000 employees based at 24 sites in seven different countries. The research and development department is a world leader in genomics/genetics and new drug discovery technologies. The company's small, therapeutically aligned Centres of Excellence for Drug Discovery conduct the middle phases of research efforts, identifying and validating potential compounds with the possibility of becoming new medicines for patients.

Interns in this company have the opportunity to help with meaningful work and make integral contributions. These intern opportunities are available at sites in the Raleigh, North Carolina, and the greater Philadelphia areas. Internship positions are full time, and last for between 10 to 12 weeks, typically beginning in May and ending in August.

HOW TO APPLY

Hard copy resumes will not be accepted. Visit the following Web site to apply online: http://www.gsk.com/careers/us-university/university_us_employment.htm. Before you start your application, you should have a cover letter and/or resume in either plain text or HTML format. The online application form will time out and cannot be retrieved after 30 minutes of inactivity.

To avoid the risk of losing your application, it's best to draft out and refine as much information as possible prior to going online. You'll receive an on-screen notification that the company has received your application. If you've provided an e-mail address, they will send you e-mail confirmation that your application is being processed.

HARVARD UNIVERSITY FOUR DIRECTIONS SUMMER RESEARCH PROGRAM

Four Directions Summer Research Program
Harvard Medical School/ Division of Medical
    Sciences
260 Longwood Avenue, MEC 432

Boston, MA 02115
(800) 367-9019, ext.2
SHURP@hms.harvard.edu
http://www.fdsrp.org/index.htm

What You Can Earn: Airfare, transportation, and lodging, plus a stipend large enough to cover food and incidentals.
Application Deadlines: Mid-February
Educational Experience: Minimum one year of undergraduate studies completed prior to start of program (June 2005) with at least one introductory science course (can include biology or chemistry) and a demonstrated interest in careers in medical sciences. This internship doesn't require the highest grades (transcripts are not requested) or the most extensive research background (research experience is not required).
Requirements: Commitment to the health of Native American communities and evidence of motivation to achieve the highest goals possible. You should not take the August MCAT immediately after this internship; the time constraints of the program do not allow adequate time for studying for this important exam.

OVERVIEW

Harvard University's Four Directions Summer Research Program is designed to give a handful of talented interns new skills, experiences, and knowledge that they can use to help themselves, their communities, and future generations of Native Peoples from all of the Four Directions. Begun in 1994, the Four Directions has more than 10 years of experience providing a uniquely tailored program to those who want to serve Native American communities through science and medicine. The program is run by medical students and members of the Native American Health Organization.

Interns participate in a full-time, two-month research program at Harvard Medical School, participating in a basic science research project under the guidance of a medical school faculty mentor. The mentor works closely with the student to ensure completion of a project over the summer period. At the end of the summer, participants will share their experiences and research in a short presentation to other members of the program and to faculty members of HMS. They will also be given other opportunities to explore their interests through activities, which could include shadowing doctors, shifts in the emergency room, and visiting surgeons in the operating room.

As an intern in this program, you'll get to experience cutting-edge research at a leading medical school, learn more about the medical school application process, be exposed to Native American healthcare issues, integrate Native traditions (including talking circles and the largest local Pow-Wow), and spend time networking with Native American students and faculty. Research projects have included sudden infant death syndrome, immune system development, nervous tissue regeneration, and pain-processing pathways.

HOW TO APPLY

Application forms and additional information are available at http://www.fdsrp.org/fdsrpapp/index.htm.

HARVARD UNIVERSITY SUMMER HONORS UNDERGRADUATE RESEARCH PROGRAM

SHURP Director
Division of Medical Sciences
Harvard Medical School
M.E.C. Room 432
260 Longwood Avenue
Boston, MA 02115
(800) 367-9019
Fax: (617) 432-2644
SHURP@hms.harvard.edu

http://www.hms.harvard.edu/dms/diversity/shurpintro.html

What You Can Earn: $3250, housing, travel expenses, and health insurance if needed.
Application Deadlines: February 2.
Educational Experience: Students considering careers in biological or biomedical research sciences who have experience in a research laboratory.
Requirements: Must participate in various sponsored activities such as an orientation session, weekly meetings, laboratory group meetings, and tours of the Boston area. You must participate for the full 10 weeks of the program, although arrival and departure dates of one week earlier or later may be arranged in a few cases if needed.

OVERVIEW

Harvard University will offer a 10-week summer research program primarily for college students belonging to minority groups who are considered underrepresented in the sciences. Summer research opportunities will be available in a variety of biological sciences, including cellular and developmental biology; cardiac and cardio-pulmonary functions and pathology; studies of blood cells; causes and treatments for high blood pressure; immunology; microbiology; molecular biology; transmembrane signaling mechanisms; and virology.

As an intern here, you'll also take part in an informal student-faculty seminar course, where you'll meet every week during supper to discuss your research projects with other student participants and faculty. You'll also participate in a weekly career discussion luncheon series, where you'll learn about the career paths of current minority faculty and graduate students and learn about the many aspects of choosing a graduate program, preparing for interviews, and completing applications.

HOUSING

Interns live in single rooms in the renovated Harvard Medical School dormitory, located across the street from the medical school quadrangle and within one or two blocks of many of the Harvard teaching hospitals and their research laboratories. Medical students, graduate students, college students participating in other summer programs, and visiting scholars also live in the dormitory in the summertime. The medical school is located in Boston.

HOW TO APPLY

Application forms are available on the SHURP homepage at http://www.hms.harvard.edu/dms/diversity/application/app.html.

Students should enclose with their application:

- A letter describing their laboratory experience, research interests and goals, and reasons for wanting to participate in this particular program.
- An updated resume.
- An official copy of latest college transcript.
- Two letters of recommendation: one from a science faculty member who can discuss your intellectual and personal suitability for the program and one from a research supervisor, another science faculty member, or (if applicable) from a science program director. Letters of recommendation should be in signed, sealed envelopes or sent separately by the recommender.

HARVARD UNIVERSITY SUMMER RESEARCH PROGRAM IN ECOLOGY

Harvard Summer Research Program in Ecology
PO Box 68
324 N. Main Street
Petersham, MA 01366

(978) 724-3595
hfapps@fas.harvard.edu
http://www.unc.edu/pmabs/northeast/Harvard3.html

What You Can Earn: $4200 for the 12-week session, with free housing at Fisher House and Raup House as well as a full meal program for participants who live on site; academic credit may be arranged with the student's home institution.
Application Deadlines: March 1.
Educational Experience: Students from diverse backgrounds attending colleges and universities across the country with a variety of science experiences. Most positions are for students currently enrolled in a community college, college, or university. A small amount of funding is available each year for recently graduated students with significant research experience.
Requirements: U.S. citizens or resident aliens.

OVERVIEW

Harvard Forest is one of the oldest and most intensively studied forests in North America. Since 1908, the scientists, students, and collaborators at the 3,000-acre forest have explored topics ranging from conservation and environmental change to land-use history and the ways in which physical, biological, and human systems interact to change Earth. The forest is located in central Massachusetts about 70 miles west of Boston, in the transition hardwood-white pine-hemlock forest region, and includes a variety of forests and wetlands. Facilities include laboratories for nutrient analysis; physiological and population ecology; isozyme, tree-ring and pollen analysis; greenhouses; herbarium; computer laboratory; library; archives; and the Fisher Museum.

Each summer, Harvard Forest offers an internship program for up to 20 undergraduate students and recent graduates to collaborate with scientists conducting ecological investigations for 12 weeks. Each student will participate in an ongoing research project with a researcher from Harvard University, the University of New Hampshire, the

Marine Biological Laboratory Ecosystem Center, or other institutions.

Interns may find themselves field sampling, conducting lab studies, analyzing data, and working on scientific writing. In addition, students attend weekly seminars and workshops given by nationally known scientists on ecosystem research, career planning, and graduate school preparation. In July, participants attend a one-day symposium on careers in ecology at the Institute of Ecosystem Studies in Millbrook, New York. At the end of the summer, students develop their research results, prepare an abstract, and present their findings at a student research symposium. Students are encouraged to give a presentation regarding their summer research project upon returning to their home institution.

Harvard Forest research focuses on the effects of natural and human disturbances on forest ecosystems, including atmospheric pollution, global warming, hurricanes, treefalls, and insect outbreaks. Researchers come from many disciplines, and specific projects center on invasive plants, pests, and pathogens; plant biology, population, and community ecology; paleoecology; land use history; biochemistry; soil science; ecophysiology; atmosphere-biosphere exchanges; aquatic studies; large experiments and permanent plot studies; retrospective studies; conservation and management; atmospheric chemistry; and soil carbon and nitrogen dynamics.

Specific projects may include the following:

Ecological and Historical Aspects of Invasion of *Alliaria petiolata* in New England

This project investigates landscape, community, and population-level interactions between *Alliaria petiolata* and native plants in New England forest habitats. Interns working on this project will use comparative methods, vegetation sampling, experimental design, and field identification of native and invasive plant species. Opportunities for independent research include but are not limited to soil fungi community sampling, mapping sites using GPS, analyzing spatial data with GIS, and leaf chemistry analysis. You'll be expected to

help with data entry and analysis, with direction from your mentor, and your summer supervisor will meet with you one to three times a week.

Disturbance Histories as a Predictor of Habitat Invasibility in a Mosaic Landscape: Cape Cod National Seashore

Nonnative species are a major threat to native species and ecosystems, and Harvard scientists are trying to understand why certain upland habitats in Cape Cod are invaded by nonnative species while others are not. As an intern, you'll help researchers set up a heathland restoration and maintain and complete two community-level experiments on nonnative species invasions in heathland and black locust habitats. You'll be gathering data five days a week, and you'll have long hours in the field, setting up experiments involving planting and weeding the assembled communities, identifying plant species, and maintaining the experiments. In addition, you'll have the option of designing a small experiment within the context of the larger project.

Hemlock Woolly Adelgid Infestations

The hemlock woolly adelgid, *Adelges tsugae*, is an invasive insect decimating hemlock forests in the eastern United States. The invasion front has passed through Massachusetts and has entered Maine, New Hampshire, and probably Vermont. The extent that trees are infested continues to increase, yet the dynamics of the spread is poorly studied. Scientists are trying to understand these processes through documentation and modeling changes in the insects' distribution, development, and survival. As an intern working on this project, you'll use existing sampling plans to monitor population increase and small-scale range expansion of HWA in hemlock stands at Harvard Forest and the surrounding area. You'll observe tree health and its relationship to adelgid density and rate-of-range expansion, and you'll work with scientists to evaluate the vertical distribution, development, density, and survival of HWA on individual trees.

Recent Forest Harvesting and Historical Land Use on Forest Composition and Invasive Species

This study investigates the ecological influence of forest harvesting in central and western Massachusetts. As an intern, you'll help conduct extensive field sampling to evaluate harvesting impacts on critical ecological characteristics, including tree regeneration, invasive species distribution, and native plant species richness and composition. You'll also determine whether the impact of recent cutting activity differs according to prior land use. The study involves active collaboration of Harvard Forest researchers with staff from The Nature Conservancy. Although the study is based at Harvard Forest, field crews will also spend a few weeks during the summer at field stations close to sampling locations. Your responsibilities will include daily travel to field sites across central and western Massachusetts to collect vegetation and soils data. You'll also help with soil sieving, drying, plant identification, data entry, and analysis.

Who Eats Whom?

This research is focused on understanding how stress (such as climate change or acid rain) changes the dynamics of food webs and alters patterns of species distribution and abundance. If you work as an intern here, you'll help conduct greenhouse and field experiments designed to determine how the structure of the invertebrate food web alters growth and form of the pitcher plant and how these shifts are related to nutrient budget of the plant. You'll be responsible for field collections of invertebrates, maintenance of experiments, and ecophysiological measurements of plants and invertebrates. You should expect to spend one or two days a week in the field and two to three days a week in the greenhouse and lab. There should be opportunities for students to develop independent research projects associated with this larger project.

The Forest is located in Petersham, a small town in central Massachusetts about 70 miles west of Boston. You'll be living on the grounds of the Harvard Forest in Fisher House or Raup House with one to three roommates. The closest town is Athol; while the forest is in a rural area, summer students often visit the college towns of Amherst and Northampton, take day trips to Cambridge and Boston, organize hikes in New Hampshire's White Mountains, and explore Maine's coastline at Acadia National Park.

HOW TO APPLY

You may apply by downloading an application at http://harvardforest.fas.harvard.edu/education/reu/reuapp.pdf. You should submit the completed application by mail, fax, or e-mail to the preceding address, along with:

- two Harvard Forest Summer Program recommendations from science professors or other appropriate persons
- a typed 250-word essay describing your career objectives, science background (including relevant courses, employment, or experiences), and why this program and the selected projects would be beneficial to you
- your resume

HOWARD HUGHES HONORS SUMMER INSTITUTE

Howard Hughes Honors Summer Institute
Associate Program Director
New York University
Department of Biology
1009 Silver Center
100 Washington Square East
New York, NY 10003-6688
http://www.nyu.edu/cas/Academic/
   HonorsProgram/hhsi/

What You Can Earn: $2,000 stipend; $1,000 research grant for supplies; room and board on New York University campus (including access to NYU facilities); campus health coverage; and travel costs to and from New York City for each participant (one time only).

Application Deadlines: Early February.

Educational Experience: Mature, well-qualified undergraduates who have completed their sophomore or junior year of college. Underrepresented minority students and women are strongly encouraged to apply. Students with an interest in research are encouraged to apply regardless of experience.

Requirements: An interest in research.

OVERVIEW

The Howard Hughes Honors Summer Institute (supported by a grant from the Howard Hughes Medical Institute) offers college undergraduates the chance to experience cutting-edge research in genomics, bioinformatics, and computational biology at New York University.

Each intern will be paired with a faculty member who shares the student's research interests. Through lab work, seminars, discussion groups, faculty lectures, and social activities, you'll learn about a variety of topics related to contemporary life sciences. The program culminates in a research festival, during which you'll present your findings to each other, faculty, and guests.

Your faculty mentor will work with you on a problem-based research project, and you'll also attend seminars, discussion groups, faculty lectures, and social activities. You'll also learn about lab safety, ethics, the importance of keeping accurate lab notes, and publishing scientific papers.

During the summer, each week there is a weekly seminar featuring the research of participating labs. Research associates, postdoctoral fellows, and graduate students present their work to students in an informal setting designed to stimulate active discussion and inquiry. In addition, once a week interns get together to discuss their individual progress. These informal sessions are designed to allow students to learn about each other's projects, ask questions about basic lab issues, and talk about the satisfaction and frustration often associated with scientific research. The associate director of the Honors Institute leads the discussions.

In addition, faculty lectures in genomics, bioinformatics, and computational biology are given during the program, featuring professors from NYU and other universities. Each lecture is followed by a reception where you'll be able to meet the speaker.

Finally, the Summer Honors Institute provides several opportunities for students to visit the city's museums, parks, and theaters.

HOW TO APPLY

Interested students must complete the application forms, available in RTF or PDF format at http://www.nyu.edu/cas/Academic/HonorsProgram/hhhsi/application.html. In addition, you must ask your college registrar to send your transcripts directly to the program coordinator. You also must request two letters of assessment, at least one of which must be from a faculty member who has taught you in a science course. It's your responsibility to ensure that all application materials, including letters of assessment and official transcripts, are received by the application deadline. On-site interviews won't be conducted.

Interns are chosen by considering their academic record, major area of concentration, and letters of assessment. Applicants will be notified of their acceptance in April.

INSTITUTE OF ECOSYSTEM STUDIES INTERNSHIP

Undergraduate Research Program
Institute of Ecosystem Studies
PO Box R, 181 Sharon Turnpike
Millbrook, NY 12545
(845) 677-7600 ext. 326

Fax: (845) 677-6455
dahlh@ecostudies.org

What You Can Earn: $3,600 for the 12-week program plus free housing in an Institute dormitory; some assistance is available for travel to and from the program.
Application Deadlines: February 15.
Educational Experience: Undergraduate freshmen, sophomores, juniors, or first-semester seniors are eligible for consideration. Minority students and women are encouraged to apply.
Requirements: U.S. citizen or permanent resident.

OVERVIEW

The Institute of Ecosystem Studies combines research and education in fulfillment of its scientific mission to create, disseminate, and apply knowledge about ecological systems. A society with a basic understanding of ecological systems and an appreciation of its role in the quality of human life is essential if natural areas are to be sustained. Founded in 1983 by the eminent ecologist Dr. Gene E. Likens, the institute is one of the largest ecological programs in the world.

Its internship program (Research Experiences for Undergraduates) is a 12-week summer program that gives students an opportunity to conduct independent research as part of a research community. Supported by the National Science Foundation and The Andrew W. Mellon Foundation, the program involves many students from colleges that don't provide undergraduate research opportunities.

During the 12-week program, interns will complete independent ecological research projects under the guidance of IES staff scientists and will be able to use the field, laboratory, and library facilities while they develop scientific inquiry and procedural skills. Students receive a great deal of support and guidance from their mentors and other IES scientists, post docs, graduate students, and research staff.

The group will also explore the broader contexts (socio-economic, intellectual, political, ethical, and personal) within which research takes place. Interns also have plenty of time to interact with other students, research scientists, and many different guest speakers.

Each student is required to prepare an oral presentation for a formal undergraduate research symposium and a final paper for inclusion in an Institute Occasional Publication.

The program tries to help students understand research so they can make good career decisions. Students who want to pursue a research career receive exceptional training, but everyone who participates gains valuable skills and experiences. The program emphasizes the community nature of scientific enterprise.

Through a case study of a regional environmental issue, a career forum, and a day spent teaching high school students from a nearby city, interns also explore the social, political, intellectual, and personal dimensions of being an ecologist. Alumni surveys indicate that the IES-REU program is the most influential factor in shaping student career choices, surpassing both prior interest and undergraduate courses and professors. More than half of the participants go on to graduate school.

Interns stay in a small dormitory (Bacon Flats) located on the grounds of the institute, next door to the Plant Science Building and the Likens Laboratory, where students conduct much of their work.

The IES-REU program gives interns opportunities to think about the process of science and its place in the world. Because of this, students have a strong grasp on the life and work of a research scientist upon completion of the program. Students participate in many activities that help broaden their perspective and deepen their understanding of the various contexts and applications of science.

Projects include the following.

Changes in Nutrient Limitation in Mirror Lake
Studies in the early 1970s found that algal production in Mirror Lake was limited by both nitrogen and phosphorus. In the 30 years since, nitrogen inputs increased and levels of development changed, and changes in the food-web structure may alter the algal standing stock. Several experiments can be

carried out to test whether there have been changes in the limiting nutrient or whether eutrophication may be of future concern for Mirror Lake. Examining pathways of nutrient input and loss provides additional areas to pursue. One interesting input of nutrients may be stocked fish. Interns will work at Hubbard Brook in New Hampshire with several trips to IES.

Community Ecology of a "Hub" Species

Recent studies have shown that the white-footed mouse is central to many important processes in eastern deciduous forest communities. Mice are a key host for blacklegged (deer) ticks and the main reservoir for Lyme disease spirochetes; they are important consumers of tree seeds, forest pests such as the gypsy moth, and eggs of some ground-nesting songbirds; and they are a preferred prey of raptors and carnivores. Because of their broad diet, they also might compete strongly with other forest vertebrates, such as the eastern chipmunk. In this project, the intern will help design a project to assess one or more of these important links between mice and their parasites, pathogens, prey, predators, and competitors.

Ecological Functions of Hudson River Marshes, Shallows, and Tributaries

The Hudson River has a large number of diverse tidal wetlands along its shores and important vegetated shallow areas where tributaries deliver their loads of nutrients and sediment. There is little understanding of how these marshes and littoral areas contribute to food webs, serve as habitat, or modify water chemistry. This project introduces students to the diversity of wetlands, streams, and shallow habitats in the Hudson Valley and teaches valuable field techniques. Depending on the interests of the intern, simple procedures for determining some of these functions could be applied to a range of sites.

Ecosystem Impacts of an Introduced Aquatic Plant in the Hudson River

Past research suggests that an introduced aquatic plant (the Eurasian water chestnut, *Trapa natans*)

may have strong effects on both the biotic interactions and chemical reactions in the Hudson River ecosystem. Interns would work on projects to better understand the impacts of this alien species and/or to develop educational materials designed for managers, educators, and the broader-interested public. Potential research projects include: the interaction of light and the oxygen balance of aquatic plants; the contribution of sediments to nutrient and oxygen in aquatic plant beds; or the interaction of aquatic plant beds and waterfowl. The projects would be done in the context of a larger ecosystem study on the chemistry, biology, and hydrology of aquatic plant beds in the Hudson River ecosystem.

Impacts of Introduced Trout on Mirror Lake

Recently, non-native rainbow trout (*Oncorhynchus mykiss*) and brown trout (*Salmo trutta trutta*) have been stocked in Mirror Lake. Studies could explore competition with or predation upon native fish and amphibian species; cascades through zooplankton to algae; utilization of terrestrial energy sources reducing interaction with other aquatic species; socioeconomic value of trout/angling versus other fish or uses of the lake; and stocked fish biomass contributing to the loading of limiting nutrients to the water column. Interns will work at Hubbard Brook in New Hampshire, with several trips to IES.

Invasive Species and Soil Biogeochemical Cycling in Urban and Rural Forests

In the Baltimore Ecosystem Study, scientists have been focusing on the role of earthworm community composition as a regulator of microbial community composition and nitrogen cycling in forest soils. Interns can participate in several different projects examining the effect of spatial heterogeneity, vegetation type, lawn maintenance, and different earthworm species on microbes. The work involves data gathering in the field (surveys and measurement of abiotic data) and measurements of soil characteristics and microbial processes in the laboratory. Students will work in Baltimore with several trips to IES.

Microbial Processes in Urban Ecosystems

The maintenance of natural microbial nutrient cycling processes in urban ecosystems is important. In this project, students can participate in several different studies that are part of the Baltimore Ecosystem Study, a long-term study of the effects of exotic species in Baltimore on soil nutrient cycling processes, microbial processes in urban riparian forests and nutrient cycling in forest, and agricultural and residential areas within the city.

The Mystery of Mystery Snails

Two species of large Asian mystery snails (*Cipangopaludina spp.*) were introduced into North America around 1900, which are now conspicuous and abundant in quiet waters across the continent, including several Hudson Valley lakes and ponds. Introduced snails have serious ecological impacts in many ecosystems around the world, but very little is known of the ecological roles or impacts of the Asian mystery snails. In this project, the intern will conduct field or laboratory research on some aspect of the role or impacts of these animals.

People and Earthworms

The idea that earthworms are "good" is common in popular literature and in gardening and K-12 ecology education. Scientists are developing a Web site about the ecological roles of worms. To help guide this development, interns will carry out their own research to reveal what different groups of people know, or think they know, about the ecology of earthworms. Areas to be explored include where the public's ideas come from and what barriers or positive pathways exist to helping people develop a more accurate view of earthworms in Northeastern ecosystems. The intern will have access to many different groups for interviews, focus-group discussions, and surveys, including youth and educators in IES education programs in New York and Baltimore; adults participating in the IES Continuing Education Program (representing general public and gardening enthusiasts); and the general public. This research will help scientists understand how people develop ideas about organisms and ecosystems and will give the student experience in social science research linked to biological inquiry.

Plant Interactions with Their Environment

Plant species not only respond to their environment; they play an active role in altering their habitat. Different plant species can have distinct effects on ecosystem processes and provide valuable services such as soil stabilization, soil water retention, pest control, and maintenance of soil fertility. An understanding of how plants provide these services can help predict the consequences of vegetation shifts, plant invasions, and loss of plant diversity. Interns may investigate a number of different topics, including the ways plant species alter ecosystem processes; how abundant a species must be to alter its environment; how agricultural management practices influence the ecosystem effects of plant species; how global change may alter species effects on nutrient dynamics in croplands; or how management practices, environmental conditions, and soil nutrients affect weed species in croplands.

Plant Population Effects on Soil Nitrogen and Carbon Cycling

It's clear that patterns of plant growth, death, and reproduction can have a large impact on biogeochemical cycling. In this project, interns will investigate how variation in seed size, seed density, and seed identity affect seedling thinning and soil dynamics of nitrogen and carbon.

HOW TO APPLY

You can obtain an application by visiting http://www.ecostudies.org/reu.html. You can submit this application electronically, but paper copies are also available by request or online as a PDF file, which may be submitted through the mail. It is not necessary to provide official transcripts with your application; you can just fill out the relevant course and grade information on the application to fulfill this requirement. However, transcripts may be requested by your mentor if you are selected for this research opportunity. Nor is it necessary to provide letters of recommendation with your application. You can simply provide three references and their contact information. If you are selected for this research opportunity, your mentor may ask for letters of recommendation at that time. However, these items are not necessary when applying, since each mentor handles this process differently.

JACKSON LABORATORY SUMMER STUDENT PROGRAM

Training and Education Office
The Jackson Laboratory
600 Main Street
Bar Harbor, ME 04609-1500
(207) 288-6250
Fax: (207) 288-6079
summerstudents@jax.org

What You Can Earn: $2500 plus room and board in a dorm (two to four students to a room).
Application Deadlines: End of January.
Educational Experience: High school seniors or seniors who have just graduated, who are at least 15 years old, or college undergraduates enrolled as full-time students with at least one semester of undergraduate school remaining before graduation.
Requirements: Must be a U.S. citizen or permanent resident.

OVERVIEW

An internationally recognized center for mammalian genetic research, The Jackson Laboratory is an independent, nonprofit institution where outstanding students conduct interdisciplinary research as apprentices in the labs of staff scientists from mid-June to mid-August. The laboratory, an NIH designated cancer-research center, is located in the coastal Maine community of Bar Harbor, adjacent to Acadia National Park. The Jackson Laboratory is home to more than 30 scientists conducting research into mammalian genetics, in the fields of cancer; bioinformatics and computational biology; developmental biology; immunology and hematology; metabolic diseases; neurobiology and sensory deficits; genomics; and resource-related research. Many of the scientists' research pertains to more than one category, and virtually all work done at the lab has a basic connection to unraveling the genetic causes of disease.

If you're selected as an intern in this nine- to 11-week program, you'll work full time on an independent research project under the supervision of a member of the laboratory scientific staff, who provides training, laboratory space, and resources. Projects are tailored to the student's background and interests. Research areas focus on advancing the knowledge of molecular, developmental, genetic, biochemical, and immunological mechanisms related to normal growth and development and human disease. Major areas of focus are cancer; bioinformatics and computational biology; developmental biology and aging; genomics; hematology/immunology; metabolic diseases; neurobiology and sensory deficits; and research associated with resource development.

The laboratory provides a stimulating environment for students interested in experiencing the day-to-day challenges of scientific research. Students live at Highseas, a Jackson Laboratory residence and historic 32-room former summer estate, overlooking Frenchman Bay and immediately adjacent to Acadia National Park. Evening talks by students, accompanied by their sponsors, enrich the intellectual environment at Highseas, and recreational outings usually are organized by the students to take advantage of Acadia National Park and coastal Maine.

HOW TO APPLY

You can access an application at http://www.jax.org/education/ssp/app.html, which you can mail to the preceding address. Notifications of decisions will be mailed in mid-March. Applications from minority students are strongly encouraged.

LEADERSHIP ALLIANCE SUMMER INTERNSHIP

The Leadership Alliance
015 Sayles Hall, Box 1963
One Prospect Street
Providence, RI 02912
(401) 863-7992
Fax: (401) 863-2244
http://www.theleadershipalliance.org/matriarch/
default.asp

What You Can Earn: Stipend, travel, and room and board provided (stipend amount varies by institutions).

Application Deadlines: February 1.

Educational Experience: Good academic standing with a GPA of 3.0 or better; must have completed at least two semesters at your respective undergraduate institutions, with a demonstrated interest and potential to pursue graduate study. The SR-EIP is not designed for students pursuing nonacademic careers in law, business administration, clinical medicine, clinical psychology, or the allied health professions.

Requirements: Must present a written report at the end of the summer-research activity and complete an anonymous program evaluation.

OVERVIEW

The Leadership Alliance is a consortium of 31 leading research and academic institutions dedicated to improving the participation of underserved and underrepresented students in graduate studies and Ph.D. programs. The Alliance sponsors a Summer Research Early Identification Program (SR-EIP), principally for these students, offering the chance to work for eight to 10 weeks under the guidance of a faculty or research mentor at a participating Alliance institution.

If you're selected as an intern, you'll work daily under the guidance of a faculty member to gain theoretical knowledge and practical training in academic research and scientific experimentation. Your experience may also include weekly seminars, regularly scheduled field trips, and social and cultural activities.

The program office will assign students to an Alliance institution with the approval of the host campus. After acceptance, the host campus will contact you with the name of the faculty mentor, research project, and research materials to review before the program begins. Through this one-on-one collaboration, you'll get theoretical knowledge and practical training in academic research and scientific experimentation.

You'll be required to present a written report and/or abstract at the end of your summer research activity, along with a program evaluation. All participants are expected to participate in the Leadership Alliance's annual national symposium and to make oral or poster presentations of their research.

The programs also offer weekly seminars and regularly scheduled field trips, as well as social and cultural activities.

The institutions set high standards and offer outstanding, closely mentored research experiences in the areas indicated in the "Research Fields" section of the application form. You should review these research areas carefully and make selections that best link your own interests and experience with the institutions' programs. You also should check each institution's Web site for specific information on research fields and mentors before submitting the application.

HOW TO APPLY

You can download the application in PDF and use your computer to fill in the form, but you must submit it by mail, along with an official transcript(s), a personal statement, a current resume, and two letters of recommendation to the preceding address. It's a good idea to mail all elements of the application together in one package, but it's not required. You can download an application at http://www.the-leadershipalliance.org/matriarch/MultiPiecePage.asp_Q_PageID_E_39_A_PageName_E_Applica-tionProcedure.

All complete applications will be initially reviewed by a committee at the executive office and will then be forwarded to the appropriate institutions for consideration. You'll get a letter from the executive office if your application doesn't meet the eligibility requirements or if the institutions are unable to match you with a mentor. All offers of placement will come directly from the institutions. Biomedical science programs notify applicants by March 1. All other disciplines notify applicants in March or April.

LUNAR AND PLANETARY INSTITUTE INTERNSHIP

LPI Summer Intern Program
3600 Bay Area Boulevard
Houston, TX 77058
(281) 486-2180
Fax: (281) 486-2127
jordan@lpi.usra.edu
https://www.lpi.usra.edu/lpiintern/application/
　　form.cfm

What You Can Earn: $500 a week stipend (and help with travel expenses to a maximum of $1000); shared low-cost housing in apartments near the institute can be arranged.
Application Deadlines: January 21.
Educational Experience: College undergraduates with at least 50 semester hours of credit interested in pursuing a science career in the sciences (spring semester graduates are also eligible). Relevant fields

of study include the natural sciences, engineering, computer sciences, and mathematics.
Requirements: Selection is based on scholarship, curriculum, and experience; career objectives and scientific interest; and match of your interest with available research projects.

OVERVIEW

The Lunar and Planetary Institute invites undergraduates to experience cutting-edge research in the planetary sciences through its summer intern program. As a summer intern, you would work one-on-one with a scientist at the LPI or at the Johnson Space Center to complete a research project of current interest in planetary science. In this program, you'll experience a real research environment, learning from some excellent planetary scientists and learning more about careers in research.

The 10-week program runs from early June to mid-August, and is located near the Johnson Space Center on the south side of Houston. On NASA's behalf, the institute leads the way in researching lunar, planetary, and solar system sciences and linking with related terrestrial programs.

If you're chosen for this program, you'll be assigned a project designed by a scientist-advisor at the institute or the Johnson Space Center. Projects could include activities such as the research into meteorites and their origins; the geology of Mars and Venus; astrobiology; lunar samples and resources; geophysical data analysis and modeling; remote sensing and spectroscopy; atmospheres of giant planets and extrasolar planets; geology of giant planet moons; image processing; interplanetary dust particles and presolar grains; and impact cratering.

HOW TO APPLY

You will need to apply using the new online application at https://www.lpi.usra.edu/lpiintern/application/form.cfm. Paper applications will not be accepted.

After you fill out the form and receive an application number, have three people submit online reference letters. (They'll need your application number and the correct spelling of your last name.) Then have your college mail an official transcript no later than January 21 to the preceding address. Interns will be notified by the end of February.

MARINE BIOLOGY LAB AT WOODS HOLE MARINE MODELS IN BIOLOGICAL RESEARCH INTERNSHIP

Department of Biology
Wake Forest University
Winston-Salem, NC 27109
browne@wfu.edu
http://www.wfu.edu/%7Ebrowne/mmbr
(336) 758-5318
Fax: (336) 758-6008

What You Can Earn: $2,000 plus room and board.
Application Deadlines: March 1.
Educational Experience: Must have completed three years at an undergraduate institution with a major in science or have the equivalent laboratory experience. Applicants with fewer than three years of college will be considered but will be expected to have strong documentation of laboratory experience.
Requirements: Women and minorities are encouraged to apply.

OVERVIEW

The Marine Biological Laboratory is an international center for research, education, and training in biology. Established in 1888 as an institute for the study of cell biology, neurobiology, and embryology, the lab hosts 200 year-round scientists and support staff, plus 800 summertime scientists and students from more than 200 institutions throughout the world.

In addition, the MBL's Ecosystem Center houses a large group of marine ecologists, microbiologists, and population geneticists. Scientists are attracted to MBL as well to the opportunity to collaborate with investigators at the other scientific institutions in Woods Hole. These include the Woods Hole Oceanographic Institute, the National Marine Fisheries Service, the U.S. Geological Survey, and the Woods Hole Research Center (devoted to research in ecology and environmental policy). In addition, there is the state-of-the-art Marine Resources Center, which provides for the latest approaches in husbandry and mariculture of marine organisms, the NIH-supported BioCurrents Research Center, and the MBL/WHOI library, one of the most complete science libraries in the world.

Each summer, up to 10 students are accepted as interns for the Marine Models in Biological Research Program, an eight-week intensive research experience for advanced undergraduates at the Marine Biological Laboratory.

If you're selected as an intern here, you'll attend lectures and seminars and conduct individual research projects under the guidance of faculty mentors matched with your coursework, experience, and/or expressed research interest. There are numerous opportunities to attend a variety of seminars and lectures taught by leading researchers. There is also the MBL Friday Night Lecture Series and a number of courses and groups who sponsor informal evening or lunch-time seminars. However, most of your time will be spent on your research project.

On the first Monday of the program, you begin work in your respective laboratories and start attending lectures in some of the MBL summer courses such as embryology, physiology, neurobiology, neural systems, and behavior. These all begin the same week as the MMBR program, as well as seminars in the neuroscience seminar series and the cell motility and cytoskeleton seminar series. The lectures are selected by the program co-directors for their value in presenting significant research areas and techniques in cell biology.

Each Wednesday a lunch seminar is arranged by the program co-directors specifically for MMBR students, during which an MBL investigator talks to students about the value of the marine model to broader research questions and presents some research observations at a level appropriate for undergraduates. Every Friday afternoon there is a group research and discussion meeting. At the first one, you'll give a brief overview of your research project, consisting of a statement of the question or problem being investigated and the organism being used. Subsequent Friday meetings are used for a variety of purposes, such as discussions on how research is funded, applying to graduate school, or applying to medical school with the objective of doing biomedical research. After the first week, you'll settle into the routine with your mentors of frequent morning lectures, a Wednesday brown-bag lunch, a Friday afternoon research seminar, and a Friday evening lecture, with the rest of the time devoted to laboratory research.

The lab maintains basic dormitory housing for summer students on campus, right on Eel Pond in Woods Hole and a stone's throw from the ocean. Rooms are shared, and MMBR students are usually assigned rooms together.

HOW TO APPLY

Click here to download an HTML application and evaluation form: http://www.wfu.edu/~browne/mmbr/applicat.html. After filling it out, mail it to the preceding address.

Applications will be evaluated after the March deadline and successful applicants will be notified beginning in April, at which time additional registration and housing information will be provided. Applications received after the deadline will be considered if space is still available. Students are accepted based on their academic credentials, letters of recommendation, and potential to benefit from an intensive research experience.

A particular effort is made each year to select at least some students who have no research experience and who come from smaller colleges, such as Lycoming College, Colby-Sawyer College, Clark

University, North Carolina A&T University, Bucknell, Hope College, College of Charleston, University of Texas at El Paso, or Fairfield University.

MICKEY LELAND ENERGY FELLOWSHIPS

Office of Fossil Energy
U.S. Department of Energy
Washington, DC 20585
(202) 586-7421
dorothy.fowlkes@hq.doe.gov
http://fossil.energy.gov/education/
lelandfellowships

What You Can Earn: Unpaid.
Application Deadlines: Early February.
Educational Experience: Currently enrolled in an accredited university as a math, science/geoscience, or engineering major with at least a 2.8 GPA.
Requirements: U.S. citizenship and minority status.

OVERVIEW

If you're interested in learning more about fossil fuels and you're a minority college student studying courses related to fossil energy, this internship could be the job for you. The U.S. energy department's office of fossil energy offers summer internships from June to August as a way for you to learn more about fossil fuels while getting hands-on experience and a potential job with the federal government after graduation.

The previous Minority Education Initiative internships were renamed after the late Houston Senator Mickey Leland in 2000, who died August 7, 1989, in a plane crash.

In the past, the department of energy established research and training grants to historically black colleges and universities and other minority institutions. In 2000, a new fellowship program was inaugurated to bring promising minority students to DOE-Fossil Energy facilities for summer internships.

HOW TO APPLY
Complete an online application at http://www.armanagement.org/mlef/default.asp.

MOUNT DESERT ISLAND BIOLOGICAL LAB RESEARCH FELLOWSHIPS FOR UNDERGRADS

Director of Education, REU Program
MDI Biological Laboratory
PO Box 35
Old Bar Harbor Road
Salisbury Cove, ME 04672
(207) 288-9880 ext. 102
Fax: (207) 288-2130
http://www.mdibl.org/edu/undergrad.shtml

What You Can Earn: NSF program: $375 a week stipend plus housing, dining, and travel; Maine Idea program: Room, board, travel, supplies, and stipend.
Application Deadlines: End of January (check individual programs for specific dates).
Educational Experience: NSF program: College undergraduates with a minimum of one year of biology and one year of chemistry; Maine IdeA program: College graduates who have completed at least one semester of undergraduate biology (chemistry is strongly suggested but not required); graduating seniors are not eligible for IDeA funds.
Requirements: NSF program: Underrepresented minorities in science are strongly encouraged to

apply. Maine IdeA program: Students must attend Bates College, Bowdoin College, Colby College, College of the Atlantic, The University of Maine, The University of Maine–Farmington, and The University of Maine–Machias. Students from other Maine colleges and universities are also invited to apply.

OVERVIEW
The Mount Desert Island Biological Laboratory is located on the north shore of Mount Desert Island in the village of Salsbury Cove, Maine. In 1898, Professor J.S. Kingsley of Tufts University invited students to the Tufts Summer School of Biology, held in South Harpswell, Maine. The summer school blossomed, and when the laboratory was moved to Mount Desert Island in 1921, the tradition of undergraduate research moved as well. Interns are given the opportunity to work and study at the MDIBL in laboratories of senior research scientists during the summer months. These scientists use marine models and cellular and molecular techniques to advance biomedical research.

There are two programs for undergraduate education to enhance scientific training in the biological and biomedical sciences: the NSF Research Experience for Undergraduates at MDIBL and the Maine IDeA Network for Biomedical Research Excellence (INBRE) Fellowships.

Maine IDeA Network for Biomedical Research Excellence (INBRE) Fellowships
The Maine INBRE supports several biomedical research training and internship programs for Maine undergraduate students. The INBRE Summer Research Fellowship is an eight- to 10-week intensive biomedical research fellowship in which students pursue independent research questions in the laboratory of an INBRE mentor. All of the programs described below provide students with a mentored and hands-on biomedical research project. Maine INBRE mentors conduct research in a variety of areas, from molecular toxicology, bioinformatics, genetics, and neuroscience. A full list of mentors and projects can be found at

http://www.maineidea.net/Undergrad/mentors. html. The mentor directory lists all Maine INBRE research mentors and describes their ongoing research projects. Interested students should read the research summaries and identify the top-three mentors with whom they would like to work this summer. Students may select any mentor on the list, irrespective of the student's or mentor's institution.

NSF Research Experience for Undergraduates

The National Science Foundation sponsors summer internships at Mount Desert Island Biological Laboratory for undergraduates interested in enhancing their scientific training in the biological and biomedical sciences. The lab provides high-quality undergraduate training for students planning careers in research or medicine.

If you're chosen for this internship in this collaborative, collegial, and camp-like environment, you'll work with scientists to design and conduct experiments together and discuss results over homemade chowder in the dining hall.

Research groups represent 65 universities, graduate schools, and research institutions in the United States, Europe, and South America. Mentors are senior research scientists chosen for excellence in undergraduate teaching and top-quality research. Between 2000 and 2003, these mentors published more than 200 peer-reviewed journal articles, and undergraduate interns are often listed as co-authors.

HOW TO APPLY
Maine IDeA Network for Biomedical Research Excellence (INBRE) Fellowships

Electronic applications may be submitted online at http://www.maineidea.net/Undergrad/ instructions.html#shortanswer. Alternatively, you may mail a hard copy that you download at http://www.maineidea.net/Undergrad/Content/ INBREapp.doc. Whichever method you choose, you must include the application form, written answers to short-answer questions, two faculty recommendations, and an official transcript. All forms are available online.

A faculty committee composed of members of each Maine INBRE institution reviews applications. Each application is read by three reviewers who assign both a score and a rank. Final decisions are made by the committee, and students are notified by e-mail one month after the application deadline. The Maine INBRE Outreach Core makes final student and mentor assignments. Final awards are typically made by one month after the deadline.

NSF Research Experience for Undergraduates

To apply for this internship, you'll first need to review the list of lab research mentors at http://www.mdibl.org/edu/mentors.shtml. You'll be asked to list a preference for three mentors or research areas on your application. Next, apply online at http://www.mdibl.org/fellowships/reu_app.shtml. You can send a transcript, recommendations, and short-answer questions either electronically or by hard copy to the preceding address. (You can download and send the application in hard copy as well.)

NASA KENNEDY SPACE CENTER SPACE FLIGHT AND LIFE SCIENCES TRAINING PROGRAM

Space Life Sciences Training Program
Tuskegee University
100 Campbell Hall
Tuskegee, AL 36088
(334) 724-4589
SLSTP@tusk.edu
http://slstp.nasa.gov

What You Can Earn: Weekly stipend to be used for food and other expenses; can receive four to six academic credits.
Application Deadlines: January 31.

Educational Experience: Undergraduates through nongraduating seniors who are pursuing a hard science or engineering degree and who have a minimum GPA of 3.0; hard science majors include animal science, botany, biochemistry, bioengineering, biology, biophysics, biostatistics, chemistry, computer science, ecology, engineering, environmental science, geology, life sciences, mathematics, pharmacy, physics, plant science, predentistry, premed, prevet, psychology, and soil science.

Requirements: U.S. citizens who are at least 18 years of age.

OVERVIEW

The Spaceflight and Life Sciences Training Program is an intensive, academically challenging six-week summer program at the Kennedy Space Center for undergraduates who want to know how to design and conduct biological research and operations in space and how to assess the environmental impacts of a launch site. The program emphasizes the unique features of experiments conducted in the space-flight environment and the challenges associated with planning and conducting long-duration space-flight missions and experiments. The curriculum also examines the use of space-related technology to study the environmental impacts of the Space Shuttle Program on the ecosystem of Kennedy Space Center.

As an intern, you'll be assigned to one of three emphasis groups: Controlled Biological Systems, Ecological Programs, and Flight Engineering/ Management Program. During a typical day, you'll complete between five and six hours of research and attend two to three hours of lectures related to spaceflight and research.

Controlled Biological Systems (CBS)

Humans will always need food, water, and air when traveling in space or establishing permanent bases throughout the solar system. For long-term missions, we'll need to develop ways to produce food, purify water, and create oxygen from carbon dioxide. Research on human life-support began in the 1950s with oxygen regeneration using algae. Since that time, the CBS program at NASA has examined growing plants for food and oxygen regeneration and using chemical and biological methods to process waste into usable resources. Three NASA centers are involved in the CBS program; Johnson Space Center, Ames Research Center, and the Kennedy Space Center. At Kennedy, a life-support effort called the CBS Breadboard Project studies crop production and biological waste processing in an integrated manner.

The Breadboard Project aims at using biological systems to recycle material: Interns working in the CBS laboratories are generally involved in the first testing of plant growth on composted material. Examples of research projects for the CBS group may include:

- mixed "salad machines" for spaceflight
- development and evaluation of space shuttle trash analog treatments
- susceptibility of bacterial pathogens from the spaceflight environment to phage-resistance
- effects of ethanol on the growth and development of radishes
- the WONDER project: wheat strain comparison study

Ecological Programs

Environmental monitoring and research has been conducted at Kennedy Space Center since the early 1970s, and The Ecological Program is responsible for developing information necessary to predict the environmental impact of activities at the space center. Ecological Program employees assess the effects of space shuttle launches and other point-source emissions and monitor the long-term effects and environmental impacts of the cumulative effects of NASA activities. This includes monitoring air quality, precipitation, and particulate sampling; surface and ground water quality; soil and sediment chemistry; flora and fauna assessments; fire ecology; threatened and endangered species population studies; and wildlife habitat management. This assessment includes remote sensing from aircraft and satellites to note change over time. Global positional system data can be directly input into a GIS system for mapping and environmental monitoring purposes.

Interns working within the Ecological Program may work in the following areas.

Air Quality
Interns research precipitation, particulate sampling, and biogenic emissions.

Aquatics
Interns here monitor water quality, manatees, horseshoe crabs, and sea turtle biology and seagrass distribution.

GIS
The GIS group gathers remote sensing imagery and manages research data.

Habitat Assessment
The habitat assessment group conducts research on threatened species such as Florida scrub-jays, Eastern indigo snakes, gopher tortoises, and the Southeastern beach mouse and is also involved in fire ecology studies.

Vegetation
The vegetation studies group is involved in studies of fire ecology, scrub habitat restoration, landscape history and dynamics, and physiological ecology.

Flight Engineering and Management Program
All aspects of biological spaceflight experiments at Kennedy are primarily supported by several groups, including the Flight Experiments Management, Hardware Engineering, and Mission Operations. These teams generally develop, manage, and process payload hardware to support NASA-funded scientific experiments. Students may work with scientists and engineers on projects associated with the supporting spaceflight experimentation.

The Flight Experiments Management Group
This group works with scientists who have experiments designated for flight experiment on the Space Shuttle or International Space Station. The group interacts with Shuttle operations teams, mission management, and safety personnel and is responsible for training the astronaut crew to perform in-flight activities for KSC-managed experiments.

The Hardware Engineering Group
This group translates experiment requirements into a suite of hardware capable of meeting those requirements. Engineers in this group design, build, and test this new hardware. This includes hardware performance testing and several different types of verification tests.

The Mission Ops
This team ensures that all ground processing of experiments at KSC goes smoothly, before and after the Shuttle mission. The group maintains an animal husbandry facility including crickets, rats, mice, fish, frogs, flies, snails, mushrooms, bacteria, and a variety of plant types. The team is ready to support launch and landing slips and maintains the back-up shuttle landing facilities at Edwards Air Force Base. Members of the Mission Ops group often assist visiting researchers to optimize laboratory conditions at KSC.

As an intern here, you'll learn that success in space research requires an integrated team of individuals with diverse knowledge, skills, and abilities. You'll spend the majority of each day actively involved in planning and executing laboratory and engineering projects that span a range of life-sciences activities of current interest to NASA.

The curriculum includes lectures from leading research scientists, managers, engineers, and astronauts from NASA centers, universities, and industry. You'll have tours of the KSC Shuttle and Payload facilities to obtain firsthand knowledge of the processes involved in conducting life-science experiments in space.

HOW TO APPLY
Download the application at http://slstp.nasa.gov/2004SLSTPStudentApplicat.pdf.

Submit the following application materials to the preceding address.

- An application typed or printed in black ink.
- An official transcript from every college or university attended up to and including the present semester (except from institutions that were attended for less than two semesters).
- A self–addressed postcard to be returned to you when all of the application materials have been received.
- A typed essay (double spaced), which will be used to evaluate your experience and writing skills. The essay should relate to your classroom, laboratory, and/or research experiences in the sciences or engineering. You should also discuss your career goals along with a statement reflecting your interest in this space program. Print your full name on each page of the essay.
- Three reference request forms or letters of recommendations from persons familiar with your academic record.

NATIONAL INSTITUTES OF HEALTH SUMMER INTERNSHIP PROGRAMS IN BIOMEDICAL RESEARCH

National Institutes of Health Summer Internships
http://www.training.nih.gov/student/internship/internship.asp

What You Can Earn: Stipends may vary slightly from one NIH internship to another but usually range from $1,400 a month for high school students to $2,800 a month for students with three or more years of graduate school. (These stipends may be lower in Arizona, Montana, and North Carolina.) Students are responsible for their own travel expenses and housing.

Application Deadlines: March 1 for NIH internships that begin in May and end in August. All candidates are advised of their status by mid-May.

Educational Experience: Although internships are not limited to certain majors, most summer positions are in research labs. Interns should therefore have successfully completed courses in biology and chemistry. There is no minimum GPA.

Requirements: U.S. citizenship (or permanent U.S. residency); enrolled at least half time in an accredited U.S. high school, college, or graduate school at time of application; must be at least 18 before June 1.

OVERVIEW

The National Institutes of Health (NIH) is the federal government's primary agency for biomedical research. If you're interested in health science, there's probably no better opportunity in the country than to intern at NIH, one of the most highly respected centers of lab research in the world. NIH offers eight-week summer internships at research laboratories around the country: at their main NIH campus in Bethesda and also in Baltimore and Frederick, MD; at Research Triangle Park (Raleigh/Durham), NC; Hamilton, MT; and Phoenix, AZ. In 2003, NIH received more than 4,000 applications for 1,000 positions in the Summer Internship Program in Biomedical Research.

If you're one of the chosen few, you're in for an exciting summer of intensive lab work. During your internship, you'll participate in meetings and seminars in your individual lab. With permission from your mentor, you may attend formal lectures and symposia at NIH. A typical day at NIH might involve compiling data gathered from another lab as well as generating some new data yourself. You might be asked to explore the meaning and usability of data with the help of other staffers, or you may work with a statistician to come up with meaningful results. Many interns are able to meet many of the patients involved in their labs' studies and interact with them and their families. You may be asked to see patients with your mentor, which can give you more exposure to the clinical side of medicine. At the end of your summer internship, you're strongly encouraged to participate in the Summer Research Program Poster Day, which allows students the chance to present their work for the NIH scientific community.

The following institutes and centers offer summer research opportunities for students in a variety of program areas:

- National Cancer Institute
- National Center for Complementary and Alternative Medicine
- National Eye Institute)
- National Heart, Lung, and Blood Institute
- National Human Genome Research Institute
- National Institute on Aging
- National Institute on Alcohol Abuse and Alcoholism
- National Institute of Allergy and Infectious Diseases
- National Institute of Arthritis and Musculoskeletal and Skin Diseases
- National Institute of Child Health and Human Development
- National Institute on Deafness and Other Communication Disorders
- National Institute of Dental and Craniofacial Research
- National Institute of Diabetes and Digestive and Kidney Diseases
- National Institute on Drug Abuse
- National Institute of Environmental Health Sciences (RTP: Raleigh/Durham, NC)
- National Institute of Mental Health
- National Institute of Neurological Disorders and Stroke
- National Library of Medicine
- Center for Biologics Evaluation and Research

- Center for Information Technology
- Warren Grant Magnuson Clinical Center

HOUSING

Although housing is not available at NIH in Bethesda, staffers will help you locate housing in the area (several local colleges rent dormitory rooms to students during the summer). NIH will send housing details if you're selected for the program. Students who participate in programs at the National Institute of Aging's Gerontology Research Center in Baltimore may find housing in the house staff apartments at the Hopkins Bayview Medical Center, located about 10 minutes from the Johns Hopkins Hospital, 15 minutes from downtown Baltimore and the hospital at the University of Maryland.

HOW TO APPLY

All internship applications are handled online at http://www.training.nih.gov/student/internship/internship.asp. The application will ask you to choose an area of scientific interest (such as cell biology) and a medical disease (such as Alzheimer's) and to select an institute where you'd like to work. NIH encourages students to contact investigators by e-mail or phone if they have an interest in working in a particular lab. Before you do so, you should review the various research programs at NIH by visiting www1.od.nih.gov/oir/sourcebook/sci-prgms/sci-prgms-toc.htm.

On the application, you'll also need to insert information about your resume and your coursework, a cover letter discussing why you're interested in the NIH internship, and two letters of recommendation from people in the scientific or academic world who are familiar with your scientific accomplishments, motivation, and skills. This might include previous employers, college professors, or high school teachers.

The deadline is March 1 for an internship beginning in May (with the exception of the National Cancer Institute, which doesn't have a deadline). Once you've submitted your application, you'll receive an e-mail confirming that your application was received. NIH isn't equipped to handle applications the old-fashioned way (on paper), but if this causes a problem, you can discuss your situation by calling NIH at (800) 445-8283.

NIH researchers review internship applications on a continuous basis. Selections are made by individual labs, not by a selection committee. If you're chosen, you're still not done; you must submit the following documents to the appropriate summer coordinator where they have been accepted:

- official school transcript
- proof of citizenship or U.S. permanent residency
- letter from your school verifying that you are in good academic standing

NATIONAL MUSEUM OF NATURAL HISTORY INTERNSHIP

National Museum of Natural History
Research Training Program
10th Street and Constitution Avenue, NW
Smithsonian Institution
Washington, D.C. 20560-0166
(202) 357-4548
Fax: (202) 786-2563
http://www.nmnh.si.edu/rtp/information/index.
  html

What You Can Earn: $3,000 plus housing, transportation, commuting costs, and research costs.
Application Deadlines: February 1.
Educational Experience: Undergraduate students interested in a career in natural history research, especially systematic biology, geology, and anthropology. Applications from women, international and minority students, and persons with disabilities are encouraged.

Requirements: Must provide proof of enrollment and coverage in the D.C. area of medical insurance in case of accident or injury.

OVERVIEW

If natural history is your passion, you might be interested in an internship at the National Museum of Natural History, part of the Smithsonian in Washington, DC. The museum's research training program offers a 10-week training course in botany, entomology, invertebrate and vertebrate zoology, paleobiology, geology, mineral science, and anthropology for students seeking a career in these natural history disciplines. As part of the program, you'll work with a Smithsonian mentor to develop confidence and competence in the natural history research process, from hypothesis to presentation.

You'll also participate in a varied series of lectures, discussions, workshops, behind-the-scene tours, and field trips featuring one-on-one interaction with Smithsonian professionals. Since the program's beginning in 1980, more than 400 students have participated and gone on to graduate school and successful careers in natural history.

Natural history research is the study of the natural world and your place in it, including the exploration, investigation, and communication of new ideas and discoveries about humans and their culture and the earth and its biology, geology, and ecology.

During the 10-week program, you'll learn more about the diversity of scientific disciplines, research techniques, and career choices available in the field of natural history. The structured curriculum covers all the natural history disciplines and includes a personalized research project that you'll design, plus group lectures, workshops, discussions, demonstrations, and tours of the NMNH specimen collections.

You'll be guided by a dedicated staff committed to every aspect of the program. In particular, you and your advisor will identify critical research questions and develop a scientific hypothesis. Examples of some possible research projects include species concepts, measuring biological diversity, bioge-ography, molecular systematics, paleoecology, forensic anthropology, global volcanism, and mass extinctions.

Next, you'll design and conduct original research, use the library, work in the museum collections, and gather and interpret data. Some projects include short-term fieldwork during the program. Other projects are followed by more extensive fieldwork at a distant site, generally in subsequent summers and usually supported by your mentors' research grants. At the conclusion of the session, you'll give a 15-minute oral presentation on the progress of your research and prepare a final report in journal style. A poster session is also held to share research results with the Smithsonian professional community.

Your adviser will interact with you each day and monitor your progress with a written hypothesis proposal, a midterm report, and a midterm evaluation. As part of your project, you may travel to scientific meetings (sometimes to observe before presenting your research findings).

Work on your research project will be complemented by a 10-week curriculum of events covering the biological, geological, and anthropological sciences through a series of research lectures, issues discussions, laboratory demonstrations, techniques workshops, tours of the collections, field trips, and social events.

Equally important to the research and curriculum is the personal interaction between interns and the museum's scientists. If you're selected to participate in the program, you'll become part of the museum's scientific community, and you'll be included in museum activities such as the Senate of Scientists, research seminars and discussion groups, special lectures by visiting scientists, exhibits preparation, and interaction with the non-scientific public.

You choose your advisor based on the person's scientific discipline, the techniques he or she uses, and the person's history of working with other students. A complete listing of all students and the research projects they pursued is also available as part of the alumni directory at http://www.nmnh. si.edu/rtp/information/index.html. Potential advisors include emeritus researchers and scientists employed by affiliated agencies such as the agriculture department, the U.S. Biological Survey, U.S. Fish and Wildlife Services, or U.S. Geological Survey, who are permanently housed within the museum and who are an integral part of its scientific community.

Through a formal lecture series, Smithsonian staff provides personal instruction on the concepts and methodologies used in natural history research. Weekly discussions and seminars are held to present topics in an open format and to help you learn about the different job opportunities available in natural history research. In the laboratory, traditional and modern methods of systematic research are demonstrated, and you'll be given the chance to learn and experiment with these various techniques. Workshops also are offered on how to prepare, use, and maintain museum specimens.

Free housing is provided during your participation in an apartment in Alexandria, VA. Typically, these apartments are four-person occupancy and include a living room, kitchen, two bedrooms, and two bathrooms. A shopping center located directly across the street from the apartment complex includes a grocery store, bank, and other conveniences.

HOW TO APPLY

All forms can be completed on-line at the program's Web site, http://www.nmnh.si.edu/rtp/information/index.html, and can be completed online and electronically transmitted directly to the RTP office.

Your application package should include a one-page cover letter, application form, and two letters of recommendation (the form is available at http://rathbun.si.edu/rtp/application_procedure/recommend_form.html) and a transcript or course and grade listing and the selection of an advisor (form available at http://rathbun.si.edu/rtp/application_procedure/advisor_list2.html). Materials also can be completed and mailed to the preceding address.

NATIONAL SCIENCE FOUNDATION RESEARCH EXPERIENCE FOR UNDERGRADUATES (REU)

National Science Foundation
4201 Wilson Boulevard
Arlington, VA 22230
(703) 292-5111
http://www.nsf.gov/crssprgm/reu/index.jsp

What You Can Earn: Stipends and travel costs, depending on host institution.
Application Deadlines: Rolling.
Educational Experience: See specific sites for details, but in general students must be undergraduate or graduate students.
Requirements: U.S. citizenship; see individual site information for more details.

OVERVIEW

The National Science Foundation (NSF) is an independent federal agency created by Congress in 1950 to promote the progress of science. With an annual budget of about $5.5 billion, the NSF funds about 20 percent of all federally supported basic research conducted by U.S. colleges and universities.

The NSF funds a large number of research opportunities for undergraduate students through its REU Sites program. An REU Site includes about 10 undergraduates who work in the research programs of the host institution. Each student is associated with a specific research project, working closely with the faculty and other researchers. Students are granted stipends and, in many cases, assistance with housing and travel. Undergraduate students supported with NSF funds must be citizens or permanent residents of the United States or its possessions. An REU Site may be at either a US or foreign location.

By using the Web page http://www.nsf.gov/crssprgm/reu/reu_search.cfm, you can check out various opportunities in your favorite subject areas. Also, you may search by keywords to identify sites in particular research areas or with certain features, such as a particular location. Students may check out opportunities in a variety of fields, including astronomical sciences; atmospheric sciences; biological sciences; chemistry; computer and information science and engineering; department of defense; earth sciences; education and human resources; engineering; ethics and values studies; international science and engineering; materials research; mathematical sciences; ocean sciences; physics; polar programs; and social, behavioral, and economic sciences.

For example, the REU in astronomy at Flagstaff brings eight undergraduate students to Flagstaff, Arizona, for individual research experiences in astronomy. The program, which is open to undergraduates at all levels, pairs students with mentors from Northern Arizona University, the Lowell Observatory, the Flagstaff station of the U. S. Naval Observatory, the astrogeology branch of the U. S. Geological Survey, or visiting members of the National Undergraduate Research Observatory. Although not every field in astronomy research is available every summer at this site, possible projects include work in planetary sciences, stellar astrophysics, extragalactic astrophysics, astrogeology, and instrumentation. In some of the projects, the students will have the opportunity to conduct observations on local telescopes. In addition to their research work, students will attend a seminar series consisting of research talks by local and visiting scientists. At the conclusion of the summer, each student will turn in a written report of their work and will give an oral presentation of the results of the research. As part of the experience, each student will receive three hours of university credit and will be housed together in a campus dormitory. Four students each year will be selected, and travel support offered, to present their work at a national professional scientific meeting.

In another example of a possible NSF internship, the REU site in archaeological research methods at Veszto, Hungary, is part of a collaborative, multidisciplinary, international research project co-organized by Florida State University,

Ohio State University, and the Munkacsy Mihaly Museum, Bekescsaba, Hungary. Ten students will have the opportunity to participate in research aimed at understanding the later prehistory of the Great Hungarian Plain. They will help excavate the Early Cooper Age settlement of Veszto-Bikeri, working side-by-side with Hungarian students as they receive instruction in survey and excavation techniques; participate in seminars taught by experts on archaeological method and theory and on the culture and history of Eastern Europe; visit museums and archaeological sites; plan and complete an independent research project; and live in the small town of Veszto and learn about life in Hungary from the villagers and Hungarian students and archaeologists. Students will be responsible not only for helping excavate the site but also for analyzing archaeological material that will provide a better understanding of prehistoric economic and social organization. They'll present papers and publish their results on the project Web site and in archaeological journals.

HOW TO APPLY

If you're interested in working in one of the NSF sites, you should apply directly to the REU site in which you're interested and should consult the directory of active REU Sites on the Web at http://www.nsf.gov/crssprgm/reu/reu_search.cfm.

NAVAL RESEARCH LAB SCIENCE AND ENGINEERING APPRENTICESHIP PROGRAM

Academia Resource Management
535 East 4500 South
Suite D-120

Salt Lake City, UT 84107
(801) 273-8911
http://hroffice.nrl.navy.mil/student/seap.htm

What You Can Earn: $1,600 academic award from the Academia Resource Management. No transportation allowance and no temporary housing are provided.

Application Deadlines: February 15.

Educational Experience: High school student in grades 9-12 who is recommended by a high school official (guidance counselor, math, or science teacher).

Requirements: U.S. citizenship or permanent status.

OVERVIEW

It's not so easy for high school students to find internships, but this program is designed to do just that. The Navy Research Lab offers select high school students a unique opportunity to explore and pursue careers in science and technology by allowing students to spend eight weeks working full-time on a variety of unclassified tasks. Under the direction of NRL scientists and engineers, students can actively engage in research problems, planning sessions, special program seminars, and writing and presentation of a final research paper. The specific programs available change throughout the year; the next year's list is available beginning in early April at http://www.armanagement.org/seap/default.htm.

Students will be chosen on the basis of grades, science and mathematics courses taken, scores on national standardized tests, areas of interest, teacher recommendations, and a personal student statement.

HOW TO APPLY

You can apply online at http://www.armanagement.org/seap/default.htm. Program information can be viewed anytime at this site; however, you'll be able to access the application form only between December and February, when applications are being accepted. Alternatively, you can print a copy of the SEAP application from this site and mail it, along with your letters of recommendation and transcripts, to the preceding address. Offers will be made in early April.

NEW YORK UNIVERSITY CENTER FOR NEURAL SCIENCE UNDERGRADUATE SUMMER RESEARCH PROGRAM

Center for Neural Science
New York University
4 Washington Place, Room 809
New York, NY 10003-6621
(212) 998-3949
surpinfo@cns.nyu.edu

What You Can Earn: A stipend for living expenses, housing in NYU dorms, a full meal plan, and reimbursement for travel.
Application Deadlines: March 31.
Educational Experience: Rising college seniors from any university with strong academic records with courses in biology, mathematics, psychology, and if possible, neuroscience, and a GPA of 3.0. Priority will be given to minority students and women.
Requirements: U.S. citizen or permanent resident.

OVERVIEW

The Center for Neural Science is the focus for teaching and research in the brain sciences at the Washington Square Campus of New York University. Formed in 1987, the center's researchers are interested in a broad range of topics in neural science, including molecular and cell biology, neurophysiology and neuroanatomy, brain imaging, human and animal behavior, and mathematics and computation.

Each summer, the center hosts a research experience program for undergraduates with an interest in neuroscience from May 31 through early August. Students apply for positions in a 10-week summer program, during which they actively participate in research projects in the laboratories of New York University science faculty.

If you're chosen as an intern for this program, you'll be matched to laboratories primarily on the basis of your background preparation and areas of interest, where you'll conduct a research project under the direction of your mentor be involved in all phases of the research process from experimental design to data analysis and communication of results. You'll also meet regularly for neuroscience seminars. At the end of the program, you'll prepare an abstract and write a journal-style report on your work, and give a 20-minute oral presentation in a special summer research conference.

HOW TO APPLY

You can submit an application electronically at http://www.cns.nyu.edu/undergrad/surp/surpapp.html. In addition, you should arrange to have the following items sent to the preceding address to complete your application:

- Two letters of reference.
- Your transcript.
- A personal statement.

Candidates will be notified in April of the internship decisions.

NEW YORK UNIVERSITY SCHOOL OF MEDICINE SUMMER UNDERGRADUATE RESEARCH PROGRAM

Summer Undergraduate Research Program
Sackler Institute
New York University School of Medicine
550 First Avenue
New York, NY 10016
(212) 263-5648
Sackler-info@nyumed.med.nyu.edu

What You Can Earn: $3,000 plus travel expenses and room and board.
Application Deadlines: Early February.
Educational Experience: Must be a highly qualified rising junior in college and have taken courses in biology, chemistry, and mathematics; research experience is preferable. Underrepresented minority students are encouraged to apply.
Requirements: Mature, well-qualified undergraduates interested in pursuing a career in the biomedical sciences (M.D./Ph.D. or Ph.D.)

OVERVIEW

The Sackler Institute of Graduate Biomedical Sciences at New York University's medical school offers programs in the basic medical sciences leading to the Ph.D. degree and, in coordination with the Medical Scientist Training Program, combined M.D./Ph.D. degrees.

Each summer, the Sackler Institute sponsors a research internship program in the basic medical sciences for undergraduate students. The program provides highly qualified students interested in pursuing careers in the biomedical sciences (M.D./Ph.D. or Ph.D.) the opportunity to conduct research while exposed to the excitement of an academic medical environment at a major research center. Students may work with faculty in the dis-

ciplines of biochemistry, cellular and molecular biology, developmental genetics, immunology, microbiology, molecular oncology, neuroscience and physiology, parasitology, and pharmacology.

Cellular and Molecular Biology

This program involves investigators in six basic science departments, and training is offered in the general areas of structure, function, and biogenesis of macromolecules and subcellular organelles and the mechanisms that regulate cell metabolism, differentiation and growth, and intercellular interactions during development.

Developmental Genetics

This program explores genetic approaches to understand developmental mechanisms, working with a variety of genetic systems including *Drosophila*, *C. elegans*, *Arabidopsis*, *Xenopus*, mouse, and zebrafish to study diverse developmental processes such as pattern formation, cell determination, cell lineage, and cell-cell interactions.

Medical and Molecular Parasitology

The department of medical parasitology studies those organisms primarily affecting developing nations, with particular emphasis on malaria and trypanosomes. Research is also conducted on pneumocystis, which produces life-threatening infections in AIDS victims and other immunosuppressed patients.

Microbiology

The microbiology program offers a wide variety of research opportunities with emphasis on the mechanisms of viral and bacterial pathogenesis, host defense mechanisms, microbial and molecular genetics, oncogenesis, growth factors, and cytokines and regulation of gene expression.

Molecular Oncology and Immunology

In this department, particular emphasis is placed on a combining these two disciplines to better understand the regulatory mechanisms involved in cellular transformation and immunological cell response. This can lead to entirely new approaches to studies of oncogenes and immunologically competent cells, while fostering the development of cancer research.

Molecular Pharmacology

This department offers multidisciplinary training in molecular pharmacology and neurobiology.

Neuroscience and Physiology

This program provides training in molecular, cellular, and organ system neuroscience and physiology strongly oriented toward research.

Structural Biology

This program studies the structural basis of molecular and cellular function using a variety of research methodologies common to structural biology.

The multifaceted program includes hands-on research on a project directed by senior faculty members of the medical center, exposure to the practice of medicine at a major teaching hospital by individual physician mentors, participation in introductory and professional-level seminars, and career seminars conducted by deans and other faculty regarding opportunities available in the biomedical sciences and how to apply to specific programs.

In most cases, you'll be matched with an investigator of your choice; otherwise, you'll be placed in a lab working in an area in which you're interested. You'll be given your own project, and you'll be expected to perform as a graduate student. At the end of the summer, you'll be expected to present your research at a poster session. If you're interested in having a physician mentor, you may request assignment to a physician in an area of medicine in which you're interested. You'll meet weekly with the physician, attend grand rounds and clinical conferences, and be able to observe the physician with patients.

You will also be escorted to concerts, museums, theater, ethnic restaurants, and other events in New York City.

HOW TO APPLY

Before linking to the application form, you'll be required to write a 500-word personal essay explaining your career plans and reasons for applying to this program. You'll need to indicate your areas of interest and describe any research experience, courses, or laboratory work that has stimulated your interest in research and discuss what graduate courses and laboratory work have best prepared you for this program. The essay should be double spaced and written with a size-12 font, and you should proof your essay, since you'll be required to upload this document to attach it to the online application.

The application is available at http://www.med.nyu.edu/Sackler/summer.html. In addition to completing the online application and the personal essay with the application, you must include two letters of recommendation and an official transcript from all colleges and universities you've attended. It's a good idea to request recommendation letters from someone with whom you've done research, as well as a letter from a professor, dean, or advisor who knows you well.

Interns will be selected based on their academic record, research experience (if any), and letters of recommendation from faculty advisors or research supervisors. Significant importance will be given to their commitment to a career in biomedical research. A committee composed of Ph.D., M.D., M.D./Ph.D. students and faculty will review applicants for admission; candidates will be notified by early March.

NUCLEAR REGULATORY COMMISSION HISTORICALLY BLACK COLLEGES AND UNIVERSITIES STUDENT RESEARCH INTERNSHIP

NRC HBCU Research Participation Program
Oak Ridge Institute for Science and Education, MS 36
PO Box 117

200 Badger Avenue
Oak Ridge, TN 37831-0117

What You Can Earn: Weekly stipend of $500 for undergraduates and $600 for graduate students; limited travel reimbursement (round-trip transportation expenses between facility and home or campus).
Application Deadlines: Third Tuesday in January.
Educational Experience: Undergraduate and graduate students from historically black colleges and universities with a 2.5 GPA majoring in computer science; engineering; earth or geosciences; health physics; materials science; mathematics; molecular/radiation biology; performance and risk assessments; physical sciences; statistics-related to nuclear material control; and accounting. Grad students must maintain a 3.0 GPA.
Requirements: U.S. citizens and legal permanent residents.

OVERVIEW

The U.S. Nuclear Regulatory Commission (NRC) was established as an independent agency in 1975, whose mission is to ensure adequate protection of public health and safety, common defense and security, and the environment in the use of nuclear materials and facilities. The NRC's responsibilities include regulation of commercial nuclear power reactors; nonpower research, test, and training reactors; fuel-cycle facilities; medical, academic, and industrial uses of nuclear materials; and the transport, storage, and disposal of nuclear materials and waste.

The NRC's Historically Black Colleges and Universities Research Participation Program offers opportunities for faculty and students to participate in research education and training at federal facilities or designated university research programs. Its purpose is to benefit historically black universities, their faculty members, their students, and their programs by involving them in NRC research and development activities. The program offers a variety of summer research opportunities

for faculty, graduates, and undergraduates to conduct research with NRC contractors. Some internships will take place on black college and university campuses, and some appointments will be at host universities under the guidance of principal investigators with Nuclear Regulatory Commission research grants.

Internships will last for 10 to 12 weeks for summer appointments; some part-time appointments are offered for one year.

HOW TO APPLY

Mail completed applications to the preceding address.

OFFICE OF NAVAL RESEARCH INTERNSHIP

Academia Resource Management
ONR Program
535 East 4500 South
Suite D-120
Salt Lake City, UT 84107
(866) 863-3570
Fax: (801) 277-5632
mariann@armanagement.org

What You Can Earn: $5,500 undergraduates and $6,500 graduates.
Application Deadlines: February 1.
Educational Experience: Junior, senior, or graduate student (students who currently are sophomores may apply if they will be juniors by the start of the summer internship) majoring in a subject relevant to the research interests of the laboratories. Candidates must be enrolled at an eligible university (see list at http://www.armanagement.org/onr/schools.htm).
Requirements: U.S. citizenship required (permanent resident alien status will also be considered by some labs).

OVERVIEW

Participating laboratories are located in California, Florida, Maryland, Mississippi, New Jersey, Pennsylvania, Rhode Island, Virginia, and Washington, D.C.

Marine Corps Warfighting Laboratory at Quantico, Virginia

This lab's purpose is to improve the naval warfare capabilities by supporting the warfare development division and conducting war games and experimentation to evaluate new tactics, techniques, and technologies. The lab has five focus areas, including military operations in urban terrain; unconventional, unexpected, innovative warfare; reconnaissance, surveillance, and target acquisition; over-the-air Internet systems; and the development of promising prototypes from experimentation to acquisition.

Naval Air Warfare Center/Aircraft Systems

Located at Patuxent River, Maryland and Lakehurst, New Jersey, the NAWCAD lab is the full-spectrum research, development, test and evaluation, engineering, and fleet support center for air platforms. The product test areas include aircraft systems (manned and unmanned); airborne technology; propulsion; flight test and engineering; avionics design and production; crew systems; and aircraft-platform interface. More than 8,000 scientists and engineers and technicians work at this lab.

Interns can help in various technical areas such as physics, chemistry, mathematics, electronics, aerodynamics, and material science engineering (software, hardware, processing, and so on). Areas of research include acoustic science and technology; advanced aircraft materials; advanced processors/computer systems technology; aircraft controls and displays; avionic systems; environmental sensing and information display; fiber optic technology; flight-control design and aerospace test and evaluation engineering; high-speed fiber optics networks; high-strength cables and harnesses; life support and human factors; manufacturing technology; microwave technology; computer technologies; and weapons system analysis, design, and integration.

Naval Air Warfare Center at Orlando

This division is the principal navy facility for research, development, acquisition, and logistics support of training systems. Scientists at the lab perform a full range of research and development activities, including basic and applied research, advanced development, prototype development, and technology transfer, in a wide variety of subjects related to training systems. This includes individual and team training methodology; virtual environment technology; advanced distributed learning; human cognition; human computer interaction; performance measurement; tactical decision-making; embedded and deployable training technologies; distributed team training strategies and technologies; intelligent tutoring in virtual and distributed simulation; sensor simulation; weapons simulation; optics; aircrew training; distributed simulation; speech recognition; and digital communications. In particular, scientists are working on diagnostic feedback displays; digital communications; distributed and deployable training technologies; distributed simulation; student/crew performance measurement; human computer interaction; human factors evaluations; scenario-based training; virtual tour-based training; and weapons simulation.

Naval Air Warfare Center/Weapons Systems

Located at China Lake and Point Mugu, California, this lab is the principal Navy research, development, test, and evaluation center for air warfare systems (except antisubmarine warfare systems) and missile weapon systems. About 5,000 civilian and 900 military personnel work here, 2,300 of whom are scientists and engineers. The Research and Technology Group, where 130 scientists, engineers, and supporting staff work, includes sensors and signals sciences, chemistry, and engineering sciences divisions.

Scientists here study many different areas of material science, including synthetic programs in energetic materials, propellant evaluation solid state and polymer chemistry, fabrication of prototype optical and electronic devices, environmental analysis, and materials characterization. Other research areas include the generation, propagation, interaction, and detection of electromagnetic waves, propulsion and terminal ballistics, signal and image processing, and applied mathematics.

There are facilities for basic and applied laser spectroscopy, including combustion diagnostics, a thin film laboratory, crystal growing facilities, machine shops, and a complete optics shop with a unique diamond single-point precision machining capability. Major facilities exist in the Research and Technology Group to support fundamental and applied studies in radar scattering; inverse radar scattering; signal processing; microwave and millimeter wave devices; combustion of propellants; flow dynamics; shock dynamics; and missile propulsion. The lab also maintains a major scientific computing facility.

Optical sciences research includes optical properties of solids, optical coatings, ellipsometry, optical scattering, laser effects, surface finishing, and optical metrology. Electrooptical technology research involves sensors and seekers, laser dyes, charge coupled devices, and compact laser devices. Scientists in the electronics area study microelectronics, compound semiconductors, and MBE-grown heterostructures. Microwave technology research possibilities include sea scatter; target modeling; inverse scattering; automatic target identification; microwave materials; electronic warfare; missile seekers; one-dimensional and synthetic aperture radars; and superdirective superconductive antenna components. In applied mechanics, scientists study detonation physics, warhead dynamics, damage mechanisms and theory, and internal explosions. Scientists in propulsion technology research the combustion of propellants, deflagration to detonation transition, combustion instability, fuels and propellant ingredient synthesis, acoustic turbulence/combustion interactions, electromagnetic propulsion, and ramjet propulsion. In the energetic materials area, scientists study fuels, explosives, polynitrogen compounds, explosives

formulation, and propellant components. Those who specialize in chemistry research instrumental analysis, electrochemistry, organic and inorganic chemistry, applied spectroscopy, and synthesis. Interns in material science may study organic and inorganic films for electronic and optical applications; nano-powders; Langmuir-Blodgett films; organic-matrix structural and energetic composites; ceramics; coatings & adhesives; metallurgy; corrosion; and IR-transparent materials. Targeting technology research includes RF; IR; laser sensors; multisensor fusion; and automatic target recognition. In human factors, scientists study multisensor targeting, manmachine interface, and decision aiding. Embedded computing involves the study of simulation and modeling, domain analysis and software reuse, artificial neural networks, fuzzy logic, software testing, and reliability. At this lab, scientists also study numerical analysis/digital signal processing: wavelet theory, pattern recognition, fractal compression, optimal smoothing/interpolation, neural networks, fuzzy logic, and genetic programming.

Naval Research Laboratory and the Stennis Space Centers

Established in 1923, the NRL—one of the largest scientific institutions within the U.S. government—still occupies its original site on the Potomac River in Washington, D.C. The corporate research lab of the navy, the NRL conducts a broad-based multidisciplinary program of scientific research in advanced technological development, techniques, systems, and related operational procedures. Additional facilities are located at Stennis Space Center in Mississippi and Monterey, CA, and other support facilities and field experiment sites throughout Maryland and Virginia.

Current research focuses on areas including computer science; artificial intelligence; plasma physics; acoustics; radar; fluid dynamics; chemistry; materials science; optical sciences; condensed matter and radiation sciences; electronics science; environmental sciences; marine geosciences; remote sensing; oceanography; marine meteorology; space technology; and space sciences.

Naval Surface Warfare Center/Carderock

The Carderock Division of the Naval Surface Warfare Center specializes in ships, submarines, and their systems. Research at Carderock includes the fields of hydrodynamics and hydromechanics; the science and technology of ship silencing and signature control; advanced electrical and mechanical systems; advanced metallic and nonmetallic materials; ship structural design and testing; ship survivability and vulnerability; and shipboard environmental quality. Scientists and engineers at this lab work in broad disciplines such as physics; chemistry; biology; mathematics and computer science; electrical and mechanical engineering; and naval architecture.

With unique laboratories and test facilities, large-scale land-based engineering and test sites, and at-sea measurement facilities throughout the United States, Carderock has been working in technology vital to the navy and the maritime industry for more than a century. The division's primary locations are its headquarters in West Bethesda, Maryland, and the Ship Systems Engineering Station in Philadelphia, Pennsylvania.

Facilities include deep-water model basins for ship hydrodynamics measurements; unmanned vehicle R&D; water tunnels for propeller R&D; and other hydrodynamic and wind tunnel facilities; deep ocean pressure tanks; a BEOWULF cluster; and other high-performance computers and modern materials science and testing laboratories.

Scientists at this lab study acoustic ship silencing; survivability, structures and materials; environmental quality; ship machinery systems (Philadelphia); ship systems and logistics; ship hydromechanics; advanced electronics instrumentation; submarine maneuvering; and electromagnetic signatures.

Naval Surface Warfare Center at Dahlgren, Virginia

The Dahlgren division is the principal navy center for surface warfare analysis; surface ship combat systems; sensor technologies; strategic systems; mines; mine countermeasures; amphibious warfare and special warfare systems; and diving. The organization was formed in 1992 with the merger of the Naval Coastal Systems Center in Panama City and the Naval Surface Warfare Center in Dahlgren. More than 10 percent of the work force is engaged in basic research, applied research, and technology. The NSWCDD research and technology departments at each site work on exploring scientific opportunities, anticipating the future, and inserting technological innovation into surface warfare systems.

Scientists at the Naval Surface Warfare Center in Dahlgren study advanced computer systems and electronic/space systems, mathematical technologies, and advanced technologies. Scientists in engineering, software development, logistics, configuration management, and systems integration at Dam Neck, VA, create and maintain computer programs for several combatant platforms and multiple versions of programs for each platform.

Naval Surface Warfare Center at Indian Head, Maryland

The Indian Head facility was established in 1890 as a naval gun-testing facility, eventually moving into a lab that developed munitions, specialized ordnance devices, and components. Located in Charles County, Maryland, 30 miles south of Washington, D.C., the warfare center involves a number of scientists studying energetics research; weapons product development; detonation science; underwater warheads; chemical/physical characterization; chemical processing/nitration; nitramine gun and high-energy propellants; extruded products; cartridge-actuated devices/propellant-actuated devices ordnance test and evaluation; weapon simulation; quality evaluation; and packaging, handling, storage, and transportation.

Its research and technology department conducts research and development on all types of energetic materials, explosives and propellants processing, explosive components, and warhead technology. The test and evaluation department plans, directs, administers, and conducts destructive and nondestructive tests and analysis required for the evaluation of propulsion systems. Scientists here also design and develop new test technologies, maintain facilities being used for test, analysis, and evaluation, and serve as the navy's primary technical resource for laboratory test and quality evaluation of the strategic systems programs' re-entry systems. The applied technology department maintains state-of-the-art facilities for the engineering, development, and transition of new formulations for chemicals, munitions, explosives, propellants, pyrotechnics, and energetic ingredients/products in support of DOD systems. The underwater warhead technology and development department comes up with warhead systems for underwater mines, torpedoes, mine neutralization, and SEAL weapons. The lab also conducts theoretical experimental research on the effects of chemical and nuclear explosion in air, water, and ground media and develops technology in applied mechanics to assess the damage to underwater targets from advanced underwater warheads.

Naval Undersea Warfare Center at Newport, Rhode Island

This is the navy's principal research, development, test, and evaluation center for submarine warfare systems, weapon systems, and surface-ship sonar systems. Scientists at this lab have designed virtually all underwater acoustic sensors and weapons systems operating in the navy today and introduced the use of a supercomputer onboard a submarine.

As an intern here, you may work in departments such as acoustics; numerical analysis; communications; optics; signal and information processing; hydrodynamics; underwater propulsion; chemistry of materials; ocean sciences and technology; and systems engineering.

Naval Surface Warfare Center at Panama City, Florida

This lab in Panama City, FL, is the main navy center for surface warfare analysis; surface ship combat systems; sensor technologies; strategic systems; mines; mine countermeasures; amphibious warfare; special warfare systems; and diving.

The organization was formed in 1992 with the merger of the Naval Coastal Systems Center in Panama City and the Naval Surface Warfare Center in Dahlgren. Scientists are involved in basic and applied research and technology, including sensor technology; superconductivity; acoustics; electro-optics; electromagnetics; hydromechanics; control systems; and signal and image processing.

Space and Naval Warfare Systems Center— SPAWAR at San Diego

At this lab, more than 2,200 scientists and engineers with degrees in physical and biological sciences and engineering study a wide range of projects, including electromagnetic and acoustic signal generation, detection, and propagation; electromagnetic and acoustic information and signal processing; ocean and biotechnology; solid-state physics and engineering; high-performance computing; human-computer interfaces and human factors; and navigation.

In addition to the preceding areas, this lab is looking for graduate students concentrating in government, international relations, public policy, and business to help with the center's strategic analysis and assessment process. Researchers at the lab are specifically looking for interns to consider working at the lab's mobile tactical networking, robotics, and advanced clinical technologies in marine mammal medicine (to work in this area, interns must be enrolled in veterinary school and preferably have completed the first year of their professional curriculum). Researchers are also looking for interns in the areas of development of decision support tools. For the internship in flow-induced bioluminescence, the graduate or undergraduate student must have a background in experimental fluid dynamics and should have a car, since some of the research will be at the Scripps Institution of Oceanography.

Stennis Space Center, Mississippi

Scientists here study ocean dynamics and prediction ocean measurement and analysis, ocean optics, and remote sensing. They also study marine geoscience, including marine sedimentology; marine seismology; marine gravity and magnetics; sediment and transport/dynamics; surf zone processes; seafloor morphology; geographic information systems; object-oriented database technology; and hydrography.

Stennis Space Center, Monterey, California

In this lab, scientists study marine meteorology, involving prediction systems, forecast support, atmospheric processes, predictability, data assimilation, numerical weather prediction, remote sensing applications, and aerosols.

U.S. Naval Observatory at Washington, D.C., and Flagstaff, Arizona

Established in 1830, the observatory is one of the oldest scientific organizations in the federal government and provides astronomical and timing data to the navy and the defense department for navigation, precise positioning, command, control, and communications. The observatory also supports research, develops instruments, and makes astronomical observations. Today, USNO is one of the leading authorities in the world in astrometry, Earth rotation measurement, precise time, fundamental reference frames, and solar system dynamics.

The observatory is a small institution, with a total technical staff of about 60 in Washington, D.C, and 20 in Flagstaff. Technical staff consists of civilian experts in astronomy and physics, who make astronomical observations in both Washington, D.C., and Flagstaff. Dark-sky observing is done at Flagstaff, where several ongoing observing programs are supported on 1.5-meter and smaller telescopes. Washington, D.C., is home to one of the most complete astronomical libraries in the world, a 26-inch refracting telescope, the U.S. Master Clock (an ensemble of over 70 atomic frequency standards), and an experimental atomic "fountain" clock.

Many USNO programs involve partnerships with other national or foreign laboratories and international organizations, and most research programs are unclassified and results are published in the open professional literature. Current areas of active research involve all-sky ground- and space-based astrometric surveys; stellar dynamics and astrophysics; binary star orbits; long-baseline radio and optical interferometry; Fourier transform spectroscopy, 2D sensor arrays (optical and near-infrared); speckle interferometry; Earth rotation dynamics; astronomical reference frames; astrometry and dynamics of solar system objects; artificial satellite orbits; photometric standards; planetary nebulae; quasar structure monitoring; atomic clock development; clock ensemble characterization and control; satellite two-way time transfer; numerical and statistical techniques; and automated daytime stellar imaging.

Washington, D.C., Naval Research Laboratory

Scientists at the Naval Research Lab study space science; plasma physics; acoustics; radar; tactical engineering; computational physics and fluid dynamics; structure of matter; chemistry; material science and technology; optical sciences; condensed matter and radiation sciences; electronics technology; information technology; space systems and technology; and remote sensing.

HOW TO APPLY

Apply online at http://www.armanagement.org/onr/. When your online application is complete, you will receive an e-mail with procedures for submitting your transcripts and letter. Both should be sent to the preceding address.

Applicants interested in the Naval Observatory should indicate on their application form whether the Washington, D.C., or Flagstaff location is preferred.

PFIZER RESEARCH AND DEVELOPMENT INTERNSHIP

Pfizer Research and Development Coordinator
Pfizer Inc.
235 East 42nd Street, MS 13-4
New York, NY 10017-5755

What You Can Earn: $1350 weekly plus college credit.

Application Deadlines: Rolling.

Educational Experience: Enrolled as a full-time undergraduate or graduate student in a degree program related to Pfizer's primary research efforts (science, business, computer science, and so on).

Requirements: Solid academic standing (3.0 GPA or above); authorized to work in the United States; satisfactory completion of a drug test and background investigation.

OVERVIEW

At Pfizer Global Research and Development (PGRD), the company's scientists, clinicians, and technicians develop new pharmaceutical and animal health products to deliver medicine to enhance the quality of life for people and animals around the world. The Pfizer Global Research and Development division of Pfizer Inc. is the principal research and development unit in the company, which periodically offers six-month co-op positions and summer internships in scientific fields such as chemistry and biology.

The internship program offers a wide range of challenging projects involving issues critical to Pfizer's research and development. As an intern, you'll gain hands-on scientific research, business, or technical experience, participating in structured projects under the guidance of a Pfizer mentor. The goal of this program is for students to experience working in a pharmaceutical-company setting and to understand the vital role of research in the drug-development process, perhaps becoming interested in careers as researchers.

The summer internships typically offer full-time (40 hours per week) experiential training opportunities for 12 weeks. You may work in one of three areas: Worldwide Development, Worldwide Research, or Functional Support Lines.

Functional Support Line

This department consists of a variety of business areas, including finance/procurement, human resources, strategic management, global operations, informatics, public affairs, and information technology.

Worldwide Development

This department must deliver a high-quality stream of new products to market using closely monitored trials of safety and efficacy to help select reliable candidates with the best potential. Only then does the department move onto the design, monitoring, and interpretation of extensive Phase III studies, often involving dozens of international study sites and thousands of people. Finally, if the results are positive, the preparation of trial reports for submission to regulatory agencies worldwide begins.

As an intern in the Worldwide Development group, you will be part of a team that must prove the effectiveness of the compounds discovered and developed by the group. Internships are available in worldwide regulatory affairs and quality assurance, clinical sciences, worldwide development operations, or biostatistics/reporting.

Worldwide Research

This department focuses on generating new ideas for drugs that address areas of significant medical need. This department uses the skills of a wide variety of chemistry, biology, and molecular science specialists to find promising treatments in major therapeutic areas including antibacterials, antifungals, antivirals, and many other drugs. Internships are available in three departments: biology, chemistry, and technology. To work in this department, you should have a background in biology, molecular biology, medicinal chemistry, analytical chemistry, biochemistry, organic chemistry, biophysics, or chemical engineering.

HOW TO APPLY

Send a resume and cover letter to the preceding address.

ROCKEFELLER UNIVERSITY SUMMER UNDERGRADUATE RESEARCH FELLOWSHIP

The Rockefeller University
Office of Graduate Studies
Box 177
1230 York Avenue
New York, NY 10021-6399
(212) 327-8086
surf@mail.rockefeller.edu
http://www.rockefeller.edu/surf

What You Can Earn: $3,000 stipend and free on-campus housing.
Application Deadlines: Early February.
Educational Experience: Currently in your sophomore year or junior year, majoring in biology or chemistry and possessing an interest in a career in basic biomedical research.
Requirements: High academic credentials and a high degree of motivation.

OVERVIEW

The Rockefeller University Summer Undergraduate Research Fellowship (SURF) program offers a unique chance for college undergraduates to conduct laboratory research.

As a SURF intern, you'll work with some of the country's top scientists in a variety of areas, such as biochemistry; structural biology and chemistry; molecular, cell, and developmental biology; immunology; virology and microbiology; neuroscience; physics; and mathematical biology.

Centered on 75 cutting-edge labs working in anything from infectious diseases to neurochemistry, the SURF program will give you a chance to explore almost any area of research you can imagine. You'll be matched according to your area of interest with faculty, postdoctoral researchers, or graduate students, who volunteer to help design and supervise your individualized summer projects for the 10-week internship. The program begins the first week in June and ends the second week in August.

Competition for these internships is keen. Each year, students are chosen from a wide variety of about 300 applicants who have diverse scientific backgrounds and training, but only 15 are accepted.

To fully experience the world of scientific research, you'll work on projects under the direct supervision of faculty, postdoctoral fellows, and/or senior graduate students, and you'll be required to discuss scientific publications at weekly Journal Club meetings. This will help you get used to speaking to a scientific audience. You'll also attend a special lecture series to hear Rockefeller faculty discuss their research and how they got involved in their particular scientific interests. At the end of the program, you'll be expected to present your research results to fellow students and mentors at a poster session. When the internship is over, you'll be strongly encouraged to return during your college breaks to complete or extend your summer research projects. This can mean you'll be developing some really helpful long-term professional relationships with Rockefeller faculty.

Interns have worked in the labs of a variety of noted Rockefeller University researchers, including Nobel Prize winners. Recent projects have included developing a composite model of the cerebellar basket cell for use in large-scale network simulations; development of yeast system to screen for g-secretase modulators; structural basis of transcriptional activation; and the effects of cytidine deaminases on gene conversion in Trypanosoma brucei; and the effects of early-life stress upon adult mu opioid receptor mRNA expression.

When you apply, you should state a preference for working in particular laboratories or areas of research, although there's no guarantee that your specific preferences will be met. The dean's office handles placement in laboratories, and you'll be matched with labs according to your research interests. You're neither expected nor encouraged to make your own lab arrangements. For a listing of faculty members and a brief description of their research, you can obtain further in-depth information by viewing the Rockefeller Web site at: http://www.rockefeller.edu/research/.

But working as a Rockefeller intern isn't all drudgery. You're also encouraged to attend social and cultural events occurring both on and off campus. Organized outings for interns include trips to see a Broadway show and a professional baseball game. The campus is located on New York City's Upper East Side amidst a culturally enriched area of Manhattan. The rest of New York City is conveniently accessible by train, bus, or taxicab.

HOW TO APPLY

First, download the application at http://www.rockefeller.edu/surf/application.php.

Submit in one envelope the completed application form along with a two-page summary describing your academic background, scientific interests, research experience, career goals, and what why you would benefit from the SURF program. You also should include an official transcript sealed by the university registrar, plus two letters of recommendation from professors or mentors who can evaluate your performance in science courses or recent research projects.

Completed applications will be reviewed in the order they are received. Final decisions will be made by early March, so it's imperative that you provide contact information (preferably e-mail or telephone) for the first two weeks of March.

ROCKY MOUNTAIN BIOLOGICAL LABORATORY SUMMER INTERNSHIP

Rocky Mountain Biological Laboratory
PO Box 519
Crested Butte, CO 81224

(970) 349-7231
Fax: (415) 750-7346
info@rmbl.org
http://www.rmbl.org/index.php?module=ContentExpress&func=display&ceid=3

What You Can Earn: $600 toward travel costs, a $3000 stipend, and all expenses at RMBL such as room, board, and tuition if you wish to receive credit for your research project.

Application Deadlines: February 15.

Educational Experience: Minorities currently underrepresented in biology (defined by the National Science Foundation as African American, Hispanic, and Native American) are encouraged to apply.

Requirements: Sincere interest in a career in field biology research and the mental and intellectual maturity to commit to hard work.

OVERVIEW

The Rocky Mountain Biological Laboratory (RMBL) was founded in 1928 to focus on research and education in the biological sciences. One of the leading field stations in North America, the laboratory owns 245 acres and more than 50 buildings, including research laboratories, offices, cabins, a library, dormitories, a dining hall, classrooms, and a store and visitors center. The lab is surrounded by national forest and wilderness, which is available for research. During the summer, 150 research scientists, students, and staff arrive to complete research, forming an active community complete with local newspaper, seminars, educational programs, and social events.

Students in this program will work with a mentor to develop a testable hypothesis, gather data, analyze it, and produce a written and oral report. The program is intended to assist students who must work through the summer to complete their education. As a result, RMBL gives special consideration to members of minorities currently underrepresented in biology (defined by the National Science Foundation as Black, Hispanic, and Native American).

HOW TO APPLY

To obtain an online application, visit this Web site: https://lisa.gendns2.com/~rmblorg/applications/CourseworkREU.php. Submit the application together with two recommendations and an essay to the preceding address. The application will be judged on the basis of financial need and on student motivation, but the essay and recommendations count significantly.

ROSWELL PARK CANCER INSTITUTE SUMMER COLLEGE INTERNSHIP

Roswell Park Cancer Institute
Summer Program Office
Elm and Carlton Streets
Buffalo, NY 14263
mary.wisnicki@roswellpark.org

What You Can Earn: At least $2,500, which varies according to program; plus room, board, and travel expenses.
Application Deadlines: February 1.
Educational Experience: Must have current junior standing; should be interested in pursuing a graduate degree in the biomedical or natural sciences.
Requirements: Must be a citizen or permanent resident of the United States.

OVERVIEW

The Roswell Park Cancer Institute is the oldest and among the largest cancer research, treatment, and educational facilities in the world, offering effective means of diagnosis and treatment while addressing both the physical and emotional needs of the cancer patients it serves.

The institute's internships, which last from early June until mid-August, are designed to introduce students to scientific research, help interns develop their own philosophy of science, give students the opportunity to experience the graduate student lifestyle, and help interns plan their graduate education and field of study. Selected students will be assigned to laboratories of graduate professors in molecular biology, genetics, biophysics, bioinformatics, experimental pathology, biochemistry, immunology, tumor biology, or pharmacology. As an intern, you'll also be able to attend classes and seminars taught by a faculty of internationally known scientists and present your research findings at a science conference and poster session. Out-of-town students stay in a supervised local college dormitory two miles from Roswell Park; social activities and field trips occur on weekends.

HOW TO APPLY

You can obtain application materials by visiting the Web site at http://www.roswellpark.org/document_3324.html.

Application forms including a $5 application fee, preaddressed stamped postcard, application, essay, transcripts, and recommendation from a science professor should be mailed to the preceding address in one envelope.

ROSWELL PARK CANCER INSTITUTE SUMMER HIGH SCHOOL INTERNSHIP

Roswell Park Cancer Institute
Summer Program Office
Elm and Carlton Streets
Buffalo, NY 14263
mary.wisnicki@roswellpark.org

What You Can Earn: Stipends and allowances for room and board are available to out-of-town students and underrepresented students from minority groups or financially disadvantaged families.

Application Deadlines: February 15.

Educational Experience: High school seniors who have demonstrated a pronounced ability and interest in science.

Requirements: U.S. citizenship or permanent resident of the United States.

OVERVIEW

The Roswell Park Cancer Institute is the oldest and among the largest cancer research, treatment, and educational facilities in the world, offering effective means of diagnosis and treatment while addressing both the physical and emotional needs of the cancer patients it serves.

During a typical summer, more than 30 high school students participate in programs designed to provide an opportunity to learn and become active participants in cancer research. The institute's intern program for high school students is particularly designed for applicants who may be the first in their families to attend college, who are from nonscience/nonprofessional families, or who are underrepresented minority students and students from financially disadvantaged backgrounds. The program, which runs from late June to mid-August, is partially funded by the National Cancer Institute.

This program has been offered at RPCI every year since 1953, as a way of giving high-ability high school juniors the chance to develop the skills, habits, and attitudes they'll need to conduct scientific research and to help them with career planning. It's also intended to interest participants in pursuing future careers in scientific cancer research.

As an intern, you'll be introduced to scientific research by working on a project supervised by graduate faculty members, who will also help you develop your own philosophy of science. You'll also have the chance to discover and experience the graduate student lifestyle and, if you've not already decided on a field of specialization, to select your undergraduate college major.

During the seven-week program, you'll work on an independent research project under the guidance of scientific staff for four days each week, spending the fifth day attending lectures, classes, and seminars. You'll also prepare critiques on various lectures you attend and present your research (poster and oral) results during a scientific conference held at the end of the program.

HOW TO APPLY

A $10 application fee must accompany your credentials with checks made payable to "RPCI – Summer Program." All admitted students will be charged a $100 activity fee, but there's no tuition. You can obtain application materials by visiting the Web site at http://www.roswellpark.org/GradEducation/HighSchoolApplicationPacket.pdf

Your completed application must be signed and mailed in one envelope by your high school guidance counselor or academic advisor. Completed applications must include a transcript of grades through the January before the internship begins, plus one science or math teacher's recommendation. You also should enclose an essay of not more than 300 words discussing why you want to participate in this program and what you hope to achieve as a future scientist, as well as briefly describing your participation in science activities, extracurricular activities, periodicals you subscribe to or read regularly, and the titles of the last two books you read not required for a class.

You must enclose a preaddressed stamped postcard that will be date-stamped and returned to you to verify that your file has been received and is complete. Only complete files will be considered.

Those chosen will be notified of their appointment by April 1.

SMITHSONIAN ASTROPHYSICAL OBSERVATORY INTERNSHIP

Program Director
SAO Summer Intern Program, MS-83
Harvard-Smithsonian Center for Astrophysics
60 Garden Street
Cambridge MA 02138
(617) 495-7094
intern@cfa.harvard.edu
http://hea-www.harvard.edu/REU/BULLETIN.
   html

What You Can Earn: $3,500 take-home pay for the nine or ten-week program, 10 percent of the stipend at the beginning and the remaining 90 percent in two equal installments at the end of June and at the end of July. The Smithsonian does not issue 1099's because the students are not on the payroll; the funds are considered fellowships. Housing at Harvard dorms is included. Travel to and from Cambridge at the beginning and the end of the summer is subsidized; the observatory sends students a round-trip air or train ticket in advance (up to $500), plus taxi fare to and from Logan airport or the train station when you arrive and leave.

Application Deadlines: February 6; decisions are made in March.

Educational Experience: Undergraduate students interested in a career in astronomy, astrophysics, physics, or related physical sciences, or with a strong interest in science and math, are encouraged to apply. Must be enrolled in a degree program leading to a bachelor's degree; seniors who will graduate in June right before the internship begins are not eligible.

Requirements: Must be U.S. citizens or permanent residents (Green Card holders).

OVERVIEW

The Smithsonian Astrophysical Observatory (SAO) is a research institute of the Smithsonian Institution headquartered in Cambridge, Massachusetts, where it is joined with the Harvard College Observatory (HCO) to form the Harvard-Smithsonian Center for Astrophysics (CfA). More than 300 scientists at the CfA are engaged in a broad program of research in astronomy, astrophysics, earth and space sciences, and science education.

Each summer a number of internships are hired to work at the observatory. Potential areas of research include observational and theoretical cosmology, extragalactic and galactic astronomy, interstellar medium and star formation, laboratory astrophysics, supernovae and supernova remnants, planetary science, or solar and stellar astrophysics. As an intern here, you'll work with an SAO/Harvard staff member on a research project for the duration of your stay. You'll also enjoy field trips, discussion evenings, and a summer colloquia series.

The observatory staff try hard to match students well with their science advisers, and to make sure that the students don't feel overwhelmed by their projects. Interns get on-the-job training and plenty of support as they work. Mentors stay in touch with their interns to help with all kinds of matters. The observatory does not expect students to have special knowledge about X-ray astrophysics or radio astronomy when they arrive. What matters most is that a student be willing and able to tackle a project with good organization skills and a curious mind. The projects are not busy-work. Students help scientists with their actual research, but the work interns do is appropriate for their academic level.

The program will provide students with the opportunity to present a paper at a scientific meeting. Summer Interns are required to write a research-style paper (approximately 10 pages long) over the course of the summer and to present the results of their work in the form of a 10-minute oral presentation at an Intern Symposium at the end of the summer.

HOW TO APPLY
There is no required application form for the SAO Summer Intern Program, although you can download a helpful form at: http://hea-www.harvard.edu/REU/form.html. You should submit the following information to the address above:

- name, permanent and school addresses, e-mail address and phone numbers
- college or university, major and minor, academic year, cumulative GPA, GPA for science and math courses, and anticipated date of graduation
- a list of the names of two faculty members or other people who have worked with you and who have agreed to send letters of recommendation
- a three-page essay (either double or single-line spacing) describing your academic and career goals, your scientific interests, relevant work experience, why you would like to participate in the SAO Summer Intern Program, and why you think you would be a good candidate for this program
- official transcript(s), spring courses you plan to take, and two letters of recommendation (from the faculty members or others you listed, as explained above)

The Smithsonian does not accept faxed, e-mailed application materials or electronic resumés. All materials need not be mailed in one package or at one time. If an application is not complete, it will not be considered.

STANFORD LINEAR ACCELERATOR CENTER SUMMER FELLOWSHIP

Stanford Linear Accelerator Center
Katherine E. Pope Fellowship
2575 Sand Hill Road, MS11
Menlo Park, CA 94025
Fax: (650) 926-4999

What You Can Earn: $500 a week stipend, transportation to and from SLAC, and lodging for the time of the appointment.
Application Deadlines: Mid-March.
Educational Experience: A sophomore or higher in a university whose faculty and students are participating in the research program at SLAC, with a cumulative college GPA of 2.5 or higher. Preference will be given to students with a project in experimental particle physics but will not be confined to physics majors.
Requirements: Must be available for a summer internship lasting for up to three months from June through August; must have a sponsor for a summer project who is a SLAC user.

OVERVIEW
The Stanford Linear Accelerator Center is one of the world's leading research laboratories. Established in 1962 at Stanford University, the center focuses on designing and operating state-of-the-art electron accelerators and related experimental facilities for use in high-energy physics and synchrotron radiation research. More than 3,000 visiting scientists from universities, laboratories, and corporations work at the center and have contributed to the research that has netted two Nobel Prizes in physics. Center scientists are making discoveries in photon science at the frontiers of the ultra-small and ultra-fast in a wide spectrum of physical and life sciences. They also are focused on making discoveries in particle and astroparticle physics to redefine humanity's understanding of what the universe is made of and the forces that control it.

The Katherine E. Pope Summer Fellowship at the Stanford Linear Accelerator Center (SLAC) was established in the memory of Katherine Pope, an undergraduate student at Smith College who was working at SLAC under the direction of her physics advisor. Katherine was killed in July 2001 as she rode a bike to the center. This fellowship remembers Katherine and encourages other undergraduates with an interest in science (especially physics) to pursue their academic interest at SLAC.

HOW TO APPLY

If this internship sounds interesting, you can apply by downloading an application at http://www-group.slac.stanford.edu/hr/forms/summerfellowshipapp.html. Or you can download it a .pdf format at http: //www-goup.slac.stanford.edu/hr/forms/summerfellowshipapp.pdf.

Mail to the preceding address the completed application, along with a college transcript and two letters of references (one must be from your summer supervisor stating that he or she is committed to your internship and project).

SUNY ALBANY SUMMER RESEARCH EXPERIENCE FOR UNDERGRADUATES

SUNY Albany Summer Undergraduate Research Program
Department of Biomedical Sciences
Wadsworth Center, C-236
Empire State Plaza, Box 509
Albany, NY 12201-0509
(518) 473-7553
reu@wadsworth.org
http://www.wadsworth.org/educate/molcel.htm

What You Can Earn: $3,400 plus travel, housing, and food allowance; students are housed within walking distance of the labs.
Application Deadlines: February 1.
Educational Experience: Undergraduates majoring in a natural science, computer science, or mathematics who will have completed their second or third year of study by the summer; students graduating the month before the internship begins aren't eligible. Applications are encouraged from students attending colleges with limited research opportunities and from students who are members of groups underrepresented in the sciences, such as women, racial minorities, and the physically challenged.
Requirements: Must be interested in attending graduate school with the goal of pursuing a career in science; must be a U.S. citizen or a resident alien.

OVERVIEW

The Wadsworth Center for Laboratories and Research in Albany is the central public-health science facility of New York. The center is unique among the state public health labs for its state-of-the-art facilities and the scope of its research programs. Participating scientists are also faculty of the biomedical sciences department (a graduate department of the University of Albany's School of Public Health).

Each year, the center offers 10-week summer internships for students interested in direct participation in a variety of research projects, as part of the National Science Foundation's Research Experiences for Undergraduates (REU) program. Students are selected from colleges across the country to work from early June through mid-August on independent research projects in the laboratories of Wadsworth scientists. You might find yourself working with microscopy and computer-image analysis of cells and macromolecules; gene expression and regulation; protein biochemistry and structure analysis; viral mechanisms and mechanisms of immunity; or neurobiology and neurotoxicology.

Recent intern projects have included structure and function of viral replicase complexes; imprinted and captured genes in development, cancer, and smallpox virulence; structure and dynamics of the ribosome, studied by cryo-electron microscopy and computer image processing; structure and catalytic mechanism of human DNA repair enzymes; molecular genetics of enzymes involved in detoxification; introns and inteins: structure, function, and applications;

trophic utilization of carotenoids in the Great Lakes; mycobacterial conjugation; yeast retrotransposons; development of a rare cell-fractionation device; microtubule formation in Foraminifera; genetics of intron mobility in bacteria; structure/function of viral replicase complexes; mouse mutations as models for studying cancer progression; mosquito-borne viruses; neuroimmunological regulation of host-defense against bacterial infections and autoimmune disease; RNA editing in trypanosomes; development of genetic analysis systems in the bacterium Treponema denticola; structure and function studies of proteins related to bacterial or viral infection and host response; and the functional analysis of murine virgin and memory T cells.

HOW TO APPLY

You can download an application at http://www.wadsworth.org/educate/molcel.htm. Once you've completed the application, submit it to the preceding address, along with a resume, official college transcripts, letters of recommendation from two faculty members, a one-page statement describing why you want to participate in this program, and a statement of your field of interest.

UNIVERSITY OF CALIFORNIA-DAVIS UNDERGRADUATE SUMMER TRAINING IN ENVIRONMENTAL TOXICOLOGY

Department of Environmental Toxicology
University of California – Davis
One Shields Avenue
Davis, CA 95616-8588
(530) 752-4521
Fax: (530) 752-3394
http://www.envtox.ucdavis.edu/niehs_summer

What You Can Earn: $1,664/month stipend, $400/month living allowance, travel, tuition, and fees.
Application Deadlines: February 28.
Educational Experience: Highly qualified college students who will have completed at least one year of undergraduate education by summer and who are exploring graduate school and careers in environmental health sciences and are from underrepresented groups.
Requirements: U.S. citizens or permanent residents.

OVERVIEW

This internship, sponsored by the University of California at Davis, allows undergraduates to study the harmful effects of chemicals on human health and the environment and learn more about toxicology—the unique science that combines the principles of biology and chemistry.

The program, which lasts eight to 10 weeks, involves a basic introduction to basic concepts in laboratory research. As an intern in this program, you'll work full time in research labs on projects of mutual interest, participate in lab research conferences, present written and oral reports on their work, attend seminars on special topics, and receive independent-study credit.

HOW TO APPLY

First, fill out the application at http://www.envtox.ucdavis.edu/niehs_summer. Then submit to the preceding address a data sheet and statement of purpose, official transcripts of undergraduate grades, financial aid transcripts, and letters of recommendation from two faculty members.

UNIVERSITY OF COLORADO AT BOULDER SUMMER MINORITY ACCESS TO RESEARCH TRAINING

SMART Program
University of Colorado at Boulder
Graduate School
Campus Box 26
Boulder, CO 80309-0026
(303) 492-4607 or 1-888-709-1997 (toll free)
smart@spot.colorado.edu
http://www.colorado.edu/graduateschool/
    SMART/SMARTWebsite/index.html

What You Can Earn: $2,800 plus room, board, tuition, travel, books, and supplies.
Application Deadlines: Mid-February.
Educational Experience: Undergraduates from schools throughout the United States and Puerto Rico who have completed 60 semester credit hours of undergraduate coursework.
Requirements: Must be from one of the following minority groups: African American, Hispanic, Asian or Pacific Islander, or American Indian or Alaskan Native.

OVERVIEW

The University of Colorado/Boulder's Summer Minority Access to Research Training (SMART) program offers 10-week research internships in science and engineering as a way of providing hands-on experience in research and an introduction to graduate education at a leading university. Typically, 20 undergraduates from schools throughout the United States and Puerto Rico take part in this challenging and informative program each summer. SMART interns conduct research projects in science engineering fields under the guidance of a faculty mentor and see firsthand graduate-student life at a major institution. Interns also interact in the social environment of a large university and in a community of minority peers.

The SMART program focuses on developing research skills and the faculty mentor/student relationship. As an intern with this program, during the first week you'll write a research project proposal, and in the next eight weeks you'll carry out that proposed project. In the final week, you'll present your research results in oral and written form. Other activities include workshops devoted to technical writing and oral presentation skills, informal evening seminars, seminars on the nature of graduate study and the application process for graduate school, and a GRE preparation workshop.

HOW TO APPLY

You can download a copy of the application in pdf format at http://www.colorado.edu/graduate school/SMART/SMARTWebsite/docs/SMART_Application.pdf. You can download the application as a word document at http://www.colorado.edu/graduateschool/SMART/SMARTWebsite/docs/SMART_Application.doc.

Next, complete a letter of interest, describing on two to three typed pages your interest in the SMART program. Your personal academic statement should explain why you want to participate in the SMART program, what you hope to gain from the program, and how this research experience will help you achieve your academic and career goals. Your statement should include a description of your specific research interests, any relevant research experience you've had in an academic or work setting, your goals after earning a B.A. or B.S., the qualities you'd contribute to the SMART program, and how those qualities would benefit the program and its participants. The letter of interest is the most important part of your application. Successful applicants are those who can demonstrate an understanding of research topics in their field and can express a particular interest in one or two areas.

Submit the completed application and letter of interest to the preceding address, along with:

- two letters of recommendation.
- transcripts from all institutions attended.
- financial aid information (if necessary for eligibility).

UNIVERSITY OF MASSACHUSETTS UNDERGRADUATE RESEARCH IN ECOLOGY AND CONSERVATION BIOLOGY

Department of Biology
University of Massachusetts at Boston
Boston, MA 02125-3393
(617) 287-6600
Fax: (617) 287-6650
maria.mahoney@umb.edu
http://www.bio.umb.edu/special_REU.htm

What You Can Earn: $3500; plus a room and board allowance of $1950.

Application Deadlines: April 1.

Educational Experience: Must be a junior or senior and must have completed at least one upper-level biology course as well as mathematics through college algebra. Women and minorities are encouraged to apply.

Requirements: Must be a U.S. citizen or permanent resident.

OVERVIEW

The University of Massachusetts at Boston, located on Boston Harbor, offers a 10-week REU program in biology to 10 undergraduate interns each summer. Each student carries out an independent research project under the close guidance of a faculty advisor.

The program stresses the integration of diverse fields of biology, demonstrating common themes across the biological sciences and especially the connections between cell and molecular biology on one hand and ecology and conservation biology on the other. Accordingly, student research projects will span a diverse array of problems in biology. Their projects are designed to help interns develop independence in making research decisions, understanding the complexities of experimental design, and appreciating their broad field of research.

In addition to carrying out research projects, you'll participate in enrichment activities designed to promote a sense of community, enhance your communication skills, help you understand the issues surrounding modern biology, and prepare you for advanced work in science. These experiences occur during weekly discussions and workshops that focus on practical, personal, and ethical aspects of research.

The program also features a three-day retreat at the Nantucket Island Field Station, other field trips in and around Boston Harbor, and final research presentations. Close mentoring relationships, as well as collegial interactions among interns, are key components of the experience. The program is designed to stimulate and support interest in biological research and to equip students to pursue research careers. The program runs from early June to mid-August, but you may adjust starting or ending times by prior arrangement. The following programs are available.

Atypical Patterns of Gene Expression in Spermatogenic Cells

This research focuses on spermatogenesis, the complex process of cell proliferation, meiosis, and cell differentiation. Using the mouse as a model system, scientists are investigating the mechanisms that regulate mRNA translation and focusing on the strikingly atypical patterns of gene expression in spermatogenic cells.

Bacterial Toxins

Scientists in this area are investigating small protein toxins produced by bacteria and then exported to the extracellular environment, where they kill other sensitive bacteria. Current work focuses on the E. coli toxin colicin V, which is being studied on both molecular and ecological levels. In particular, this lab combines methodologies of molecular biology and genetics to study the genetic regulation of toxin synthesis and the transport system that exports toxins across membranes. In addition, scientists are analyzing mixed communities of bacteria to study the role of the toxin in microbial interactions, as well as the conditions that modulate toxin production.

Community Assembly and Susceptibility to Invasion or Global Environmental Change

This research focuses on how plant species become established in or excluded from communities and how global environmental changes affect ecosystems. In California grasslands, scientists are studying how the initial composition and diversity of a plant community determines which introduced species become established and which species dominate the community after several years. In Massachusetts, scientists are examining how global environmental changes such as climate change, increasing atmospheric carbon dioxide concentrations, and increasing nitrogen pollution affect old-field ecosystems.

Concealment by Countershading

This research focuses on two mechanisms that have been proposed to account for the concealing effect conferred on animals with coloration that is both dark and pale (countershading), which may improve concealment by reducing contrast against the background when an animal is viewed from both below and above. In this research, scientists are comparing the conspicuousness of countershaded three-dimensional spheres versus countershaded two-dimensional discs relative to three other colorations by recording the sequence of discovery when human participants picked out the objects when placed against a splotchy black and white background.

Conservation Genetics

This research in Costa Rica involves assessing plant-mating systems and the impact of habitat loss and fragmentation on plant pollination mechanisms, breeding systems, and seed dispersal. Scientists examine the molecular basis of evolution of unisexuality from a heteromorphic, hermaphrodite system in the genus Cordia and how landscape-level processes such as fragmentation might disrupt the reproductive system. The project integrates molecular and landscape-level approaches. Interns will have opportunities to conduct fieldwork in Costa Rica, studying breeding systems in environments that span a gradient of disturbances. In Boston, they can use molecular tools to study evolution of breeding systems and population genetic structure.

Control of Cellular Organization

Although most cells contain the same basic set of organelles, the internal architecture of a particular cell type reflects the specific properties of the cell. This research seeks to answer questions of how signal-transduction processes are used for spatial and temporal regulation of cellular organization, using molecular, genetic, and biochemical methods to understand the regulation of cellular architecture in the budding yeast S. cerevisiae.

Genetic Bases of Biodiversity

This research combines components of field work, greenhouse experiments, and molecular biology to examine the genetic bases of biodiversity. At the genomic level, scientists study the evolution of suites of selectively critical interacting genes that affect the genetic structure and fitness of species. In plants, genes responsible for shifts from outbreeding to inbreeding or from hermaphroditic to dioecious are one focus. Genes that bestow resistance to pathogens and the genetic bases of host-pathogen interactions are another.

Genetic Diversity and Adaptation of Bacteria

This research focuses on genetic diversity of hydrocarbon-degrading bacteria, rhizosphere bacteria, and coliforms in the environment. Interns will examine the abundance, distribution, and/or dynamics of specific bacteria in coastal waters, sediments, or on plant roots and will design experiments for the laboratory or field to answer questions about genetic diversity and bacterial adaptation in the environment. Students will use microbiological and molecular methods, including DNA fingerprinting tools to address these problems in microbial ecology.

Growth Control in Plants

Because land plants cannot move to avoid harsh environmental conditions, they have evolved highly regulated cellular mechanisms (primarily cell division and elongation) to modify growth patterns of root and shoot organs. Scientists use cellular, molecular, and genetic tools to understand the contribution of cell division to the regulation of organ growth during seedling development. They are also studying the role of the motor proteins kinesins in cytoskeletal changes during organ formation and are using molecular methods to search for genes that can be used in bioengineering plants to biodegrade petroleum-based pollutants. All three projects use the plant-model system Arabidopsis thaliana.

Mechanisms of Gene Regulation

This research explores several aspects of gene expression regulation in eucaryotes, using plants and animals. Some investigations focus on transcription initiation for pre-mRNA synthesis in plants and animals. The overall goal is to learn how a plant responds to environmental stimuli, where scientists can model the system to study how the signal pathway activates repressed genes to respond to a challenge.

Molecular Evolution of Alzheimer's-related Genes and Circadian Rhythms in Primates

This research focuses on applying bioinformatics approaches to conduct integrated evolutionary and functional studies. In particular, one research project is studying the molecular evolution of Alzheimer's-related genes in primates, in which evolutionary analysis is used to provide new perspectives on functional studies of Alzheimer's disease. Another project looks at molecular evolution of circadian rhythm in primates, in which scientists hope to address certain intriguing primate-evolution issues. Students will use PCR, gel electrophoresis, DNA sequencing, nucleotide substitution estimation, and molecular phylogenetic analysis to address their research problem.

Pollutants in Aquatic Systems

This research focuses on maintaining the quality of the environment and understanding interactions of aquatic ecosystems. The focus of current research is the effect of acidic precipitation and includes monitoring water systems and aquatic organisms. These experiments are a continuation of a 10-year acid rain study. Interns will focus on the relationship among acid rain, transient pH changes, and pond biota.

HOW TO APPLY

Download the application at http://www.bio.umb. edu/Documents/2_application.doc or call or e-mail the lab for a hard copy. Send a completed application form to the preceding address, along with the following: a resume; a letter describing your background, career goals, interests in biology, and preferences among listed research topics; a current undergraduate transcript; and letters from two faculty members familiar with your academic performance.

UNIVERSITY OF MASSACHUSETTS MEDICAL SCHOOL SUMMER ENRICHMENT PROGRAM

Office of Outreach Programs
University of Massachusetts Medical School
55 Lake Avenue North
Worcester, MA 01655
(877) 395-3149
http://www.umassmed.edu/outreach/sep.cfm

What You Can Earn: Upon successful completion of the program, each participant will receive a stipend and a certificate of achievement.
Application Deadlines: February 15.
Educational Experience: Sophomore and junior undergraduate college students interested in health careers. You must have completed a minimum of eight credit hours of organic chemistry (desirable) and 30 hours of college work.
Requirements: Must be either a Massachusetts resident or attending a Massachusetts college or university and be designated underrepresented. (Underrepresented individuals include those from economically disadvantaged backgrounds, first-generation college graduates, or underrepresented minorities in medicine, nursing, and biomedical research.) All participants are required to stay in the dormitory.

OVERVIEW

This is a four-week residential program designed to reach and encourage students early enough in their academic careers and to help them increase their qualifications for admission to graduate and medical schools.

It seeks to increase the number of underrepresented individuals successfully entering the health profession and biomedical research. Underrepresented individuals include those from economically disadvantaged backgrounds, first-generation college graduates, or underrepresented minorities in medicine, nursing, and biomedical research. The program helps students make the adjustment from an undergraduate experience to professional school. The tuition-free, four week program includes enrichment classes in science, seminars, and lectures. Additionally, the program offers participants the opportunity to interact daily with medical students, scientists, physicians, and other healthcare professionals.

The SEP is held Monday through Friday from 8:30 A.M. to 5:00 P.M. from early June through July 1. The SEP provides participants with medical and graduate school admission requirements and an opportunity to become familiar with a professional school setting. Academic enrichment focuses on communication skills, study skills, time management, and test-taking skills. Science enrichment focuses on physics and its application to physiology. All participants receive cardiopulmonary resuscitation (CPR) certification. Step-by-step sessions on completing the application process and writing a personal statement for the American Medical College Admissions Service (AMCAS) are presented. Practice medical-school interviews and workshops on financing a graduate/professional education are also offered.

HOUSING

The University of Massachusetts Medical School does not have dormitories. Participants are housed in dormitories at local colleges.

HOW TO APPLY

You can download a copy of the application at https://www.umassmed.edu/outreach/apply/sepapp.cfm.hr. Required supplemental documentation includes an official college transcript, three letters of recommendation (two from faculty), a GPA calculation sheet (available online at https://www.umassmed.edu/outreach/apply/sepapp.cfm.hr), and a resume and a personal statement discussing briefly your background, tentative career plans, and explaining any unusual aspects of your preparation and record.

Each application will be reviewed during the month of March by the selection committee; face-to-face interviews may be conducted by the program coordinator. Students will be notified of their selection during the month of April.

For assistance with the application process, call the office of outreach programs at the University of Massachusetts Medical School (Worcester) at (508) 856-2707 or (toll free) (877) 395-3149 (press 2).

UNIVERSITY OF MASSACHUSETTS MEDICAL SCHOOL UNDERGRADUATE SUMMER NIH RESEARCH FELLOWSHIP PROGRAM

University of Massachusetts Medical School
Office of Outreach Programs
55 Lake Avenue North, Room S1-842
Worcester, MA 01655
(508) 856-2707; toll free: 877-395-3149, press 2
Fax: (508) 856-6540
http://www.umassmed.edu/outreach/sep.cfm

What You Can Earn: $4,000 plus subsidized housing at about $50 a week at local dormitories, plus travel to Worcester up to $500.
Application Deadlines: March 15.
Educational Experience: College undergraduates.
Requirements: Must be U.S. citizens or permanent residents of the United States; must be minority; immunization records and physical exam required.

OVERVIEW
The University of Massachusetts Medical School NIH Summer Research Fellowship Program offers a noncredit, 10-week structured research experience from early June to mid-August as a way of providing minority undergraduate students exposure to opportunities in biomedical research. The program consists of hands-on laboratory research experience with an investigator serving as a mentor, role model, and adviser.

As an intern in this program, you'll get in-depth exposure to the actual practice of scientific research; the university hopes that the excitement, challenge, and creativity of the enterprise will convince you to consider basic research in the sciences as a viable career choice.

You'll be placed in laboratories for 10 weeks at the University of Massachusetts Medical Center with an investigator serving as a mentor, role model, and advisor. As an intern here, you'll be required to attend all seminars, lectures, group discussions, brown-bag luncheons, socials, and field trips. You'll also need to create and present a professionally prepared scientific poster.

HOW TO APPLY
Applications must be submitted online at https://www.umassmed.edu/outreach/apply/srfpapp.cfm.

UNIVERSITY OF TEXAS-HOUSTON HEALTH SCIENCE CENTER SUMMER RESEARCH PROGRAM

University of Texas HSC at Houston— Medical School
Summer Research Program
6431 Fannin St., JJL 450

Houston, TX 77030
(713) 500-3192
summer.research@uth.tmc.edu
http://www.med.uth.tmc.edu/srp/ug.htm

What You Can Earn: $2500 stipend.
Application Deadlines: Mid-February.
Educational Experience: College sophomores, juniors, and nongraduating seniors who have at least 12 hours in a science discipline. With AP credit, freshman can apply to the program. Undergraduate freshman who successfully completed the UT-Houston Summer Program for High School Students may apply.
Requirements: Must be a U.S. citizen or an international student enrolled at an accredited undergraduate institution in the U.S. All undergraduate students must be 18 years of age by the start of the program and must be able to work at least 40 hours a week in a research lab.

OVERVIEW

UT-Houston is a large academic institution located in the Texas Medical Center near Houston's museum district and includes six schools: medical, dental, nursing, biomedical sciences, public health, and allied health sciences. Each year, about 60 undergraduate students from Texas and across the nation spend 10 weeks during the summer gaining intensive hands-on laboratory experience under the direction of seasoned faculty researchers and teachers. All undergraduate students perform at least 40 hours per week in a research lab.

In addition, interns also attend weekly, one-hour seminars on cutting-edge biomedical research topics. At the conclusion of the 10-week program, students write a brief abstract, listing their name and a description of their project, for inclusion in the annual UT-Houston Summer Research Program Abstracts. Students will be provided with instructions and an outline and will have faculty help in preparing their abstract.

HOW TO APPLY

To apply, complete an on-line application (no paper applications will be accepted) at http://www.med.uth.tmc.edu/srp/appprocess.htm. In addition to the application, you should have original transcripts, a 250-word personal statement to be sent by e-mail, and two letters of reference. These can be sent by e-mail but must come directly from you.

U.S. DEPARTMENT OF ENERGY'S SCIENCE UNDERGRADUATE LAB INTERNSHPS (SULI)

Department of Energy
http://www.scied.science.doe.gov/SciEd/erulf/about/html

What You Can Earn: $400 a week, plus housing allowances (or direct housing) and transportation; round trip travel costs are paid for students who live more than 50 miles away; local transportation is provided.
Application Deadlines: Naval Reactor lab, November 15.
Educational Experience: Must be currently enrolled as an undergraduate student with a cumulative GPA of 2.5 or above. Students majoring in natural science, engineering, mathematics, or computer science have the best chance of being selected.
Requirements: Must be interested in a career in science, technology, engineering, or mathematics; be at least 18 years of age at the start of the program; be a U.S. citizen or permanent resident alien; and have health insurance. Students are required to participate for the full term of the program.

OVERVIEW

The U.S. Department of Energy's (DOE) Science Undergraduate Laboratory internships are available at a number of national laboratories (described below) and at DOE headquarters.

Interns may choose to work in a variety of basic scientific research programs, including physical and life sciences, mathematics, computer science, and engineering. Also available are applied research programs related to coal, conservation, environmental impact and technology, fission, or fusion technology.

This program places students in paid internships in science and engineering at any of several DOE facilities. As an intern in one of these labs, you'll work with scientists or engineers on projects related to the laboratories' research programs; each lab offers different research opportunities.

The lab summer programs last from late May to mid-August; fall programs run from August through December, and spring programs from January through May. The exact start date will depend on the laboratory and will be given to participants who have been accepted at that specific laboratory. Participants should expect to spend more than 40 hours per week and more than eight hours a day in activities or research related to their internships. Some of the labs described below offer only SULI internships during the summer; others also accept interns for the fall or spring terms.

Both you and your mentor will be asked jointly to prepare a research paper and abstract by the end of the appointment. Some laboratories have poster sessions for students or require oral presentations at the end of the appointment.

Ames Laboratory

Scientists at this lab research energy-related problems by exploring chemical, engineering, materials and mathematical sciences, and physics. Established in the 1940s with the successful development of the most efficient process to produce high-purity uranium metal for atomic energy, Ames Lab now pursues much broader priorities than the materials research for which it is so well known. Lab scientists are actively involved in research, science education, and the development of applied technologies. Integrated within a university environment, the lab is located in Ames, Iowa, on the campus of Iowa State University.

Argonne National Laboratory

This lab performs a variety of research in four basic areas. Its basic science research includes experimental and theoretical work in materials science, physics, chemistry, biology, high-energy physics, mathematics, and computer science. The lab's scientific facilities department designs, builds, and operates sophisticated research facilities that would be too expensive for a single company or university to maintain. The lab's energy resources programs help ensure a reliable supply of efficient and clean energy for the future and include developing advanced batteries and fuel cells, as well as advanced electrical power generation systems. The environmental management area includes research into alternative energy systems; environmental risk and economic impact assessments; hazardous waste site analysis and remediation planning; electrometallurgical treatment to prepare spent nuclear fuel for disposal; and new technologies for decontaminating and decommissioning aging nuclear reactors. The Argonne lab is located about 25 miles southwest of Chicago's Loop.

Brookhaven National Laboratory

Scientists at this major multidisciplinary laboratory have earned four Nobel Prizes, as they carry out basic and applied world-class research in physical, biomedical, and environmental sciences, as well as energy technologies. Brookhaven sponsors programs for students and faculty in physics, biology, chemistry, medical science, and environmental science.

As an intern in this lab, your duties may range from working with physicists to investigate the nature of matter at its newest accelerator to investigating the structure of proteins with biologists. Brookhaven National Laboratory is located on Long Island.

DOE Headquarters—Naval Reactors Internship

If you're interested in nuclear engineering and reactor design, the internship at the Naval Reactors (SULI-NR) might be of interest. These internships are available only in Washington, D.C., during the summer term.

Candidates must be U.S. citizens in their junior or senior year, working toward a major in aerospace, ceramic, chemical, civil, computer, electrical, mechanical, metallurgical, nuclear, or optical engineering; chemistry; computer science; materials science; or physics.

The internship at Naval Reactors doesn't involve lab research but instead focuses on program management and science policy. As an intern here, you'll spend 10 weeks during the summer working with the engineers, scientists, and naval officers responsible for the design, construction, maintenance, refueling, and decommissioning of nuclear propulsion systems used in U.S. Navy ships and submarines.

Fermi National Accelerator Laboratory

Scientists here conduct basic research in high-energy physics, in a lab that houses the world's highest-energy particle accelerator, used by more than 2,500 scientists to study the structure of matter and the forces that govern the universe. Experiments at Fermilab can involve hundreds of scientists from all over the world who work for years designing and constructing large detectors and then analyzing the resultant data. As an intern here, you'll get the chance to work on projects that support these particle-physics experiments in areas such as engineering, applied physics, and computing. In addition, the Fermilab site offers the chance to study the environment, particularly in the hundreds of acres of restored tall-grass prairie. Located in Batavia, Illinois, Fermilab is 30 miles west of Chicago's loop.

Idaho National Laboratory

As an intern at this multipurpose national laboratory, you'll help participate in specialized science and engineering solutions for the DOE. This lab offers research opportunities in the environment, subsurface science, nuclear energy systems, advanced computing and collaboration, advanced waste management solutions, biotechnology, and engineering. INL specializes in environmental management and stewardship. In partnership with Argonne National Laboratory, it also specializes in nuclear energy. It is home to one of the largest concentrations of technical professionals in the northern Rocky Mountain region. Located in Idaho, the INL covers 889 square miles of the Snake River Plain between Idaho Falls and Arco, Idaho. Offices and laboratories are also in Idaho Falls, Idaho.

Lawrence Berkeley National Laboratory

Lawrence Berkeley National Laboratory's research and development includes new energy technologies and environmental solutions with a focus on energy efficiency, electric reliability, carbon management and global climate change, and fusion. Frontier research experiences exist in nanoscience, genomics and cancer research, advanced computing, and observing matter and energy at the most fundamental level in the universe. Ernest Orlando Lawrence founded Berkeley Lab in 1931. Lawrence invented the cyclotron, which led to the Golden Age of particle physics, the foundation of modern nuclear science, and revolutionary discoveries about the nature of the universe. Berkeley Lab's Advanced Light Source is its premier national facility located centrally on the lab site overlooking the San Francisco Bay.

Lawrence Livermore National Laboratory

This research and development lab focuses on national security and the safety and reliability of the nation's nuclear weapons and applies its expertise to prevent the spread and use of weapons of mass destruction while strengthening U.S. security. Scientists at this lab study programs in advanced defense technologies, energy, environment, biosciences, and basic science, serving as a resource to the U.S. government, to industry, and to academia. The lab is located east of San Francisco.

Los Alamos National Laboratory

At this lab, located in the Jemez Mountains of northern New Mexico, you'll have the chance to work at a multidisciplinary research facility with a team of top scientists and engineers on critical issues involving national security, environment, infrastructure, and security. Internship opportunities are available in a variety of areas, including biology; chemistry; computer science; physics; mathematics; materials science; environmental science; and chemical, civil, computer, electrical, mechanical, nuclear, and software engineering. Candidates should be independent problem solvers who can function well on a team and possess good communication skills.

National Renewable Energy Laboratory

Interns at this leading lab for renewable energy research will help develop new energy technologies to benefit both the environment and the economy. Scientists at NREL conduct research in more than 50 areas, including photovoltaics; wind turbine and blade research; energy; biomass-derived fuels and chemicals; energy-efficient buildings; advanced vehicles; industrial processes; solar thermal systems; hydrogen technologies fuel cells; superconductivity; geothermal; distributed energy resources; measurement and testing of renewable energy systems; hybrid systems; basic energy research; and waste-to-energy technologies. The lab's 300-acre main campus lies at the foot of South Table Mountain in Golden, CO, a western suburb of Denver.

Oak Ridge National Laboratory

The largest of DOE's national laboratories, Oak Ridge develops new energy sources, technologies, and materials in the biological, chemical, computational, engineering, environmental, physical, and social sciences. As an intern here, you might help work in a variety of areas, including materials science and engineering; neutron science; life sciences; computer and computational science; environmental sciences; chemical sciences and chemical engineering technology; fusion science and technology nuclear physics; instrumentation and measurement science; and technology social sciences. Oak Ridge is located in East Tennessee, about 25 miles from Knox-

ville, near the Great Smoky Mountains National Park.

Pacific Northwest National Laboratory

A world leader in environmental science research, this lab has built an international reputation in environmental sciences by focusing on chemistry, biology, computer sciences, and a wide range of other fields. If you intern here, you may choose an appointment in atmospheric science and global change; computational sciences; experimental chemistry; marine sciences; molecular biology; environmental studies; remediation; environmental microbiology; wildlife and fisheries biology; materials research; process science and engineering; economics; or political science. The lab is located at the confluence of the Columbia, Snake, and Yakima rivers in Washington.

Princeton Plasma Physics Laboratory

This Collaborative National Center for Plasma and Fusion Science focuses on developing an attractive fusion energy source, in addition to conducting research in plasma science. This lab supports graduate education primarily through Princeton University's Program in Plasma Physics in the astrophysical sciences department. In addition, through the interdepartmental program in Plasma Science and Technology, this lab supports students in affiliated engineering and science departments pursuing research in plasma physics.

Stanford Linear Accelerator Center

This basic research laboratory is operated for the DOE by Stanford University, known internationally for its research in particle physics, accelerator physics and engineering, and the applications of synchrotron radiation to studies of matter at the atomic and molecular scale with a wide variety of applications in biochemistry, materials science, and environmental science as well as in fundamental condensed-matter physics. Astrophysics is a relatively new area of interest at this lab; a detector for the planned Gamma Large Area Space Telescope (GLAST) is currently being built there.

Candidates for an internship at this lab should be majoring in physics, chemistry, biochemistry, biophysics, computer science, or electrical/mechanical engineering; at least one year of college-level physics is required. Interns here are housed as a group on the Stanford campus, with access to Stanford facilities for the summer. The lab itself is located about two miles from the central campus of Stanford University. As an intern here, you'll be working in some aspect of the lab's experimental program. Particle physics experiments are large-scale, multiyear projects, but interns can get involved in many aspects of detector upgrades or maintenance, data analysis, or simulation studies. Computer science students may be placed in projects related to data handling and/or simulation.

Accelerator physics includes the maintenance and upgrades of existing on-site facilities; design studies for future facilities; and research on novel accelerator designs. Some electrical or mechanical engineering internship projects are available in this area.

Synchrotron radiation provides an intense photon beam with a continuous spectral distribution extending from IR to hard X-rays. A variety of spectroscopic and imaging techniques allow this radiation to be used to determine structural and electronic properties of various materials such as microstructures, ultra-thin layers or small clusters. The Stanford Synchrotron Radiation Laboratory (SSRL) is the division of SLAC responsible for synchrotron radiation studies and has internship openings for physics, chemistry, and biochemistry as well as for biophysics majors. High-intensity synchrotron radiation can be applied to detect trace impurities on Si wafer surfaces and to determine the structure of protein molecules or amorphous materials.

In biology, form and function are closely related, even at the molecular scale. Studies of the structure of biological macromolecules from proteins lead to better understanding of disease processes and the ability to design treatments.

Materials science studies with synchrotron radiation range from surface science to X-ray physics with applications for the structure of metal, metal oxide, and semiconductor surfaces and interfaces as well as their interactions with small molecules or chemical reactivates in the gas phase.

The ability to track the migration of pollutants such as heavy metals in the environment can allow development of targeted remediation efforts. High-intensity synchrotron radiation enables the detection of very low concentration pollutants with high sensitivity, which allows more accurate tracking.

Astrophysics opportunities at SLAC all involve the GLAST project scientists. In the future, a new astrophysics institute will offer further opportunities. GLAST will study the array of gamma-ray sources in the universe with improved sensitivity and improved localization. At present, the very energetic gamma-ray burst sources that are seen are poorly understood. GLAST can contribute much to understanding these effects. Projects may range from analysis of data from previous related experiments to testing of GLAST components.

Thomas Jefferson National Accelerator Facility

This basic research laboratory is designed to probe the nucleus of the atom as a way of learning more about quarks, the particles that make up protons and neutrons in the atom's nucleus. The accelerator delivers a continuous beam to a target. When the beam collides with its target, particles scatter. By studying the speed, direction, and energy of the scattered particles, scientists learn more about the nucleus. This lab is located in Newport News, Virginia, between Williamsburg and Norfolk/Virginia Beach on the coast of Virginia between the deep-channeled James and York Rivers and the Chesapeake Bay.

HOW TO APPLY

To apply for any of the DOE lab programs, submit an electronic application at the Department of Energy Web site at http://www.scied.science.doe.gov/SciEd/erulf/about.html.

You must select a specific term when you apply. The application process runs on a 12-month cycle, which means that applications open on June 1 and close around May 20. To increase your chances of being selected, it is a good idea to select at least two lab choices on your application.

References should be submitted by someone familiar with your academic achievements and your academic ability, such as college faculty members who teach science, technology, engineering, or mathematics courses. However, you may use former high school teachers, lab assistants, teaching assistants, or employers (especially if they are in a research setting).

For summer interns, selection will consist of two rounds. In round one, your first-choice lab will view your application. In round two, both your first- and second-choice laboratories will look at your application. Throughout the process, you can receive only one offer. If you're selected in the first round, your application will not appear in the second round.

Fall and spring semesters have an open process with no rounds. Your application will be judged on your educational experience, research interests, and references. Researchers are looking for someone interested in the kind of research they are conducting and who will benefit from their expertise and facilities.

Naval Reactors Internship

To apply, complete the application for the summer term and check the box in question #22 to indicate that your application should include consideration for the SULI-NR program. Students who are not selected for SULI-NR will automatically have their completed applications evaluated for the standard SULI program at one of the other DOE national labs.

VIRGINIA INSTITUTE OF MARINE SCIENCE INTERNSHIP

Summer Intern Program
Office of the Graduate Dean
Virginia Institute of Marine Science
Gloucester Point, VA 23062
Fax: (804) 684-7097
http://tethys.vims.edu/reu/apply.cfm

What You Can Earn: A stipend of $3075 for the 10-week program (paid on the first and 16th of the month), housing in a dormitory on the main campus, and transportation between campuses. In addition, most interns will receive travel costs to and from the program.
Application Deadlines: Mid-February.
Educational Experience: College juniors and seniors are preferred because of their better course preparation, but all students, including those traditionally underrepresented in the marine sciences, are encouraged to apply.
Requirements: None specified.

OVERVIEW

The Virginia Institute of Marine Science is one of the largest coastal and estuarine science institutions in the world, with more than 65 faculty members and a graduate student body of more than 130. With its state-of-the-art oceanographic instrumentation and analytical facilities, a large fleet of coastal research vessels, a world-class marine science library, and a location near a variety of habitats ranging from freshwater tributaries to the coastal ocean, it can make a great summer internship experience! The School of Marine Science is a part of the College of William and Mary.

Each year, 12 to 16 undergraduates with the Summer Intern Program study with faculty mentors for a summer research experience. As a summer intern, you'll experience an individualized research experience along with a variety of group activities. You'll work closely with a mentor and often within the context of a research team, and you'll be expected to develop an individual project. Depending on the project, the summer may involve lots of hands-on experience in the field or laboratory or both. You'll have access to one of the best marine science libraries in the country, as well as extensive computer facilities. You'll be expected to work with your mentor to develop a project idea in the form of a brief research prospectus, conduct research, and then present results in a final program that is open to the VIMS community. Interns also prepare a summary research paper that is maintained in the program archives. In some cases, this has been the basis for a subsequent publication in scientific literature.

Internships are available in many areas of marine science, including biological, geological, chemical, physical, environmental science, fisheries, and management. The program is funded by the National Science Foundation's Research Experience for Undergraduates program, VIMS, The College of William and Mary, private donors, and grants to individual faculty. Potential areas of internships include the following.

Aquaculture
Cultivation of native and non-native species; effects of food quality on growth and reproduction of species in culture.

Benthic Ecology
Ecology of soft sediments, marshes, oyster reefs, or seagrass meadows; effects of pollution, nutrients, or disturbance on biodiversity and structure of invertebrate soft-sediment and vegetated communities; predator-prey interactions; effects of environmental factors growth and reproduction; effects of food-web structure on community function; bioenergetics of estuarine organisms.

Biogeochemistry and Marine or Environmental Chemistry
Cycling of carbon, nutrients, and contaminants; effects of microbial processes on carbon, nutrients, and oxygen in estuarine ecosystems; sources and characteristics of organic carbon in marine and estuarine sediments; biogeochemical processes governing the transport and fate of contaminants in the environment.

Biology, Immunology, and Disease Processes
The effects of environmental factors on disease in marine organisms; effects of nutrition and energy reserves on host/parasite interactions in shellfish and fish; and the immunological responses to disease.

Conservation Ecology
The utility of marine sanctuaries for estuarine species; ecology and restoration of seagrasses; wetland or dune restoration; index development for effective management and conservation of estuarine habitats.

Fisheries
The application of techniques in molecular biology to help resolve problems in fishery science; factors affecting the population dynamics of commercial species; biology and ecology of billfish, tunas, sharks, and turtles.

Geology/Geological Oceanography
The effects of hydrodynamics on geomorphology and particle transport in estuaries; shoreline behavior (erosional hotspots) and its relationship to underlying geology; processes controlling sediment dispersal in coastal systems.

Hydrology
The effects of the coastal landscape on groundwater processes.

Physical Oceanography
Modeling physical processes such as estuarine circulation, waves, water residence time, and sediment transport in estuaries and lagoons; interactions of physical and biological processes.

Plankton Processes
You may choose to study the ecology of microbes, phytoplankton, and zooplankton; the effects of light availability and nutrients on plankton growth rates; temporal and spatial variations in zooplankton communities in estuaries; zooplankton predator-prey interactions; effects of zooplankton nutrient and carbon cycling in marine and estuarine environments.

Policy and Management
It's not all work under a microscope—you can choose to investigate integrated coastal zone

management, integrating science, and policy and public resource management.

HOW TO APPLY
Download the application at http://tethys.vims. edu/reu/apply.cfm. After filling it out, mail the following items together in a single envelope to the preceding address.

- Two letters of recommendation in sealed, signed envelopes; these letters should be from science faculty at your college or university and should address your academic and research capabilities/potential.
- An official copy of your transcript (this may be an original released to student).

WELLESLEY COLLEGE BIOLOGICAL SCIENCES INTERNSHIP

Wellesley College
Department of Biological Sciences
106 Central Street
Wellesley, MA 02481
(781) 283-3154
Fax: (781) 283-3642
kthomason@wellesley.edu
http://www.unc.edu/pmabs/northeast/wellesley.
  html

What You Can Earn: Stipend plus housing allowance.
Application Deadlines: February 27 by 4:30 P.M.
Educational Experience: Applicants should have completed introductory biology courses and have had at least one other course in the area of specialization. Graduating seniors are ineligible. Prefer-

ence will be given to those beginning or continuing academic year independent research.
Requirements: Must be a U.S. citizen or permanent resident.

OVERVIEW
As a research intern at Wellesley, you'll help conduct research in the lab of one of the faculty advisors, participate in the group seminar-journal club and in seminars presented by biologists in research careers, attend field trips to a biotechnology company, industry, and/or ecological site, and work on a poster session in final week of project.

Participants will be expected to contact their sponsor the spring before the summer internship begins and to begin suggested readings in preparation for the summer program.

HOW TO APPLY
Download and complete an application at http://www.unc.edu/pmabs/northeast/wellesley.html. Mail it to the preceding address, along with three letters of recommendation from faculty, a resume, a personal statement, and an official transcript of grades. Be sure to note any research experience.

WHITNEY LABORATORY MARINE BIOMEDICAL RESEARCH EXPERIENCE FOR UNDERGRADUATES

Undergraduate Coordinator
The Whitney Laboratory
9505 Ocean Shore Blvd.
St. Augustine, FL 32086-8623
(904) 461-4000

Fax: (904) 461-4052

http://www.whitney.ufl.edu/reu/REUprogram.
htm

What You Can Earn: Competitive stipend, travel expenses, and housing allowance.
Application Deadlines: February 20 for the summer internship; at least two months before the start of other session internships.
Educational Experience: None specified.
Requirements: Must be a U.S. citizen or permanent resident.

OVERVIEW

The Whitney Laboratory, a research institute of the University of Florida, offers training in marine biomedical research and biotechnology to students interested in exploring careers in science. The lab provides hands-on research experience using cellular, molecular, and neurobiology.

As an intern here, in cooperation with a faculty supervisor, you'll choose a project that fits with ongoing investigations and can be completed within the 10- to 12-week training period. You may work at any time during the year, but you should plan to stay for at least 10 weeks (preferably longer).

HOW TO APPLY

To apply, first fill out the information form at http://www.whitney.ufl.edu/reu/forms.htm. The form should be submitted electronically from the Web site or faxed or mailed to the preceding address. This form helps the lab determine if you satisfy National Science Foundation requirements for funding your position and establish an address for future communication.

Next, you should submit your application materials at least two months before your anticipated starting date. These materials include:

- your resume, including a list of courses and your grades
- letters of reference from two people able to evaluate your academic performance and potential
- a letter briefly describing your interests and goals and how work at the Whitney Laboratory would help you to achieve these goals
- a list of the two or three projects (see list below) at the Whitney Laboratory that interest you the most, with an explanation of your selection.

Choose from these projects:

- physiology and biochemistry of olfaction
- structure and function of ion channels
- biochemistry of vision
- membrane transport and microanalytical technology
- synaptogenesis and synaptic physiology
- molecular and cell biology of complex systems
- molecular evolutionary ecology and marine biotechnology
- neurogenomics, nanotechnology, and neuronal evolution
- structure and function of neuropeptide receptors
- cellular neurobiology and signal transduction.

SPORTS

BOSTON CELTICS INTERNSHIP

Boston Celtics, Human Resources
151 Merrimac Street
Boston, MA 02114
Fax: (617) 722-4348
http://aol.nba.com/celtics/news/opportunities_
001019.html

What You Can Earn: Unpaid.
Application Deadlines: Rolling.
Educational Experience: Must be enrolled in a degree program as a junior or senior undergraduate or a graduate student. You must be eligible to receive course credit toward your degree for the successful completion of the internship. See individual departments for more specific requirements.
Requirements: Excellent communication, organizational, and computer skills; a serious interest in the field of the internship for which you would like to be considered; hard working, dedicated, and self-motivated; and able to function productively in a challenging environment. Prior experience in sports is preferred but not required. In addition to working the full 40-hour workweek, interns are required to work all home games; summer interns are required to work 40-hour workweeks.

OVERVIEW

A charter member of the Basketball Association of America (which evolved into the NBA), Boston flies more title banners from the rafters of its home arena than any other franchise.

The mission of the Boston Celtics internship program is to educate its participants in all aspects of operating a professional sports organization. Through observation and practical experience, interns learn how to function in a professional environment that requires a high energy level, the ability to perform under pressure, and the utilization of essential time-management skills. Through these developments, the Boston Celtics strive to prepare their interns to compete for positions in the professional sports industry.

The Celtics accept interns in marketing, sales, community relations, media relations, operations, and basketball operations departments each semester (fall lasts from September through December, spring from January through May, and summer from May through August).

Community Relations

In this department, you'll help manage and track all charitable donations and help manage various programs such as Stay in School, Read to Achieve, and community ticket programs. You'll also handle incoming inquiries for the department. For this internship, the Celtics prefer interns with experience working with nonprofit organizations and who are comfortable working with and managing children and young adults.

Corporate Sales/Business Development

As an intern in this department, you'll help provide marketing support to corporate sales and business development staff in creating sales tools to support sponsorship sales efforts. You'll help develop market research, database marketing, and sales forecasting tools, and you'll support game-night sponsorship activities. For this position, the Celtics prefer an MBA candidate or undergraduate working toward a B.S. in marketing or finance.

Information Technology

Interns here will help provide day-to-day computer support and network administration and conduct general OS, application, phone/voice mail and e-mail administration. You must be a candidate for a bachelor's degree in computer science or electrical engineering, with proficiency in Windows hardware and software support with basic networking.

Marketing

As an intern here, you'll get experience in marketing, promotions, and event management. You'll help with coordinating game operations, half-time entertainment, game-night giveaways, and in-game entertainment, and you'll be responsible for assisting with some administrative duties.

Media Relations
Interns in this department help staff with all duties relating to media relations, help disseminate media information, and work on publications and Web sites. You also must be ready to assist with any other duties as needed.

Sales
In this internship, you'll help support account executives with day-to-day activities and game-night duties and check out new leads for group sales via the Internet. You'll also use the ticketing system and database to help handle incoming calls and inquiries, coordinate mailings designated by sales staff and management, process payments and ticket requests from existing clients, and help with season-ticket holders and ticketing events. You'll also help support the sales and marketing department on game nights.

Sponsorship Sales and Service
As an intern here, you'll help create and prepare sales presentations, create and maintain material directory, and update and maintain a collateral tracking system for sponsor programs and sponsor review books. You'll also help with game-night sponsor hospitality events and promotions and other game-night sponsor needs; help with sponsor communications regarding ad materials, specs and logos; update and post sponsor content on Celtics.com; monitor execution of in-arena sponsored elements; and maintain sponsor storage areas.

Statistics
Interns in this department will help design and execute statistical analysis, gather and format data, decide an analysis approach, execute analysis, and interpret results. Candidates should have a degree in, or be a candidate for a degree in, statistics or another major with focus on statistical analysis

(such as econometrics). You also must have experience in executing successful statistical-analysis projects.

Ticket Operations
Interns here will help resolve client concerns or issues related to their accounts, provide operational support related to all season and group-ticket accounts, maintain computerized records of all season and group accounts, and help with ticket promotions and community events, as well as other special events as requested.

HOW TO APPLY
To apply for an internship, forward your resume and cover letter to the preceding address.

CBS-4 (KCNC-TV) SPORTS DEPARTMENT INTERNSHIP

KCNC-TV Sports Internship Coordinator
1044 Lincoln Street
Denver, CO 80203
(303) 830-6464; (800) 444-5262
Fax: (303) 830-6593
http://news4colorado.com/employment/local_
    story_116121756

What You Can Earn: Unpaid.
Application Deadlines: January 1 for spring session; April 1 for summer session; August 1 for fall session.
Educational Experience: A junior or senior in college.
Requirements: Minimum GPA of 2.5 for fall and spring application and 3.0 for summer application; three nine-hour days a week for three months.

OVERVIEW

CBS-4 is Channel 4 (KCNC-TV) in Denver, Colorado. As an intern in the sports department, you'll be responsible for logging sporting events, helping producers and anchors produce a newscast and shadowing a reporter on stories.

HOW TO APPLY

To apply, mail an application to the preceding address (e-mailed applications will not be accepted). An application must include a cover letter, resume, official transcript, letter of recommendation from a professor or previous employer, and a letter from a different professor than indicated above (or an academic advisor) stating that the internship is for credit at the school you are attending.

CHICAGO BEARS GRAPHIC DESIGN INTERNSHIP

Chicago Bears
Halas Hall
1000 Football Drive
Lake Forest, IL 60045
(847) 295-6600
http://www.chicagobears.com

What You Can Earn: Unpaid.
Application Deadlines: May 31.
Educational Experience: College student seeking a degree in graphic design.
Requirements: Knowledge of the printing process and working knowledge of Quark, Adobe Illustrator, Adobe Photoshop and Adobe InDesign in a Mac environment. Must be able to take direction and balance multiple projects; exceptional communication and organizational skills, commitment to quality creative work, and ability to meet daily deadlines are required.

OVERVIEW

The Chicago Bears were one of the original teams in the National Football League (NFL) when it formed in 1933. Coached by the legendary George Halas from 1933 until his retirement in 1968, the Bears have won six NFL championships and are represented in the Pro Football Hall of Fame by 26 players.

The Chicago Bears are offering an internship in graphic design within their Internet/new media department. Interns will collaborate with the director of creative services to ensure that the appropriate message is communicated and the brand image is consistent. Responsibilities include design of marketing collateral, logos, advertising, Web graphics, newsletter, magazines, and other Chicago Bears print and Web media.

HOW TO APPLY

Apply online at http://footballjobs.teamworkonline.com/teamwork/jobs/apply.cfm?jobid=5659&aid=1459&supcat=325&subcat=2211.

CHICAGO BULLS TICKET SALES REPRESENTATIVE INTERNSHIP

Chicago Bulls, Internship Coordinator
1901 W. Madison Street
Chicago, IL 60612-2459
http://aol.nba.com/bulls/news/internship_010328.html

What You Can Earn: Minimum wage as a draw against commissions earned ($6.50 per hour), a flat fee tiered commission structure for all sales that exceed the minimum wage draw, and weekly/monthly bonus potential. Parking and lunch at the United Center are provided daily, free of charge, and employees will receive two complimentary tickets for each home Bulls game.

Application Deadlines: Rolling.

Educational Experience: A four-year college degree. Sports administration, business, advertising, marketing, communications, or liberal arts degrees are preferred.

Requirements: An interest in sports marketing or a career in sales, excellent verbal and written skills, willingness to be a team player, a positive attitude, self-confidence, professionalism, integrity, motivation, and a very strong work ethic. Sales experience, although not required, is very helpful.

OVERVIEW

The Chicago Bulls made their NBA debut in 1966, but their most significant move in came in the 1984 college player draft, when the team selected Michael Jordan from the University of North Carolina. Jordan, arguably the greatest player in NBA history, led the Bulls to six league championships in eight years.

The Bulls offer internships for ticket representatives, to be responsible for soliciting new season and group ticket business by telephone; each intern is expected to make a minimum of 50 new phone calls a day (leads are provided). Interns also will handle all incoming requests for season and group ticket information and provide additional support to the ticket and marketing departments when necessary.

The internship begins in July and ends in February, Monday through Friday from 9:00 A.M. until 5:00 P.M. Although there are no guarantees for full-time employment once the internship ends, individuals who excel are considered for future positions or placement with another organization.

HOW TO APPLY

Send a cover letter and resume to the preceding address.

COLORADO SPRINGS SKY SOX INTERNSHIP

Colorado Springs Sky Sox Baseball Club
4385 Tutt Boulevard
Colorado Springs, CO 80922
(719) 597-1449, ext. 351
http://www.skysox.com/subpage.
asp?page=internships#

What You Can Earn: Unpaid.
Application Deadlines: Rolling.
Educational Experience: None specified.
Requirements: See specific requirements for individual internships below.

OVERVIEW

The Sky Sox are the Triple-A affiliate of the Colorado Rockies that play in the Pacific Coast League. Formerly the Hawaii Islanders, the Sky Sox moved to Colorado Springs in January of 1988. They play their home games at Sky Sox Stadium, located 10 miles east of downtown Colorado Springs; their offices are located in the stadium complex. There are three classifications of minor league baseball: Triple A, Double A and Single A. The Pacific Coast League consists of Triple-A teams, one level below the major leagues. The Sky Sox have been affiliated with the Colorado Rockies of the National League since 1993.

The Sky Sox offer the opportunity to learn the business of baseball from the ground up to seven full-time interns. Internships are available for a season, all beginning in early January and ending sometime in September. The internships include corporate sales (advertising, promotional sponsorships, ticket plans), preseason ticket-book sales (Bonus Books), group sales, and work in one of the following areas: public relations, promotions, operations, or box office.

The Sky Sox expect that interns consider themselves a part of the staff. Within minor league baseball, the front-office staff performs duties at all levels of management and maintenance. From time to time, staff members will be required to help sell tickets, help in the on-site restaurant, interact with players and coaches, and pull tarp over field and other tasks, in addition to their primary duties. Everyone working in minor league baseball wears many different hats, and a willingness to go above and beyond one's normal duties is expected.

Box Office

During the preseason, you'll help with advertising and group sales and prepare ticket packages. During the season, you'll help handle box office ticket transactions; prepare ticket packages; print group tickets; schedule birthday parties; handle all pass lists (front office, home clubhouse, and visiting clubhouse); coordinate ticket outlet distribution; reconcile daily tickets and cash; and handle group sales and front desk shifts.

Candidates should have the ability to solve problems, good interpersonal skills, the ability to think on one's feet, and basic computer skills (Word and Excel).

Group Sales

During the preseason, you'll help with group sales, corporate event planning, and ticket office and catering operations. Sales are the highest priority during this time. During the season, you'll also help with printing of group tickets, daily coordination of group events including set-up, client support, and customer relations.

Candidates should be able to solve problems and think quickly, have good inter-personal skills, be self-motivated., and have good basic math and computer skills (Word and Excel).

Operations

During the preseason, you'll help with advertising and group sales and help hire and train game-day employees in March and April. During the season, you'll help manage game-day employees/stadium staff, supervise parking lot operations, work with grounds crew on daily game-day field preparation, do stadium maintenance, upkeep stadium sky box

suites, set up closed circuit TV system, and handle group sales and front desk shifts.

Candidates should have basic mechanical ability and a willingness to get their hands dirty, good interpersonal skills, and self-motivation.

Promotions

During the preseason, interns will be responsible for advertising sales; group sales; planning/coordinating the season in-game promotional schedule; maintaining the fan rewards program database; preparing memorabilia for the Sky Sox Youth Foundation Auctions; and collecting ad copy for scorecard/insert.

During the season, you'll help participate in daily promotional meetings; coordinate with corporate sponsors; prepare for daily promotional activities (such as on-field games/activities, pregame giveaways, and upkeep of promotional items/equipment); schedule concourse table space and national anthem singers; maintain the fan rewards program database; and coordinate with local schedule outlets.

Candidates should be able to multitask, have good interpersonal skills and problem-solving capabilities, and be able to think on their feet.

Public Relations

As an intern in this area, you'll work from 8:30 A.M. to 5:00 P.M. during preseason in advertising sales, group sales, preparing team publications (media guide, program, and season ticket holder newsletter), and collecting sponsor ad copy (print/radio). Corporate sales are the highest priority during this time. In-season duties include updating daily statistical books; preparing daily game/media notes; maintaining working press box; coordinating with local/national media outlets; writing press releases; updating the official team Web site (http://www.skysox. com); operating souvenir sales carts (every other game); coordinating with flagship station on radio spot rotation; and shifts in group sales and front desk.

Candidates should have good writing, interpersonal, and computer skills (Word, Excel,

PageMaker, and Web site maintenance software), and be self-motivated.

HOW TO APPLY

Download an application at http://www.skysox. com/content/intern_application.pdf and submit it to the preceding address.

INDIANA PACERS INTERNSHIP

Indiana Pacers, Internship Coordinator
1 Conseco Court
125 S. Pennsylvania Street
Indianapolis, IN 46204
(317) 917-2500

What You Can Earn: Unpaid; commission for sales internships.
Application Deadlines: See specific internships below.
Educational Experience: See specific internships below.
Requirements: See specific internships below.

OVERVIEW

The Indiana Pacers joined the NBA for the 1966–67 season. The team was one of four from the rival American Basketball Association to be accepted into the NBA when the two leagues merged. After struggling for their first 15 seasons, the Pacers became one of the top teams in the Eastern Conference, reaching the conference finals five times and the NBA finals in 2000.

Those selected to be a Pacers intern will acquire practical knowledge through hands-on experience and will gain the invaluable skills necessary to compete for jobs in the sports industry when their program is completed. The Indiana Pacers offer internship positions in ticket sales; premium sales; event planning; game operations; broadcast production; sponsorship sales and promotions; community relations; media relations; basketball video; and sports marketing. While you will see some similarities in their descriptions, most of their internship positions are different in their responsibilities and time commitments.

Athletic Training

Interns in this area will help the training staff of the Indiana Pacers run their department and will assist in the daily operation of the department. Special projects will be assigned. Interns in this area should be pursuing a degree in physical therapy or athletic training.

Broadcast Production

These interns will help the broadcast department log all Pacers game and production tapes; maintain the video edit suite, video library, and tape stock; and serve as production assistant for all Pacers programming.

Interns will work at least 20 hours a week in one of three sessions: September through December, January through April, or June through August. The production intern must be available in four-hour shifts (minimum) and during some home games.

Interns will be responsible for logging all Pacers game and production tapes and maintaining the video edit suite, video library, and tape stock and will serve as production assistant for all Pacers programming, including Pacers television network broadcasts, Pacers cable, and Pacers Full-Court TV show. Interns also may help with video research, script writing, and grip work for location shoots.

Candidates should be majoring in video production or related majors or have production backgrounds. Candidates also should have an excellent attitude, extensive knowledge of basketball and the NBA, good written and verbal communication skills, and the willingness and ability to work flexible schedules. Knowledge of broadcast cameras, VTRs, editing systems, character generators, lighting, and computers is desired.

Community Relations

Interns in Community Relations will assist this department in planning and implementing community-related events, help with game day/night responsibilities, and perform project work for the community relations department and the Pacers Foundation.

Positions are for 40 hours a week, from either September through January (first half of the season), January through May (second half of the season), or May through August. Dates are somewhat flexible.

Interns in this area contribute to the writing of in-game announcements, public service announcements, and so on for the community relations department and Pacers Foundation. You'll also help coordinate and implement community relations programs and Pacers Foundation events, help coordinate internal autograph sessions, and work some game nights and help the department with implementation of game day/night elements. You'll also report on and research information pertaining to the community relations department and Foundation and help other front-office departments as needed. General office duties will include data entry; answering phones; copying; filing; faxing; maintaining mailing lists; collating; distributing packets and mass mailings; responding to fan mail; and helping with various aspects of the newsletter.

You should be creative and detail oriented and have excellent organizational skills, strong written and verbal skills, excellent computer skills, and the ability to work a flexible schedule, including some weekends and evenings. The ability to meet deadlines and work on multiple tasks in a timely manner is preferred, as is some experience in special events planning.

Marketing, sports administration, communications, or related business majors are preferred.

Community Relations – Indiana Fever

Interns in this area will help the community relations department plan and implement community relations events for the Indiana Fever. Interns will be involved with grassroots marketing efforts geared to increase interest in the WNBA and Fever, both during the season and off-season. Interns will have game day/night responsibilities (if applicable) as well as perform project work for the department.

You'll work 40 hours a week during one of three sessions: August through January, January through May, or May through August. Dates are somewhat flexible.

As an intern here, you'll help coordinate internal autograph sessions and work some game nights and help the community relations department implement game day/night elements. You'll also help other front-office departments as needed and help coordinate and implement community relations programs and Pacers Foundation events. In addition, you may report on and research information pertaining to community relations and the Pacers Foundation, perform general office duties, and contribute to the writing of in-game announcements and public service announcements.

Candidates should have strong written, verbal, computer, and organizational skills, and be creative, detail oriented, and able to work flexible schedules (with some evenings and weekends), meet deadlines, and work on multiple tasks in a timely manner. Candidates should be current undergraduate or graduate students majoring in marketing, sports administration, communications, or business; some experience in special events planning is helpful.

Event Coordinator/Meeting Planner

Interns in the event department will assist managers in event planning to schedule, plan, and implement all types of events taking place at Conseco Fieldhouse. You'll be responsible for dealing with patrons at events and working with event coordinators on production details. You'll work with the box office, deal with various promoters and meeting planners, and work with promoters and agents regarding event scheduling and event calendars. You'll help input data to maintain accuracy of calendars and scheduling and do general office work such as data entry, answering phones, copying, filing, faxing, collating, and distributing departmental information.

Internships in this position run January through May, May through July, and August through December and are 40 hours a week (including weekends and evenings; schedule must be flexible). Candidates should have some production knowledge (concert; radio; television; theatre; game operations); be computer literate with knowledge of Windows, Excel, the Internet, and e-mail, and have strong organizational skills. You must be able to track and manage details of events from start to finish and work with managers to make events run smoothly. Excellent communication and organizational skills are required.

Candidates should be majoring in sports marketing, recreation, or hospitality. Professional volunteer or student event coordination experience and work experience in an entertainment or sports venue are preferred.

Fever Video

This intern will help record Indiana Fever practices for Fever coaching staff. Interns will assist with basic edits and maintenance of tape stock and video room. Fever video interns must be available to assist with Indiana Fever home games and therefore must be flexible with schedule (including weekends). Extensive knowledge of Microsoft Windows programs is required. Candidates must be eager to learn and operate various types of digital-editing equipment. Basketball/coaching experience is a plus.

Game Operations and Promotions

Interns in this department will help coordinate talent bookings for Pacers and/or Fever home games, help with the Pacers and Fever mascots on their appearances, help with invoicing and contracts as necessary for appearances and talent bookings, and help coordinate and execute game timeouts, contests, game activities, and events prior to, during, and after games.

Interns will work 20 to 30 hours a week during either the full season (September 1 through May 1) or the summer (May 1 through August 30).

You'll also sit in on all game-operations meetings as well as marketing meetings. You'll be given various assignments and projects to work on, including interaction and information exchange with other NBA teams and WNBA teams.

Candidates should have excellent writing, phone, and computer skills (Microsoft Word) and be detail oriented and able to keep track of multiple calendars and deal with internal and external clients in a professional manner. You should be a marketing, sports administration, or related business major.

Group Ticket Sales

Interns will work with the ticket sales and service staff in all aspects of group sales-related events. The successful candidate should have solid marketing and interpersonal skills.

Human Resources

Interns in this area will help the human resources department with various day to day generalist duties as well as work on relevant projects within the department.

Internet Marketing

With three Web site covering the NBA Pacers, WNBA Fever and Conseco Fieldhouse events, this small department has large responsibilities working with all areas of Pacers Sports & Entertainment. Candidates should have a wide variety of interests, including writing, Web design, graphics, publishing, database management, and e-mail marketing.

Media Relations

Interns in media relations will help in game-day setup of the media work room, get post-game quotes from visiting coaches and players, distribute monthly media clippings, and help in compiling statistical/historical information. You also may help with administrative tasks such as data entry, copying, filing, faxing, and so on.

Interns work at least 35 hours a week, from either September through January, January through end of season, or mid-June through August or September.

Candidates should be college juniors, seniors, or graduate students majoring in media/public relations, communications, or journalism. You should have strong writing skills, interviewing experience, good communications skills (verbal and written), and be adaptable, able to meet deadlines, able to work under pressure, and available for long hours. Computer and basketball knowledge is a plus.

Merchandising

Interns in this area will support the merchandising department, helping with the selection of items to be carried in the company's retail outlets, helping with projects involving warehousing and inventory-control management, and helping with retail sales, as well as supporting the department on a variety of special projects. This internship opportunity is for the fall semester only.

Pacers Foundation

Interns will assist with grant review, accommodation, and evaluation; help contribute to the long-term strategy of the Pacers Foundation; help with the foundation's annual report and the community relations newsletter; correspond with organizations around the state about scholarship programs; and plan special-event functions. For either the summer or fall, you will work between 20 and 40 hours a week, from 8:30 A.M. to 5:00 P.M. Some nights and weekends are required, depending on events.

Interns here will help with grant review, grant recommendation and evaluation, and correspondence to high schools and universities regarding scholarship programs, as well as with editing information for the annual report and community-relations newsletter. In addition, interns may help with day-to-day administrative duties, preplanning for special-event fund-raisers, correspondence with donors and grant recipients, and development of foundation strategy, along with the long-range planning committee. Interns will be required to perform community relations department activities and game-related activities. Candidates should have excellent writing and organizational skills, some familiarity with the nonprofit sector, and proficiency in Microsoft Excel and Access.

Premium Sales/Club Seat Sales

Interns in the premium sales department will assist with premium sales and service events and activities, including receptions and game-night activities, and will help support the department's efforts in providing excellent service to all their premium seat holders. Interns in this area also will help with planning and implementing new ideas, attending out of office sales calls, and working on any number of department-related projects. Interns will work 40 hours a week, either during January through May, May through August, or August through January.

As an intern, you'll help with premium sales activities and events, including receptions and game-night activities. You'll also take part in brainstorming, planning and implementing ideas and proposals in the department, attending out of office sales calls, and completing a project that applies some knowledge of a problem or opportunity currently confronting the department.

Candidates should be majors in business, sales, or sports marketing; sales experience is a plus. You should have strong verbal and written communication skills, excellent organization and computer skills, and be a creative and outgoing self-starter.

Sponsorship Sales

Interns in the sponsorship area will help with sponsor activities and events, including receptions, game-night entertainment, and so on. You'll also initiate, implement, and complete a project designed to solve a problem or create an opportunity in the sponsorship sales and promotions area. Internship dates are somewhat flexible, but generally run from September 1 to December 31 (first half of season); January 1 to May 15 (second half of season); or May 15 to August 31. All internships require 20-plus hours a week.

As an intern in this department, you'll help implement and complete a project that applies some knowledge of a problem or opportunity currently confronting the sales department. This project must be significant and have an ongoing practical value to the Pacers following the completion of the internship. You'll also help with sponsor activities and events, including receptions, game-night entertainment, and so on. You'll also attend two or three out-of-office calls with an account executive and possibly attend one with the director of sponsorship sales. You'll help brainstorm, plan, and implement sponsor-related promotions and sales proposals. In addition, you'll be responsible for general office duties such as data entry, answering phones, copying, filing, faxing, collating, and distributing departmental information.

Candidates should be majoring in business, sports marketing, or sales. You must have strong communications and computer skills and be creative, a self-starter, well-organized, and enthusiastic.

Ticket Sales

These interns will help the ticket sales department with ticket sales activities and events. Enthusiasm for sales and sales experience are helpful. Internships are 20 to 30 hours a week (flexible) from either May 1 through August 15, September to December, or January through May. Dates are flexible according to college schedules.

Internships in this department will help implement and complete a project that applies some knowledge of a problem or opportunity currently confronting the sales and promotion department. This project must be significant and have ongoing practical value to the Pacers following the completion of the internship. You'll also be responsible for general office duties such as data entry, answering phones, copying, filing, faxing, maintaining lists, collating, and distributing departmental information. Telephone sales (for commission sales positions only) are also included. You'll help with ticket sales activities and events, including receptions and game-night entertainment, and help in brainstorming, planning, and implementing ticket sales plans, ideas, and proposals.

Candidates should be enthusiastic, creative, outgoing, well organized, and self-starters, with strong verbal and written communication skills and excellent computer knowledge. Candidates should be majoring in business, sports marketing, sales, or related areas.

HOW TO APPLY

You may submit your resume, indicating the individual department in which you're interested, to the preceding address. Or you may send your resume via e-mail to Pgroeschen@pacers.com. If you apply via e-mail, you should attach your resume and specify the internship title in the subject line.

Any candidate selected as a finalist will be interviewed at the Pacers front office in Indianapolis; travel or accommodations will be at the intern's own expense, during both the selection process and internship.

The following internships have more specific application requirements.

Broadcast Production

All applicants will be reviewed by a broadcasting panel and will be invited for preliminary interviews. Two weeks after the final interviews, the intern will be selected and all applicants will be notified by phone.

Community Relations

Although this department accepts applications year round, you should submit your formal application at least three months before the period for which you are applying. Applicants will receive acknowledgment of receipt of their applications.

Community Relations—Indiana Fever

You should submit your resume two to three months prior to the period for which you are applying. Applications will be kept on file until one month before the start of an internship period. At that time, between six to eight students will be selected to come in, at their own expense, for the interview process. Finalists will be contacted by phone to schedule an interview. If you aren't selected for an interview, you'll be notified in writing.

Event Internship

Apply by October 31 for January; by March 31 for May; and by June 30 for August. All resumes will be reviewed, and the top applicants will be called to set up an interview. In some cases, phone interviews may be considered when the cost of travel is unreasonable.

Game Operations and Promotions

You should submit a formal application four months before the starting date. All applicants will receive acknowledgment of receipt of their applications, which will be kept on file until two months before the start of an internship period. At that time, you'll be selected to come in, at your own expense, for the interview process.

Media Relations

You must have your cover letter and resume mailed to the preceding address six months prior to the semester you wish to do your internship. All students will be notified by telephone of their interview status if they meet the criteria. Otherwise, a letter will be mailed to you. If you are selected for an interview, an appropriate time for the interview will be set up. You will need to travel at your own expense.

Pacers Foundation

Applications for this internship are rolling; you may apply anytime.

Premium Sales/Club Seat Sales

Applications are accepted year round, but the Pacers suggest you submit your formal application at least two to three months prior to the period for which you are applying. Qualified candidates will be contacted by phone to set up a formal interview. About six to eight people will be selected to come in at their own expense for an interview, three or four weeks prior to the start of the internship program. Finalists will be contacted by phone to schedule an interview. If you are not selected for an interview, you will be contacted in writing.

Sponsorship Sales

Although this department accepts applications year round, you should submit your formal application at least two to three months before the period for which you are applying. Six to eight students will

be selected to come in at their own expense for an interview, three to four weeks before the start of the internship program. Finalists will be contacted by phone to schedule an interview. If you are not selected for an interview, you will be notified in writing.

Ticket Sales

Although this department accepts applications year round, you should submit your formal application at least two to three months before the period for which you are applying. Candidates will be selected to come in at their own expense for an interview, two months before the start of the internship program. Finalists will be contacted by phone to schedule an interview. If you are not selected for an interview, you will be notified in writing.

KANSAS CITY BLADES INTERNSHIP

Kansas City Blades Internship Coordinator
1800 Genesse
Kansas City, MO 64102
Fax: (816) 842-6673

What You Can Earn: Unpaid but academic credit is available.
Application Deadlines: Rolling.
Educational Experience: Unspecified.
Requirements: 20-40 hours a week; game-night internships require 10 hours a week plus evenings and weekends.

OVERVIEW

The Kansas City Blades have been active members in the local community since 1990 and serve as a catalyst for community pride and spirit. From clinics, school assemblies, and community festivals to hospital visits, grand openings, and in-arena events, the Blades are involved in hundreds of programs and events throughout the community each season that enhance the mental, physical, and social welfare of Kansas City citizens.

Game Night Only

Between October and May, three intern positions are available in the game operations and marketing department, where you'll help with on-ice promotions, fund-raising events, giveaway distribution, and mascot escorts.

Off Season Internships

The Kansas City Blades offer one or two internship positions between May and September in the marketing department. As an intern here, you'll help plan promotional events during the summer, attend promotional events, research for sponsorship sales, design the monthly Kids Club Newsletter, and help sales staff with mailings to current and potential ticket buyers.

Season Internships

Full-time internships are available between August to May in the marketing department, helping with games, designing the monthly Kids Club Newsletter operations, planning and attending promotional events, and promoting games.

HOW TO APPLY

Send your resume to the preceding address.

KROENKE SPORTS ENTERPRISES INTERNSHIP

KSE Internship Program
1000 Chopper Circle
Denver, CO 80204

Fax: (720) 931-1547
internships@pepsicenter.com
http://www.pepsicenter.com/About/Intern_Desc.
   asp?EmploymentID=int3

What You Can Earn: Unpaid.
Application Deadlines: April 11.
Educational Experience: You must be able to receive academic credit for the experience; specific educational requirements vary by department and are listed below.
Requirements: Proof that you're covered under your school's workers compensation insurance. Other specific requirements vary by department and are listed below.

OVERVIEW

Kroenke Sports Enterprises is the Rocky Mountain West's leading provider of live sports and entertainment events, where you'll see the Denver Nuggets, Colorado Avalanche, Colorado Mammoth, Colorado Rapids, Pepsi Center, and the Altitude Sports & Entertainment network.

The KSE Summer Internship Program consists of a range of internship opportunities in departments throughout the organization. The following are brief descriptions of KSE internships. The duties are tentative and can change depending on business needs.

Altitude Affiliate Marketing

This internship teaches students about the relationship between a TV network and its affiliates. You'll help with affiliate research, monthly newsletters and press releases, special events, and updating materials on affiliate Web site. Business majors are preferred.

Altitude Production

This internship gives students hands-on experience in studio production and live events. You may log tapes, record television feeds, write scripts, and perform research. Candidates should be radio, TV, film, or communications majors.

Altitude Programming

This internship allows students to see what goes into developing a programming lineup. You'll be involved in researching TV listings (local, regional, and national), programming opportunities, and programming partner Web site. You'll also compile and mail programming documents.

Community Relations

This internship teaches students about community affairs, fund-raising, special events, and other charitable initiatives of KSE. The ideal intern should have strong communication and interpersonal skills and a desire to help the community.

Corporate Sales/Sponsorship Marketing

This internship shows students what goes into the relationship with sponsors, including research, promotions, special events, and customer service. Business majors are preferred.

Corporate Travel

This internship allows students to learn about corporate travel sales and service, the Apollo airline reservation system, and international travel and bookings. You should have strong communication and customer service skills.

Event Operations

This internship teaches students what goes into putting on an event at Pepsi Center. You may be involved in event planning, facility surveys and research, game-day productions, and special projects as needed.

Game Entertainment

This internship teaches students about promotions and entertainment at Colorado Rapids games. You may be involved in securing halftime entertainment and anthem singers, as well as preparing in-game promotions and throwing T-shirts. You should be comfortable in front of large crowds and must be able to work two hours before and through the completion of all Colorado Rapids home games.

Information Technology

This internship allows students to get hands-on experience in hardware/software installation, support, and troubleshooting. Strong communication skills are needed, and any previous IT training is a plus.

Lacrosse Operations

This internship gives students a close look at the daily operations of a professional sports team. You may also be involved in the development of a new KSE venture, National Development Program (NDP) Lacrosse.

Premium Sales and Service

This internship allows students to work with the Suite and Club Seats sales team. You may be involved in sales and service, arena/event operations, and setting up the club level on event days.

Rapids Media Relations

This internship teaches students the relationship between the Colorado Rapids soccer club and the local/national media. You'll be involved in writing media guides, press releases, and updating coloradorapids.com. The ideal candidate is a journalism or communications major, and the ability to speak and/or write in Spanish is a plus.

Youth and Fan Development

This internship allows students to work with KSE's youth initiatives, including the Denver Nuggets, Colorado Avalanche, and Colorado Mammoth Kids Clubs, Avalanche street hockey program, Junior Nuggets, Break the Ice, Rapids Dribble Pass & Score, and school and mascot appearances. The ideal intern should enjoy working with children and be available for nights and weekends.

HOW TO APPLY

To apply for the summer internship program, send a cover letter and one-page resume via e-mail, mail, or fax to the preceding address. If there are specific internships you're interested in, mention them in your cover letter. Students selected for an interview will be contacted by a hiring manager within a few weeks after the deadline.

LOS ANGELES LAKERS INTERNSHIP

Los Angeles Lakers
Attn: Internship Program
555 North Nash Street
El Segundo, CA 90245
(310) 419-3100

What You Can Earn: Unpaid.
Application Deadlines: Rolling.
Educational Experience: Undergraduates and grad students (within two years of graduation).
Requirements: Must live in the Los Angeles area.

OVERVIEW

Six-time NBA champs, the Los Angeles Lakers are one of the world's most prestigious sports franchises. The Lakers' purple-and-yellow uniforms have been worn by stars such as Jerry West, Elgin Baylor, Magic Johnson, Kareem Abdul Jabaar, James Worthy, Shaquille O'Neal, and Kobe Bryant.

The franchise moved from Minneapolis to Los Angeles before the start of the 1960–61 NBA season. The Los Angeles Lakers have been one of the league's elite teams, thanks to its roster of all-time greats. Since moving from Minneapolis, the Lakers have won nine NBA titles.

Interns work in the public relations office at least one day a week as well as on game nights, which occur about eight times a month. Also, interns work at all home Laker's games, dinners at the arena on game nights, and other Lakers functions (Stay in School, Jam Session, and so on).

HOW TO APPLY

Submit your resume, cover letter, and recommendations to the preceding address.

NASCAR DIVERSITY INTERNSHIP

NASCAR Diversity Internship
1801 W. International Speed Blvd
Daytona Beach, FL 32114
jobs@nascar.com

What You Can Earn: Unpaid.
Application Deadlines: March for the summer session.
Educational Experience: College students of any major.
Requirements: An interest in the motorsports industry; must be of Alaskan Native, American Indian, Asian/Pacific Island, African American, Hispanic, or other minority descent.

OVERVIEW

The National Association of Stock Car Auto Racing (NASCAR) is a sanctioning organization for various classes of automobile racing throughout the United States, including the Nextel Cup and Busch Series. Founded in the Southeast, NASCAR racing has spread in popularity throughout the country. The organization is committed to attaining greater diversity within its organization and throughout the industry. To help with this endeavor and assist in growing the industry's representation of communities of color, NASCAR has created the NASCAR Diversity Internship Program to run from June through August. This program will provide meaningful opportunities for qualified candidates to work with NASCAR's sanctioning body, NASCAR sponsors and licensees, NASCAR teams and tracks, and other motorsports-related companies.

Minority college students will work in a 10-week summer program designed to introduce them to the world of NASCAR and the exciting career opportunities available throughout the motorsports industry. The program offers internship opportunities in broadcasting, communications, competition, design, engineering, event management, fund-raising, general business, licensing, marketing, media services, public relations, sales, and sports marketing.

HOW TO APPLY

You can always check for current internship openings by visiting http://employment.nascar.com. If you are interested in a particular internship, you can e-mail your resume to the preceding address; be sure to include the position you are applying for and your salary history.

NASCAR INTERNSHIP

NASCAR Internships
1801 W. International Speed Blvd.
Daytona Beach, FL 32114
jobs@nascar.com

What You Can Earn: Unpaid.
Application Deadlines: Rolling.
Educational Experience: Must have completed at least your sophomore year of college and must currently be an undergraduate or graduate student in good standing with at least a 3.0 cumulative GPA.
Requirements: An interest in the motorsports industry computer proficiency in Microsoft Office applications.

OVERVIEW

The National Association of Stock Car Auto Racing (NASCAR) is a sanctioning organization for various classes of automobile racing throughout the United States, including the Nextel Cup and Busch Series. Founded in the Southeast, NASCAR racing has spread in popularity throughout the country.

The program offers a number of internship opportunities in broadcasting, communications, competition, design, engineering, event management, fund-raising, general business, licensing, marketing, media services, public relations, sales, and sports marketing. A sample of possible internships appears as follows.

Fall Public Relations Internship (Daytona Beach)

This intern will help in daily public relations activities, including writing press releases, correspondence, and various projects.

Summer Public Relations (Charlotte, North Carolina)

This public relations intern will help with daily public relations activities, including writing press releases, correspondence, and various projects to assist the public relations department.

Summer Brand/Consumer Marketing (Charlotte)

This intern will help with daily brand and consumer marketing activities, helping account executives with both market and media research results and related research projects.

Fall Series Operations (Daytona Beach)

This intern will help with daily series operations activities, helping account executives and coordinators and developing individual projects.

Fall Publishing (Charlotte)

This intern will help on all publishing projects and approvals, work with publishers on production needs and requests, and coordinate projects between offices. The intern also will update and maintain the NASCAR publishing library, conduct research for new business, retail programs, and the publishing industry as a whole, and will track all editorial materials in publications and create presentations for partners.

HOW TO APPLY

You can always check for current internship openings by visiting http://employment.nascar.com. If you are interested in a particular internship, you can e-mail your resume to the preceding address; be sure to include the position you are applying for and your salary history.

NEW YORK RANGERS INTERNSHIP

New York Rangers Human Resources Department
Madison Square Garden
2 Penn Plaza
16th Floor
New York, NY 10121
newyorkrangers@thegarden.com
http://www.newyorkrangers.com/employment.asp

What You Can Earn: $25 a day.
Application Deadlines: First week of November for spring session (January through May); first week of March for summer session (June through August); first week of June for fall session (September through December).
Educational Experience: Students must be enrolled in undergraduate or graduate programs. Undergraduate juniors and seniors are preferred, but qualified sophomores can be considered.
Requirements: Between 25 and 40 hours per week; students must be eligible to earn credit through their university by submitting letters of credit eligibility from their academic advisers, indicating how many credits they will earn.

OVERVIEW

The New York Rangers were one of the National Hockey League's "Original Six," a term used to describe NHL teams prior to the league's expansion in 1967. The Rangers joined the NHL in 1926 and won three Stanley Cups, emblematic of the NHL championship, over the next 14 years. It would be 54 years until the Rangers won another Stanley Cup, a drought that ranks as one of the most famous in sports.

The New York Rangers Internship Program offers students real business exposure within the various departments of Madison Square Garden. Internships are available within the New York Rangers organization in administration/team operations, marketing, and public relations.

HOW TO APPLY

E-mail or mail applications for Madison Square Garden's internship program to the preceding address. To become a Madison Square Garden intern, review your academic status with your professor/advisor and mail your resume along with the required letter of credit for further consideration. Your resume will be reviewed. If a suitable position is available, you will be contacted by human resources for an interview.

ORLANDO MAGIC INTERNSHIPS

Orlando Magic, Human Resources
Attn: Internship Program
8701 Maitland Summit Blvd.
Orlando, FL 32810
Fax: (407) 916-2884
employment@orlandomagic.com

What You Can Earn: $750 a month plus Sportsplex Athletic Club access, game tickets during Magic season, and a 25 percent discount at RDV Sportsplex retail stores.
Application Deadlines: Apply by May or June for an internship for the entire season or by January or early February for the summer (May-August/September).

Educational Experience: College juniors, seniors, and graduate students, along with recent college graduates (up to 18 months following graduation date).

Requirements: Must work game nights, including weekends and holidays.

OVERVIEW

The Orlando Magic joined the NBA as an expansion team for the 1989–90 season. By drafting seven-foot, one-inch Shaquille O'Neal out of Louisiana State University, the team was an instant contender. In 1995, O'Neal led the Magic to the NBA finals, where they lost to the Houston Rockets.

Orlando Magic interns will acquire practical knowledge through hands-on experience and gain invaluable skills necessary to compete for jobs in the sports industry when their program is completed. Interns will work at least 40 hours a week from September 1 to May 31 (the entire NBA season) or from June 1 to August 31; dates are somewhat flexible.

Internship positions are offered in arena operations/retail; broadcasting radio and tv production; business strategy; communications; community and government relations; corporate sales; fan relations; human resources; Latin affairs; marketing; Orlando Magic Youth Foundation; publicity; and strength and conditioning. Most intern positions differ in their responsibilities and time commitments.

Arena Operations/Retail

You'll help the arena operations manager with event planning and game preparations, serve as a security checkpoint for all home games and distribute credentials, and help manage all aspects of program sales, including scheduling and supervision of game-night staff, receiving shipments of programs, and preparing monthly reports. You'll also help prepare merchandise for game-day sales, be responsible for inventory control and handling money, help schedule and supervise game-night staff positions for security check-in, and help manage the online shop, including site management

and order processing. You'll also be responsible for general office duties.

Management, marketing, sports administration, communications, or related business majors are preferred. Candidates should have strong written and verbal skills, strong communication and organizational skills, solid knowledge of Microsoft Word and Excel, and the ability to work independently and lift up to 25 lbs. Event-management experience and forklift certification are preferred.

Broadcasting Radio and TV Production

As an intern here, you'll help the assistant director of broadcasting and the radio producer for Magic radio broadcasts. You'll be responsible for gathering pregame/post-game sound and conducting game-day interviews for all home games played at the TD Waterhouse Center. You'll help gather production elements for all radio broadcasts and productions (including halftime features), feed to and retrieve sound from the NBA retrieval system, archive and log sounds bites and game broadcasts for future productions, maintain organization of audio suite and audio library, and write and produce commercials for Magic broadcasts, including upcoming game-promotion spots. You'll also help the chief engineer complete engineering projects for video and radio.

Audio production, journalism, communications, or a related major or production background is preferred, but prior engineering experience is not required. Candidates should be enthusiastic and have a solid knowledge of basketball, excellent verbal and written communication skills, and knowledge of audio recording equipment (minidisc, DAT, and so on). Tape editing, digital audio work stations, and some on-air experience are pluses.

Business Strategy

Interns in this area will help the director of business strategy and the corporate office with projects, ongoing research, analysis, and strategic planning. You'll perform detailed research on new business strategies (via Internet and or/other resources), help with both long- and short-term strategic planning, provide additional support to the director of business strategy, help maintain the office and project files, prepare correspondence, and communicate with internal and external stakeholders. You'll also help organize all project communication. Game-night responsibilities will vary depending on the scope of current projects.

This internship is reserved for recent college grads or graduate students with business, sports management, or related majors. Candidates should have strong accounting and budgeting skills, excellent oral and written communication skills, and the ability to work independently, demonstrate initiative, handle multiple tasks and prioritize goals, and be proficient in Microsoft Word, Microsoft Excel, and PowerPoint.

Communications

In-season interns will help with *Magic Magazine* (the team magazine) and *Hoop* (the game program); all interns will help with the Internet site, media guide, and department manuals. You'll also help with the NBA draft media-viewing party and summer league (summer only); prepare daily news clippings from local, national and international news media and the Internet; participate in planning, setting up, and controlling all aspects of press conferences; write press releases and follow through with the editing process; distribute press conference and post-game quotes to local and national media; and coordinate video and slide libraries. You'll also help with game-day/night operations; be responsible for media credentials; be responsible for keeping and updating team statistics during the NBA season (in-season interns); help create public relations plans and follow through with specific community projects; organize and implement High School Media Day (in-season interns only); and perform general office duties as needed.

Candidates should be college senior or graduate students or recent college graduates in sports management, public relations, communications, journalism, or related majors. Candidates should have excellent writing and communication skills and be self-starters who can meet deadlines and think creatively; available to work long, irregular hours; able

to handle several simultaneous projects; work well with others; and be proficient in Microsoft Word, Excel, and QuarkXPress. Previous SID experience is preferred; basketball knowledge is a plus.

Community & Government Relations

Interns will help coordinate and evaluate all community relations programs, including holiday programs, community ticket programs, NBA Read to Achieve, Awareness Months, and OMYF events. You'll also help with monthly events by coordinating communication to schools, gathering incentive items for the youth involved, recruiting volunteers if needed, working with creative services on any signage needed, and assisting in the development of the agenda and other logistics. Interns also will manage the ticket program by developing relationships with community partners, database management, distribution and tracking tickets, and reporting the number of tickets used per home game to your supervisor. Helping with *Magic Magazine* and Web site articles for all community relations programs is another part of the internship, along with general office duties. In addition, you'll work all home games by being the main contact through radio communication to troubleshoot any issues as they relate to community relations and help evaluate and track all programs.

Candidates should be college seniors or graduate students (or recent college graduates) with marketing, sports administration, communications, or related business majors. Candidates should have strong written and verbal communication skills, flexibility to work long hours, and the ability to meet deadlines, balance multiple tasks, and think and write creatively. Proficiency in Microsoft Word and Microsoft Excel is required; experience with special event planning, community relations, community service work, public relations, multitasking, and database management are preferred but not required.

Corporate

As an intern in this area, you'll help organize sponsor activities and events and update and distribute weekly reports on inventory sold and sponsor promotions. You'll also help update current sponsor lists and the *Magic Magazine* distribution list, attend client meetings, gather information, and write the corporate sales *Magic Magazine* spotlight page each month. You'll maintain and create a supply of welcome kits and sales kits, make all necessary deliveries, fulfill any internal or external requests, and work all Magic game nights (duties include staffing the corporate sales ticket window, game-night set up, and take down of signs and promotions). You'll complete a significant project that applies some knowledge of a problem or opportunity currently confronting the corporate sales division. You'll also participate in weekly departmental sales and game-related marketing meetings, attend all planned intern-related functions, and promote ticket sales as they relate to the ticket synergy program.

Candidates should be college juniors or seniors, graduate students, or recent college graduates with business, marketing, or sales-related majors. Candidates should have strong verbal and written communication skills, and be a creative and outgoing self-starter. Candidates should be well organized, with an enthusiasm for sales and proficiency in Microsoft Word; knowledge of Microsoft Excel, PowerPoint, and mail merges is a plus.

Fan Relations

Interns in this area will help fan relations representatives by answering questions and help service representatives' accounts and develop strong client relationships with season ticket account holders, through regular communication and contact opportunities, including telephone, e-mail and in-game visits. Interns also will be responsible for working at all Magic home games, staffing the TD Waterhouse Centre/Magic Will Call, Guaranteed Giveaways table, Guest Service windows, and fan relations booth on the concourse. In addition, interns will help review surveys of season ticket holders and communicate with season ticket holders to gauge satisfaction levels and to inform them of upcoming season ticket holder exclusive events. Interns will also answer phones and respond to e-mails, process incoming mail and faxes, track

general trends regarding fan comments, and help with all season ticket holder events, including first-year orientation and open practices. Finally, interns will help organize and distribute season ticket holder gifts and birthday cards; help plan, organize, and execute season ticket holder events.; help the Orlando Magic booster club Hoop Troop as the Magic liaison for game-night needs and membership meeting assistance; and help with departmental marketing strategies and fan communication efforts, including the orlandomagic.com fan relations page and *Magic Magazine*.

Candidates should have completed course work in marketing, communications, or similar fields; have excellent computer skills (Word and Excel required); excellent oral and written communication skills; proven organizational and time-management skills; research and analysis skills and experience; the ability to handle and prioritize multiple assignments; and excellent interpersonal skills. Attention to detail and the flexibility to work long and irregular hours are necessary. Marketing experience is preferred.

Human Resources

Interns in this area will help with all aspects of recruitment (scheduling of drug testing and background checks, respond to inquires, application data/file management); help with new hire packets; recruitment filing system; and create new hire personnel files. Interns also will help with job fairs and special recruiting events, answer employment questions, and create a job description book and online files. Interns also will help with benefits administration; monthly benefit enrollment for new hires and preparation related to the session; the audit and process of monthly insurance billing; coordinate 401(k) quarterly distribution instruction mailings; and attend College of Knowledge sessions. Interns also coordinate the Magic Game Ticket distribution, compile data for exit summary reports; help with terminations, I-9, and medical filing; with merit review process; and help with Game Night and special project duties as needed.

Candidates should be juniors or seniors pursuing bachelor's degrees in human resources, organizational, development, or related fields. Candidates should be able to maintain confidentiality and have excellent oral and written communication skills. Organizational skills and attention to detail, proficient computer skills (word processing and spreadsheets), proven people skills, cooperative attitude with team-oriented disposition, and the ability to work extra hours as needed are essential.

Latin Affairs

Interns in this area will serve as support to all members of the division in order to gain insight and experience into the operation of a major sports operation as it relates to Latin Affairs issues. If you're chosen as an intern in this department, you'll help organize sponsor activities and events, attend client meetings, make all necessary deliveries, and fulfill any internal or external requests and help with the creation of the Latin Nights. You'll also work with the creative services department to fulfill sponsor-related signs and promotional needs and handle general office duties. You'll participate in weekly departmental sales and game-related marketing meetings and help with game day/night operations (season interns only).

You'll also help with daily maintenance of orlandomagic.com en espanol, including developing original site content and keeping up with current knowledge of online innovations and technology, creating special event Web pages (Draft, Summer League, and Playoffs), weekly five-game scheduler, and more. You'll also post and translate post-game quotes, press-conference quotes, and press releases and perform daily site updates (post-practice reports, headlines, calendar, promotions, polls, and all secondary pages).

Candidates should be juniors, seniors, graduate students, or recent college graduates with business, marketing, or sales majors. Candidates should also have outstanding verbal and written communication skills and be organized, enthusiastic, creative, outgoing, and bilingual (reading, writing, and speaking both Spanish and English proficiently). Proficiency in Microsoft Word is required; knowledge of Microsoft Excel, PowerPoint, and mail merges is a plus.

Marketing

Interns in this area will coordinate content and materials for the production of collateral pieces, signs, and promotional items and work closely with outside vendors in producing and delivering materials for the creative services department while communicating progress to the creative services manager. Interns will help with in-game market research, input advertising media placement information into a database to track marketing return on investment, help analyze market research data, and help update a monthly creative services cost-savings-analysis report. Interns also will participate in game-night responsibilities, including game-night research, game operations, activities, fan fest, monitoring the image and artwork management database, and producing banners, signs, and so on.

Candidates should be juniors, seniors, graduate students, or recent college graduates majoring in advertising, communications, graphic design, or related areas. Candidates should have excellent phone skills and be able to deal with the public in a professional manner; be detail oriented and able to think and write creatively; and be able to work in a fast-paced environment. Proficiency in Microsoft Word and Excel, and knowledge of Adobe Illustrator, Adobe InDesign, Photoshop, and Access are a plus but not required; knowledge of the NBA is required.

Orlando Magic Youth Foundation

Interns in this area will help coordinate various fund-raising events, including in-game and online auctions and raffles, the Black Tie & Tennies Charity Gala, and the Players Championship for Charity Golf Tournament. Interns also will help with the grant cycle, site visits, and generating revenue for the foundation. You'll be responsible for all autograph and donation requests, including tracking requests, coordinating delivery or pick-up of items, managing inventory, and reporting items donated. You'll also help create and manage databases for the golf tournament and the gala, which includes silent auction donations items and donor contact information items as well as final bid and buyer contact information. You'll maintain current knowledge of league and team foundation events and generate ideas on how to improve existing programs, follow current trends in the sports and entertainment industries to aid in procuring auction items, and research other national sports teams' fund-raising activities to enhance those of the OMYF. You'll also manage the silent auction process for the golf tournament and gala; generating solicitation letters; receiving; assessing value; tracking; displaying items; payment collection; and item delivery and generating thank you letters to donors and buyers.

In addition, you'll help manage game-night auctions and raffles and solicit fans to purchase raffle tickets and bid on items at the table, and you'll manage online auctions by securing creative Orlando Magic items to place on site and coordinate league affidavits and certificates of authenticity. You'll monitor the bidding process and handle the payment process, distribution of items, and thank you letters to the buyer. You'll help with all aspects of the golf tournament and gala as necessary and help in the grant cycle and site-visit phases as necessary.

Candidates should be college seniors, graduate students, or recent college graduates in marketing, public relations, sports administration, or communications; proficient computer skills in Word and Excel are required. Candidates also should have excellent oral and written communication skills; proven organizational and time-management skills; excellent interpersonal skills; the ability to handle and prioritize multiple assignments; and excellent attention to detail.

HOW TO APPLY

To apply for an internship program(s), please e-mail, fax, or mail a resume with a cover letter detailing which internship(s) you are interested in to the preceding address. Any candidate selected as a finalist may be asked to interview in Orlando at his or her own expense. Candidates for the communications internship should include writing samples with their resumes.

PERFORMANCE RESEARCH INTERNSHIP

Performance Research
25 Mill Street
Queen Anne Square
Newport, RI 02840
(401) 848-0111
Fax: (401) 848-0110
http://www.performanceresearch.com/
    internship-info.htm

What You Can Earn: $750; academic credit possible.
Application Deadlines: Rolling.
Educational Experience: No specific academic background is required.
Requirements: Strong writing skills, a great attitude toward work, a sincere interest in learning, a high energy level, and a minimum of 45 hours a week (8:30 A.M. to 5:45 P.M.). Any weekend work trips are mandatory and additional to the 45 hours a week.

OVERVIEW

As the world leader in consumer-based sponsorship evaluation, Performance Research has conducted more than a million personal interviews and hundreds of focus groups on sports-sponsorship issues. The company's clients include more than 50 worldwide corporate sponsors, including Anheuser-Busch, AT&T, Bank of America, Eastman Kodak, Pepsi-Cola, and Visa, as well as leading properties and cause-related organizations.

Realizing there is little opportunity for learning about sponsorship research in college, Performance Research has set up an internship program for those interested in pursuing careers in the sponsorship industry.

Positions for interns are open just one or two times each year. As an intern, you'll travel throughout the United States to sports and special events, collecting data by conducting sponsorship interviews with sports fans or event attendees (all travel and accommodation expenses are paid during research trips). You'll work within the company's in-house telephone research facility, helping to generate research tabulations, and design and write sponsorship research reports and presentations using PowerPoint and Word. Full internships are for 10- to 12-week periods, depending on the time of year.

HOW TO APPLY

To apply for an internship, complete an on-line application form at http://www.performance research.com/intern-application.htm, stating the dates of the internship program that's best for you. You also need to provide a one- to 10-page writing sample, anything you've written that you're proud of. It doesn't have to be about sponsorship, marketing, or research.

PHILADELPHIA PHANTOMS INTERNSHIP

Philadelphia Phantoms Internship Coordinator
Wachovia Spectrum
3601 South Broad Street
Philadelphia, PA 19148

What You Can Earn: Unpaid.
Application Deadlines: Rolling.
Educational Experience: Juniors, seniors, or graduate students; must receive academic credit (students are required to provide documentation of receiving academic credit for the internship experience).
Requirements: Some game nights and/or weekends may be required.

OVERVIEW

The Philadelphia Phantoms play in the American Hockey League, which is one level below the National Hockey League. The Phantoms have been in existence since the 1996 season and affiliated with the Philadelphia Flyers of the National Hockey League. A number of internships are available including positions in marketing, public relations, and sales.

Marketing (Including Complex, Premium Seating/Hospitality, and Wings)
Interns will help promote family shows and arena sporting events; help in day-of-event operations with promotions, operations, and security departments; conduct demographic and psychographic research for various department projects; and participate in the brainstorming sessions related to proposed marketing projects.

Public Relations
Interns will help pitch story ideas to national, regional, and local media; help with brainstorming, planning, and executing Wachovia Spectrum/Center publicity events; help with media tours and publicity mailings; handle correspondence concerning the Wachovia Spectrum/Center and other related issues; and keep a comprehensive record of events that occur at the Wachovia Spectrum/Center.

Sales (Including Advertising Sales, Event Services, and Premium Seating)
Interns will help coordinate special events and promotions for all Wachovia Spectrum/Center family shows and sporting events; develop new concepts for advertising venues at the Wachovia Spectrum/Center; and organize, prepare, and maintain stock on all Wachovia Center sales information.

HOW TO APPLY

You may apply for these internships online at http://comcast-spectacor.teamworkonline. com/teamwork/jobs/apply.cfm?jobid=5997&ai

d=807&supcat=429&subcat=3010. During the online-application process, you'll be asked to select one of the positions as your first and second choice.

PHILADELPHIA 76ERS INTERNSHIP

Philadelphia 76ers Internship Coordinator
3601 S. Broad Street
Philadelphia, PA 19148

What You Can Earn: Unpaid.
Application Deadlines: Rolling.
Educational Experience: Juniors, seniors, or graduate students; must receive academic credit (students are required to provide documentation of receiving academic credit for the internship experience).
Requirements: Some game nights and/or weekends may be required.

OVERVIEW

The 76ers moved to Philadelphia from Syracuse for the 1963–64 season, replacing the Philadelphia Warriors, who moved to San Francisco. The 76ers won NBA championships in 1967 and in 1983. The 76ers also have the dubious distinction of the league's worst record ever (nine wins and 73 losses in 1973). A variety of internships are available with the Philadelphia 76ers.

Electronic Media/Arena Vision

As an intern here, you'll be responsible for editing and logging highlights from each Flyers/76ers game, helping the producer during game nights, and learning how to operate cameras, editors, audio, routing switchers, and graphics.

Finance

Interns here will maintain data files, prepare bank reconciliations, analyze various accounts, enter accounts payable invoices in the accounting system, help with payroll editing on Kronos time and attendance system, help prepare payroll on Ceridian P/R system, and perform clerical duties and responsibilities as assigned.

Graphic Services

As an intern in this department, you'll help the graphic designer in advertisement design, editorial layout, and brochure design; maintain computer files; help produce four-, two-, and single-color pieces; actively participate in brainstorming sessions related to proposed graphic services projects; and help produce game and event related materials.

Human Resources

Interns here will help provide support to the employment manager by screening incoming applications and resumes, including daily updates of database and mailing responses; help post positions to the employment opportunities Web site; coordinate the internship program; help the staff with various individual projects involving research and design; plan an Internship Orientation event; and handle incoming calls and answer inquiries.

Information Technology (Including Web Development, Digital, Media, and Information Systems)

Interns in this area will help prepare computerized mailing lists and mailing labels, customize Lotus spreadsheets and write Lotus macros, write documentation for custom systems, and help update and maintain the department database.

Marketing (Including Complex, Premium Seating/Hospitality and Wings)

Interns will help promote family shows and arena sporting events; help in day-of-event operations with promotions, operations, and security departments; conduct demographic and psychographic research for various department projects; and participate in the brainstorming sessions related to proposed marketing projects.

Operations

Interns will help the operations department with event-related activities, help create a production book concerning events held at the Wachovia Spectrum/Center, maintain clear and precise reports on event activities, help with changeover responsibilities, and help staff with various projects involving research and design.

Public Relations

Interns will help generate and pitch story ideas to national, regional, and local media; help with brainstorming, planning, and executing Wachovia Spectrum/Center Publicity Events; help with media tours and publicity mailings; handle correspondence concerning the Wachovia Spectrum/Center; and keep a comprehensive record of events that occur at the Wachovia Spectrum/Center.

Sales (Including Advertising Sales, Event Services, and Premium Seating)

Interns will help coordinate special events and promotions for all Wachovia Spectrum/Center family shows and sporting events, develop new concepts for advertising venues at the Wachovia Spectrum/Center, and organize, prepare, and maintain stock on all Wachovia Center sales information.

HOW TO APPLY

You may apply for these internships online at http://comcast-spectacor.teamworkonline.com/teamwork/jobs/apply.cfm?jobid=5997&aid=807&supcat=429&subcat=3010.

During the online-application process, you'll be asked to select one of the following positions as your first and second choice: electronic media/area vision; finance; graphic services; human resources; information technology; marketing; operations; public relations; and sales. (If you'd be willing to work in any of these positions, type ANY.)

SAN DIEGO CHARGERS INTERNSHIP

San Diego Chargers Internship Coordinator
4020 Murphy Canyon Road
San Diego, CA 92123
Cassidyk@Chargers.NFL.com

What You Can Earn: Unpaid.
Application Deadlines: April 29.
Educational Experience: Rising college seniors or seniors intending to enter a graduate or professional school in the fall or graduate or law students returning to school in the fall. First consideration will be given to undergraduate students with an overall GPA of at least a 3.0 and 3.3 in their major; graduate students with a GPA of at least 3.3; law students in the top half of their class.
Requirements: Must be legally permitted to work in the United States.

OVERVIEW

The San Diego Chargers moved from Los Angeles after their inaugural season in 1961. The Chargers were one of eight teams in the American Football League (AFL), created to rival the National Football League. The Chargers, who won the AFL title in 1963, joined the NFL for the 1970–71 season, when the AFL and NFL merged. Interns will work about 40 hours a week, from June to August, in a variety of positions with the Chargers.

HOW TO APPLY

Download a summer internship application at http://www.chargers.com/employment/intern.cfm. E-mail the completed application along with your resume and an unofficial transcript to the preceding address, with "2005 Summer/Seasonal Internship Application" in the subject line. If you're chosen to interview for an intern position, you must then submit an official transcript prior to the scheduled interview. Do not telephone regarding the status of your application; only applicants chosen to interview for intern positions will be contacted.

TOLEDO MUD HENS BASEBALL CLUB INTERNSHIP

Toledo Mud Hens Internship Coordinator
406 Washington Street, Fifth Floor
Toledo, OH 43604
http://www.mudhens.com/FrontOffice/
   Employment/

What You Can Earn: Unpaid.
Application Deadlines: February for the summer session.
Educational Experience: Not specified.
Requirements: Not specified.

OVERVIEW

The Toledo Mud Hens Baseball Club is the Triple-A affiliate of the Detroit Tigers. The Mud Hens' first year of baseball began in 1896. Since then, many famous individuals have played for the Hens, including Jim Thorpe, Casey Stengel, Kirby Puckett, and Kirk Gibson. The Mud Hens were made world famous when Toledo native Jamie Farr appeared on the hit TV show *M*A*S*H* wearing a Mud Hens jersey.

Interns play a large role in the success of any minor league baseball organization. Positions include marketing, public relations, corporate sales, stadium operations, groundskeeping, and merchandising. Interns who have completed the Mud Hens internship program have gone on to successful careers with many organizations, including *Sports Illustrated*; the Michigan International Speedway; Detroit Tigers; Lansing Lugnuts; Richmond Braves; Chicago White Sox; New Orleans Saints; Hagerstown Suns; Pittsburgh Pirates; and Cleveland Browns.

HOW TO APPLY

To apply for an internship, download the internship application from the Web site http://www.mudhens.com/FrontOffice/Employment/InternBrochure.pdf. Submit the completed application and your resume to the preceding address.

TECHNICAL

AEROSPACE CORPORATION INTERNSHIP

Aerospace Corporation
Manager, Staffing Administration
PO Box 92957, M1/050
Los Angeles, CA 90009-2957
(310) 336-1614
Fax: (310) 336-7933
suzan.h.barbee@aero.org
http://www.aero.org/careers/intern.html

What You Can Earn: Competitive salary.
Application Deadlines: Rolling.
Educational Experience: College students, at the sophomore level and above, studying science and engineering, computer science, mechanical engineering, aerospace engineering, information systems, or mathematics.
Requirements: None specified.

OVERVIEW

The Aerospace Corporation has provided independent technical and scientific research, development, and advisory services to national-security space programs since 1960. The company operates a federally funded research and development center for the U.S. Air Force and the National Reconnaissance Office and supports all national-security space programs. The company also applies more than 40 years of experience with space systems to projects for civil agencies such as NASA and the National Oceanic and Atmospheric Administration, commercial companies, universities, and some international organizations in the national interest. The company doesn't manufacture anything, but it provides technical expertise on a consultant basis. The company offers research in all facets of space systems, including systems engineering, testing, analysis, and development; acquisition support; launch readiness and certification; anomaly resolution; and the application of new technologies for existing and next-generation space systems.

Summer intern positions are available at company headquarters in El Segundo, California, and at Chantilly, Virginia. Job assignments are designed to give students the opportunity to work in scientific, technical, or administrative areas of the company. The difficulty and level of responsibility of each job depends on the needs of the project and on the student's career interests and level of experience.

HOW TO APPLY

To apply, fax or mail your resume with cover letter to the above address.

AGILENT TECHNOLOGIES INTERNSHIP

Agilent Technologies
395 Page Mill Road
Palo Alto, CA 94303
(650) 752-5000
http://www.jobs.agilent.com/students/usa.html

What You Can Earn: Competitive salary plus holiday pay, medical insurance, relocation assistance including lump sum payment, round trip travel, roommate- and housing-sourcing services, as well as housing and transportation allowances to help offset the cost of short-term housing; service credit earned toward benefits once full-time employee status is reached; and access to on-site health and fitness facilities.
Application Deadlines: Rolling.
Educational Experience: You must have completed your freshman year in college with strong academic achievement in a technical or business curriculum pursuing a B.S., B.A., M.S., M.B.A., or Ph.D., and be majoring in electrical, mechanical,

industrial, computer, or chemical engineering; chemistry; biological science; materials science; physics; management information systems; computer information systems; information technology; or computer science.

Requirements: None specified.

OVERVIEW

Agilent Technologies, once a part of Hewlett-Packard, specializes in test, measurement and monitoring devices, semiconductor products, and chemical analysis tools for the communications, electronics, and life sciences industry. Agilent delivers critical tools and technologies that sense, measure, and interpret the physical and biological world. The company's innovative solutions enable a wide range of customers in communications, electronics, life sciences, and chemical analysis to make technological advancements that drive productivity and improve the way people live and work.

Depending upon your major, as an intern here you'll gain 10 consecutive weeks of full-time employment in research and development, manufacturing, marketing, quality, materials, facilities, information technology, finance, or human resources. The goal of this program is to hire students into regular jobs after graduation.

HOW TO APPLY

To talk to Agilent about internships, you can schedule an appointment when they visit your campus. For a schedule of campus visits, check out http://www.jobs.agilent.com/events/usa.html#campus. The company also appears at major employment events and conferences held by such groups as the Society of Hispanic Professional Engineers, National Society of Black Engineers, Society of Women Engineers, and at the American Indian Science and Engineering Society.

To check out current internships being offered and to apply online, visit http://www.jobs.agilent.com/search/uscampus.html.

AMAZON.COM SOFTWARE DEVELOPMENT ENGINEER INTERNSHIP

Amazon.com
1200 12th Avenue South
Suite 1200
Seattle, WA 98144-2734
(206) 266-2335
http://www.amazon.com

What You Can Earn: Unpaid.
Application Deadlines: Rolling.
Educational Experience: Must have junior-level standing or above in a computer science, computer engineering, EE, or math degree (or related technical discipline).
Requirements: Strong fundamental knowledge of software design, coding (C, C++, Java on Unix platform), relational databases, and quality assurance. Intern experience building production software is strongly preferred. Technical people with a passion for creating a fantastic customer/end-user experience are encouraged to apply.

OVERVIEW

Amazon.com, one of the fastest-growing companies in the country, is a personalized virtual marketplace attracting more than 35 million customers a year. Originally an online bookstore, the company has branched out into a variety of other items but remains passionate about using technology in new ways.

Internships are available at this giant online retailer, which is looking for exceptional students interested in software development to join its growing technology organization for the summer in many different areas. As an intern here, you might find yourself working on anything from forecasting systems to recommendation technologies, from GUI development to database systems.

As an Amazon.com intern, there will be little distinction between you and full-time Amazon.com employees. You can expect to interact with your mentor and participate as part of the development team as a responsible employee, providing analysis, design, programming, and quality assurance. The company will expect you to be open minded, willing to take risks, and start working on real projects right away.

The internship lasts three months, primarily during the summer, although start dates are flexible. If you're interested in an internship during other times of the year, you can apply and simply indicate your availability.

HOW TO APPLY

If you're interested in this internship, e-mail your cover letter and resume to college@amazon.com.

APPLE COMPUTER INTERNSHIP

Apple Computer
1 Infinite Loop MS: 84-3CE
Cupertino, CA 95014
college@apple.com
http://www.apple.com/jobs/internship.html

What You Can Earn: $750 to $1,400 weekly, depending on education an work experience, plus round-trip travel expenses and benefits (including medical insurance) and discounts on Apple products.
Application Deadlines: Rolling.
Educational Experience: Most successful interns have a computer or information systems technology college background or engineering (computer engineering, electrical engineering, or mechanical engineering). Apple does hire interns from nontechnical areas as needed, including MBAs or undergraduates studying finance, media arts, or graphic design, among others. Successful intern candidates from non-engineering fields tend to have some technical knowledge or experience.
Requirements: You must be a full-time student enrolled in a four-year university degree program. If you've already completed your undergraduate degree, you must be enrolled in an accredited graduate program for the following term in order to apply for an internship. Apple doesn't offer internships to high school students at this time.

To apply, you also must be a U.S. citizen or national, a U.S. permanent resident, a student who has been granted asylum, or a refugee. People with temporary work authorizations, such as students in practical training status (F1, J1 visas) will be considered only if enrolled in graduate programs.

OVERVIEW

It's probably no surprise that the employee-friendly, innovative Apple Computer company is also a terrific place for interns. If technology is your mantra, look no further for a great internship experience! As an Apple intern, you'll play a key role in developing the latest hardware and software while immersing yourself in Apple's high-energy environment. You'll be working with teams that challenge you and appreciate your ideas and contributions. Internships are available in both technical and nontechnical positions, including software and hardware, marketing, sales, and administration.

Apple is located in Cupertino, California, in the heart of the Silicon Valley, with easy access to San Francisco, national parks, beaches, and mountains. Apple has a casual work environment on a beautiful campus with a world-class cafe, sport courts, state-of-the-art fitness center, and a company store. What's more, there's a casual dress code; no suits required!

This company believes that internships should be challenging, offering quality hands-on experience that can be taken back to school, to another internship, or to a full-time job, whether at Apple or at another company. To achieve that, Apple interns work on teams that develop cool Apple products. Apple interns are assigned roles and functions on small teams with other full-time employees.

Apple's formal intern program is held during the summer, beginning in May and June and lasting at least 12 weeks. Apple occasionally hires interns to work at other times of the year, but this isn't a formal program.

Apple's university relations department hosts a variety of activities for interns each summer. As an intern, you might participate in team contests, with fabulous Apple products as prizes. You might attend an Executive Speaker Series, where you'll get a 'view from the top' from executive team members across the company. Technical talks and presentations are given throughout the summer, where you'll learn more about Apple's creative products and processes. Many Apple interns are eventually offered permanent employment.

At Apple, you will work with one of the major groups, including software engineering, applications engineering, product marketing, and developer relations.

Applications Engineering

This group develops, tests, and enhances Apple's consumer and professional software applications, such as Final Cut Pro, the iLife Suite of iTunes, iPhoto, and iMovie, and DVD Studio Pro. They typically hire interns as software engineers to help test and develop the next generation of applications for Apple.

Developer Relations

This group provides technical support and business and marketing resources for nearly 20,000 Apple developers. Their activities include marketing programs, technical and marketing briefings, escalation and resolution of technical issues, and hardware and software seeding. They typically look for interns who can be partnership managers or who can provide technical services to developers.

Finance

These are the money experts, providing financial and strategic support to the company by forecasting, performance reporting, and offering investment analysis. This group hires both undergraduate and graduate students as financial analysts.

Product Marketing

This group collects global customer and developer requirements and feedback that affect future product development. They're looking for exceptional candidates for product marketing manager positions.

Software Engineering

This group produces Apple's operating system and OS X and typically looks for engineering interns for OS X Server, Core Mac OS, OS Technologies, technical publications, and graphics and imaging.

HOW TO APPLY

Apple regularly appears at campus job fairs all over the country, and you can visit one of these events to schedule an interview. To check out whether and when Apple is coming to your school, visit http://www.apple.com/jobs/campus_events.html.

Once you've scheduled an interview, you should learn about the company before you meet with an Apple representative. Go to Apple.com and find out all you can about their latest products, including hardware, software, and music offerings. Review the job descriptions and make sure you're comfortable with the job requirements. Create a list of questions to ask about Apple, the job, Cupertino, and more; you get to interview the company as well!

You can search the Apple job database to see what's currently available at https://jobs.apple.com/cgi-bin/WebObjects/Employment.woa/wa/intern.

If you find something that looks interesting, you can apply directly online (see contact information below). If you don't see exactly what you're looking for, e-mail your resume and tell Apple what your interests are.

AT&T UNDERGRADUATE RESEARCH PROGRAM

AT&T Laboratories
32 Avenue of the Americas
New York, NY 10013-2412
(212) 387-5400
http://www.research.att.com

What You Can Earn: Stipend plus travel to the internship. Housing is not included, but AT&T makes arrangements with local universities to provide dorm housing and also provides a database of alternative housing options.
Application Deadlines: The formal deadline is March, but to have the best chance at a position, you should apply before mid-January.
Educational Experience: College juniors through graduate students.
Requirements: You must be a woman or a minority and have demonstrated interest in communications sciences, computer science, computer engineering, electrical engineering, information science, mathematics, operations research, physics, statistics, human computer interaction, or industrial engineering.

OVERVIEW

Participating students work on individual projects that are parts of the ongoing research in the lab, designed so that they can be completed over the 10-week course of the summer. As a participant, you'll get valuable exposure to the challenges and rewards of a scientific career and you'll be part of a quest to make a significant contribution to your field of study.

Current areas of research at AT&T Labs include: IP networks; artificial intelligence; broadband access; distributed IP-based virtual environments and communities; human-computer interface; mathematics and information sciences; mobile wireless networks; information; optical networking; photonics; secure systems; wireless technology; and visualization.

AT&T hires many summer research interns from all over the country, most of whom work with individual members of staff on specific research projects related to the ongoing research program in the organization. (A few work in groups.) The typical internship is 10 to 12 weeks during the summer; at the end of the internship, students normally give a 20 to 30 minute talk on their work.

HOW TO APPLY

Applications for these summer internships are made online. Before you start, you should contact your two technical references to let them know that they'll be receiving an electronic request for a reference letter from the AT&T database. The requests will arrive within seconds of your resume submission, so contacting them before you start might head off some questions. Once you're ready to start applying, click here: http://www.research.att.com/~kbl/cgi-bin/resume.pl.

After your resume is submitted, you will receive instructions by e-mail for submission of a personal statement as an optional addendum to your resume. This also provides you with a mechanism for updating your resume after submission. AT&T encourages you to use this mechanism to submit additional information on your interests and expertise.

A number of technical staff members maintain relationships with particular academic departments, where they serve as recruiters, making periodic trips to talk with students. Some of the recruiters use the Web-based interview scheduling system (check out http://www.research.att.com/academic). Others will merely post signs around a department, so watch your bulletin boards as well.

BALL AEROSPACE INTERNSHIP

Ball Aerospace
1600 Commerce Street
Boulder, CO 80301
(303) 939-4000
http://www.ballaerospace.com/hr_recruit.html

What You Can Earn: Competitive salary, company product discounts, relocation reimbursement, housing assistance, and possible future employment.
Application Deadlines: Rolling.
Educational Experience: College juniors, seniors, and graduate students majoring in computer engineering, computer science, aerospace engineering, chemical engineering, mechanical engineering, electrical engineering, laser electro-optics, optics, or physics (but check internship listings for exact requirements).
Requirements: U.S. citizenship, effective communication skills, and team skills. Computer program experience with Mathcad, Matlab, or similar programs is a benefit for some internships; check online internship listings for details.

OVERVIEW

Ball Aerospace & Technologies Corp.'s is a global leader providing advanced imaging, communications, and information solutions to the government and commercial aerospace markets. They conduct domestic and international business in the defense, civil space, and commercial arenas. Ball Aerospace supports national policy-makers, military services, NASA, and other U.S. government agencies, as well as numerous aerospace industry allies.

Internships are available in a variety of technical disciplines, such as software engineering, electrical engineering, and materials engineering. All summer intern opportunities last 10 to 12 weeks and are available at the company's Colorado offices.

Throughout the summer, management takes the opportunity to meet with the interns; topics of these meetings vary depending upon the interests of the students. There are also occasions to tour company facilities in Boulder, Broomfield, Westminster, and Golden. At the end of the session, students present their completed project to managers, coworkers, and other students.

HOW TO APPLY

If you are interested in working at Ball Aerospace, you can check out internship possibilities at a college career fair (click here for the schedule: http://www.ballaerospace.com/hr_fairs_college.html). Or you can submit your resume for consideration by checking out available internships at http://www.recruitingsite.com/csbsites/ball_aerospace/Search.asp. After clicking on a particular internship, you'll be taken to a page where you can apply online.

BECHTEL INTERNSHIP

Frederick Bechtel Corporation
Human Resources
5275 Westview Drive
Frederick, Maryland 21703-8306
becoppap@bechtel.com

Glendale Bechtel Staffing Support Center
PO Box 7700
Glendale, AZ 85312-7700
staffpx@bechtel.com

Government Services Bechtel Staffing Support Center
PO Box 7700
Glendale, AZ 85312-7700
staffpx@bechtel.com

Hong Kong Bechtel
Human Resources
Suite 3501, 35/F Jardine House
1 Connaught Place
Central, Hong Kong

(852) 2970-7000
Fax: (852) 2840-1272

Houston Bechtel Corporation
Human Resources
PO Box 2166
Houston, TX 77252
staffpx@bechtel.com

London Bechtel House
PO Box 739
245 Hammersmith Road
London W6 8DP
United Kingdom
erecruit@bechtel.com

Melbourne Bechtel
Human Resources
Level 4, Boeing House
363 Adelaide Street
Brisbane QLD 4001
Australia
austjobs@bechtel.com

San Francisco Bechtel Staffing Support Center
PO Box 7700
Glendale, AZ 85312-7700
staffpx@bechtel.com

Singapore Bechtel
Attn: Human Resources
137 Telok Ayer Street
#07-05
Singapore 068602
(65) 6332-1220
Fax: (65) 6332-1335

What You Can Earn: Competitive salary.
Application Deadlines: Rolling.
Educational Experience: Must be enrolled in a formal college or university cooperative education program and must have satisfactorily completed at least one year of study in engineering or computer science. Bechtel hires interns only from local colleges and universities in closest proximity to the hiring Bechtel office.
Requirements: None specified.

OVERVIEW

Founded in 1898, Bechtel is one of the world's premier engineering, construction, and project management companies. Its 40,000 employees are teamed with customers, partners, and suppliers on a wide range of projects in nearly 60 countries. Bechtel has completed more than 22,000 projects in 140 countries, including Hoover Dam, the Channel Tunnel, Hong Kong International Airport, the San Francisco Bay Area Rapid Transit (BART) system, the reconstruction of Kuwait's oil fields after the Gulf War, Jubail industrial city (Saudi Arabia), and the Alma aluminum smelter for Alcan Inc. (Quebec, Canada).

This global engineering and construction firm provides science and engineering interns with practical, hands-on experience and exposure to Bechtel, while giving the company an opportunity to evaluate a student's professional potential.

HOW TO APPLY

Mail or e-mail a letter to the College Relations Department at the address of the closest staffing center, explaining your interest in the company's internship program, or requesting more information about the program. If you e-mail your letter, be sure it is in ASCII text format and left justified. Selection priority will be given to students within one year of graduation, to recipients of Bechtel scholarships, and to students who have previously worked for Bechtel and have been identified as high performing and/or having high potential.

CALLAWAY ADVANCED TECHNOLOGY INTERNSHIP

Calloway Advanced Technology
3 High Street
Old Lyme, CT 06371
(860) 434-9002

http://www.callawaycars.com/Engineering_
  Services/services.htm

What You Can Earn: Unpaid but discounts available on Callaway merchandise, such as T-shirts, caps, and so on.

Application Deadlines: Rolling.

Educational Experience: College students, recent graduates, and graduate students majoring in electrical/computer engineering, engineering (general), industrial/manufacturing engineering, and mechanical engineering

Requirements: None specified.

OVERVIEW

Callaway Advanced Technology, part of the Calloway Companies, which includes Callaway Cars, is an automotive engineering firm specializing in the design and manufacture of high-performance cars and engines. The Callaway team creates cars, products, systems, and components that exemplify technological sophistication, artistry in design, and craftsmanship in fabrication. Students will get to work alongside automotive engineering experts for a 12-week experience offered in the spring, summer, or fall. Eventually, about half of all interns will be offered full-time jobs.

HOW TO APPLY

Submit your resume with a cover letter to the preceding address.

CISCO SYSTEMS INTERNSHIP

Cisco Systems Inc.
170 West Tasman Drive
San Jose, CA 95134
(408) 526-4000
(800) 553-NETS

(800) 553-6387
college@cisco.com
http://www.cisco.com/college/intern-co-op_
  program.shtml

What You Can Earn: Competitive salary plus paid time off and paid holidays. However, you aren't eligible for other company-sponsored benefits. College credit is also possible.

Application Deadlines: Rolling.

Educational Experience: None specified.

Requirements: None specified.

OVERVIEW

Cisco Systems Inc. is the worldwide leader in networking for the Internet. Networks are an essential part of business, education, government, and home communications, and Cisco Internet Protocol–based (IP) networking solutions are the foundation of these networks. Cisco hardware, software, and service offerings are used to create Internet solutions that allow individuals, companies, and countries to increase productivity, improve customer satisfaction, and strengthen competitive advantage. Cisco was founded in 1984 by a small group of computer scientists from Stanford University. Since the company's inception, Cisco engineers have been leaders in the development of Internet Protocol (IP)–based networking technologies. This tradition of IP innovation continues with industry-leading products in the core areas of routing and switching.

Cisco Systems has ongoing opportunities for interns who wish to gain valuable work experience while continuing their education. Interns are given the opportunity to work on interesting projects that are of real value to the company. You will work side-by-side with experienced employees while getting the chance to learn more about your career plans. As an intern at Cisco, you'll be involved in a career-related work assignment supervised by a professional with expertise in your career interest.

An intern can either be a part-time or full-time position, which can take place at any time during the calendar year. Your internship can last from three to six months, for which you may or may not receive college credits (depending on your university's guidelines). Intern opportunities are available in the San Jose, California; Chelmsford, Massachusetts; and Research Triangle Park, North Carolina locations and are ongoing in engineering, information systems, and manufacturing.

HOW TO APPLY

If you're interested in an internship at Cisco, you should attend national recruiting conferences and job fairs or sign up for a meeting at your university campus. Check out the campus schedule at http://www.cisco.com/college/campus_schedule.shtml.

If the company isn't visiting your campus, you can fill out an online Profiler at http://tools.cisco.com/careers/applicant/ciscorm/careers/applicant/index.jsp. The Profiler tailors its questions to you, and when your profile is complete it will be routed to college recruiters at the company.

Alternatively, if you already have a resume written, you can e-mail it to the address above in plain-text (ASCII) format.

DELL COMPUTER INTERNSHIP

Dell Computer Corporation
One Dell Way
Round Rock, TX 78682
http://www.dell.com

What You Can Earn: Stipend plus expenses for travel to and from the Dell internship location; fully furnished corporate apartment with two bedrooms, two bath, washers and dryers, and housekeeping service every other week (housing is based on a roommate plan unless a family plan is needed); 10-percent discount on Dell products; corporate health club membership at a discounted rate; intern executive speaker series that includes a Q&A session with Michael Dell and Kevin Rollins; plus intern events and orientation.

Application Deadlines: Rolling.

Educational Experience: Sophomore or junior college students with a 3.0 GPA and graduate students currently enrolled in a full-time academic program at an accredited college or university with at least one semester of school remaining before graduation; must have good academic standing in a field of study consistent with Dell's needs for intern assignments.

Requirements: Unspecified.

OVERVIEW

Dell is the world's leading computer systems company and designs, builds, and customizes products and services to satisfy its customers. Since 1994, Dell has been identifying, recruiting, and hiring university students for internship positions. By establishing working relationships with colleges and universities, Dell gains exposure to talented students. Dell sponsors and participates in many on-campus activities, including career fairs, information sessions, events with student organizations, meetings with faculty and campus officials, and on-campus interviews.

Interns share the same job responsibilities as full-time employees and will be given real work with business-related problems to solve. As an intern, you'll be continually working with full-time employees to accomplish the goals outlined in your performance plan. Internships at Dell last between 10 to 12 weeks during the summer (May to August).

Undergraduate and graduate student internship opportunities are available in the IT and engineering departments in both the company's Austin and Nashville locations. The internship will help you evaluate Dell's work processes, management style, culture, values, and work ethic. At the same time, Dell will have a chance to assess your performance during the summer and to evaluate your problem-solving skills, the extent of academic training and abilities, and your overall fit in the Dell organization.

At the end of a successful internship, some students may receive full-time offers for employment.

HOW TO APPLY

If you're interested in internship opportunities at Dell, you should meet with the company representatives at one of their scheduled campus events; full-time interviewing takes place on campus during the fall semester each year. You can apply for an internship by registering with your school's career services office.

Alternatively, you can submit your resume online through the Careers Direct link. Go to http://www1.us.dell.com/content/topics/topic.aspx/global/hybrid/careers/content/6a40a237-caa1-4333-83d9-4f90ee6c8b31?c=us&l=en&s=corp#top.

DOW CHEMICAL COMPANY INTERNSHIP

Dow Chemical Company
2030 Dow Center
Midland, MI 48674
(989) 636-1000
http://www.dow.com

What You Can Earn: A competitive salary.
Application Deadlines: Rolling.
Educational Experience: Undergraduates (excluding freshmen) and graduate students in a wide range of career fields, including chemical engineering, chemistry, computer engineering, electrical engineering, and computer science.
Requirements: None specified.

OVERVIEW

The Dow Chemical Company was founded in Midland, Michigan in 1897 and remains headquartered in the same town more than 100 years later. Dow manufactures food, transportation, health and medicine, personal and home care, and building and construction products, among others. Dow is a leader in science and technology, providing innovative chemical, plastic, and agricultural products and services to many consumer markets. With annual sales of $40 billion, Dow serves customers in 175 countries. Dow and its 43,000 employees are committed to the principles of sustainable development and seek to balance economic, environmental, and social responsibilities. Dow people around the world develop solutions for society based on Dow's inherent strength in science and technology.

At Dow, you'll be able to take advantage of training and development opportunities while working with a mentor/teacher. You'll gain business knowledge and be involved in projects with a global scope and reach. You can apply for internships in various career areas such as engineering, research and development, and information technology. Dow internships are typically offered during the summer months at various locations.

HOW TO APPLY

To search for an open internship, or to submit your profile, visit http://www.dow.com/careers/studentjobs.htm.

EASTMAN KODAK INTERNSHIP

Eastman Kodak Company
2/15/KO - Mailstop: 00539
343 State Street
Rochester, NY 14650
http://www.kodak.com

What You Can Earn: Competitive salary based on your major and education level; round-trip travel expenses (from your school/home to Kodak and back); help in locating housing.

Application Deadlines: Rolling.
Educational Experience: Full-time rising college sophomores, juniors, seniors, or graduate students (master's or Ph.D.) with at least a 3.0 GPA.
Requirements: Must be able to work a minimum 10-week work block during the year and must complete and pass a drug screen.

OVERVIEW

Eastman Kodak is a world leader in imaging and provides customers with the solutions they need to capture, store, process, output, and communicate images, anywhere, anytime. The company delivers cost-effective solutions (including consumables, hardware, software, systems, and services.

Kodak offers positions in a range of science and technology fields, including computer science, engineering (general), industrial/manufacturing engineering, mathematics, optics, and science. As an intern, you'll have the opportunity to participate in activities that will expose you to other company business units and groups, Lunch & Learn sessions, and company tours, plus meet and interface with other students in social events and activities.

Outside of work, you'll have the opportunity to participate in activities that will expose you to area highlights, thanks to the CIP Council of new employees, mentors, managers, and students—all encouraging interaction between Kodak peers.

HOW TO APPLY

To be considered for an internship at Kodak, you must place your profile/resume in Kodak's online database at https://sjobs.brassring.com/EN/ASP/TG/cim_home.asp?PartnerId=515&SiteId=251&codes=. Cooperative internship positions may be posted at selected colleges/universities and at www.kodak.com/go/careers. To see if Kodak is coming to your college, click here:

http://www.kodak.com/US/en/corp/careers/events/index.jhtml.

FERMILAB SUMMER INTERNSHIPS IN SCIENCE AND TECHNOLOGY

Equal Opportunity Office
Fermilab
MS 117
PO Box 500
Batavia, IL 60510-0500
630-840-3415
Fax: 630-840-8365

What You Can Earn: Salary plus partially subsidized housing arranged by the laboratory; paid airfare and/or ground transportation to and from the laboratory; and cars for use between local housing and the laboratory.
Application Deadlines: February 25.
Educational Experience: Satisfactory completion of at least one full year of college, current enrollment in a four-year college or university with at least a 3.0 GPA, and a balanced course load of science and nonscience electives.
Requirements: Good recommendations from one or more scientific staff. Preference is given to qualifying U.S. citizens of Native American, Hispanic, and African-American ethnicities.

OVERVIEW

The Fermi National Accelerator Laboratory is dedicated to the understanding of the fundamental nature of matter and energy. It provides resources for researchers to conduct basic research at the frontiers of high-energy physics and related disciplines. Originally named the National Accelerator Laboratory, Fermilab was commissioned by the U.S. Atomic Energy Commission in1967. In 1974, the laboratory was renamed in honor of 1938 Nobel Prize winner Enrico Fermi, one of the preeminent physicists of the atomic age.

The Fermilab summer internships in science and technology (SIST) program focuses on giving opportunities in science and technology to the minorities that historically have been underrepresented in science in the United States—Hispanic, African-American, and Native American. This program has been developed to familiarize these minority students with opportunities at the frontier of scientific research and to provide experiences that support their choice of science as a career. About 20 internships are offered in physics, electrical engineering, computer programming, and mechanical engineering. Interns work with Fermilab scientists or engineers on a project within the context of laboratory research.

The SIST committee, consisting of Fermilab scientists and engineers, selects the best candidates from the pool of applicants. The intern will join a Fermilab staff member in some scientific, engineering, or computer work to carry out experiments, to improve the operation of the particle accelerator, or to support and develop specialized research. Interns are assigned projects appropriate to their interests and academic levels.

The 12-week program consists of a work assignment, an academic lecture series, and a final report that you'll present orally to the Fermilab staff and submit to the lab in writing. Reports from previous years are available at the lab's Web site. There are no grades or quizzes.

The SIST Committee will follow your progress to help ensure you get the maximum benefit from the program. The internship program is expected to be the primary source for candidates for the Fermi National Accelerator Laboratory Graduate Fellowships for Minority Students and for GEM Consortium fellowships.

HOW TO APPLY

To apply, visit http://sist.fnal.gov/applicants/how_to_apply.html and follow the directions to complete the online application form. You'll need to submit the following to the address above:

- Application form: This can be the online form available at http://mccrory.fnal.gov/sist2005/login.php or the paper form (available at http://sist.fnal.gov/forms/PDF/InternForm.pdf.
- Official university transcripts: Be sure to provide transcipts from all the colleges you have attended.
- Letters of recommendation: You need to have two letters of recommendation, preferably from college professors, but other sources are acceptable. One recommendation ideally should be from a professor in your major field.
- Essay: This is specified on the application form. A tip: Be personal and be interesting!
- Resume: You must submit a professional resume with your application. Your work experiences, and how you describe them, are very important in understanding your qualifications.
- Course descriptions: Submitting a description of your courses is optional, but it certainly helps the company know about the classes you have taken.

For more helpful tips on completing the application, visit http://sist.fnal.gov/applicants/tips.html.

IBM EXTREME BLUE INTERNSHIP

IBM Corporation
1133 Westchester Avenue
White Plains, NY 10604
1-800-IBM-4YOU
888-839-9289

extremeblue@info.ibm.com
http://www-913.ibm.com/employment/us/
    extremeblue/index.html

What You Can Earn: IBM offers a competitive salary (based in part on current academic level) including relocation and housing assistance, overtime pay, paid holidays, sick leave, and much more.

Application Deadlines: Rolling.

Educational Experience: Undergraduates (excluding freshmen) and graduate students in a wide range of career fields. Preference is given to candidates within 12 months of their graduation date.

Requirements: Passion; strong experience in a technical industry in C, C++, or Java™ software development; advanced computer science skills; experience and passion for technology; and a history of giving back to the technical community through teaching, mentoring, and tutoring experiences. Students also should have completed complex independent software projects.

OVERVIEW

The Extreme Blue internship program is IBM's incubator for talent, technology, and business innovation. It challenges project teams of interns (along with their technical and business mentors) to develop new high-growth businesses. What began in 1999 with 25 summer interns in Cambridge, Massachusetts, now serves more than 200 students in 12 worldwide labs year-round.

IBM considers its internship program a valuable recruiting tool to find qualified candidates who fit the organizational style of the company. Interns not only have a chance to gain valuable professional experience but also to take part in IBM educational programs, social events, and workshops. Some may have the opportunity to travel.

Internships are available in chemical engineering; computer science; electrical/computer engineering; industrial/manufacturing engineering; mechanical engineering; and metallurgical/materials engineering.

In general, hours are flexible, but work can be intense at times, as teams strive to complete their projects by the end of the summer. Individual teams decide together on their hours and schedule, but all students must work a minimum of 40 hours per week. (September to March), fall (March to May).

Each project will be extremely challenging, so we expect interns to focus on a single project during the program. Given the laboratory environment, you will be exposed to all projects and are expected to lend assistance when it is required or where you are uniquely qualified. You will also have personal access to the senior engineering team serving as project mentors.

The Extreme Blue program will give you the opportunity to interact with both senior engineers, executives, and other exceptional students from across the country, access to scientists and business leaders as part of the ongoing lecture series, and a competitive compensation package.

Extreme Blue projects are varied—focusing on topics such as emerging business opportunities, including e-business on demand, grid, autonomic computing, and other emerging technologies. Extreme Blue projects also represent and potentially affect all of IBM's core businesses, including hardware, software such as Linux, services, and research. Your impact on the project will be immediate. In the first days, you and your fellow interns will set a series of goals: baseline, target, and stretch. Your project sponsors and mentors will be banking on your fresh ideas to make your project extreme—so your input is critical. And at the end of the project, you'll have a chance to show off your work to the decision makers that matter within the company.

You'll participate on a small team to conceive and deliver the technology, business plan, and go-to-market strategy for an emerging business opportunity. Extreme Blue project teams mix business and technical disciplines with a variety of experience from undergraduate and graduate interns—all lead by IBM's technical and business experts. Sessions run from January to April and June to August. Each program runs approximately 10 to 12 weeks and varies by location, which might be in Austin, Texas; Raleigh, North Carolina; or San Jose, California.

HOW TO APPLY

Apply online at http://www-913.ibm.com/employment/us/extremeblue/apply/questionnaire.html. All applications are screened individually, but the company cannot respond to every individual directly. The Extreme Blue internship is an extremely competitive program and requires that you meet the minimum qualifications in order to be considered.

For a schedule of recruiter visits to your campus, go to http://www-913.ibm.com/employment/us/extremeblue/calendar.html.

INTEL INTERNSHIP

Intel
2200 Mission College Boulevard
Santa Clara, CA 95052
(800) 628-8686
http://www.intel.com

What You Can Earn: Competitive salary; vacation and holiday time; earned credit toward a sabbatical; relocation assistance; access to Intel University classes for professional and personal development; opportunities to network with Intel managers and other interns at informational sessions; career fairs; social events; and recreational activities.

Application Deadlines: Rolling (although Intel usually searches for and recruits summer interns between January and March).

Educational Experience: College students enrolled in a four-year college or university with at least a 3.0 average, majoring in chemical engineering, computer engineering, computer science, electrical engineering, industrial engineering, material science, mechanical engineering, or physics.

Requirements: U.S. citizenship.

OVERVIEW

For more than 35 years, Intel Corporation has developed technology that enabled the computer and Internet revolution, which has changed the world. Founded in 1968 to build semiconductor memory products, Intel introduced the world's first microprocessor in 1971. Today, Intel supplies the computing and communications industries with chips, boards, systems, and software-building blocks that are the basis of computers, servers, and networking and communications products. These products are used to create advanced computing and communications systems.

Intel is a leader in semiconductor manufacturing and technology and has established a competitive advantage through its scale of operations, the agility of its factory network, and consistent execution worldwide. Intel has 11 fabrication facilities and six assembly and test facilities worldwide. Intel produces the silicon for its high-performance microprocessors, chipset, and flash memory components in its fabrication facilities. After the silicon-based products are created, they are sent to Intel's assembly and test facilities, where each wafer is cut into individual microprocessors, placed within external packages, and tested for functionality.

Intel Corporation offers undergraduate and graduate students the opportunity to join their staff for a professional work experience in one of several technical disciplines. Both 10 to 12 week internships and three nine-month co-op opportunities are available year-round, although most interns participate in the summer. Intel's student programs are well established; more than 60 percent of all previous interns have ended up working for Intel after they graduate. Internships are located in Arizona, California, New Mexico, Oregon, and Washington.

HOW TO APPLY

You can check Intel's U.S. recruitment calendar at http://appzone.intel.com/uscalendar/calendar.asp to see when an Intel recruiter will be in your area, but you'll still need to submit your resume online, even if you meet a recruiter and provide your resume in hard copy.

You can go to https://jobs.intel.com/jobs/signon.iccw to submit your resume online now. Intel regularly searches its database for qualified candidates. If an opportunity matches your skills, you will be contacted by a staffing representative. Your resume will be kept on file for at least six months, so it is not necessary to resubmit your resume within six months unless it has changed.

LAM RESEARCH INTERNSHIP

Lam Research Corporation
Corporate Headquarters
4650 Cushing Parkway
Fremont, CA 94538
(510) 572-0200
http://www.lamresearch.com

What You Can Earn: Competitive salary.
Application Deadlines: Rolling.
Educational Experience: Must be at least a rising sophomore, enrolled in school for the following semester/quarter; majors typically are in physics, materials science, or chemistry or chemical, electrical, or mechanical engineering.
Requirements: None specified.

OVERVIEW
Founded in 1980, Lam Research Corporation is a leading supplier of wafer fabrication equipment and services to the worldwide semiconductor industry. Headquartered in Fremont, California, the company is known for its innovative etch technologies. The company also offers a next-generation wafer cleaning solution, which can be used throughout the semiconductor manufacturing process. Lam maintains a network of facilities throughout the United States, Asia, and Europe to meet the complex and changing needs of its global customer base.

Lam offers internship opportunities in a number of technical fields to students at all university academic levels. During the internship, you'll work with a business group and be exposed to a broad view of the company through workshops and seminars. Interns are assigned career-related projects supervised by a professional experienced in that field. At the end of the summer, Lam interns present their research to company executives.

You can start your experience at Lam at the end of your freshman year, and you may come back each summer until graduation, where you'll get new projects each summer. As a Lam intern, you'll also be eligible to receive one of two annual scholarships awarded via an essay contest on your involvement with the company's values.

HOW TO APPLY
To submit your qualifications for an internship, copy your resume into the online text box at http://www.lamresearch.com/main.cfm?section=7&subsection=3&subsubsection=0&subnav=subnav_7.cfm&contenturl=careers_3.cfm. Once you have entered your resume information, indicate your educational background and functional area of interest. If your qualifications match a current need, you will be contacted by human resources. Otherwise, your resume will be retained for a three-month period.

LEXMARK INTERNSHIP

Lexmark International Inc.
740 New Circle Road NW
Lexington, KY 40550
recruiting@lexmark.com.
http://www.lexmark.com

What You Can Earn: All student positions are paid, depending on your total credit hours earned and your length of service with Lexmark. In addition, all students moving more than 50 miles to work at Lexmark are eligible to receive a relocation package; all students who live more than

50 miles outside of Lexington also receive housing at an extended-stay hotel, just minutes from Lexmark. Students staying at the hotel receive free breakfast and appetizers every Wednesday, plus housekeeping, cable, and access to swimming and fitness facilities. Other perks include sporting tournaments, pizza parties, movies, Kings Island, and Cincinnati Red's baseball games.

Application Deadlines: Rolling.

Educational Experience: College students with at least a 3.0 GPA, majoring in mechanical engineering, electrical engineering, computer engineering, chemical engineering, material science, chemistry, or computer science.

Requirements: Permanent U.S. work authorization; see specific intern openings for details.

OVERVIEW

In a little more than a decade, Lexmark has become a leading developer, manufacturer, and supplier of printing solutions, including laser and inkjet printers as well as associated supplies and services, for offices and homes in more than 150 countries.

Lexmark offers two primary products: business and consumer printers. The company's printing solutions and services division delivers high-powered solutions, services, and supplies to large corporate enterprises and small and medium businesses worldwide. Its consumer printer division develops and delivers innovative, easy-to-use, and affordable black-and-white and color inkjet products and supplies for homes, home offices, and small and medium businesses. The company maintains about 12,000 employees worldwide to support its products and customers in more than 150 countries.

Lexmark's summer internship program offers employment for at least 40 students in a variety of technical fields. Normally, interns work at the company for three to four months between the months of May and August.

HOW TO APPLY

To find out if Lexmark recruiters are coming to your school to discuss internships, click here for a recruitment schedule: http://www.lexmark.com/US/hr/employ/current_student/at_your_campus.html. To apply for an internship, complete the online application at https://careers.lexmark.com/HRFRAMES/apply_default.html.

When the company receives your on-line application, you will be notified via e-mail that they've received it. A recruiter will review your qualifications against the internship openings and determine if you need to come in for an interview. On the day of your interview, you'll meet with several Lexmark people to discuss your background and qualifications. If the company thinks your skills are what they're looking for, they'll present an offer with complete compensation and benefits information.

LOCKHEED MARTIN INTERNSHIP

LMMO-LaSPACE
Department of Physics and Astronomy
Louisiana State University
Baton Rouge, LA 70803-4001
http://laspace.lsu.edu/intern

What You Can Earn: The successful applicant will receive a competitive stipend determined by their classification and field of study. Assistance with housing will be provided for those who must live and attend school farther than 50 miles from LMMO.

Application Deadlines: February 11.

Educational Experience: Rising juniors or rising seniors at a Louisiana university, with at least a 2.5 GPA, majoring in physical sciences (physics, chemistry, or computer science); engineering (aeronautical, chemical, electrical, mechanical, industrial, or material); or materials science.

Requirements: U.S. citizenship. In addition to relevant coursework, a student should have demonstrated an interest in or commitment to science, technology, or engineering through participation in science fairs, clubs, laboratory work, awards, tutoring/mentoring, internships, or other related experience.

OVERVIEW

Although Lockheed Martin is world-renowned for their aerospace advancements, they also specialize in satellite telecommunications and microgears for artificial hearts. They're also the world's largest producer of public-sector systems engineering, software, and integration. The company was formed in March 1995 with the merger of two of the world's premier technology companies: Lockheed Corporation and Martin Marietta Corporation. In 1996, Lockheed Martin completed its strategic combination with the defense electronics and systems integration businesses of Loral.

Lockheed offers summer internships in a variety of technical fields for a 10-week summer internship, including aerospace, computer, electrical, mechanical, and nuclear engineering; computer science; and other technical degree areas.

HOW TO APPLY

Submit a copy of your resume plus an unofficial transcript from your university to the preceding address. Your resume should include

- address and contact information (include phone and e-mail) permanent address
- educational history (including coursework taken)
- previous employment
- relevant skills
- extracurricular activities
- interests/career plans
- naturalized U.S. Citizens must include proof of naturalization

While unofficial transcripts are acceptable for initial application, selected interns will need to supply an official transcript before beginning the

program. Preference may be given to applicants who specify that they are interested in two consecutive summer internships.

To see when the company may be recruiting at a college near you, check out http://www.lockheedmartin.com/wms/findPage.do?dsp=fec&ci=12939&sc=400

LOS ALAMOS NATIONAL LABORATORY HIGH SCHOOL CO-OP PROGRAM

Student Program Staffing
Los Alamos National Laboratory
MS P219
Los Alamos, NM 87545
bmontoya@lanl.gov
http://www.lanl.gov/education/jumpstart/
    studapp_procedures.shtml

What You Can Earn: $6.88 an hour ($14,320 a year); post-high-school program $7.77 an hour ($16,170 a year); plus holiday pay.
Application Deadlines: April 1 for summer internship.
Educational Experience: Must be a rising high school senior in good academic standing. Students who have graduated high school but have not been accepted to college are also eligible (see details below). Regional students from alternative schooling, including home-schooled students, are also welcome to apply (with guidance counselor approval).
Requirements: Must be at least 16 years old and a U.S. citizen.

OVERVIEW

The high-school cooperative program at Los Alamos National Laboratory (LANL) offers qualified high school seniors an opportunity to develop work-related skills and to gain experience in a variety of technical and administrative careers. High school co-op appointments can be full time during the summer between a student's junior and senior years and may continue on a part-time basis during the senior academic year. Internship and coop programs are administered through the education program office (STB/EPO).

The high school co-op program provides regional qualified high school seniors the opportunity to develop skills and gain work experience, while receiving exposure to a variety of technical and administrative career fields. This popular program provides employability skills and assists local area high school students with the school-to-work transition. Participants who successfully complete the program may be eligible to receive high school credit from their school. The participating high schools establish eligibility criteria to receive this credit.

The high school co-op program also offers recent high-school graduates an opportunity to work at LANL. Students in this category have graduated from high school, but have not yet been accepted to or enrolled in an undergraduate college program. Postgraduate students can remain in this program for one year and are encouraged to take classes during that year. After a student provides proof of acceptance into an undergraduate program, the student can move to the undergraduate student program.

All student program participants in every category are paired with a laboratory mentor who serves as a guide and resource to students.

HOW TO APPLY

For a schedule of when Los Alamos may be visiting your school, check out http://www.lanl.gov/education/precollege/hsrecruit_calendar.shtml.

Participating high schools receive application information and materials during annual scheduled campus visits by LANL representatives. Materials cannot be picked up from the Laboratory's Student Programs Office. Applicants are screened by designated high school representatives for aptitudes and interests, grade point average, and number of credits toward graduation.

Students interested in applying for the high school co-op program will need a resume, a completed LANL supplemental employment form, a skills profile, and a current transcript. Applications must be submitted through a high school counselor and received by the deadline.

Once an application is submitted to the student programs office, it is made available for all interested LANL hiring officials to view. Hiring officials are LANL employees who have the funding and work available to hire a student. Hiring officials can search for qualified applicants using different search criteria (such as area of interest, major, university, skills, and so on). Once hiring officials have narrowed their search, they may contact the student directly to conduct a phone interview. When a selection has been made, the hiring official will submit a hiring package to the student programs office. The package is then reviewed by the student programs office, and an official offer letter is processed and mailed to the student. Students review and accept the offer, include a start date, and return the signed offer letter to the student programs office within two weeks of receiving the letter. Once the offer letter is received by the student programs office, the student is scheduled for the new hire and orientation process.

LOS ALAMOS NATIONAL LABORATORY INTERNSHIP

Student Programs, HR Staffing
Los Alamos National Laboratory
MS P290
Los Alamos, NM 87545
progsinfo@lanl.gov
http://www.lanl.gov/education/jumpstart/
    studapp_procedures.shtml

What You Can Earn: High school graduates who will be starting college in the fall can earn $8.59 an hour ($17,870 yearly); college students who have completed their freshman year and have earned 24 credit hours earn $11.01 an hour ($22,910 yearly); those just completing their sophomore year with at least 48 cumulative credits earn $12.89 an hour ($26,820 yearly); those just completing their junior year with 72 cumulative credits earn $15.76 an hour ($32,790); those just completing their senior year with at least 96 cumulative credits earn $18.64 an hour ($38,780 yearly); and those with a bachelor's degree but not yet in grad school earn $19.60 an hour ($40,770 yearly).

Application Deadlines: April 1 for summer internship; for all other internship dates, your application materials are accepted year-round and will be kept on file for one year from date of receipt.

Educational Experience: Must have graduated high school by the start of the UGS internship and be able to provide documentation of acceptance into an undergraduate academic program and enroll in college or university courses. Recent college grads who have not yet started graduate school are also eligible for post-baccalaureate internships. You must have a cumulative GPA of 2.0 upon completion of your first year and 2.5 upon completion of subsequent years or proof of good academic standing from your college or university.

Requirements: None specified.

OVERVIEW

From its origins as a secret Manhattan Project laboratory, Los Alamos National Laboratory (LANL) has attracted world-class scientists who have applied their energy and creativity to solving the nation's most challenging problems. As one of the U.S. Department of Energy's multiprogram, multidisciplinary research labs, Los Alamos thrives on having the best people doing the best science to solve problems of global importance. The University of California (UC), which has operated the laboratory since its founding by UC physicist J. Robert Oppenheimer, has contributed signifi-

cantly to the scientific quality of the laboratory's work and technical staff.

Los Alamos combines security awareness, intellectual freedom, and scientific excellence to generate scientific and engineering solutions for the nation's most pressing problems. Maintaining the nation's nuclear stockpile is the most important responsibility of Los Alamos. Certifying that the nation's nuclear weapons remain safe and reliable without underground testing remains the biggest technical challenge. The laboratory is the second-largest manufacturing site in the nuclear weapons complex.

The undergraduate student (UGS) program in technical fields at LANL offers summer, part-time, and full-time internships for undergraduate students. This year-round program gives students the opportunity to obtain valuable work experience while they pursue their undergraduate degree. The UGS program includes a post-baccalaureate category for college graduates who have not yet been accepted to or enrolled in a graduate program. Participants have the opportunity to conduct research and gain valuable work experience at LANL. Participants may remain in this category for up to one year. All student program participants in every category are paired with a laboratory mentor.

HOW TO APPLY

Fill out and submit the online application at https://www.hr.lanl.gov/stuapp/default.asp, and send your transcripts to the above address. If your university doesn't include a calculated GPA on your transcript, you should contact your registrar's office in writing to request this information.

Once an application is submitted to the student programs office, it is made available for all interested LANL hiring officials to view. Hiring officials are LANL employees who have the funding and work available to hire a student. Hiring officials can search for qualified applicants using different search criteria (such as area of interest, major, university, skills, and so on). Once hiring officials have narrowed their search, they may contact the student directly to conduct a phone interview. When a selection has been made, the hiring official will submit a hiring package to the student programs office. The package is then reviewed by the student programs office, and an official offer letter is processed and mailed to the student. Students review and accept the offer, include a start date, and return the signed offer letter to the student programs office within two weeks of receiving the letter. Once the offer letter is received by the student programs office, the student is scheduled for the new hire and orientation process.

LUNAR AND PLANETARY INSTITUTE SUMMER INTERN PROGRAM

Lunar and Planetary Institute
3600 Bay Area Boulevard
Houston, TX 77058
(281) 486-2180
jordan@lpi.usra.edu
http://www.lpi.ursa.edu

What You Can Earn: $500 a week stipend to cover living expenses and assistance with travel expenses, to a maximum of $1000. Shared low-cost housing in apartments near the LPI can be arranged.
Application Deadlines: January.
Educational Experience: College undergraduates with at least 50 semester hours of credit and recent graduates interested in pursuing a career in the sciences. Major should be in the areas of the natural sciences, engineering, computer sciences, or mathematics.
Requirements: None specified.

OVERVIEW
The Lunar & Planetary Institute is a NASA-funded institute that studies and promotes education and public involvement in lunar, planetary, and terrestrial studies. It's a focus for academic participation in studies of the current state, evolution, and formation of the solar system. The institute includes a computing center, extensive collections of lunar and planetary data, an image-processing facility, an extensive library, education and public outreach programs, resources, and products. The LPI also offers publishing services and facilities for workshops and conferences. Located near Johnson Space Center on the south side of Houston, the LPI leads the scientific community in research in lunar, planetary, and solar system sciences and linkage with related terrestrial programs.

At the institute, student interns have the opportunity to engage in hands-on research work with scientists from the institute and the nearby Johnson Space Center. Interns will be assigned a project designed by a scientist/advisor at LPI, working on projects that probably will include research in meteorites and their origins (petrology and geochemistry); the geology of Mars and Venus (volcanoes, faults, volatiles); astrobiology; lunar samples and resources; geophysical data analysis and modeling; remote sensing and spectroscopy; atmospheres of giant planets and extrasolar planets; geology of giant planet moons; image processing; interplanetary dust particles and presolar grains; and impact cratering.

HOW TO APPLY
Paper applications aren't accepted. Fill out the online form at https://www.lpi.usra.edu/lpiintern/application/form.cfm, and receive an application number. Have three people submit online reference letters (you can obtain a reference form at https://www.lpi.usra.edu/lpiintern/references/form.cfm). References will need your application number and the correct spelling of your last name. Next, have your college mail LPI an official transcript, which must be received by the application deadline.

Notification of selection will be made by the end of February. You should be prepared to make a decision regarding the offer to participate within two days of notification.

MARATHON OIL CORPORATION INTERNSHIP

Marathon Oil Corporation
5555 San Felipe Road
Houston, TX 77056-2723
(713) 629-6600
http://www.marathon.com

What You Can Earn: Competitive salary.
Application Deadlines: Rolling.
Educational Experience: High school or college students who thrive in an environment full of challenges and professional development prospects.
Requirements: None specified.

OVERVIEW

Marathon Oil Corporation is engaged in the worldwide exploration and production of crude oil and natural gas, as well as the domestic refining, marketing, and transportation of petroleum products. Headquartered in Houston, Marathon is among the leading energy industry companies, applying innovative technologies to discover valuable energy resources and deliver the highest quality products to the marketplace.

Marathon offers exciting internships at many company offices for students interested in pursuing engineering, geosciences, health and environment, or information technology. Interns can look forward to a paid summer internship at Marathon, corporate mentorship, networking opportunities, and the potential for a full-time position after graduation.

Engineering

Depending on your skill and interest, interns at Marathon immediately become involved in diverse and challenging projects including joining a team of experienced engineers and geoscientists responsible for an offshore field development projects in a production-, reservoir-, or facility-engineering capacity. Interns can participate as integral members of a team evaluating and making recommendations on acquisitions and other business development opportunities.

Geosciences

Interns in this department contribute to meaningful projects that are designed and implemented to deliver significant opportunities and results for both the intern and the company. Projects include interpreting 3-D seismic data for high-profile offshore prospects, conducting Gulf of Mexico field studies, and interpreting log and seismic data for deep gas plays in onshore North America.

Health, Environment, and Safety

Interns in this area may work in either the environmental or safety areas. In these assignments, students gain broad exposure to issues involving implementation of company policy. Environmental projects may include soil sampling, air emission surveys, report writing, site remediation, permitting, regulatory reviews, waste disposal, employee exposure monitoring, and procedural updates. Safety duties may include facility audits, assisting with training, industrial hygiene research/monitoring, report writing, and incident investigations. Where possible, health, environment, and safety interns will be trained across both functional areas.

Information Technology

At Marathon, interns and entry-level full-time employees in Information Technology immediately become involved in strategic projects such as implementing connectivity and delivering applications to remote locations, developing Web applications, and performing business analysis of processes and procedures. Marathon looks to information technology professionals to bring fresh perspectives and innovative ideas technology application to help meet the company's goals and objectives.

HOW TO APPLY

For a list of scheduled campus visits, see http://www.marathon.com/Careers/Career_Opportunities/

College_Students_Entry_Level. Students should submit a resume and letter of recommendation to the address above.

MARATHON OIL CORPORATION/UNCF CORPORATE SCHOLARS PROGRAM

Marathon Oil Corporation/UNCF Corporate Scholars Program
8260 Willow Oaks Corporate Drive
Fairfax, VA 22031
http://www.marathon.com/Careers/Career_
Opportunities/College_Students_Entry_Level/
Internships/UNCF_Corporate_Scholars_
Program

What You Can Earn: Scholarships of up to $10,000 and transportation and housing stipends of up to $2,500.

Application Deadlines: Between September 1 and mid-January.

Educational Experience: Sophomores majoring in chemical, civil, electrical , mechanical, or petroleum engineering; health, environment, and safety; geology; or geophysics; and seniors or graduate student candidates with plans to earn a master's degree in geology, geophysics, mathematics, or physics. Students must maintain at least a 3.0 grade point average. The scholarship is restricted to the following major fields of study: chemical engineering; civil engineering; electrical engineering; mechanical engineering; petroleum engineering; health, environment and safety; geology, geophysics, mathematics, and physics.

Requirements: Must be African American, Asian Pacific Islander American, American Indian/Alaska Native or Hispanic American.

OVERVIEW

Marathon Oil Company works with the United Negro College Fund in offering the Marathon Oil Corporation/UNCF Corporate Scholars Program. The program is designed to reduce the financial barriers for minority students with academic promise and significant financial need. It is also meant to increase the representation of minorities in chemical, civil, electrical, mechanical, or petroleum engineering; health, environment and safety; geology; geophysics; and mathematics or physics disciplines and allow Marathon to develop relationships with minority students to increase the company's entry-level pool of prospective minority employees.

Each student will be paired with a mentor, exposing the students to outstanding examples of achievement and to career- and leadership-building opportunities. During the summer, in addition to working closely together, mentors and interns will be encouraged to spend informal time together participating in recreational and cultural activities to build and nurture relationships that will endure throughout each student's educational career and beyond.

HOW TO APPLY

Applicants must complete an online application, have a faculty member complete a letter of recommendation, and submit a current transcript and resume to the address above. Online applications are available during the annual application period at https://internships.uncf.org/CSP/login.aspx?id=15.

MICROSOFT INTERNSHIP

Microsoft Corporation
One Microsoft Way
Redmond, WA 98052-6399
(800) 642-7676
http://microsoft.com

What You Can Earn: Competitive salary plus relocation and travel expenses (including taxi fare to Microsoft from the airport; mileage rates if you drive); fully furnished housing, including basic cable, electricity, water, and housecleaning services; health club memberships at very nice gyms; free beverages; free T-shirts; bus passes to anywhere; educational training and workshops; and merchandise discounts; plus, either a subsidized rental car plan or a bike purchase plan during your stay. They'll also contribute toward shipping expenses to help get your stuff to and from your new location and send you to training seminars for free.

Application Deadlines: Rolling.

Educational Experience: College undergraduates at any level majoring in computer science or engineering (although you do not have to be a computer science major).

Requirements: A deep passion for technology as well as a drive to solve the issues involved in getting world-class software ready to ship.

OVERVIEW

Microsoft, founded in 1975 by Bill Gates and Paul Allen, is the world's largest software developer. Microsoft is busy building the next generation of cutting-edge technologies, from mobile devices to business servers to better game-development platforms. It also has a well-established intern program that appoints about 700 interns a year, who work in either California or Washington for 12 weeks in the summer, just like full-time employees on group projects (usually in software design and testing). With more than 300 products in production, Microsoft offers so many different things to work on that interns may have trouble making up their minds which to choose!

Applying for Microsoft internships is competitive, but the benefits are outstanding, and the internship program is a gateway to full-time employment after graduation.

In the past quarter century, Microsoft has grown from a small start-up to a Fortune 500 success by creating innovative software and working diligently to help customers realize their full potential.

During that first crazy week, the company will orient you to your job and to Microsoft in general. You'll be teamed up with a full-time mentor from your group who will show you the ropes, give you advice, and help you get the most out of your internship. Along the way, interns are invited to parties and special events sponsored by Microsoft or their particular team. It's a great way to meet other people and get to know the Northwest at the same time.

At Microsoft, interns are treated just like full-time employees. You have enormous responsibility, project ownership, and impact; in fact, the only difference between you and a full-time employee is that you're here for a few months instead of years. You'll be given real work with tremendous problems to solve, and you'll be working right alongside full-time employees as part of a team charged with delivering world-class software on schedule. Because Microsoft wants you to become very involved with your project, they'll ask that you commit to a specific group during your internship. It's the best way to make sure you have the opportunity to make a real contribution. However, there will be plenty of opportunities to attend discussions about different Microsoft technologies and to pick the brains of other employees working around campus.

There are a number of areas in which you might work, including the following.

Program Manager

If you're looking for a position where you're at the center of the action, think about working with the program manager. As keeper of the product vision, the program manager designs and applies breakthrough technologies to new software solutions while tracking the product plan, driving communication among all team members, and working to define features.

Software Design Engineer

If you're the creative type, think about working with software design engineers (SDEs), who write code, construct data structures and algorithms, and work closely with the program manager to define and prioritize features.

Software Design Engineer in Test

A Software Design Engineer in Test (SDET) combines software design engineering with software test engineering. You'll break the product down (including creating tools such as automation, stand-alone programs, and device drivers), then work with software design engineers to take the product to beta stage.

But there's more than just work at Microsoft, although much of its culture is dedicated to technology (which is why you'll find employee-driven think tanks and new product ideation sessions). Besides being a driven culture, however, the company encourages employees to indulge their playful spirit as well. Microsoft sponsors "puzzle day" (a one-day puzzle-solving competition for summer interns, with great prizes), sports teams, a volunteer network, a theatre troupe, an orchestra, and a singing group (the Microtones).

HOW TO APPLY

Before writing your resume, spend some time thinking about your goals and your strengths. You should compile a resume and cover letter that tells Microsoft who you are as well as offer ways you can contribute. You should include a short statement of your objective, including the job title and location you're seeking. If you're interested in more than one job or location, rank them in order of preference. Next, explain your experience (both academic and real-world). Cover the extracurricular projects you've worked on, and definitely include any other internships you've had and any on-the-job responsibilities. Explain the roles you played in each, what you contributed, and what you learned.

Once you've written your resume, there are several ways to get it into the hands of a Microsoft recruiter. You can simply hand your resume over when you attend a Microsoft recruiting event, either at your school or in your area (check out the schedule to see when Microsoft will be at your school at http://www.microsoft.com/college/YourSchool.aspx). If you do attend a recruiting event, it's not unusual for recruiters to conduct interviews on the spot, so be prepared! Research the company's business and product groups, and have an idea of what roles you might be interested in. This will also help you ask questions about life at Microsoft.

If you can't attend a recruiting event, or you don't want to wait until one is scheduled in your area, you can also submit your resume online at http://www.microsoft.com/college/app_overview.mspx.

After you submit your information, Microsoft will match your qualifications with the specific position or positions you want. You need to send only one resume, even if you're interested in multiple jobs or different locations. A recruiter will contact you if Microsoft is interested in scheduling an interview. (For helpful interview tips, visit: http://www.microsoft.com/college/int_tips.mspx.)

First-Round Interviews

The recruiter will want to figure out if Microsoft is a place where you'll flourish and if they have an opportunity that aligns with your current goals. They want to hear about you—what types of projects have inspired you, what self-directed missions may have influenced your career direction, and whether you had a moment of epiphany when you KNEW what you wanted to be when you grew up. They'll want to know how Microsoft fits into your vision and what excites and motivates you.

First-round interviews are usually held over the phone or at your school and are typically casual. Besides thinking about your career goals, you should do some research about Microsoft and its various product groups and businesses. After your conversation, your interviewer will consider your skills and interests, along with their current business needs, and determine the roles and business groups for which you might be considered. You can generally expect to hear from your recruiter within two weeks if you will be asked back for a second-round interview.

Second Round Interviews

If your first interview went well and Microsoft has a position that seems good for you, you'll be invited to meet for a second day of interviews, which will give you a chance to meet some sharp Microsoft people, look at the campus, and get an inside perspective of what the company is all about. During the second-round interview, you'll meet people from a couple of different product groups. The groups you are matched with will be determined by your skills and interests, as well as by available opportunities within the company. It's not uncommon to meet four or five people. Because you're on site, second interviews really give you a feel for what life is like at Microsoft, so ask questions and look around.

After your visit, your recruiter will follow up with your interview results within two weeks. If they make you an offer, they'll work with you to help you make your decision. You will have one week to make a decision.

MOTOROLA INTERNSHIP

Motorola
1299 East Algonquin Road, Second Floor
Schaumburg, IL 60196
(800) 331-6456
http://www.motorola.com

What You Can Earn: Competitive salary, healthcare benefits, investment options and work/life programs, plus extras that make your career rewarding, such as on-site fitness centers, sports and recreation teams, and product discounts.
Application Deadlines: Rolling.
Educational Experience: All levels of college students or graduate students may apply, but the company is especially interested in engineering majors (electrical, computer, mechanical, chemical, and so on). Students should have a GPA of at least 3.2 and have held a leadership position in a student organization (such as an engineering society, fraternity or sorority, sports team, and so on.)

Requirements: Enthusiastic, dynamic, innovative candidates who think critically and creatively and have had at least one prior intern or co-op term.

OVERVIEW

If you dream about inventing new technology, creating new markets, and participating in a new competitive landscape, you might consider an internship at Motorola. Originally founded in 1928 as the Galvin Manufacturing Corporation, today Motorola is a large manufacturer of wireless and other communication hardware, a Fortune 100 global communications leader that provides seamless mobility products and solutions across broadband, embedded systems, and wireless networks. "Seamless mobility" means you can reach the people, things, and information you need in your home, auto, workplace, and everywhere in between, using smarter, faster, cost-effective, and flexible communication. Today, Motorola is composed of four businesses: Connected Home Solutions, Government & Enterprise Mobility Solutions, Mobile Devices, and Networks.

Internships are offered three times a year, in spring for 16 weeks (January through April), in summer for 12 weeks (May through August), and in fall for 16 weeks (September through December). During the co-op term, the student works full time. Co-op terms at Motorola alternate with semesters in school. Most universities provide some semester credit for co-op terms.

As a co-op or summer intern, you will have an opportunity to apply your education to solving real-life problems. Internships are available in a wide range of areas, such as student engineers, hardware engineering, and development engineering. Positions are primarily available in Illinois and Florida, although opportunities can arise in any of the 21 states where the company operates. A wide range of internships are available; to check out what's available, visit http://careers.peopleclick.com/client40_motorola/external/ola/Welcome.xml.

Motorola claims to strive to "make things smarter and life better." It does this by developing high-tech wireless, broadband, and automotive solutions for individuals, on the job, at home, and in your car. The company maintains a business-casual work environment, emphasizing integrity, dignity, and respect for the individual, business ethics, diversity, and continuous professional development.

HOW TO APPLY

To be considered for an internship, visit Motorola's Career Portal at http://careers.peopleclick.com/client40_motorola/external/ola/Welcome.xml and register with the site. At the career portal, you can sign up for a "Job Agent" to e-mail you when future internship openings are posted that meet your interests, view the status of your application to specific openings, and store up to five resumes.

At this Web site, you can search and apply for posted positions that meet your requirements, or you can simply drop off a copy of your resume by clicking Submit CV/Resume at the top of the Job Search or Search Results screens.

When openings arise, recruiters search the database for available candidates. If your qualifications align with the requirements for the position, either a manager or recruiter will contact you directly. If a match isn't made, your resume will remain in the system for other recruiters to search. If you applied for a specific position and registered with the site, you can check back with Motorola's Career Portal to view the status of your application.

NATIONAL INSTRUMENTS INTERNSHIP

Human Resources Coordinator
National Instruments
11500 North Mopac Expressway
Austin, TX 78759-3504
Fax: (512) 683-7500

What You Can Earn: Competitive salary plus paid holidays, medical/dental benefits for full-time interns, relocation assistance. (Students coming from schools outside of Texas receive $1,000, less taxes, to help with relocation. Those coming from schools within Texas, but outside the Central Texas area, receive $750, less taxes.)
Application Deadlines: Rolling.
Educational Experience: A full-time student currently enrolled in an accredited degree program (preferably engineering).
Requirements: U.S. citizens or nationals, U.S. lawful permanent residents (LPR), temporary residents granted legalization under IRCA, asylees or refugees.

OVERVIEW

Today, it takes a sophisticated mix of computers, networks, and machines to manufacture anything from light bulbs to lightwave communications. National Instruments (NI) is revolutionizing the measurement and automation industry with virtual instrumentation, a concept that gives customers the freedom to define solutions that meet their particular needs, using industry-standard technology. National Instrument's vision is to create innovative computer-based products that improve everyday life by improving technology.

Their customers include engineers, scientists, and technology professionals in diverse industries who use NI software and hardware tools to research, design, manufacture, test, and improve a wide array of products and services. The company's strategy is to innovate, constantly improve, and deliver a steady stream of new products that deliver greater productivity and higher value.

At NI, interns get to work on real projects with a fair amount of independence, which is why you must have lots of initiative and talent to qualify. An internship with this company can help you hone both your technical and entrepreneurial skills as you work with leading edge technologies. In addition, National Instruments offers a relaxed work environment and countless activities and training opportunities. Internship terms are offered in fall, spring, and summer.

Internships are offered in applications engineering, information technology, manufacturing engineering, and research and development.

Applications Engineering

In application engineering, you'll be working with your own projects and you'll get to see the impact they have on the company. Some intern projects have even resulted in that person filing for patents.

Information Technology (IT)

IT positions are available throughout the company. Whether you intern as part of the applications group, in operations, or in the infrastructure group, you have the opportunity to learn about many functional areas, using different technologies and working with more than 35 international offices. IT interns take full ownership of their projects, which include anything from requirements gathering through project implementation. Internships are available in each of the IT groups, working with programmer/analysts, systems administrators, and business analysts. You'll have flexible start and end dates, but the projects assigned usually span a three-month period. Projects are assigned throughout many areas of the business with the overall goal of integrating the company's systems into one single IT solution.

Manufacturing Engineering

Manufacturing engineering interns at NI have the opportunity to work on projects such as designing, developing, and qualifying cutting-edge manufacturing technology; reducing cycle time and improving throughput and costs; or introducing and integrating new products into manufacturing.

Research/Development

National Instruments creates innovative computer-based products that improve everyday life, giving customers a better solution for measuring and automating the world around them. As an intern in research and development, your technical exper-

tise can help the company create better, faster, and more accurate ways to make measurements.

HOW TO APPLY

To apply, you may fax or mail your resume and cover letter to the above address, or send these materials electronically. To submit your resume electronically, go to http://digital.ni.com/universities/library.nsf/basic?openform&intern&node=33300_us and browse the opportunities available under Intern-Co-op. Go to the position in which you're interested, and then click on the "Apply for this Job" link at the bottom of the position description. Send plain ASCII files only. You will receive an instant message letting you know that we received your resume when you apply for the position. If the company believes your skills and experience may match their needs, they will contact you at that time.

NATIONAL RENEWABLE ENERGY LABORATORY INTERNSHIP

National Renewable Energy Laboratory
1617 Cole Boulevard
Golden, CO 80401-3393
(303) 275-3000
http://www.nrel.gov/about.html

What You Can Earn: Competitive salary; one-time, round trip transportation might be available for participant depending on eligibility (residing more then 50 miles from the National Renewable Energy Laboratory work site).
Application Deadlines: Rolling.
Educational Experience: Undergraduates who have completed their sophomore year by the time the internship begins in the summer, and graduate students, who are enrolled full-time in a U.S. college or university, and who plan to continue

full-time education immediately after the internship. Must be enrolled in a minimum of 12 credit hours as an undergraduate and 9 credit hours as a graduate student. Preferred minimum GPA of 3.0 in the last completed semester. Students should be majoring in one of the following fields: aerospace, biomedical, chemical, electrical, computer, metallurgical, materials, or mechanical engineering; biology; chemistry; or physics.

Requirements: U.S. citizenship or U.S. permanent residency.

OVERVIEW

National Renewable Energy Laboratory (NREL) is the nation's primary laboratory for research, development, and transfer of renewable energy and energy efficiency technologies. Established in 1974, NREL began operating in 1977 as the Solar Energy Research Institute. It was designated a national laboratory of the U.S. Department of Energy (DOE) in 1991, when its name was changed to NREL. Today, NREL is the principal research laboratory for the DOE Office of Energy Efficiency and Renewable Energy. NREL is managed for DOE by the Midwest Research Institute and Battelle.

Typical internships might include a position at NREL's Energy and Environmental Applications Office or at the National Bioenergy Center at NREL. At NREL, interns can work 40 hours per week during the summer and breaks, and a maximum of 25 hours per week for undergraduate students and 30 hours per week for graduate students during the academic year.

HOW TO APPLY

Go to the NREL Web site at http://www.nrel.gov/hr/employment/rpp/internships.html to search for open positions; applications are accepted as positions become available. When applying for an internship position that you have found on this Web site, you should follow the instructions for submitting your resume at the bottom of the internship vacancy page. In general, when

applying you should send your resume and a cover letter to the address above, stating your areas of interest, along with the prior semester school transcripts (these do not need to be official). You should include a requisition number on your resume if you're applying for a specific open position.

NATIONAL SEMICONDUCTOR INTERNSHIP

National Semiconductor
2900 Semiconductor Drive
PO Box 58090
Santa Clara, CA 95052-8090
(408) 721-5000
http://www.national.com

What You Can Earn: Competitive salary plus paid holidays, medical/dental benefits for full-time interns, relocation assistance (if eligible).
Application Deadlines: Rolling.
Educational Experience: A full-time student currently enrolled in an accredited degree program (preferably engineering).
Requirements: U.S. citizens or nationals, U.S. lawful permanent residents (LPR), temporary residents granted legalization under IRCA, asylees or refugees.

OVERVIEW

National Semiconductor, the industry's premier analog company, creates high performance analog devices and subsystems. National's leading-edge products include power management circuits, display drivers, audio and operational amplifiers, communication interface products and data conversion solutions. National's key analog markets include wireless handsets, displays and a variety of broad electronics markets, including medical, automotive, industrial, and test and measurement applications.

Headquartered in Santa Clara, California, National Semiconductor will place you on a small team of experienced professionals where you'll contribute to developing products that people will use every day. The company primarily looks for electrical engineering students for assignments in circuit design, product engineering, test development engineering, applications engineering, and technical marketing. The intern program is very flexible; assignments can be full time or part time and can alternate on a quarterly or semester basis.

HOW TO APPLY

Search for specific internship openings by visiting http://www.national.com/careers/search.html. Register at this Web site http://www.national.com/careers/register.html to receive information about internships, and to apply for available internships.

NCR INTERNSHIP

NCR
1700 S. Patterson Blvd
Dayton, OH 45479
(80) 225-5627
http://www.ncr.com

What You Can Earn: Competitive salary.
Application Deadlines: January.
Educational Experience: Undergraduate computer science and engineering majors.
Requirements: None specified.

OVERVIEW

NCR (founded as the National Cash Register Company) provides transaction and data warehousing solutions for thousands of companies throughout the world. NCR provides hardware, software, and solutions to simplify transactions across the coun-

ter, by telephone, at a kiosk or ATM, or over the Internet, NCR combines customer outreach with powerful data warehousing solutions to help companies use this information to better understand and serve each customer.

The NCR Corporate Summer Intern Program is an integral part of NCR's recruitment strategy and a great opportunity for you to spend the summer working on projects related to your career interests in engineering or computer systems. In addition to assigned projects, you'll participate in program events designed to network with other interns, learn about NCR's business and culture, and support the community through volunteer events.

HOW TO APPLY

Internship opportunities will be posted on http://www.ncr.com/careers/interns.htm as soon as they are available; you can apply at the same site. You can check out the company's recruiting schedule to see when NCR is coming to your school at http://www.ncr.com/careers/camptour.htm.

ORACLE CORPORATION INTERNSHIP

Oracle Corporation
500 Oracle Parkway
Redwood Shores, CA 94065
(650) 506-7000
interns_us@oracle.com
http://www.oracle.com

What You Can Earn: Competitive salary plus housing (fully furnished corporate apartments), paid car/bike rentals, paid round-trip travel expenses from school; the program also can include helicopter ride over/under the Golden Gate Bridge, festive lunches and dinners, and special events such as San Francisco sightseeing and trips to Disneyland/SeaWorld.

Application Deadlines: March 15.
Educational Experience: Students with computer science or equivalent majors attending college in North America.
Requirements: None specified.

OVERVIEW

Oracle, the world's leading developer of database management software and services, was founded in 1977 with a vision of finding faster, easier, less expensive, and more powerful ways to access and manage information. The company built the first commercial relational database system and sold the first products using structured query language, which is now the industry standard. The company recognized the value of low-cost, client/server systems over proprietary mainframes, and pioneered portable software that today runs on practically all hardware, from PCs to mainframes. In recent years, Oracle championed parallel software as the breakthrough that will power very large database applications such as data warehousing and information-on-demand. Recently, the company introduced the Oracle universal data server, an extremely powerful software platform with the ability to integrate and consolidate all types of data for thousands of users over any network, including the World Wide Web.

Each summer, the company hires about 35 to 40 outstanding interns to work for three months in the summer, experiencing the thrill of developing cutting-edge software. Interns typically work alongside Oracle staff on projects related to software development, design, and service.

HOW TO APPLY

To apply, e-mail your resume to the above address, attaching your resume as text or Word, or paste content directly into the e-mail. Do not send your internship resume through other resume links on the recruiting Web site provided for permanent job applicants. Selection is based entirely on your resume, and no interviews are conducted. Students who are selected for internships will be notified by April 1. Although each resume is reviewed, we receive a vast number of applications and are only able to notify applicants who are selected for the internship.

PACIFIC GAS AND ELECTRIC COMPANY INTERNSHIP

Pacific Gas and Electric Company
One Market, Spear Tower, Suite 2400
San Francisco, CA 94105-1126
(415) 267-7070
http://www.pge.com/careers/college/summer_
  internships

What You Can Earn: Competitive salary plus paid holidays and medical benefits.
Application Deadlines: Rolling.
Educational Experience: Currently enrolled with good academic standing in an accredited university, or with a graduation date within the last six months by the time your internship starts.
Requirements: Strong work ethic, initiative, motivation, ability to work well in a team environment, strong written and verbal communication skills, and active involvement in extracurricular activities.

OVERVIEW

Pacific Gas and Electric Company is one of the largest combination natural gas and electric utilities in the United States. The company, a subsidiary of PG&E Corporation, serves approximately 15 million people throughout a 70,000-square-mile service area in northern and central California.

Pacific Gas and Electric Company offers summer internships to undergraduate students in a number of technical field. Interns with this company perform project-focused assignments in the utility field, which provide hands-on experience. As an intern, you'll have the opportunity to contribute and you'll be surrounded by people who are committed to helping you learn. In addition, as an intern, you'll increase your prospects for a full-time position upon graduation. Positions are available throughout northern and central California, with many located in San Francisco at corporate headquarters. Internships typically last 10 to 12 weeks.

HOW TO APPLY

Summer internship positions are posted on the corporate Web site during the month of January preceding the summer when the internship will take place. Once the internships are posted, you should review the various opportunities and select the ones you are interested in and for which you qualify.

To apply, submit your resume and cover letter using the company's online resume submission process.

After you submit your resume, it is entered into the company database. If your resume is a potential match for a current open internship position, you'll be contacted in February or May to schedule an interview.

If you have questions, you may communicate with the company by using the online e-mail form available at http://www.pge.com/careers/college/comments/index.html.

PACKER FOUNDATION ENGINEERING INTERNSHIP

The Packer Internship Program
Attn: Recruiting Director
1950 N. Washington
Naperville, IL 60563
pejobs@packereng.com
http://www.packerfoundation.org/internships/
    index.cfm

What You Can Earn: Competitive salary.
Application Deadlines: Rolling. Generally, internships start by mid-May or early June and end by mid-August or early September.
Educational Experience: Most college interns are engineering and science majors. High school students can work as interns in the laboratory services department, where they are exposed to testing and experiments. High school students considering an engineering curriculum in college may find this an excellent way to figure out if engineering is a possible career.
Requirements: You should have basic writing and computer skills and be a self-starter with a strong sense of personal responsibility, vision, and assertiveness. You should be a freethinker, focused both academically and practically, a communicator, a team player, accomplishment-oriented, and above all a leader.

OVERVIEW

Packer Engineering is a multidiscipline, multifaceted engineering company with locations in Ann Arbor, Michigan; Columbia, Maryland; and Naperville, Illinois, serving a broad range of manufacturers, process industries, insurers, litigants, researchers, and developers throughout the United States and around the world. This business-casual environment of 120 employees includes engineers and technicians in a variety of engineering and science-related disciplines.

The internship program consists of about 15 to 25 students, each with different skills and backgrounds, who are given the opportunity to work on projects which will help them excel. Several members of the Packer staff started as summer interns and became full-time employees after graduation. Because Packer Engineering is a multidisciplinary engineering consulting and technical services company, interns are involved in a wide range of disciplines and engineering fields.

Although interns have the opportunity to work with many different people inside and outside the company, they'll also be given a mentor in their area. The mentor will be responsible for guiding the student on a one-to-one basis, responsible for developing tasks and projects composed of multiple tasks for the student. Paired with mentors in their area of study, interns work full time on real projects with real clients. Their tasks may include billable projects, research and development, marketing, field inspections, and laboratory work. Interns also participate in professional-development seminars on topics such as career management and professional ethics and work together on group presentations to build teamwork, leadership, and communication skills.

Site visits to local corporations allow interns to experience other types of industries and testing facilities. But it's not all work—interns and mentors have picnics and weekly volleyball games to provide plenty of opportunity for fun with coworkers.

HOW TO APPLY

For details, visit: http://www.packereng.com/jobsintern.cfm. Submit your resume to the preceding address, along with a cover letter describing your personal and academic short-term and long-term goals, as well as what you wish to realize from the internship.

PRATT & WHITNEY CO-OPS AND INTERNSHIPS

Pratt & Whitney
400 Main Street
East Hartford, CT 06108
(860) 565-4321
(800) 565-0140
http://www.pw.utc.com

What You Can Earn: Competitive salary.
Application Deadlines: July through November for spring semester (January through June);

January through May for fall semester (July through December). Summer internships are also available.

Educational Experience: Must be currently pursing a degree at an accredited college or university in one of the following disciplines: engineering (aerospace, chemical, computer, industrial, mechanical, manufacturing, or materials), computer science, or information technology. Engineering students should be familiar with ProEngineer or AUTOCAD design.

Requirements: Excellent communication and problem-solving skills; working knowledge of all Microsoft software applications. Candidates should be self-starters and have the ability to work with minimal direction. Leadership and teamwork skills are a must.

OVERVIEW

Pratt & Whitney is a pioneer in flight and in technology—the world's leading producer of engines for corporate jets, commuter aircraft, and helicopters, powering space vehicles, and military and commercial aircraft,. Over the years, the company has patented hundreds of innovations, from heat-resistant coatings to aerodynamic blades, to make air travel more cost effective, more comfortable, and more dependable. Today, Pratt & Whitney engines power nearly half of the world's commercial fleet. Every few seconds, more than 20,000 times a day, a Pratt & Whitney-powered airliner takes flight somewhere in the world. The company's military engines are used in the Air Force's F-15 and F-16, and its F119 and F135 engines will power the frontline fighters of the future, the F/A-22 Raptor and F-35 Joint Strike Fighter. Its rocket engines send payloads into orbit at 20,000 miles per hour. Its gas turbines are also used to generate electricity in a growing number of locations.

To ensure its ability to shape the future of aerospace technologies, the company focuses on recruiting ambitious, innovative achievers for intern and co-op programs. There are various co-op and internships positions available at Pratt & Whitney in almost all locations. Working side-by-side with the industry's top people in some of the world's most technologically advanced facilities, you'll earn a good income while you learn the very latest techniques in the business. Through a combination of classroom work and practical experience, with alternating periods of attendance at college and co-op employment at Pratt & Whitney, you'll have opportunities to integrate theory and practice, confirm your career choices, and help finance your education.

As part of its co-op and intern programs, you'll benefit from supervised and comprehensive on-the-job training in your field of professional endeavor, and you'll be encouraged to contribute your fresh ideas in an environment that ignites the imagination and brings innovative results.

HOW TO APPLY

To check out internship vacancies, click on http://careers.hodes.com/pratt-whitney. To apply online, click on http://careers.hodes.com/pratt-whitney/apply_online_1.asp?JobID=533134&User_ID=. This Web site requires you to paste your resume (text only) onto the electronic application.

SANTE FE INSTITUTE INTERNSHIP

Summer Research Opportunities for Undergraduates

Santa Fe Institute
1399 Hyde Park Road
Santa Fe, NM 87501
(505) 946-2746
reuinfo@santafe.edu
http://www.santafe.edu

What You Can Earn: Modest living stipends plus housing in single-occupancy rooms with shared bathrooms at St. John's College, a partial board plan, use of a car, plus some support of round-trip travel expenses from the home institution.

Application Deadlines: February 18.
Educational Experience: Undergraduate students interested in science, excluding graduating seniors.
Requirements: U.S. citizenship. Women and minorities are especially encouraged to apply. Because Santa Fe lacks a full public transportation system, autos are provided to participants on a shared basis. However, if possible you should try to bring your own car.

OVERVIEW

The Santa Fe Institute (SFI) is a private, nonprofit research institute founded by Los Alamos Lab scientist George Cowan, and other scientists, who wanted to create a place where scientists could pursue problem-driven science directed at the "hard" problems. Since its founding in 1984, its researchers have defined the frontiers of complex systems research, which tries to understand what unites artificial, human, and natural systems. By their very nature, these problems transcend any particular field. For example, if scientists understand the fundamental principles of organization, they will better grasp cell function in biology and magnets in physics. This research relies on theories and tools from across the sciences. Part of the rise of the complex systems research agenda can be tied to the use of theoretical computation as a new way to explore such systems.

Typically, there are about 35 researchers in residence year round, with about twice that number during the summer months. SFI is an institute without walls, and hosts about two dozen workshops a year, an external faculty of 60, annual summer schools, and many other activities.

As an intern here, you'll work with faculty mentors on an individual research project focused on some aspect of complex systems. SFI's broad program of research is aimed at understanding both the common features of complex systems and at comprehending the enormous diversity of specific examples. Possible focus areas include adaptive computation; computational aspects of complexity; energy and information in biological computation; scaling laws in complex phenomena; network structure and dynamics; robustness and innovation in biological and social systems; and the dynamics of human social interactions including state and market formation, economics as a complex system, and the evolution of language. This program is highly individualized. Each student works with one or more faculty mentors on a specific, mutually selected project. The project may be based on a suggestion from the SFI mentor, an idea from the student intern, or a combination of the two. The initial weeks of the program will be devoted to meeting potential mentors and determining the choice of project. Participants are expected to be in residence approximately 10 weeks, within an early-June to mid-August time frame.

HOW TO APPLY

You can use the institute's online application form on the "job openings" page of http://www.santafe.edu/education/reu/2005/index.php to submit most of your materials electronically (including a feature which allows your referees to upload letters of recommendation directly to your file). The institute strongly encourages you to apply online in order to speed up your application.

Otherwise, you may mail your materials to the above address, including

- a current resume
- a statement of your current research interests and what you intend to accomplish during your internship (suggested length one to two pages)
- three letters of recommendation from scholars who know your work
- official transcripts from each college or university you attended

If you mail your application material, be sure to include your e-mail address and fax number. Do not bind your application materials. If you apply by postal mail, transcripts and letters of recommendation may be included in the application package in sealed envelopes, or they may be sent directly to the address above.

SILICON GRAPHICS INC. (SGI) INTERNSHIP

Silicon Graphics Inc.
1500 Crittenden Lane
Mail Stop: 410
Mountain View, CA 94043
(650) 933-7777
http://www.sgi.com

What You Can Earn: Competitive salary, plus other benefits that may include relocation, housing, and transportation assistance. Participants are eligible for one paid day off per month of employment and paid holidays.

Application Deadlines: Rolling.

Educational Experience: You should at least have completed your freshman year in college (most interns are juniors with some of their core curriculum under their belts) with a technical major. Masters, MBA, or Ph.D. students are also eligible.

Requirements: None specified.

OVERVIEW

Silicon Graphics Inc. is a world leader in hardware (severs, workstations) and software (for Internet, entertainment, and design applications) solutions for many different industries including, manufacturing, life sciences, energy, defense and intelligence, and media. This leader in high-performance computing, visualization, and storage provides technology that enables the most significant scientific and creative breakthroughs of the 21st century. Whether it's sharing images to improve brain surgery, finding oil more efficiently, studying global climate, providing technologies for homeland security and defense, or enabling the transition from analog to digital broadcasting, SGI is dedicated to addressing the next class of challenges for scientific, engineering, and creative users. With offices worldwide, the company is headquartered in Mountain View, California. Its technology is used to design and build safer cars and airplanes, discover new medications and oil reserves, understand and better predict the weather, and provide movie special effects.

SGI has a well-established intern program involving more than 200 participants each summer. The company provides a unique professional work experience and offers educational and social activities to involve interns in the team-oriented atmosphere that's part of SGI's corporate culture. The intern program typically runs from May to August or June to September, for 10-12 weeks. Internships are available across the United States, although most take place in Mountain View, California; Eagan, Minnesota; or Chippewa Falls, Wisconsin. As an intern here, you might work in microprocessor design, design verification, and diagnostics; software kernel development for Linux and IRIX, or technical support, IS support, or tech writing.

HOW TO APPLY

SGI does not review or make any record of unsolicited mailed-in resumes; instead, you should apply online at http://www.sgi.com/company_info/employment/f_apply.html and paste your resume. When the company gets your application, it's entered into a database; from there, they will evaluate it against appropriate positions that open anytime during the year.

TEXAS INSTRUMENTS INTERNSHIP

Texas Instruments Incorporated
12500 TI Boulevard
Dallas, TX 75243-4136
(800) 336-5236
http://www.ti.com

What You Can Earn: Competitive salary (you're paid based on the number of hours/units/credits you've completed toward your degree, plus raises); paid relocation (airfare, truck rentals, and gas and mileage if you drive); relocation assistance (TI helps you find an apartment, and even a roommate, if you want, and can help with settling in). You'll also get employee benefits (students are treated as regular, full-time employees with all of the benefits TI offers, except health insurance, including paid vacations and holidays, profit sharing, and tuition reimbursement for qualified courses during your work term, including co-op tuition). You're also eligible to participate in TI's Employee Stock Purchase Plan, plus its fitness and health program as well as the credit union. When you go back to school, they'll put you on an educational leave of absence so that many of your benefits continue uninterrupted, and you continue to accrue service time, qualifying for more benefits, while you're finishing your degree.

Application Deadlines: At least four months before your internship starts.

Educational Experience: Successfully pursuing an undergraduate or graduate degree in engineering or science (students in other disciplines may occasionally be accepted) with a 3.0 GPA.

Requirements: Values must be consistent with TI's ethics and business philosophy. Students should be able to hit the ground running, take initiative, dream and make that happen, work with changing technologies and markets, be unafraid of taking risks, and value and support each other.

OVERVIEW

Texas Instruments Incorporated is the world leader in digital signal processing and analog technologies, the semiconductor engines of the Internet age. In addition, Texas Instruments focuses on sensors and controls and educational and productivity solutions. It's also a leader in the real-time technologies that help people communicate, moving fast to drive the Internet age forward with semiconductor solutions for large markets such as wireless and broadband access and for emerging markets such as digital cameras and digital audio.

The company offers an intensive student co-op and internship program for undergraduate and graduate students pursuing engineering or science-related degrees. TI prefers that students co-op, which means you'll go to school a semester, then work a semester for two terms (five to eight months). You'll find offices in Arizona, California, Colorado, Illinois, Massachusetts, North Carolina, and Texas. At TI, you'll be able to work while you're still in school, as a real employee, not in some paper-pushing job but in a real job, with your hands on great technology. And if you have the right stuff, once you graduate, the company will offer you a permanent spot.

HOW TO APPLY

TI recruits on campus, so check with your career center for representative contacts. If you're interested in talking to a TI recruiter during a campus visit, check out the recruitment schedule: http://www.ti.com/recruit/docs/campvis.shtml.

To apply for an internship, submit your resume to the preceding address, including:

- Your current GPA, degree level and discipline (such as BSEE)
- Anticipated graduation date
- Any co-op, intern, or other work you've done related to your major

When TI gets your resume, a supervisor will review it and match your qualifications with open internships; students are selected by supervisors. If you're selected, the company makes an offer; once you accept a position, you'll work with your supervisor to pick a date when you'll report to work at TI.

XEROX INTERNSHIP

Xerox
800 Long Ridge Road
Stamford, CT 06904

203-968-3000
http://www.xerox.com

What You Can Earn: Competitive salary ($700 to $1,000 a week) for summer internships and work-study; benefits change according to location. No salary for internship for academic credit.
Application Deadlines: Rolling.
Educational Experience: Full-time undergraduate juniors and seniors enrolled in a college-level program leading to a bachelor's degree or higher in math sciences; chemical engineering; civil/environmental engineering; computer science; electrical/computer engineering; industrial/manufacturing engineering; mechanical engineering; or information management. You must intend to continue academic pursuits until completion of the degree requirements.
Requirements: Successfully passing a drug test and background investigation, providing proof of work eligibility, and satisfactorily completing all offer forms.

OVERVIEW

Xerox Corporation is a $15.7 billion technology and services enterprise that develops innovative technologies, products, and services. Xerox provides the document industry's broadest portfolio of offerings, including digital systems (with color and black-and-white printing) and publishing systems; digital presses and "book factories"; multifunction devices; laser and solid ink network printers; and copiers and fax machines. Xerox's services help businesses develop online document archives, analyze how employees can most efficiently share documents and knowledge in the office, operate in-house print shops or mailrooms, and build Web-based processes for personalizing direct mail, invoices, brochures, and more. Xerox also offers associated software and support and supplies such as toner, paper, and ink.

The company offers its College Experiential Learning Programs (XCEL) as summer Internships and Work/Study programs to undergraduate and graduate students. These internships provide Xerox with an opportunity to recruit and evaluate students for potential full-time new college positions, and they provide college students with an income, plus real-life, on-the-job experience in their field of study. Internship-for-Credit (unpaid) positions are also offered, in which a student visits Xerox for research or learning/training experience.

Summer Internship

This paid position is available only from May to August on the East Coast and June to September on the West Coast, for 10 to 12 weeks (10 weeks is the minimum).

Work-Study

This paid position will have you working part time (fewer than 20 hours a week) while attending school full time. Occasionally, summer interns continue to work for Xerox part time once they start school in the fall; these participants "convert" from internship status to a work-study status at that time.

Internship for Credit

This unpaid position allows you to visit Xerox for research or a learning/training experience. Although you'll not be paid, you'll get academic credit from your institution.

HOW TO APPLY

You can apply by submitting your resume online at http://www.xerox.com/go/xrx/template/009.jsp?view=Feature&Xcntry=USA&Xlang=en_US&ed_name=Careers_University_Internships.

PART IV

FURTHER RESOURCES

APPENDIXES

APPENDIX A
INTERNET RESOURCES

This two-volume set offers a listing of some of the most well-known and exciting internships and summer jobs available in the United States in a wide range of areas. But as many entries as we've included, there are many more out there in just about every city in the United States and around the world. With this volume, we're trying to provide you with a taste of internship options you maybe never knew existed.

Before applying for any internship, you'll want to do more research to make sure that it is really something you want to pursue. You should learn as much as you can about the internship or summer job in which you're interested so that as you talk to people in those particular fields, you can ask informed and intelligent questions that will help you make your decisions. You also might want answers to questions not addressed in the information provided here.

If you search long enough, you can find just about anything using the Internet, including additional information about the internships in this book. The Internet is also a wonderful resource for networking; many internship sites have bulletin boards where students can interact with former interns or provide bios and quotes from former interns about what they liked about their experience. Some sites even offer online chats where you can communicate with former or current interns in real time. But as you use these forums and chats, remember that anyone could be on the other side of that computer screen, telling you exactly what you want to hear. It's easy to get wrapped up in the excitement while you're in a forum or a chat, interacting with people that share your interests and dreams. Remember to be cautious about any personal information you provide in forums and chats, and never give out your full name, address, or phone number. And of course, never agree to meet someone you've met online.

As you use the Internet to search information on the perfect career, keep in mind that, as with anything you find on the Internet, you need to consider the source from which the information comes.

Some of the most popular Internet search engines include

- http://www.alltheweb.com
- http://www.altavista.com
- http://www.ask.com
- http://www.directhit.com
- http://www.dogpile.com
- http://www.excite.com
- http://www.google.com
- http://www.goto.com
- http://www.hotbot.com
- http://www.looksmart.com
- http://www.lycos.com
- http://www.mamma.com
- http://www.msn.com
- http://www.vivisimo.com
- http://www.yahoo.com
- http://www.allsearchengines.com

The Internet offers a wealth of information on internships, with countless sites devoted to helping you find the perfect internship or summer job experience using your interests, skills, and talents. The sites listed here are some of the most helpful ones that the authors discovered while researching the jobs in this volume. These sites are offered for your information and are not endorsed by the author or publisher.

American Society of Newspaper Editors (ASNE)

http://www.asne.org

Provides an internship guide listing paid internships at daily newspapers by state and application deadline. Also available online.

Associated Collegiate Press Guide to Internships at the Top Newspapers and Magazines

http://commfaculty.fullerton.edu/tclanin/jobs/internguide03.pdf

http://www.studentpress.acp

A guide to getting a variety of journalism internships at a variety of newspapers and magazines.

Association for International Practical Training

http://www.aipt.org

Nonprofit organization offering internships in 65+ countries. Also offers assistance with work permits.

Best Bets for Internships Abroad

http://www.transitionsabroad.com

University of California, Irvine International Opportunities Program. Site outlines internship programs and Web sites for great international internships.

British Universities North America Club

http://www.bunac.org

BUNAC makes work and travel programs possible for students in England, Scotland, Wales, Northern Ireland, Australia, and New Zealand.

CDS International

http://www.cdsintl.org

Web site that specializes in internships in Germany, with opportunities in commerce and business.

Council on International Educational Exchange

http://www.iaeste.org

This work-abroad program supplies the necessary work documents and practical information on finding work and housing.

4International Careers and Jobs

http://www.4icj.com

Choose your country of interest to find links in 18 different categories such as job boards, companies, internships, temporary, government, and newspapers. The site also lets you know whether or not the services offered by the linked organizations are free to use.

French American Chamber of Commerce

http://www.faccparisfrance.com

This organization arranges internships in France.

Fun Jobs

http://www.funjobs.com

Fun Jobs lists fun summer jobs at ranches, camps, ski resorts and more, with information about positions, requirements, benefits, and responsibilities. You can apply online for most of the positions. In addition, the "Fun Companies" link will let you look up companies in an A to Z listing, or you can search for companies in a specific area or by keyword. The company listings offer you more detailed information about the location, types of jobs available, employment qualifications, and more.

GoAbroad

http://www.goabroad.com

At this Web site, you can search for internships abroad, among many other things, such as country-specific travel guides and tools such as rail-pass information and student ID cards.

Idealist.org (Action without Borders)

http://www.idealist.org

This helpful Web site lists a wide variety of resources, products, organizations, and interns in more than 165 countries, with lots of helpful info on cultural and travel issues abroad.

Institute of International Education

http://www.aipt.org

This Web site offers information on internships, practical training, and volunteering for more than 1300 programs, most of which charge tuition and give academic credit.

Internabroad.com

http://internabroad.com

This Web site is a terrific source for international internships. Search for paid and volunteer, academic and nonacademic internships, as well as college credit practical training programs around the world. The Web site also includes resources and lots of helpful info about working and traveling abroad.

International Association for the Exchange of Students for Technical Experience

http://www.iaeste.org

IAESTE offers worldwide internships to juniors and seniors in engineering, architecture, mathematics, computer sciences, and natural and physical sciences.

International Cooperative Education

http://www.4icj.com

Arranges paid internships in Germany, Switzerland, Belgium, Luxembourg, Finland, and Japan. One year college-level German, French, or Italian and/or two years minimum college-level Japanese required.

International Volunteer Programs Association

http://www.volunteerinternational.org

An alliance of nonprofit, nongovernmental organizations based in the Americas involved in international volunteer and internship exchanges. This Web site is filled with information about volunteering abroad, tings to know, resources, and much more.

Internship Programs.com

http://internships.wetfeet.com

With this award-winning Web site, students can check out listings of internship programs or individual internship openings and can post resumes for employers looking for interns. In addition, this Web site allows you to search an extensive database of internships, read internship reviews, create a real-intern profile, or research companies and careers on Wetfeet.com.

Internships in Francophone Europe

http://www.ifeparis.org

This organization offers a semester-long academic internship program to students and recent graduates of North American schools.

Job Monkey: Cool Summer Jobs in the U.S. and Abroad

http://www.jobmonkey.com

Job Monkey claims to be your gateway to "The Coolest Jobs on Earth," which includes listings for summer jobs around the country and around the world.

Life-in Jobs UK

http://www.livein-jobs.co.uk

This Web site offers info on seasonal employment opportunities in hotels in England, Scotland, and Wales (three-to six-month positions), including waiting tables, bartending, or being a receptionist or chef.

National Association of Hispanic Journalists Job Bank

http://www.nahj.org

Job/Internship/Fellowship/Workshop listings for NAHJ members. Opportunities in all media.

Pennsylvania Newspaper Association

http://www.pa-newspaper.org

PNA Foundation Newspaper Internship Guide (Free directory of internships offered by PNA members.)

Resortjobs.com

http://www.resortjobs.com

This Web site offers a database of summer job listings at worldwide resorts, ski areas, camps, parks, cruise ships, and hotels.

Society of News Jobs Foundation

http://www.snd.org/jobs/jobs.lasso

SND Foundation Internship Directory (free) of newspapers with internships in graphics and design. Search on the word "intern" in the job title field.

Southern Cone Internships

http://www.internabroad.com/listingsp3.cfm/
listing/12061

This Web site gives students the opportunity for professional work experience in Buenos Aires, Argentina or Santiago, and Chile. A fee is charged for participation in the language immersion course, as part of the internships.

Southern Newspaper Publishers Association

http://www.snpa.org

Provides a list of internship programs offered by SNPA member newspapers.

Summerjobs.com

http://www.summerjobs.com

This Web site offers a database of summer teaching, tourist, and service sector jobs all over the world.

Teen Jobs, Quintessential Careers for Teens

http://www.quintcareers.com/teen_jobs.html

This site has job and career advice for teens, including part-time and summer employment.

Transitions Abroad

http://www.transitionsabroad.com

A very detailed site with information for those wanting to work, study, or travel abroad. Includes listings of programs offering opportunities as well as a classifieds section.

Virginia Press Association

http://www.vpa.net/internships

Provides the *Journalism Internship Guide*, a list of newspaper internship opportunities throughout Virginia.

APPENDIX B
FURTHER READING

INTERNSHIPS AND SUMMER JOBS

Culbreath, Alice N. and Saundra K. Neal. *Testing the Waters: A Teen's Guide to Career Exploration.* New York: JRC Consulting, 1999.

Dawicki, Ed. *Adventures Unlimited: The Guide for Short-Term Jobs in Exotic Places.* iUniverse, 2003.

Mannion, James. *The Everything Alternative Careers Book: Leave the Office Behind and Embark on a New Adventure (Everything: School and Careers).* Cincinnatti: Adams, 2004.

WRITING RESUMES

Adams, Robert L. *The Complete Resume Job Search Book for College Students: The A-To-Z Career Guide for College Students and Recent Grads Who Want to Stand Out.* Cincinnatti: Adams Media, 1999.

Cochran, Chuck, and Donna Peerce. *Heart & Soul Resumes: 7 Never-Before-Published Secrets to Capturing Heart & Soul in Your Resume.* Mountain View, Calif.: Davies-Black, 1998.

Criscito, Pat. *Designing the Perfect Resume: A Unique 'Idea' Book Filled With Hundreds of Sample Resumes Created Using Wordperfect Software.* Hauppauge, N.Y.: Barrons, 1995.

Deluca, Matthew. *Best Answers to the 201 Most Frequently Asked Interview Questions.* New York: McGraw-Hill, 1996.

Fein, Richard. *100 Quick Tips for a Dynamite Resume.* Atascadero, Calif.: Impact Publishers, 1998.

Fry, Ron. *101 Great Answers to the Toughest Interview Questions.* Clifton Park, N.Y.: Thomson Delmar Learning, 2000.

Gonyea, James C. and Wayne M. Gonyea. *Electronic Resumes: A Complete Guide to Putting Your Resume On-Line.* New York: McGraw-Hill, 1996.

Hinds, Maurene J. *The Ferguson Guide to Résumés and Job-Hunting Skills: A Step-by-Step Guide to Preparing for Your Job Search.* New York: Facts On File, 2005.

Morin, Laura. *Every Woman's Essential Job Hunting & Resume Book.* Cincinnati: Adams Media, 1994.

Nemnich, Mary B., and Fred Jandt. *Cyberspace Resume Kit: How to Make and Launch a Snazzy Online Resume.* Indianapolis: JIST Works, 1998.

Schuman, Nancy, and Adele B. Lewis. *From College to Career: Winning Resumes for College Graduates.* Hauppauge, N.Y.: Barrons, 1993.

WRITING COVER LETTERS

Beatty, Richard. *175 High-Impact Cover Letters.* 3d ed. Hoboken, N.J.: John Wiley and Sons, 2002.

Besson, Taunee. *Cover Letters Made Easy.* Hoboken, N.J.: John Wiley and Sons, 1999.

Block, Jay. *101 Best Cover Letters.* New York: McGraw-Hill, 1999.

Enelow, Wendy S. *201 Winning Cover Letters for $100,000+ Jobs: Cover Letters That Can Change Your Life!* Indianapolis: Wendy S. Enelow, 1998.

Greene, Brenda. *Get the Interview Every Time: Fortune 500 Hiring Professionals' Tips for Writing Winning Resumes and Cover Letters.* Chicago: Dearborn Trade, 2004.

Hansen, Katherine and Randall Hansen. *Dynamic Cover Letters: How to Sell Yourself to an Employer by Writing a Letter That Will Get Your Resume Read, Get You an Interview, and Get You The Job.* Berkeley: Ten Speed Press, 2001.

Kennedy, Joyce Lain. *Cover Letters For Dummies.* Hoboken, N.J.: Wiley, 2000.

Toropov, Brandon. *Last Minute Cover Letters.* Clifton Park, N.Y.: Thomson Delmar, 1998.

Yate, Martin John. *Cover Letters That Knock 'Em Dead.* 3d ed. Cincinnatti: Adams Media, 1998.

PREPARING FOR INTERVIEWS

Block, Jay A. *Great Answers! Great Questions! For Your Job Interview.* New York: McGraw-Hill, 2004.

DeLuca, Matthew J. and Nanette F. Deluca. *24 Hours to the Perfect Interview: Quick Steps for Planning, Organizing, and Preparing for the Interview That Gets the Job.* New York: McGraw-Hill, 2004.

DeLuca, Matthew J. *Best Answers to the 201 Most Frequently Asked Interview Questions.* New York: McGraw-Hill, 1996.

Kador, John. *201 Best Questions To Ask On Your Interview.* New York: McGraw-Hill, 2002.

Gottesman, Deb. *The Interview Rehearsal Book.* New York: Berkley Trade, 1999.

Almost all offices of the governor accept interns; contact the governor in your state to see if an internship is possible. (The names of the governors were accurate at the time of publication.)

Alabama
Gov. Bob Riley
State Capitol
600 Dexter Avenue
Montgomery, AL 36130-2751
office_of_the_governor@gov.state.ak.us
http://www.gov.state.ak.us

Alaska
Gov. Frank Murkowski
State Capitol
PO Box 110001
Juneau, AK 99811-0001
http://www.governor.state.al.us/email/contact_form.htm
http://www.governor.state.al.us

Arizona
Gov. Janet Napolitano
1700 West Washington
Phoenix, AZ 85007
http://www.governor.state.az.us/post/feedback.asp
http://www.governor.state.az.us

Arkansas
Gov. Mike Huckabee
State Capitol
Room 250
Little Rock, AR 72201
mike.huckabee@state.ar.us
http://www.arkansas.gov/governor/staff/index.html

California
Gov. Arnold Schwarzenegger
State Capitol
Sacramento, CA 95814
governor@governor.ca.gov
http://www.governor.ca.gov/state/govsite/gov_homepage.jsp

Colorado
Gov. Bill Owens
136 State Capitol
Denver, CO 80203-1792
governorowens@state.co.us
http://www.colorado.gov/governor

Connecticut
Gov. M. Jodi Rell
210 Capitol Avenue
Hartford, CT 06106
Governor.Rell@po.state.ct.us
http://www.ct.gov/governorrell/site/default.asp

Delaware
Gov. Ruth Ann Minner
Tatnall Building
William Penn Street
Dover, DE 19901
gminner@state.de.us
http://www.state.de.us/governor/comments.shtml
http://www.state.de.us/governor/index.shtml

District of Columbia
Mayor Tony Williams
http://dc.gov/mayor/talk.htm
http://dc.gov/mayor/index.shtm

Florida
Gov. Jeb Bush
The Capitol
Tallahassee, FL 32399-0001
jeb.bush@myflorida.com
http://www.myflorida.com/b_eog/owa/b_eog_
    www.html.main_page

Georgia
Gov. Sonny Perdue
203 State Capitol
Atlanta, GA 30334
http://www.gov.state.ga.us/contact_dom.shtml
http://gov.state.ga.us

Hawaii
Gov. Linda Lingle
State Capitol
Executive Chambers
Honolulu, HI 96813
http://www.hawaii.gov/gov/gov/email
http://gov.state.hi.us

Idaho
Gov. Dirk Kempthorne
State Capitol
700 West Jefferson 2nd Floor
Boise, ID 83702
http://gov.idaho.gov/ourgov/contact.htm
http://gov.idaho.gov

Illinois
Gov. Rod Blagojevich
State Capitol
207 Statehouse
Springfield, IL 62706
http://www.illinois.gov/gov/contactthegovernor.
    cfm
http://www.illinois.gov/gov

Indiana
Gov. Joseph Kernan
206 State House
Indianapolis, IN 46204
http://www.ai.org/gov/contact/index.html
http://www.ai.org/gov/index.html

Iowa
Gov. Thomas Vilsack
State Capitol
Des Moines, IA 50319-0001

Kansas
Gov. Kathleen Sebelius
State Capitol, 2nd Floor
Topeka, KS 66612-1590
http://www.ksgovernor.org/comment.html
http://www.ksgovernor.org

Kentucky
Gov. Ernie Fletcher
The Capitol Building
700 Capitol Avenue, Suite 100
Frankfort, KY 40601
http://governor.ky.gov/contact.htm
http://governor.ky.gov

Louisiana
Gov. Kathleen Blanco
PO Box 94004
Baton Rouge, LA 70804-9004
http://www.gov.state.la.us/govemail.aspWeb
    Sitehttp://www.gov.state.la.us

Maine
Gov. John Baldacci
1 State House Station
Augusta, ME 04333
governor@maine.gov
http://www.state.me.us/governor/index.html

Maryland
Gov. Robert Ehrlich
State House
100 State Circle
Annapolis, MD, MD 21401
http://www.gov.state.md.us/mail
http://www.gov.state.md.us

Massachusetts
Gov. Mitt Romney
State House
Room 360

Boston, MA 02133
http://www.mass.gov/Agovwebmail/
    WebMailPageControl.ser?level=101
http://www.mass.gov/portal/index.jsp?pageID=g
    ov2homepage&L=1&L0=Home&sid=Agov2

Michigan
Gov. Jennifer Granholm
Governor's Office
PO Box 30013
Lansing, MI 48909
http://www.michigan.gov/gov/0,1607,7-168-
    21995---,00.html
http://www.michigan.gov/gov

Minnesota
Gov. Tim Pawlenty
130 State Capitol
75 Rev. Dr. Martin Luther King, Jr. Boulevard
St. Paul, MN 55155
tim.pawlenty@state.mn.us
http://www.governor.state.mn.us

Mississippi
Gov. Haley Barbour
PO Box 139
Jackson, MS 39205
http://www.governorbarbour.com/Data/Services/
    Services.asp
http://www.governorbarbour.com

Missouri
Gov. Bob Holden
Missouri Capitol Building
Room 216
Jefferson City, MO 65101
mogov@mail.state.mo.us
http://go.missouri.gov/index.htm

Montana
Gov. Judy Martz
PO Box 0801
Helena, MT 59620
http://www.discoveringmontana.com/gov2/staff/
    contact.asp
http://www.discoveringmontana.com/gov2

Nebraska
Gov. Mike Johanns
PO Box 94848
Lincoln, NE 68509-4848
jodee@mail.state.ne.us
http://gov.nol.org/mail/govmail.html
http://gov.nol.org

Nevada
Gov. Kenny Guinn
State Capitol
101 North Carson Street
Carson City, NV 89701
http://gov.state.nv.us/contact.htm
http://gov.state.nv.us

New Hampshire
Gov. Craig Benson
State House
Concord, NH 03301
benson@nh.gov
http://www.state.nh.us/governor

New Jersey
Gov. Richard Codey
PO Box 001
Trenton, NJ 08625
http://www.state.nj.us/governor/govmail.html
http://www.state.nj.us/governor

New Mexico
Gov. Bill Richardson
Office of the Governor
State Capitol Building
Santa Fe, NM 87503
http://www.governor.state.nm.us/
    constituentcontact.html
http://www.governor.state.nm.us

New York
Gov. George Pataki
State Capitol
Albany, NY 12224
http://161.11.3.75/
http://www.state.ny.us/governor
http://www.state.ny.us/governor

North Carolina
Gov. Michael Easley
Office of the Governor
20301 Mail Service Center
Raleigh, NC 27699
http://www.governor.state.nc.us/email.asp?to=1
http://www.governor.state.nc.us

North Dakota
Gov. John Hoeven
Governor's Office
600 E. Boulevard Avenue
Bismarck, ND 58505
governor@state.nd.us
http://www.governor.state.nd.us

Ohio
Gov. Bob Taft
77 S. High Street
Columbus OH 43215
http://governor.ohio.gov/contactinfopage.asp
http://governor.ohio.gov

Oklahoma
Gov. Brad Henry
State Capitol Bldg.
Oklahoma City, OK 73105
http://www.governor.state.ok.us/message.php
http://www.governor.state.ok.us

Oregon
Gov. Ted Kulongoski
State Capitol Building
900 Court Street NE
Salem OR 97301
http://www.governor.state.or.us/Gov/contact_
    us.shtml
http://www.governor.state.or.us

Pennsylvania
Gov. Edward Rendell
225 Main Capitol
Harrisburg, PA 17120
http://sites.state.pa.us/PA_Exec/Governor/
    govmail.html
http://www.governor.state.pa.us

Rhode Island
Gov. Don Carcieri
Office of the Governor
222 State House
Providence, RI 02903
http://www.governor.state.ri.us/contact.shtml
http://www.governor.state.ri.us

South Carolina
Gov. Mark Sanford
Office of the Governor
PO Box 11829
Columbia, SC 29211
http://www.scgovernor.com/Contact.
    asp?sitecontentid=33
http://www.scgovernor.com

South Dakota
Gov. Mike Rounds
Office of the Governor
500 East Capitol
Pierre, SD 57501
http://www.state.sd.us/governor/Main/forms/
    RequestForm.asp
http://www.state.sd.us/governor

Tennessee
Gov. Phil Bredesen
State Capitol
Nashville, TN 37243
phil.bredesen@state.tn.us
http://www.state.tn.us/governor

Texas
Gov. Rick Perry
Office of the Governor
PO Box 12428
Austin, TX 78711
http://www.governor.state.tx.us/contact
http://www.governor.state.tx.us

Utah
Gov. Olene Walker
210 State Capitol
Salt Lake City, UT 84114

http://www.utah.gov/governor/contact.html
http://www.utah.gov/governor

Vermont
Gov. James H. Douglas
109 State Street, Pavilion
Montepelier VT 05609
http://www.vermont.gov/governor/contact.html
http://www.vermont.gov/governor

Virginia
Gov. Mark Warner
Office of the Governor
State Capitol
Richmond, VA 23219
http://www.governor.virginia.gov/Contact/
    Contact.html
http://www.governor.virginia.gov

Washington
Gov. Gary Locke
Office of the Governor
PO Box 40002
Olympia, WA 98504
http://www.governor.wa.gov/contact/contact.
    htm http://www.governor.wa.gov/

West Virginia
Gov. Bob Wise
West Virginia State Capitol
Charleston, WV 25305
http://www.wvgov.org/New_eform.cfm
http://www.wvgov.org

Wisconsin
Gov. Jim Doyle
Office of the Governor
115 East State Capitol
Madison, WI 53702
http://www.wisgov.state.wi.us/contact.
    asp?locid=19
http://www.wisgov.state.wi.us

Wyoming
Gov. Dave Freudenthal
Wyoming State Capitol
Cheyenne WY 82002
http://wyoming.gov/governor/staff/staff.asp
http://wyoming.gov/governor/governor_home.
    asp

Puerto Rico
Gov. Sila Calderon
La Fortalenza
San Juan, PR 00901
http://fortaleza.govpr.org
http://fortaleza.govpr.org

Virgin Islands
Gov. Charles Turnbull
Government House
21-22 Kangens Gade
Charlotte Amalie, U.S. Virgin Islands 00802
http://www.usvi.org

INDEXES

INTERNSHIPS AND SUMMER JOBS BY APPLICATION DEADLINE

MARCH

APRIL

MAY

NOVEMBER

INTERNSHIPS AND SUMMER JOBS BY EDUCATION LEVEL

HIGH SCHOOL STUDENTS

COLLEGE STUDENTS
Freshmen

Sophomores

Juniors

Seniors

UNSPECIFIED FOR COLLEGE STUDENTS

GRADUATE STUDENTS

INTERNSHIPS AND SUMMER JOBS BY SALARY

UNPAID

$1 TO $999

$1,000 +

INTERNSHIPS AND SUMMER JOBS BY COUNTRY (NON-U.S.)

INTERNSHIPS AND SUMMER JOBS BY STATE

COLORADO

CONNECTICUT

DELAWARE

DISTRICT OF COLUMBIA

FLORIDA

GEORGIA

NORTH CAROLINA

ORGANIZATION INDEX

S

T

U

V